Revised Sixth Edition

Flea Market Trader

Edited by

Sharon & Bob Huxford

COLLECTOR BOOKS

A Division of Schroeder Publishing Co., Inc.

The current values in this book should be used only as a guide. They are not intended to set prices, which vary from one section of the country to another. Auction prices as well as dealer prices vary greatly and are affected by condition as well as demand. Neither the Editors nor the Publisher assumes responsibility for any losses that might be incurred as a result of consulting this guide.

On the cover: Holiday postcards $3.00-5.00 each; World War II battleship identification model $20.00-25.00; Novelty figurine $30.00-35.00; Gordon's peanut jar $25.00-35.00; Big Little Books $15.00-25.00 each; Geisha Girl teapot $15.00-25.00; Decoy $50.00-75.00; Stoneware pitcher $150.00-250.00; Tobacco baseball cards $5.00-10.00 each; Barry Goldwater political doll $20.00-25.00; Chilly Willie salt shaker $20.00-25.00; Philippine flag $10.00-25.00.

Additional copies of this book may be ordered from:

COLLECTOR BOOKS
P.O. Box 3009
Paducah, Kentucky 42001

@$9.95 Add $2.00 for postage and handling.

Copyright: Schroeder Publishing Company, Inc., 1990

Introduction

The Flea Market Trader is a unique price guide, geared specifically for the convenience of the flea market shopper. Several categories have been included that are not often found in general price guides, while others on antiques not usually seen at flea markets have been omitted. The new categories will serve to introduce you to collectibles that are currently coming on, the best and often the only source for which is the market place. As all of us who religiously pursue the circuits are aware, flea markets are the most exciting places in the world to shop; but unless you're well-informed on current values those 'really-great' buys remain on the table. Like most pursuits in life, preparation has its own rewards; and it is our intention to provide you with the basic tool of education and awareness toward that end. But please bear in mind that the prices in this guide are meant to indicate only a general value. Many factors determine actual selling prices -- values vary from one region to another, dealers pay various wholesale prices for their wares, and your bargaining skill is important, too.

We have organized our listings into general categories for easy use; if you have trouble locating an item, refer to the index. We assume that prices quoted by dealers are for mint items unless damage is noted. So our listings, when no condition code is present, reflect prices of items in mint condition. NM stands for minimal damage, VG indicates that the items will bring 40% to 60% of its mint price, and EX should be somewhere between the two. Nothing is listed in poorer condition than VG. Glassware is assumed clear unless a color is noted. Only generally accepted abbreviations have been used. Photos other than those we have taken are acknowledged on page 4, and we would like to take this opportunity to thank each author, dealer, and auction house who allowed us to use their photographs.

The Editors

Photo Credits

Antique and Collectible Marbles, Edward Grist, pg 183

Antique and Collectible Thimbles, Averil Mathis, pg 165

Blue Willow, Mary Frank Gaston, pg 313

Brian-Riba Auctions, Inc., Historical Ephemera, P.O. Box 53, Main St., South Glastonbury, CT 06073, pg 21,58,78,223,233

Carnival Chalk Prizes, Thomas G. Morris, pg 61

Children's Dishes, Margaret and Kenn Whitmyer, pg 51

Children's Glass Dishes and Furniture, Doris Anderson Lechler, pg 73,74

Col. Doug Allard, P.O. Box 460, St. Ignatius, MT 59865, pg160,161

Collector's Encyclopedia of Depression Glass, Vol. 6 and 7, Gene Florence, pg 101-109

Collector's Encyclopedia of Fiesta, 6th Edition, Sharon and Bob Huxford, pg 125,126

Collector's Encyclopedia of Hall, Margaret and Kenn Whitmyer, pg 148

Collector's Encyclopedia of Nippon, 3rd Edition, Joan Van Patten, pg 198

Collector's Encyclopedia of Noritake, Joan Van Patten, pg 199

Collector's Encyclopedia of Occupied Japan, 2nd Edition, Gene Florence, pg 202

Collector's Encyclopedia of Pattern Glass, Mollie Helen McCain, pg 210-218

Collector's Guide to Country Stoneware and Pottery, Don and Carol Raycraft, pg 287

Collector's Guide to Paper Dolls, Mary Young, pg 205-208

Du Mouchelles, 409 Jefferson Ave., Detroit, MI 48226, pg 80

Effanbee Dolls, Patricia Smith, pg 113

Garths Auctions, Inc., 2690 Stratford Road, Box 369, Delaware, OH 43015, pg 239

Glassworks Auctions, P.O. Box 187, East Greenville, PA 18041, pg 136

Goofus Glass, Carolyn McKinley, pg 143

Greg Tunks, Publisher, *Credit Card Newsletter*, 150 Hohldale, Houston, TX 77022, pg 94

Head Vases, Kathleen Cole, pg 151

Illustrated Guide to Cookie Jars, Ermagene Westfall, pg 185

Medical, Dental, and Pharmaceutical Collectibles, Don Fredgant, pg 187

Metal Molds, Eleanore Bunn, pg 190

Miscellaneous Man, George Theofiles, Box 1776, New Freedom, PA, 17349, pg 172

Petretti's Coca-Cola Collectibles Price Guide, Alan Petretti, pg 85,86

Railroad Collectibles, 2nd Edition, Stanley Baker, pg 241,244, 245

Richard A. Bourne, Co., Inc., Estate Auctioneers & Appraisers, Box 141, Hyannis Port, MA 02647, pg 54,81,221

Salt and Pepper Shakers, Helene Guaraccia, pg 228,269

Scouting Collectibles, R.J. Sayers, pg 272

Standard Baseball Card Price Guide, Gene Florence, pg 33,34

Standard Encyclopedia of Carnival Glass, Bill Edwards, pg 62-65

Standard Knife Collector's Guide, Stewart and Ritchie, pg 170

Straight Razor Collecting, Robert Doyle, pg 247

Willis Henry Auctions, 22 Main St., Marshfield, MA 02050, pg 275

World War II German Military Collectibles, Robert McCarthy, pg 195,196

300 Years of Kitchen Collectibles, Vols 1 and 2, Linda Campbell Franklin, pg 146,178

ABC Plates

Popular in the 1800s as well as the early years of this century, plates with the ABCs in their borders encouraged children toward learning their letters even during mealtime. They were made from a variety of materials, but examples in earthenware with a colorfully-printed central motif are most collectible, especially those dealing with sports, transportation, or a famous person, place, or thing.

Wild Animals — The Lion, BP Co., Tunstall, England, 7", $75. 00.

Cup & saucer, Germany . . .**55.00**
Dish, Dolly Dingle, signed Drayton, Buffalo **37.50**
Mug, gold trim, ABC rim, marked Germany **25.00**
Mug, milk glass, alphabet . .**45.00**
Mug, tin, 1¾" **75.00**
Plate, Aesop's Fables, Fox & Grapes, ca 1875 . . . .**55.00**
Plate, Archery, multicolor, Meakin, 6¼" **85.00**
Plate, boy & girl play with hoop, tin, 3" **60.00**
Plate, boys play marbles, multicolor, Elsmore, 5⅞" **65.00**
Plate, Cricket Game, Staffordshire, 7½" **125.00**

Plate, Crusoe Rescues Friday, Staffordshire, EX **85.00**
Plate, deer & tree, glass, 6" .**50.00**
Plate, dog, ABC rim, glass .**15.00**
Plate, Fox & Geese, 8" **85.00**
Plate, girl swings, tin, 3½" .**35.00**
Plate, granite ware, EX . . .**145.00**
Plate, Hobnail, glass, 6¼" . .**30.00**
Plate, Humpty Dumpty, 8" .**38.00**
Plate, hunt scene, blue transfer, 7½" **95.00**
Plate, Liberty, tin, 5½" **60.00**
Plate, Little Bo-Peep, numbers 1-9, ABC rim, glass **55.00**
Plate, Little Red Riding Hood, ABC rim, 7¼" **65.00**
Plate, Major General NP Banks, black transfer, 5", EX . .**88.00**
Plate, newspaper boy on city street, pottery, 7" **85.00**
Plate, Niagara From the Edge of the American Fall, 7½" **85.00**
Plate, Oriental Hotel, ABC rim, pottery, 7½" **75.00**
Plate, Punch & Judy, Staffordshire, 7½" **45.00**
Plate, Robinson Crusoe Viewing the Island, 8" **75.00**
Plate, Sancho Panza & Dapple, glass, 5¼" **45.00**
Plate, Washington in center, ABC rim, tin, 6" **85.00**
Plate, Who Killed Cock Robin?, tin, 8" **60.00**
Plate, 2 riders on steeplechase, green & brown, 7½" **50.00**
Set, bunny with mouse, Lord Nelson Pottery, 4-pc **75.00**

Abingdon Pottery

Produced in Abingdon, Illinois, from 1934 to 1950, this company made vases, cookie jars, utility ware, and lamps.

Ash tray, #326, Greek, undecorated, 4¼x3" **25.00**

Planter, donkey and basket, #699, 7", $25.00.

Ash tray, #509, elephant figure, black **65.00**

Ash tray, #510, donkey figure, black, ... **75.00**

Basket, #582D, decorated . . **32.00**

Bookends, #363, colt, undecorated, 5¾", pair **60.00**

Bookends, #374, cactus planter, undecorated, 7", pair . . **32.00**

Bookends, #428, Fern Leaf . **30.00**

Bowl, #527, hibiscus, pink . . **25.00**

Bud vase, #482, decorated . . **24.00**

Cookie jar, #471, Mammy, chartreuse **70.00**

Cookie jar, #495, Fat Boy, red. **72.50**

Cookie jar, #611, Jack-in-the-Box, 11" **75.00**

Cookie jar, #663, Humpty Dumpty, decorated **65.00**

Cookie jar, #674, Pumpkin . **45.00**

Cookie jar, #677, Daisy, undecorated, 8" **25.00**

Cookie jar, #695, Mother Goose, goose at side **110.00**

Cornucopia shell, #449, 5" . . **17.50**

Figurine, #98, upright goose, undecorated, 5" **22.50**

Figurine, #99, goose, head down, pink **17.00**

Flowerpot, #150, cattails . . . **12.00**

Pitcher, #200, ice lip, 2-quart with ice lip **20.00**

Planter, #490, Dutch girl, wall mount, 10" **17.50**

Refrigerator pitcher, #RE1, blue & white **30.00**

Teapot tile, #401, coolie, undecorated, 5x5" **27.50**

Vase, #110, Classic, Deco, blue gloss, small **25.00**

Vase, #112, Classic, green, miniature **12.00**

Vase, #179, floral, 10" **22.00**

Vase, #389, geranium, cream . . **45.00**

Vase, #421, Fern Leaf **30.00**

Vase, #463, star, 7" **15.00**

Vase, #634, Heirloom **25.00**

Wall pocket, #431, Fern Leaf, undecorated, 7½" **17.50**

Wall pocket, #586D, lily . . . **30.00**

Advertising Collectibles

Since the late 1800s, competition

among manufacturers of retail products has produced multitudes of containers, signs, trays, and novelty items, each bearing a catchy slogan, colorful lithograph or some other type of ploy, all flagrantly intent upon catching the eye of the potential customer. In their day, some were more successful than others; but today it is the advertising material itself rather than the product that rings up the big sales — from avid collectors and flea market shoppers, not the product's consumers!

See also Coca-Cola; Labels; Planters Peanuts.

Ad Cards

Clark's Thread, Hard To Beat, 4½x3", $3.00.

Austen's Forest Flower Cologne, lady picking flowers **3.00**
Beymer, Bauman & Co, woman painting sign, man looking on **4.00**

Celluloid Collars & Cuffs, shows map of Europe with flag .**4.00**
Diamond Black Leather Oil, Garfield monument **4.00**
Dr Winchell's Teething Syrup, man holding screaming baby .**5.50**
Frank Miller's Crown Dressing for Shoes, shoe form, 7" . . .**10.00**
Garland Stoves & Ranges, baby in highchair **6.50**
Horsehead Tobacco, horse's head chewing plug **9.00**
International Baking Powder, boy playing flute **2.50**
Keller's Sure Cure for Diphtheria & Croup, ca 1880 . . . .**4.00**
Kinney Bros Cigarettes, 5 die-cuts, different ladies **5.00**
Lydia Pinkham's Vegetable Compound, sailboats **3.50**
Newsboy Plug, Where Is Mother?, 5 puppies **5.00**
Pabst Best Tonic, lady **7.50**
Stolwerck's Chocolates, Columbian Expo **7.00**
Veteran Tobacco, uniformed soldier & windmill **8.00**
Wilbur's Chocolate **6.00**
Wilson's Beef, sneaking Indian stealing beef **7.00**

Casara Quinine card, 5½x8", $25.00

7

Banks

Armour Meat, service truck.. **45.00**
Bokar Coffee, tin **12.00**
Buffalo Sled Co, celluloid ..**80.00**
Calumet Baking Soda **110.00**
Carnation Evaporated Milk, tin,
  EX **25.00**
Cheverolet, car, 1953 .....**65.00**
Dutch Cleanser, tin **65.00**
GE Refrigerator, cast iron, 4¼",
  NM **95.00**
Grapette, elephant, clear w/slotted
  metal lid **20.00**
Log Cabin Syrup, glass **22.00**
Parsley Brand Salmon, tin .**45.00**
Patton Paints, colorful litho on tin,
  EX **35.00**
Red Goose Shoes, plastic goose,
  4¾", EX **20.00**
Rival Dogfood, tin, can form. **10.00**
Schmidt Beer, beer bottle shape,
  24" **18.00**
Structo Motor Oil, tin **20.00**
Tower Motor Oil, EX **12.00**

Calendars

BF Goodrich, 1947 ....**10.00**
Clark's Thread, 1908 .....**31.00**
Doe Wah Jack Stoves **290.00**
Ernest's Meat Market, color inte-
  rior of country store, 1939,
  NM **24.00**
Harvard Brewing Co Pure Malt
  Beverages, portrait of a lady,
  1907 ....**45.00**
Hercules Powder, oil rigger & ex-
  plosives, 1915 ....**90.00**
Hood's, 1898 ....**35.00**
Hood's, 1905 ....**45.00**
New Idea Farm Equip, 1949.**15.00**
Pepsi-Cola, hunting & fishing scene,
  ca 1940 ....**32.00**
Pompeian Soap, Mary Pickford pic-
  ture, 1917 ....**50.00**
Robothan & Sons Dairy, Dionne
  Quintuplets, 1937 .....**12.00**
Selz Shoes, 1923, 36x12" ..**135.00**

Times Square, night scene, in frame,
  1930 ....**125.00**
Wrigley's, 1923 ....**5.00**

Springfield Fire & Marine Insurance Co., 1849, 19x13", $95.00.

Clock

Canada Dry, electric **53.00**
Carstair's White Seal Whiskey,
  11x15" **35.00**
Dr Pepper **45.00**
El Producto Cigars, lighted, 16x
  16" **27.50**
Four Roses **40.00**
Gold Star Ice Cream **50.00**
Jersey Farms, glass in metal frame,
  round, EX **47.50**
Joys Beverages, electric ..**55.00**
Keystone Paint, electric light-up,
  celluloid **45.00**
Moxie, electric light-up, Great New
  Taste, ca 1968 ....**10.00**
Mr Boston, 8-day, marked Gilbert,
  22x10" **175.00**
Old Charter Whiskey **55.00**
Rival Dog Food **65.00**
Schlitz Beer, electric light-up, lu-
  cite, 16½x7" **25.00**
Vantage Cigarettes, round, battery,
  EX **25.00**

Wilson Whiskey, lighted, electric
    light-up, NM **55.00**
7-Up, wood frame **70.00**

Dolls

Bazooka Bubble Gum, Bazooka Joe,
    cloth, ca 1970, 18" **6.00**
Big Boy Restaurant, Dolly, fabric,
    red dress, marked, 14" ..**8.00**
Campbell's Soup Co, Campbell Kid
    Scottish dress, 1960 ...**27.50**
Chesty Potato Chips, Chesty Boy,
    rubber, ca 1950, 8" **17.00**
Chicken of the Sea, Mermaid,
    printed cloth, 1974, 15" .**8.00**
Close-Up, Close-Up Cuddle-Ups,
    plush fabric, ca 1975 ...**6.50**

**Captain Crunch, vinyl bank, 7",
$8.00.**

Kellogg's, Woody Woodpecker,
    stuffed cloth, 1966, 13" ..**8.00**
Mohawk Carpet Company, Mohawk
    Tommy, fabric, 16" **8.00**
Nestle Co, Nestle Quik Rabbit, 'Q'
    on shirt, 24" **8.00**
Pillsbury Co, Poppin' Fresh in chef
    hat, knit cloth, ca 1972 ..**8.00**
Quaker Oats, Cap'n Crunch, plastic
    bank, ca 1975, 7½" **6.50**
Rexall Drug Co, vinyl baby with
    painted eyes, 7½" **6.00**
Tony's Pizza, Mr Tony, vinyl
    squeaker toy, 1970, 8" ..**4.00**
Vlasic Pickles, Vlasic Stork, inflat-
    able, 1977, 53" **8.00**

Green Sprout, plastic, 7", $5.00.

Hawaiian Punch, Punchy, printed
    cloth, ca 1970, 13" **8.50**
Hot Tamale Candies, Tamale Kid,
    stuffed cloth, 16" **7.00**
Keebler Co, Keebler the Elf, painted
    vinyl, marked, 6½" **8.50**
Kellogg's, Toucan Sam, fabric, ca
    1960, unmarked, 9" ...**10.00**

Fans

Acme Beer, cardboard, oval hole for
    holding **15.00**
Caterpillar Tractor **15.00**
Cherry Smash, paper, early..**40.00**
Coon Chicken Inn **20.00**
Emerson's Julep **25.00**
Hires, Dutch girl **11.00**

9

Hufnagel's Ice Cream, couple eating ice cream, ca 1925 . **32.00**
Kenny's Tea **3.50**
Lime Cola, palm trees, NM . **25.00**
Morrel Meats **20.00**
Moxie, boy on rocking horse, 1922, EX **15.00**
Moxie, Muriel Ostriche, in hat, 1918, EX **25.00**
Moxie, Muriel Ostriche, in landscape, 1916 . . . . **37.00**
Royal Crown Cola, All American, EX **20.00**
Tums 10¢ a Roll, picture of children in wagon, cardboard . . . **10.00**
20-Mule Team Borax, with Maud, ca 1900 . . . . **12.00**

Match Holders

**Old Judson, J.C. Stevens, 5x3",
$75.00.**

Ceresota Flour **130.00**
DeLaval, tin, 1908 . . . . **175.00**
Dokash Stoves **100.00**
Dr King's New Discovery . **225.00**
Dr Pepper **42.00**
Dr Shoop's Coffee **100.00**

Ellwood Steel Fences **55.00**
Fatima Cigarettes, white porcelain with gold trim, 6x6x5" . **42.00**
Fatima Turkish Blend Cigarettes, Van Pottery, 3½x6x5" . . **50.00**
Golden Wedding Coffee, tin. **35.00**
Her First Born Steel Range, tin, lady cooking on stove . . **68.00**
Kool Cigarettes, penguin, EX. **16.00**
Milwaukee Harvesting . . . **100.00**
New Process Gas Range, gray & red painted tin **52.00**
Old Judson, man, woman, & child, JC Stevens **75.00**
Packham's Table Waters, ceramic, blue on off-white, 2x3" . **12.00**
Sharples' Separators, mother & girl in farm scene **175.00**
Universal Stoves **175.00**

Match Safes

Anheuser Busch, large eagle flying off large A, silver **100.00**
Berlin Iron Bridge Company, celluloid, EX **72.00**
Blumenthal & Bickart, brass, 2½x1½" **36.00**
Bueber Watch Case, brass, decorative scrollwork, 3x1½" . **12.00**
Chicago Pneumatic Tools, nickel & brass **22.50**
Glenwood Ranges & Heaters, nickel & brass, EX **37.50**
Sunnybrook Pure Food Whiskey, tin, M **25.00**
Wylie Coal, brass, dated 1890. **20.00**

Paperweights

Bell System, C&P Telephone Co & Associated Co **55.00**
General Motors Building, brass, NM **35.00**
Libby, McNeil & Libby, Chicago; gold-painted steel, 3" . . **27.00**
Montana Banking, Paid-Up Capital, brass **75.00**

Red Cross Stoves, red cross & embossed letters on black metal,
NM 12.00
Scottish Union Insurance, brass,
rectangular 75.00
Ward's Vitovim Bread, red, white &
blue, glass, ½x2¼x4" ...10.00

Pin-Backs

Butterine 20.00
Deadshot Powder 40.00
Dumbo DX 20.00
Dupont 75.00
Moxie boy's head, early 25.00
Peters Cartridges 40.00
Peters Referee Shells 55.00
Shoot UMC 30.00
Studebaker 25.00

Pocket Mirrors

Atlanta Paper Co, sepia litho of
factory, 4" 17.50
Creme Simon 15.00
Cutler's Cutlery 35.00
Dr Daniel's Vet Medicine, lady with
horse & dog 45.00
Ghiradellis 35.00
Holeproof Hosiery, EX 15.00
Invincible Automobile Oil ..25.00
Kansas Expansion Flour ...15.00
Morrell's Pride 25.00
Nehi Ginger Ale 10.00
Red Seal Lye 25.00
Rosen's Pure Zizel Bread ...35.00
Shaefer Pianos, upright piano, oval,
EX 47.50
Starrett Tools 25.00
Union Shoes 25.00
Vassar College 6.00
Wyandotte Clothing House, oval,
EX 16.00

Signs

Blue Star Coal, large blue star,
EX 22.50

Nehi, lithographed cardboard,
under glass, framed, ca 1920, 15x22",
$150.00.

Camel Cigarettes, So Mild, So Good,
23½x42" 20.00
Canada Dry Hi-Spot, 1946, 24x7",
EX 20.00
Chesterfield Cigarettes, cardboard,
lady & pack, 24x24" ...35.00
Clabber Girl Baking Powder, tin,
1952, 12x30" 25.00
Crusade Tobacco, crusader knight,
ca 1900, 13½x7" 25.00
Five Roses Flour, porcelain, Indian
with flour, 42x26", G ..25.00
Foot Rest Hosiery, tin, girl & swing,
11x17" 275.00
Good Housekeeping, tin, anti-smok-
ing 20.00
Green River Soda, cardboard, ca
1940, 7x10" 15.00
Hance Bros Cough Drops, card-
board, girl & boy, 28x20". 55.00
Hanna Paints, embossed tin, ca
1940, 3x12" 12.00
Highball Ginger Ale, tin, square,
EX 12.00
Kool Cigarettes, tin,1940s ..17.00
Lime Cola, Drink Lime Cola in
Bottles 5¢ 40.00
Lime Julep, embossed tin, ca 1920,
6x21" 27.00
Miller Lite, electric, raised logo &
hops, 12x16" 15.00
Mobil Flying Red Horse, porcelain,
EX 25.00
Mound City Horseshoe Paints, tin,
yellow & black 57.00
Murad Cigarettes, paper, lady with
Christmas box, 10x20" .40.00

Northern Assurance Co, red, black,
    & white, porcelain **55.00**
Polar Ice Cream, aluminum, ca
    1930, EX **22.50**
Robin Hood Flour, porcelain, 28x15",
    EX **40.00**
Squirt, with bottle, 4x17" ..**17.50**
Superior Grain Drills, wood, white
    letters on black **95.00**
Texaco, porcelain, ca 1930 ..**52.00**
Tivoli Ale, tin, fox hunt scene, ca
    1930, 28x20" **175.00**
Triner's Bitter Wine, cardboard, ca
    1920, signed **25.00**
Turkey Red Cigarettes, cardboard,
    13x16" **120.00**
Westchester Fire Insur, porcelain,
    black & white, 14x20" ..**120.00**
Worcester Salt, paper, railroad
    scene **275.00**
Wynola, cardboard, man & woman
    on the beach, 12x16" ..**12.00**
7-Up, colorful tin, Fresh Up, It Likes
    You, 6x18" **60.00**
7-Up, porcelain, 20x28" **35.00**

Thermometers

Crush, blue & white on orange,
    9½x3½" **32.00**
Dad's Root Beer, metal **30.00**
Dr Pepper, white on yellow, rec-
    tangular center, 9" diameter,
    EX **36.00**
Drink Double Cola, You'll Like It
    Better; red on white, 26x8",
    EX **23.00**
Kentucky Club Tobacco, blue &
    white painted metal, 34x8",
    EX **43.00**
Mission Beverages, orange &
    yellow bottle on white, 17x5",
    EX **37.00**
Moxie, Remember Those Days,
    orange, round **20.00**
Nesbitt, white letters on orange
    bottle, 26x7", EX **18.00**
Purolator **30.00**
Winston **15.00**

Tin Containers

Old Master Coffee, 6", $30.00.

Acme Coffee, 1-pound **25.00**
Amalie Non-Fluid, 6x6" **15.00**
American Deluxe Coffee, red, white,
    & blue can, 1-pound ...**12.00**
Apollo Marshmallows **35.00**
Arm & Hammer, 8-ounce ..**60.00**
Bee Brand Insect Powder, cylinder-
    shaped can, unopened ..**8.00**
Bond Street Tobacco **15.00**
Borden's Malted Milk **60.00**
Borozin, pictures baby **10.00**
Buckingham Tobacco, pocket tin,
    EX **38.00**
Buckingham Tobacco, sample,
    pocket tin **80.00**
Campfire Marshmallows, 5-pound
    size **15.00**
Chesterfield Flat 50s **7.00**
City Club Tobacco, pocket tin,
    EX **60.00**
Cuticura Talc, woman with baby,
    EX **52.00**
Early Morning Pure Coffee, Dubuis-
    son, 8-ounce **35.00**
El Roi Tan Cigars **15.00**
Hi-Plane Tobacco, single engine,
    pocket tin **30.00**

Horlick's Malted Milk **75.00**
Imperial Ginger, 5x5x1" . . . **10.00**
Long's Ox-Heart Cocoa, 5-pound
size **70.00**
M&V Brand Oysters, with lid, 1-
pint size **20.00**
Martin's Capsules, birds in nest,
EX **10.00**
McCormick Insect Powder, un-
opened **5.00**
Monarch Peanut Butter, 1-pound
size **65.00**
Mount Cross Coffee, 3-pound
size **35.00**
Napoleon Honey Dew Tobacco, with
lid, 4x5" **45.00**
Nash Coffee, key open, 1-pound
size **18.00**
National Biscuit Company Fruit
Cake, round, flat **18.00**
New Era Potato Chips, 1-pound
size **20.00**
Partridge Lard, 8-pound . . . **25.00**

**Squirrel Confections, Clear Gums,
4x3¼x1", $50.00.**

Pic-O-Bac Tobacco, pocket tin,
EX **45.00**
Puritan Tobacco, yellow and black,
EX **35.00**
Serv-Us Coffee, screw lid, 1-pound
size **40.00**
Sparkling Gems Confection, 3-
pound **25.00**
Stag Tobacco, pocket tin, short
style **45.00**

Stag Tobacco, pocket tin, tall
style **50.00**
Union Leader-Uncle Sam Tobacco,
pocket tin **50.00**
Victor Vacuum Coffee, multicolor,
EX **60.00**
Watkin's Malted Milk **17.00**

**Bayle Peanut Butter pail, 4¾",
$185.00.**

Tip Trays

Ballantine Beer, wood **65.00**
Big Jo Flour, Wabash Roller Mills,
shows sunrise **35.00**
Braumeister-Independence Brew-
ery Co, Milwaukee, WI . **35.00**
Cottolene Shortening, woman &
child in cotton field **85.00**
Davenport Malt & Brewery Co, lady
with roses & beer **95.00**
Fairy Soap, girl on soap bar, round,
4¼" **40.00**
Garland Stoves & Ranges . . **50.00**
Globe-Wernicke Bookcases, 4¼",
EX **15.00**
Gobel Beer, 4½" **35.00**
Heburn House Coal, gold eagle atop
coal **30.00**
Hupfel Brewing Co, red & gold trade-
mark **50.00**
Kling's Prost Beer, 4¼" **25.00**

Mellwood Distillery, whiskey bottle, NM 47.50

Monroe Brewery Co, lady sitting on winged wheel 110.00

Muelebach's Pilsner, shows product 55.00

Pfeiffer Brewing Co, shows product, NM 65.00

Quickmeal Stoves 42.00

Round Oak Stoves 45.00

Ruppert's Beer, Hans Flato cartoon 42.00

Universal Stoves & Ranges .50.00

Young Rip Rap, hunting dog on point, 3x4" 20.00

Rockford High Grade Watches, $38.00.

Trays

Brown's Mule Tobacco, with 16 mules, 12x12" 38.00

Calumet Brewing Co, cavalier scene, 12x17" 250.00

CD Kenny, seated Victorian lady, 4", NM 65.00

Cherry Blossom 35.00

Congress Beer, label, 12" ..46.00

Dawson's Ale & Lager, lady & man dining 95.00

DeCoursey's Ice Cream 36.00

Ehret's Beer 85.00

Fairy Soap, change size 65.00

Haberle Congress Brewery Company 42.00

Holland Ice Cream 15.00

Iroquois Brewery Co, Buffalo, NY; Indian head 27.00

Lion Brewery, lion pushing barrel, oval 86.00

Miller High Life Beer, girl on moon, ca 1950, 13" 55.00

Nectar Brewery Co, Elmira, NY; barrel on elf's shoulder .40.00

Old Reading Beer, red & white on blue, 13" diameter 55.00

Orange Crush 35.00

Pepsi-Cola, group of children, ca 1940 ......32.00

Sunshine Beer, 15" 50.00

Yuengling's Beer, horse head...60.00

Akro Agate

This company operated in Clarksburg, West Virginia, from 1914 to 1951, manufacturing marbles, novelties, and children's dishes, for which they are best known. Though some were made in clear solid colors, their most popular, easy-to-identify lines were produced in a swirling opaque type of glass similar to that which was used in the production of their marbles. Their trademark was a flying eagle clutching marbles in his claws.

Chiquita, creamer, opaque green, 1½" 5.00

Chiquita, creamer, opaque turquoise, 1½" 12.00

Chiquita, cup, 1½", with saucer, 3⅛", opaque green 6.00

Chiquita, plate, transparent cobalt, 3¾" 6.00

Chiquita, 21-piece set in opaque green, $85.00; 16-piece set in transparent cobalt, $100.00.

Chiquita, sugar bowl, transparent cobalt, no lid, 1½" **10.00**

Chiquita, 16-piece set, baked-on colors **70.00**

Concentric Rib, creamer, white, 1¼" **5.00**

Concentric Rib, cup, opaque colors other than green or white, 1¼" **5.00**

Concentric Rib, cup, white, 1¼", with green saucer, 2¾" **5.00**

Concentric Ring, large cereal, solid opaque colors, 3⅛" **18.00**

Concentric Ring, large cup, opaque lavender, 1⅜" **30.00**

Concentric Ring, sugar bowl with lid, marbleized blue, 1⅞" . **45.00**

Concentric Ring, small plate, solid opaque colors, 3¼" **5.00**

Concentric Ring, small plate, transparent cobalt, 3¼" **12.00**

Concentric Ring, small 16-piece set, solid opaque colors . . . **105.00**

Interior Panel, large cereal, transparent topaz, 3⅜" **15.00**

Interior Panel, large plate, azure blue, 4¼" **12.00**

Interior Panel, small cup, marbleized red & white, 1¼" . . **25.00**

Interior Panel, small saucer, yellow, 2⅜" **5.50**

Interior Panel, small sugar bowl, marbleized blue, 1¼" . . **25.00**

JP, cup, transparent red or brown, 1½" **30.00**

JP, plate, various baked-on colors, 4¼" **4.00**

JP, saucer, transparent red or brown, 3¼" **8.00**

JP, sugar bowl, transparent red or brown, with lid, 1½" . . . **38.00**

JP, teapot, transparent red or brown, 1½" **50.00**

Miss America, cup & saucer. **37.50**

Miss America, saucer, marbleized orange & white **11.00**

Octagonal, large cereal, 3⅛" . **6.00**

Octagonal, large creamer, closed handle, light blue **12.00**

Octagonal, large teapot **12.00**

Octagonal, small creamer, dark green, 1¼" **12.00**

Octagonal, small sugar bowl, dark green, 1¼" **8.00**

Octagonal, small tumbler, lime
green, 2" **12.00**
Raised Daisy, plate, blue, 3" . **8.00**
Raised Daisy, tumbler, 2" . **18.00**
Stacked Disc, cup, opaque green,
1¼" **5.00**
Stacked Disc, pitcher, opaque green,
2⅞" **8.00**
Stacked Disc, sugar bowl, pumpkin,
1¼" **14.00**
Stacked Disc, teapot, white,
3⅜" **9.00**
Stacked Disc, tumbler, white,
2" **4.00**
Stacked Disc & Interior Panel, large
cereal, blue, 3⅜" **35.00**
Stacked Disc & Interior Panel, large
creamer, blue, 3⅜" **35.00**
Stacked Disc & Interior Panel, large
plate, blue, 4¾" **18.00**
Stacked Disc & Interior Panel, cup,
transparent cobalt, 1¼" . **18.00**
Stacked Disc & Interior Panel, sugar
bowl, blue, 1¼" **30.00**
Stippled Band, large creamer, transparent green, 1½" **15.00**
Stippled Band, large cup, transparent amber, 1½" **6.00**

Stippled Band, large plate, transparent green, 4¼" **4.50**
Stippled Band, large sugar bowl,
transparent amber, 2" . **17.00**
Stippled Band, small tumbler, transparent amber, 1¾" **6.00**

Aluminum

From the late 1930s until early
in the 1950s, kitchenwares and
household items were crafted from
aluminum, usually with relief-
molded fruit or flowers on a hammered background. Today many
find these diversified items make
an interesting collection. Especially
desirable are those examples
marked with the manufacturer's
backstamp or the designer's signature.

Butter tub, hammered, embossed
leaves **16.00**
Candy dish, leaf shape, hammered,
unmarked **7.00**
Casserole, side handles, with lid,
floral relief **12.50**

**Casserole, marked Continental Silver Co. Inc., Wild Rose, Brilliantone,
$12.50.**

Chafing dish, cylinder base, wood handles, electric, Russel Wright **120.00**

Crumber & brush, #444, hammered, Rodney Kent **22.50**

Ladle, 14" **4.50**

Percolator, wood handle, with basket, 1-cup **12.00**

Pitcher, water; plain, hammered, large **10.00**

Relish, fruit relief, hexagonal, scalloped, Cromwell **8.50**

Tray, elaborate relief, 11½" diameter **10.00**

Tray, embossed roses, flowers, & scrolls in center, 13x6" . . **7.00**

Tray, flowers & eagle, hammered, 11x11" **10.00**

Tray, with handles, tulip relief, hammered, Kent, 14" . . **30.00**

Wastebasket, floral relief, Everlast, 11x11" **22.50**

Animal Dishes with Covers

Popular novelties for part of this century as well as the last, figural animal dishes were made by many well-known glass houses in milk glass, slag, colored opaque, or clear glass. These are preferred by today's collectors, though the English earthenware versions are highly collectible in their own right.

American hen, milk glass . . **85.00**

Bird with berry, milk glass, Greentown **300.00**

Cat, milk glass, marked Pat'd Aug 6, 1889, 8" long **100.00**

Cat on hamper, chocolate glass, Greentown **350.00**

Cat on ribbed base, blue, Westmoreland Specialty **95.00**

Chick & eggs, milk glass, Westmoreland **90.00**

Chick emerging from horizontal egg, milk glass **95.00**

Cat, white head, blue body and base, Westmoreland, $90.00.

Dog on wide-ribbed base, amber, Westmoreland **45.00**

Donkey, powder jar; clear . . **12.00**

Duck, milk glass, amethyst head, glass eyes, 10¾" long . **215.00**

Duck, milk glass, McKee . . **150.00**

Duck on cattail base, milk glass, 5½" **65.00**

Duck on wavy base, milk glass, Westmoreland **75.00**

Eagle with young, milk glass, glass eyes, Westmoreland . ., . . **85.00**

Elephant, standing, 9" **45.00**

Hand & dove, milk glass, Westmoreland **50.00**

Hen on a basketweave base, milk glass **35.00**

Hen on cattail base, milk glass **65.00**

Hen on diamond basketweave nest, milk glass, Greentown. **135.00**

Hen on nest, milk glass, Westmoreland, 7" **45.00**

Lamb, blue with milk glass head, 5½" long, $135.00.

Recumbent cow, vaseline, 4½x6½", $200.00.

Hen on wide-ribbed base, Degenhart **15.00**

Lamb on picket fence base, milk glass **85.00**

Lion on ribbed base, milk glass, Atterbury **130.00**

Lovebirds, powder jar **15.00**

Quail, milk glass **65.00**

Rabbit, clear, Vallerysthal .**95.00**

Rabbit, milk glass, Imperial, 9" long **85.00**

Rabbit emerging from horizontal egg, milk glass **125.00**

Rabbit on domed lid, milk glass, Greentown **150.00**

Rabbit with mule ears on picket fence base, milk glass ..**70.00**

Rooster, blue opaque **45.00**

Rooster, clear with paint, Challinor, Taylor & Co, 8" ...**95.00**

Rooster on ribbed base, milk glass, Westmoreland **65.00**

Swan, clear frosted, Vallerysthal, 5½" long **95.00**

Turkey, standing, clear, Cambridge, large **150.00**

Turkey, standing, clear, Cambridge, small **45.00**

Turkey, milk glass **85.00**

Turtle, rectangular base ...**70.00**

Art Deco

The Art Deco movement began at the Paris International Exposition in 1925 and lasted into the 1950s. Styles of apparel, furniture, jewelry, cars, and architecture were influenced by its cubist forms and sweeping, aerodynamic curves. Sleek greyhounds and female nudes (less voluptuous than Art Nouveau nudes), shooting stars and lightning bolts, exotic woods and lush fabrics — all were elements of the Art Deco era. Today's fashions, especially in home furnishings, reflect the movement; and collectors delight in acquiring authentic examples to recreate the posh Art Deco environment.

Belt buckle, multicolor Bakelite **15.00**

Bookends, hand-painted nudes in garden, basalt, pair ...**42.00**

Candle holder, chrome, stylized fish-form handles, 4", pair ..**35.00**

Cigarette lighter, Catalin, 3", $25.00.

Cigarette lighter, painted enamel
on chrome, marked **47.50**

Cocktail shaker, chrome, wood
handle, wood lid finial . **37.50**

Cocktail shaker, sterling, 30-ounce,
10½" **190.00**

Compact, embossed floral design on
sterling silver **75.00**

Compact, green enamel over
chrome **10.00**

Cuff links, sterling, marked Georg
Jensen **47.50**

Figurine, flamingo, pink, porcelain,
10½" **45.00**

Flower frog, dancing girl, porcelain,
marked Germany, 8" . . **30.00**

Humidor, solid bronze, wood lined,
5x7½" **65.00**

Inkwell, Bakelite, with plumed
pen **18.00**

Inkwell, brass with milk glass insert **95.00**

Inkwell, hammered copper & cast
brass, hinged lid **75.00**

Lamp, white cube with black scottie
dog **67.00**

Letter rack, brass, 3 divider sections, marked ES Gesh **55.00**

Powder box, silver butterfly on blue
enameled metal, oval . . **20.00**

Powder jar, frosted green glass,
clown lid finial **42.00**

Powder jar, frosted pink glass,
Egyptian head finial . . . **45.00**

Powder jar, onyx, metal lady
finial **40.00**

Purse, wire mesh with chain
handle **37.50**

Table lamp, electric, copper,
marked Armour Bronze Core
1928 . . . . **90.00**

**Lamp base, bronze with green
patina, no mark, 13", $125.00.**

Art Nouveau

'New Art' originated in the late
1890s in the L'Art Nouveau shop on
the Rue de Provence in Paris and
lasted until the 1920s. The style
took themes from nature — flowers,
insects, fruits, animals, and female
nudes — and used them in flowing,
sensuous, asymmetrical forms. It influenced every aspect of fashion —
jewelry, furniture, art, silver, glass,
bronzes, and ceramics — and many

examples remain to delight today's collectors.

Lamp, patinated metal figural, green marble base, French, 1900, 40", $650.00.

Ash tray, portrait relief of lady, pewter **22.00**
Bottle, perfume; applied sterling flowers on crystal **40.00**
Cake plate, stylized lilies, round, 11" **75.00**
Calendar, Larkin, 1906 ....**35.00**
Candelabra, silverplated, 5-light, ca 1910 ....**180.00**

Candlestick, lotus blossom relief, brass, 10½" **87.00**
Card tray, nude to side, pewter finish metal, 4½x7" **72.00**
Cigar holder, draped lady, metal, unmarked **85.00**
Crumber, handled, embossed flowers, silverplated, 11" ...**15.00**
Inkwell, bust of youth relief, metal, attributed de Feure, 9" long **220.00**
Knife, pen; 2 blades, sterling silver **37.50**
Match safe, brass **35.00**
Match safe, embossed portrait bust of lady, sterling silver ..**65.00**
Note pad, embossed florals, German silverplate **45.00**
Plaque, cherub & lady in relief, chalkware **48.00**
Razor, folding; lady's face in relief on celluloid handle **22.50**
Shaving mug, decorated with crocus, marked Derby & Silverplate **42.50**
Shoe horn, full-length nude, sterling silver **80.00**
Tray, handled & footed, traditional relief, 12" **35.00**
Tray, lady in long gown, tin litho, 1910, 10" diameter **60.00**

Autographs

Autographs of famous people from every walk of life are of interest to students of Philography, as it is referred to by those who enjoy this hobby. Values hinge on many

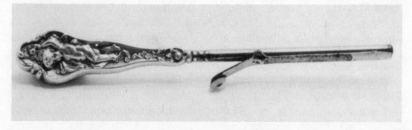

Curling iron, sterling with embossed cherub, 7", $50.00.

things — rarity of the signature and content of the signed material are major considerations. Autographs of sports figures or entertainers often sell at $10.00 to $15.00 for small signed photos. Beware of forgeries. If you are unsure, ask established dealers to help you.

Jimmy Carter, autographed letter signed as President-Elect on church stationery, scarce, $1,800.00.

Allen, Rex; inscribed signed photo, 8x6" **8.50**
Astaire, Fred; signed on a 3x5" card **5.00**
Bacall, Lauren; signed black & white photo cut from a book . .**25.00**
Baker, Carroll; signed glossy black & white photo **8.50**
Bergman, Ingrid; signed on 3x5" card **30.00**
Bolger, Ray; signed glossy black & white photo as Oz scarecrow, 8x10" **25.00**
Boone, Richard; inscribed signed glossy black & white photo, 8x10" **18.50**
Bradley, Tom; inscribed signed black & white photo **7.50**
Burnett, Carol; inscribed signed glossy black & white photo, 8x10" **12.50**
Capp, Al; signed on 2x4" slip of paper **10.00**

Cash, Johnny & June Carter; both names signed on black & white photo **15.00**
Christy, Howard Chandler; signed on card **25.00**
Cobb, Lee J; inscribed signed black & white photo, 8x10" . .**15.00**
Colonna, Jerry; inscribed signed photo **15.00**
Coogan, Jackie; inscribed & signed photo from the film 'The Kid' **12.50**
Elgart, Les; inscribed & signed on card **15.00**
Flanagan, Edward J; signed 3x5" card **15.00**
Ford, Betty; inscribed & signed photo **20.00**
Ford, Henry II; inscribed signed color photo, 8x10" **8.00**
Harvey, Paul; inscribed & signed photo **15.00**
Helms, Jesse; signed color photo, 8x10" **8.50**

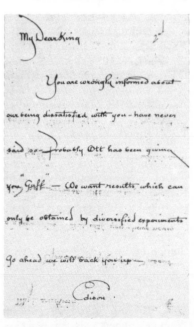

Thomas Edison, autographed letter signed, dated 1885, $500.00.

21

Heston, Charlton; signed glossy
black & white photo ...**15.00**
Holt, Victoria; signed glossy black
& white photo, 5x7" ...**18.50**
Humphrey, Hubert H; signed on
5x7" card **15.00**
Hunter, Kim; signed black & white
photo, 8x10" **6.00**
James, Harry; inscribed signed
photo, 5x7" **12.00**
Jong, Erica; inscribed signed black
& white photo, 8x10" ...**8.00**
Koch, Edward; inscribed signed
black & white photo **7.50**
Lynde, Paul; inscribed signed black
& white photo, 8x10" ..**22.50**
MacGraw, Ali; signed glossy black
& white photo, 8x10" ..**18.50**
Mathis, Johnny; signed black &
white photo, 8x10" **15.00**
Meadows, Audrey; inscribed signed
photo, 8x10" **12.50**
Meredith, Burgess; signed color
photo from the film 'Rocky,'
8x10" **15.00**
Minelli, Liza; inscribed signed black
& white photo, 8x10" ..**10.00**
Newhart, Bob; inscribed signed
photo, 8x10" **8.50**
O'Brien, George; signed photo, black
& white, 5x7" **12.00**
Oswald Porter, Marina; signed on
card **25.00**
Price, Vincent; signed photo, vintage, 2x2" **15.00**
Rayburn, Sam; signed on Speaker
of House stationery ...**15.00**
Rickles, Don; inscribed signed glossy
black & white photo ...**10.00**
Sinclair, Upton; handwritten signed
post card **20.00**
Slaughter, Frank G; signed black &
white photo, 4x5" **10.00**
Struthers, Sally; inscribed signed
glossy black & white photo,
8x10" **12.50**
Wagner, Robert; signed black &
white photo, 8x10" **15.00**
West, Dottie; inscribed signed black
& white photo, 8x10" ...**8.00**

Williams, Andy; inscribed signed
black & white photo ...**12.50**

Automobilia

Many are fascinated with vintage automobiles, but to own one of
those 'classy chassis' is a luxury not
all can afford! So instead they enjoy
collecting related memorabilia such
as advertising, owners' manuals,
horns, emblems, and hood ornaments. The decade of the 1930s
produced the items that are most in
demand today, but the fifties models have their own band of devoted
fans as well. Usually made of porcelain on cast iron, first-year license
plates in hard-to-find excellent
condition may bring as much as
$200.00 for the pair.

**Chevrolet Motor Car calendar,
dated 1920, 31x16", $160.00.**

22

Sales folder for 1938 Chryslers, 18x21", NM, $40.00; for 1937 Chrysler Airstreams, 12x17", $35.00.

Ash tray, Flying Red Horse, metal, small 10.00

Ash tray, John Deere Vanbrunt, steel 10.00

Ash tray, tire, BF Goodrich Silvertown 600-16 .... 15.00

Badge, employee; Dodge Brothers, star shaped 20.00

Badge, supervisor; REO, enameled metal 25.00

Booklet, Why Women Prefer the Ford V-8 .... 15.00

Booklet, 1932 Ford Instruction, NM 28.00

Calendar, desk; 1948 Packard, metal with logo 15.00

Catalog, Corvair, 1960, full color, NM 5.00

Coin, Futuramatic 88 Oldsmobile, brass 10.00

First aid kit, Tabloid First Aid #716, ca 1925 .... 12.00

Hood ornament, 1950 Pontiac Indian Head 22.00

Horn, brass with rubber bulb, 18", NM 27.50

Ink blotter, Sunoco Blue Motor Fuel, EX 8.00

Keychain, coin-holder/scraper; Flying Red Horse 6.00

Keychain, license plate; Iowa, 1945, NM 10.00

Keychain, registration holder; Hudson, ca 1950 ...... 15.00

Manual, owner's; Chevrolet 1953, EX 15.00

Manual, owner's; Oldsmobile 1936, EX 35.00

Manual, repair; Chevrolet 1930, EX 35.00

Manual, shop; Buick 1946 .. 10.00

Manual, shop; Chevrolet 1930, 275 pages 35.00

Map, Shell, Wisconsin, 1940 . 4.00

Medallion, 10th Anniversary, Chrysler, brass, 1924 .. 25.00

Model, promotional; Ford Galaxie 50 2-door hardtop, 1962, NM 35.00

Motometer, Minute Man 6 . 45.00

Pencil, Cadillac Script Bullet, early, NM 15.00

Pencil, Conoco, wood, ca 1950, unsharpened 5.00

Pin, 1933 Chevrolet Watch the Leader 15.00

Plate, dinner; Buick, script logo, ceramic 45.00

Post card, photo of 1967 Mustang convertible 2.50

Program, Indy 500 Official, 1951, EX 10.00

Radiator emblem, Hupmobile, enameled metal 45.00

Screwdriver, Studebaker, metal handle 25.00

Spark plug, Diamond, EX ... 5.00

Tire gauge, brass, marked A Schrader's Son, Brooklyn, New York 35.00

Toy truck, Mobil Gas Flying Red Horse, tin, EX 35.00

Aladdin teapot, $38.00.

Autumn Leaf

Autumn Leaf dinnerware was a product of the Hall China Company, who produced this extensive line from 1933 until 1978 for exclusive distribution by the Jewell Tea Company. The Libbey Glass Company made co-ordinating pitchers, tumblers, and stemware. Metal, cloth, plastic, and paper items were also available. Today, though very rare pieces are expensive and a challenge to acquire, new collectors may easily reassemble an attractive, usable set at a reasonable price.

Blanket, twin size	50.00
Bowl, cereal; 6"	8.00
Bowl, fruit; 5½"	3.00
Bowl, metal; set of 3	65.00
Bowl, salad; 3½-pint	14.00
Bowl, vegetable; 10½"	60.00
Bowl, vegetable; oval, 10½"	12.00
Bowl, vegetable; 9"	60.00
Cake plate, 9½"	10.00
Canister, metal, round, with ivory plastic cover	10.00
Canister, metal, round, with matching cover, 6"	15.00
Casserole, 10-ounce	8.00
Casserole, 2-pint	55.00
Coaster, metal, 3⅛"	4.00
Creamer, New Style	8.00
Creamer, Old Style, 4¼"	15.00
Cup & saucer	8.00
Custard cup	4.00
Fruit cake tin, metal	10.00
Gravy boat	15.00
Hot pad, oval	10.00
Marmalade jar, 3-piece	45.00
Mug, beverage	45.00
Mustard jar, 3½"	45.00
Napkin, ecru muslin	20.00
Pickle dish, oval, 9"	16.00
Pie baker, 9½"	18.00
Place mat, paper, scalloped	22.00
Plate, 10"	10.00
Plate, 6"	4.00
Plate, 7"	4.00
Plate, 8"	8.00
Plate, 9"	7.00
Platter, 11½"	14.00
Platter, 13½"	16.00
Range set, pair of shakers & covered drippings jar	32.00
Shakers, Casper, pair	16.00
Shakers, range; w/handle	16.00

Cookie jar, $100.00.

Tablecloth, cotton sailcloth with gold
    stripe, 54x54" **60.00**
Teakettle, enamelware **75.00**
Teapot, long spout, 7" **45.00**
Tidbit tray, 2-tier **35.00**
Toaster cover, plastic, fits 2-slice
    toaster **25.00**
Towel, tea; cotton, 16x33" ..**35.00**
Trash can, red metal **65.00**
Tumbler, Brockway, 13-ounce
    size **15.00**
Tumbler, Brockway, 16-ounce
    size **18.00**
Tumbler, Brockway, 9-oz. ..**14.00**
Tumbler, gold frost etched, flat
    bottom, 10-ounce **30.00**
Tumbler, gold frost etched, footed
    bottom, 10-ounce **45.00**

Aviation Collectibles

Collectors of aviation memorabilia search for items dealing with
zeppelins, flying machines — aircraft of any type, be it experimental,
commercial, civilian, or military.
From airplane parts and pilot's gear
to photos and magazines, there is a
multitude of material relative to
this area of interest.

Armband, US Army Air Force AWS
    Observer, WWII AAF ...**2.00**
Aviator cap, green-colored baseball
    type, WWII USN **10.00**
Bag, survival dye marker; current
    issue, USAF **5.00**
Boots, flight; Russian **140.00**
Clothing card, WWII RAF, 1942,
    EX **25.00**
Compass, aircraft; WWII Japanese,
    EX **90.00**
Compass, astro; in original wood
    case, WWII RAF **65.00**

Compass, directional; WWII German 40.00
Flap switch, Spitfire 20.00
Gloves, Nomex flight 15.00
Handbook, AAF Combat Air Intelligence, WWII 25.00
Helmet, flight; light blue mesh cloth, RAF, ca 1950 .... 15.00
Life vest, current issue, USN Aircraft 15.00
Model, RAF Hurricane, black cardboard, 1/72 scale 10.00
Oxygen masks, type A-10 standard, WWII AAF 35.00
Parachute, Luftwaffe backpack type, WWII, ca 1943 .. 325.00
Photo, A3D-2 Skywarrior in flight, black & white, 8x10" ... 3.00
Pilot wings, yellow & silver on blue cloth, WWII Japanese Army, NM 30.00
Poster, aircraft ID; WWII AAF, 1942, EX 5.00
Signal lamp, type C-3, complete in box, WWII AAF 65.00
Sleeping bag, Luftwaffe, WWII, EX 200.00
Surgeon wings, gold-plated pinback, WWI USN 10.00
Survival knife, 2 blue metal blades & black grips, WWII AAF, EX 55.00
Survival moccasins, white cloth, leather bottoms, USAF 15.00
Throat microphone, type T-30, WWII AAF 10.00
Uniform, dress blue supply; USN, complete 35.00
Vickers machine gun links, 10 links in original box, WWI .. 10.00
Wing badge, American Boy Junior Pilot-Future Pilot 18.00

Avon

Originally founded under the title California Perfume Company, the firm became officially known as Avon Products, Inc., in 1939, after producing a line of cosmetics marketed under the Avon name since the mid-twenties. Among collectors they are best known not for their cosmetics and colognes but for their imaginative packaging and figural bottles. Also collectible are product samples, awards, magazine ads, jewelry, and catalogues.

American Ideal Set, green silk-lined box, 1919 .... 400.00
Atomizer, green frosted bottle, 1928, 2-ounce, 5¾" 70.00
Bay Rum, clear glass, cork stopper, rare, 1912, 16-ounce .. 145.00
Boot Spray cologne, 1968, 3-ounce figural 3.00
Bubble Bath, bottle with blue cap, 1950, 4-ounce 20.00
Christmas Cheer, boxes of sachet powder, 1929 .... 35.00
Cocker Spaniel, white glass & cap, 1978 .... 6.00
Cotillion Bath Oil, plastic bottle, 1962, 6-ounce 4.00
Cotillion Cologne, pink cap, 1948, 6-ounce 55.00
Cotillion Perfume, metal cap, 1934, ¼-ounce 50.00
Crystal Candle Holders, clear crystal, 1980, 10", pair ... 120.00
Diary Clock, gold, 1968 .... 42.00
Firefighter Decanter, 6-ounce size, 1975 .... 4.00
Heart Stick Pin Award, sterling silver, 1978 .... 25.00
Jolly Surprise Set, pink & white box, 1952 .... 40.00
Merry Christmas Mug, glass mug, 1977 .... 5.00
Mickey Mouse Bubble Bath, 4½-ounce, 1970 .... 5.00
Paul Revere Bell Decanter, 4-ounce, 1979 .... 6.00
Playmate, carrying case, 1956, M 80.00
Short Pony Decanter, 4-ounce figural, 1969 .... 4.00

Smile Pendant Award, red & gold, 1978 .... **12.00**
Three Bears, white plastic bottles blue caps, 1967, 4¼" **5.00**
Timothy Tiger, Germany, yellow plastic soap dish, 1973 . **12.00**
Top Style Set, box, 1956 ... **20.00**
World Bank, plastic globe of Europe, 1976 .... **10.00**

Azalea China

Manufactured by the Noritake Company from 1916 until the midthirties, Azalea dinnerware was given away as premiums to club members and home agents of the Larkin Company, a door-to-door agency who sold soap and other household products. Over the years, seventy chinaware items were offered as well as six pieces of matching hand-painted crystal. Early pieces were signed with the blue 'rising sun' Nippon trademark, followed by the Noritake M-in-wreath mark. Later the ware was marked Noritake, Azalea, Hand Painted, Japan.

Basket, #193 .... **145.00**
Bowl, #310 .... **50.00**
Bowl, #439 .... **235.00**

Bowl, oatmeal; #55 .... **18.00**
Bowl, salad; #12 .... **32.00**
Bowl, vegetable; #101 ..... **40.00**
Cake plate, #10 .... **50.00**
Candle holder, #114, pair .. **30.00**
Celery tray, #99 .... **50.00**
Compote, #170 .... **60.00**
Creamer & sugar bowl with gold finial, #401 .... **115.00**
Cruet, #190 .... **175.00**
Cup & saucer, #2 .... **18.00**
Egg cup, #120 .... **40.00**
Gravy boat, #40 .... **50.00**
Milk jug, #100 .... **175.00**
Mustard jar, #191 ...... **48.00**
Plate, dinner; #13 .... **20.00**
Plate, soup; #19 .... **18.00**
Platter, #17 .... **55.00**
Platter, #311 .... **180.00**
Sandwich tray, #112 ..... **60.00**
Shakers, #11, pair **28.00**
Teapot, #15 .... **80.00**
Teapot tile, #169 .... **45.00**
Toothpick holder, #192 ... **90.00**
Vase, #187 .... **125.00**

Badges

Wild West badges and those once worn by officials whose positions no longer exist — City Constable, for instance — are tops on the lists of today's badge collectors. All law-

Celery tray, #444, 10", $240.00.

27

enforcement badges are considered collectible as well. Badges have been made in many materials and styles since the 1840s when they came into general use in this country. They were usually of brass or nickel silver, though even silver and gold were used on special order. Stars, shields, octagonals, ovals, and disks are the most common shapes.

Allied Detective Agency Guard, silver finish, pin-back **25.00**
Automobile Investigator, silver finish shield **45.00**
Chauffeur, IN; silver finish, triangle, pin-back, 1935 . . . . **12.00**
Chauffeur, OH; silver finish, oval, 1950, 1¾" **8.50**
Constable, TN; state seal in center, silver finish shield **20.00**
Court Officer, PA; seal in blue enamel on silver **75.00**
Defense Corps, Dept of Public Safety Albany on shield **50.00**
Deputy Constable, CO; 6-point star, silver finish **35.00**
Deputy Sheriff, Sullivan Co, TN; star shape clip-on **18.00**
Deputy Sheriff, Tehama Co; nickel star, 2½" **35.00**
Deputy US Marshall, Pecos, TX; made of half dollar . . **150.00**
Deputy US Marshall, peso coin with cut star in center, EX . **100.00**
Detective Guard, PA; state seal, Allied Agency Inc **27.00**

Drivers License, KY; state seal, round, brass, 1963 . . . . . **7.50**
Fire Inspector, dog wearing helmet, black, engraved . . **10.00**
Fireman, Auxiliary Fire Co Clifton Forge, VA; 1½" **15.00**
Junior G Man, metal shield shape, Melvin Purvis **27.00**
Patrolman, shield shape, eagle at top, screw back **18.00**
Police, Bristol, VA, Police #10; star shape **18.00**
Police, Dept of Motor Vehicles, KS; star shape **25.00**
Police Chief, Camas, WA; eagle atop shield, star in center . **225.00**
Railroad Sergeant, B&O RR; gold finish shield **150.00**
Railway, 'PA Railroad Police' in relief on shield, large . **175.00**
Revenue Inspector, AR #341; engraved columns on shield, silver metal **50.00**
Sheriff, Lincoln Co, MT; 6 ball-point star **50.00**
Special Police, General Hospital, MA; silver metal shield. **10.00**
Watchman, 'Works Projects Administration,' round **22.50**

Banks

The most popular (and expensive) type of bank with today's collectors are the mechanicals, so called because of the antics they perform when a coin is deposited. Over three

14k badges, about $250.00 for any example.

28

hundred models were produced between the Civil War period up to the first World War. On some, arms wave, legs kick, or mouths open to swallow up the coin — amusing nonsense intended by the inventor to encourage and reward thriftiness. The registering bank may have one or more slots and, as the name implies, tallys the amount of money it contains as each coin is deposited. Many old banks have been reproduced — beware! Condition is important; look for good original paint and parts.

Some of the banks listed here are identified by C for Cranmer, D for Davidson, L for long, and M for Moore, oft-used standard reference books.

Mechanical Banks

Always Did 'Spise a Mule, D-250, bench, EX **750.00**
Bad Accident, D-20, mule pulls man & cart, child on ground beside **1,450.00**
Bamboula, D-21 ......**1,000.00**
Birdie Putt, cast iron/polychrome paint, 9" **85.00**
Boy on Trapeze, D-50, painted cast iron, VG **1,600.00**
Bulldog, D-69, standing, coin on tongue, cast iron/worn paint, 3½" **500.00**
Cat & Mouse, D-104, painted cast iron, 8¼", VG **1,500.00**
Cat Boat, painted cast iron, tin sail, 11", EX **95.00**
Creedmore, D-137, cast iron, VG paint, Stevens, patented 1877, 10" **600.00**
Dark Town Battery, D-146, cast iron, worn paint, 9⅞" **1,950.00**
Eagle & Eaglets, D-165, cast iron, EX paint, Stevens, patented 1883, 10" **750.00**
Fisherman, cast iron, polychrome paint, 12¼" **95.00**
Football Player, D-192, fake bank, converted toy **150.00**

Monkey and Coconut, D-332, VG, $1,700.00; Clown on Globe, D-127, G, $1,400.00.

Fun Producing Savings Bank, D-205, tin **750.00**

Grenadier, D-223, soldier aims rifle at tree, EX **650.00**

Hall's Excelsior, D-228, painted cast iron, 3¾", EX **275.00**

Home Bank, D-242, no dormers, cast iron, EX **800.00**

Horse Race, D-246, straight base style **2,700.00**

Humpty Dumpty, D-248, painted cast iron, EX **750.00**

Joe Socko, D-262 ....**750.00**

Jolly Nigger, cast aluminum with worn paint, Starkies Patent, 6¾" **85.00**

Jolly Nigger with High Hat, D-272, aluminum, EX **275.00**

Leap Frog, D-292, EX ...**2,100.00**

Mason, D-321, painted cast iron, 7½", EX **4,000.00**

New Creedmore, D-358 .**1,200.00**

Organ Bank, D-368, boy & girl, monkey wearing red jacket, 7⅝" **700.00**

Pelican with Arab, D-381, painted cast iron, EX **2,800.00**

Rabbit in Cabbage, D-408, 4½", NM **350.00**

Safety Locomotive, D-422.**2,000.00**

Speaking Dog, D-447, cast iron with worn paint, 7" **925.00**

Strike, cast iron with polychrome paint, 11½" **95.00**

Teddy & the Bear, D-459, painted cast iron, Stevens Patent, 10", VG **800.00**

Uncle Tom, painted cast iron, star base plate, EX **400.00**

William Tell, D-565, painted cast iron, VG **600.00**

Registering Banks

Astronaut Daily Dime **20.00**

B&R Mfg, NY, 10¢ register .**10.00**

Bed Post, M-1305, 5¢ register **65.00**

Get Rich Quick Bank, by Marx, patented, 3½", $55.00.

Beehive Savings, M-681, nickel-plated cast iron with paint traces, 5" **125.00**

Bucket, 1¢ register, cast iron, Japan, pat applied, 2¾" ..**80.00**

Daily Dime Clown **16.00**

Honeycomb, C-105, 5¼" ...**100.00**

Junior Cash, M-930, nickel-plated cast iron, 4¼", VG **65.00**

Kettle, painted nickel-plated cast iron, 5¢ register, 3½" ..**20.00**

Popeye, 10¢ register, EX ...**30.00**

Prudential, nickeled cast iron, pat Feb 25, 1890, 7", VG ...**45.00**

Rockford Nat'l Bank, 10¢ register, EX **24.00**

Spinning Wheel, tin litho with 2 scenes, square, W Germany, 4¼" **25.00**

Trunk, Phoenix, M-947, 10¢ register, worn nickel plate, painted, 5" **95.00**

Wee Folks Money Box, tin litho, square, English, 5" **50.00**

Still Banks

Amish Boy, holds pig, sits on hay bale **65.00**

Aunt Jemima, M-176, cast iron, worn paint, 5¼" **70.00**

Baby Emerging from Eggshell, C-535, EX **35.00**

Baseball Player, L-640, cast iron, paint traces, 5¾" **135.00**

Bear, M-713, standing, cast iron, worn brown paint, 6⅜" . **65.00**

Beggar Boy, L-643, boy kneels, holds hat, 7", EX **65.00**

Billiken, M-81, Good Luck, cast iron, old repaint, 6½" **35.00**

Black Boy, M-84, 2-faced, worn black & gold paint, 3⅛" **65.00**

Boy Scout, M-45, cast iron, paint traces, 5⅞" **80.00**

Bulldog, L-72, cast iron, 4" . **35.00**

Camel, M-768, cast iron, worn gold, red & orange paint, 5" . **45.00**

Carpet Bag, C-352, bronze, 3½", EX **45.00**

Cat, M-366, seated, cast iron, worn multicolor paint, 4⅛" . **145.00**

Clock, M-1537, cast iron, repaint, hand missing, 4½" **85.00**

Colonial House, M-993, cast iron, EX old paint, 3" **95.00**

Crown Bank, M-1227, cast iron, gray paint, worn trim, 3½" . . **45.00**

Dock Yak, L-692, cast iron, 4⅝", EX **220.00**

Owl, cast iron with gold paint, Be Wise Save Money, 5", $185.00.

Donkey, M-499, cast iron, green paint, 4½" long **50.00**

Dutch Boy, M-180, cast iron, pastel-colored paint, 5½", EX . **50.00**

Eiffel Tower, M-1074, cast iron, metallic finish, 9" **650.00**

Elephant, M-455, swivel trunk, cast iron, black paint, gold trim, 4" **155.00**

Elephant, M-472, cast iron, worn gray paint, 4⅛" long . . . **15.00**

Elephant with Howdah, M-457, cast iron, gold trim, 2⅜" **55.00**

Fido, M-193, cast iron, polychrome paint, modern, 4⅞" **45.00**

Frog, M-692, Iron Art, cast iron, green paint, 7" long . . . **55.00**

General Pershing, L-815, cast iron, 7¾" **195.00**

Globe, M-812, cast iron, worn striped bronze finish, 5⅜" **110.00**

High Rise, M-1219, cast iron, EX metallic paint, 5½" **65.00**

Horse, M-506, prancing, cast iron, EX gold paint, 4⅝" . . . **165.00**

Horse, M-532, cast iron, gold paint, 3" **115.00**

House, W-408, 2-story dwelling, cast iron **85.00**

Indian, L-751, cast iron, 6". . **150.00**

Lamb, M-595, cast iron, worn white paint, 3⅛" **95.00**

Lion, M-755, cast iron, EX gold paint, red trim, 5⅛" **35.00**

Lucky Joe, glass **15.00**

Mourner's Purse, L-1481, lead, 1902, 5" **50.00**

Our Kitchener, M-1313, cast iron, 6½" **145.00**

Pirate Chest, tin **32.00**

Rabbit, M-568, cast iron, paint traces, 3¾" **65.00**

Radio, M-821, cast iron, blue paint & gold traces, 3¼" **95.00**

Sailor, M-27, cast iron, worn paint, 5¼" **105.00**

Scotty, L-118, cast iron, 3¼", EX **65.00**

Sharecropper, W-18 . . . . . . **195.00**

Statue of Liberty, M-1164, cast
iron, worn gold, 6" . . **115.00**
Stove, Parlor; L-1004, cast iron, 7",
EX **75.00**
Tank, M-1437, cast iron, worn gold
paint, 4½" long **85.00**
Trolley Car, L-1605, cast iron, no
wheels, 2½" **250.00**
US Mail, M-839, cast iron, worn red
paint, 3½" **25.00**
Woolworth Building, M-1045, lead,
worn silvering, 4" **35.00**
Yellow Cab, L-1570, cast iron, 4",
VG **400.00**

Barber Shop

Though few fans of barber shop
memorabilia have any personal
recall of the old-time tonsorial
establishments, the fancy blown
glass barber bottles, tufted velvet
chairs, and red, white, and blue
poles that once hung at their doors
kindle a spark of nostalgia among
them.

See also Shaving Mugs; Razors.

Ash tray, William Marvy Barber
Supplies, 5" diameter . . **12.00**
Bottle, cranberry glass, Hobnail,
7½" **52.50**
Bottle, Witch Hazel, clambroth, with
stopper **40.00**

**Child's chair mounted on lion, J.L.
Hudson, ca 1915, 48" long, $4,000.00.**

Bottle, Witch Hazel, hand-painted
milk glass, applied lip. . **130.00**
Chair, carved oak with gold-colored
upholstery, NM **750.00**
Child's chair booster, adjustable,
leather-covered seat . . . **30.00**
Display card, Gold'N Honey Blade,
original in box **42.00**
Jug, Mascaro Tonique for the Hair,
blue on off-white, 10" . . **50.00**
Neck duster, turned cherry wood
handle, 10" **15.00**
Pamphlet, What Kind of Beard Have
You?, 15 pages, 3½x6" . **16.00**
Pole, turned wood, 3-color paint,
crown with ball top, 1900s,
44x4" **495.00**
Razor sharpener, Automatic Kriss
Kross **12.50**
Safetee Shaving Cabinet, painted
woodgrain on tin, USA . **22.00**
Shaver, Stahly Stroke, vibrating,
EX, in original box **75.00**
Shaving mirror, barber pole base,
gold trim, marked CTP. . **54.00**
Spittoon, brass, 4x10" **16.00**
Strop, leather, Brandt's Automatic,
1912, in original box . . . **16.00**
Trade catalog, Biedermeier, 48
pages, German, 1909 . . **20.00**
Trade catalog, Chrometal Barber
Shop Equipment by Kochs,
1938 . . . . **75.00**

Baseball Cards

The first baseball cards were issued in the late 1800s by cigarette
and tobacco companies who packed
them with their products, primarily
to promote sales. The practice was
revived for a few years just before
WWI and again just in time to be
curtailed by the Depression. From
1933 until the onset of WWII and
from early in the 1950s to the present, chewing gum companies produced sports cards, the most popular of which are put out by Bowman

and Topps. The colored photo cards from the thirties are the most treasured, and any of a baseball great or Hall of Famer is the most valued in any particular issue.

Batter-Up, 1934-36, #6, Bill Terry, VG **28.00**

Bowman, #100, Mike Garcia, 1954, VG **1.25**

Bowman, #102, Bobby Thompson, 1955, VG **1.50**

Bowman, #102, Jim Hegan, 1953, EX/NM **12.75**

Bowman, #114, Willard Nixon, 1954, EX/NM **4.00**

Bowman, #122, Bill Serena, 1953, EX/NM **22.50**

Bowman, #129, Russ Meyer, 1953, VG **4.75**

Bowman, #133, Willie Jones, 1953, EX/NM **17.50**

Bowman, #137, Al Corwin, 1954, VG **1.00**

Bowman, #147, Bert Singleton, 1949, VG **10.00**

Bowman, #156, Del Rice, 1951, VG **3.00**

Bowman, #159, Dutch Leonard, 1952, VG **1.65**

Bowman, #160, Eddie Stankey, 1952, VG **2.50**

Bowman, #166, Stan Rojek, 1951, VG **3.00**

Bowman, #169, Hank Edwards, 1950, EX/NM **6.50**

Bowman, #169, Sid Hudson, 1951, VG **3.00**

Bowman, #18, Don Mueller, 1952, EX/NM **9.00**

Bowman, #184, Willie Mays, 1955, VG **18.00**

Bowman, #186, Richie Ashburn, 1951, VG **3.50**

Bowman, #199, Ted Gray, 1949, EX/NM **3.75**

Bowman, #204, Andy Pafko, 1952, VG **2.50**

Bowman, #213, Monte Kennedy, 1952, EX/NM **6.50**

Bowman, #141, Fred Hutchinson, 1951, EX/M, $10.00.

Bowman, #219, Gene Woodling, 1951, VG **3.25**

Bowman, #243, Johnny Groth, 1950, VG **2.25**

Bowman, #308, Al Lopez, 1955, VG **5.50**

Bowman, #37, Pee Wee Reese, 1955, VG **4.50**

Bowman, #41, Eddie Yost, 1951, EX/NM **8.00**

Bowman, #43, Bob Feller, 1952, VG **9.00**

Bowman, #44, Joe Dobson, 1950, VG **5.00**

Bowman, #44, Roy Campanella, 1952, VG **15.00**

Bowman, #47, Sammy White, 1955, VG **1.00**

Bowman, #59, Ed 'Whitey' Ford, 1955, VG **5.50**

Bowman, #60, Yogi Berra, 1950, EX/NM **120.00**

Bowman, #89, Lou Boudreau, 1955, VG **4.00**

Donruss, #0, Rollie Fingers, 1984, VG **1.00**

Donruss, #1, Wally Joyner, 1986, VG 1.50

Donruss, #181, Vince Coleman, 1986, EX/NM 2.00

Donruss, #190, Dwight Gooden, 1985, VG 3.50

Donruss, #254, Pete Rose, 1985, EX/NM 1.25

Donruss, #27, Kal Daniels, 1986, VG 1.50

Donruss, #32, Tony Fernandez, 1984, VG 2.00

Donruss, #324, Tony Gwinn, 1984, EX/NM 2.50

Donruss, #38, Bo Jackson, 1986, EX/NM 3.00

Donruss, #380, Glenn Davis, 1986, EX/NM 1.50

Donruss, #538, Tim Raines, 1981, EX/NM 5.00

Donruss, #651, Don Mattingly, 1985, EX/NM 2.50

Donruss, #66, Will Clark, 1987, EX/NM 2.00

Donruss, #68, Darryl Strawberry, 1984, VG 6.00

Fleer, #131, Don Mattingly, 1984, VG 5.00

Fleer, #15, Ellis Burks, 1987, EX/NM 1.25

Fleer, #212, Bret Saberhagen, 1985, EX/NM 2.00

Fleer, #28, Vince Coleman, 1985, EX/NM 3.75

Fleer, #30, Alvin Davis, 1984, EX/NM 5.00

Fleer, #39, John Franco, 1984, EX/NM 2.00

Fleer, #61, Jimmy Key, 1984, EX/NM 5.00

Fleer, #641, Mark Grace, 1988, EX/NM 2.50

Fleer, #648, Rob Deer, 1985, EX/NM 1.50

Fleer, #649, Jose Canseco, 1986, VG 5.50

Score, #1, Don Mattingly, 1988, EX/NM 1.25

Score, #645, Gregg Jeffries, 1988, EX/NM 1.50

Sportflics, #158, Dave Cochrane, 1987, EX/NM 2.50

Sportflics, #158, Tim Pyznarski, 1987, EX/NM 2.50

Sportflics, #178, Steve Lombardozzi, 1986, EX/NM 5.00

Sportflics, #75, Wally Joyner, 1987, EX/NM 1.50

Sportflics, #97, Darryl Strawberry, 1986, EX/NM 1.25

Topps, #101, Max Lanier, 1952, VG 4.50

Topps, #102, Bill Kennedy, 1952, VG 4.50

Topps, #104, Hank Foiles, 1957, EX/NM 2.00

Topps, #121, Cletis Boyer, 1957, EX/NM 2.50

Topps, #13, Wally Burnette, 1957, EX/NM 2.00

Topps, #135, Richie Ashburn, 1963, EX/NM 2.75

Topps, #14, Dave Concepcion, 1971, EX/NM 4.00

Topps, #140, Wes Covington, 1958, EX/NM 2.00

Topps, #141, Joe Frazier, 1956, EX/NM 2.50

Topps, #380, Hank Aaron, 1959, EX/M, $50.00.

34

Topps, #141, Joe Jay, 1954, EX/
NM 6.00

Topps, #143, Rollie Hemsley, 1954,
VG 1.25

Topps, #144, Leroy Powell, 1956,
EX/NM 2.50

Topps, #158, Tom Carroll, 1955,
VG 3.50

Topps, #16, Murry Dickson, 1951,
VG 3.50

Topps, #167, Mike Brumley, 1964,
VG 3.50

Topps, #168, Joe Cunningham,
1958, EX/NM 2.00

Topps, #171, Red Sox team, 1957,
EX/NM 4.00

Topps, #175, Marv Throneberry,
1958, EX/NM 5.00

Topps, #185, Ken Holtzmann, 1967,
EX/NM 1.00

Topps, #19, Johnny Bruchia, 1952,
VG 12.50

Topps, #194, Don Newcombe, 1975,
EX/NM 2.00

Topps, #2, Pete Rose, 1969, EX/
NM 3.00

Topps, #20, Jose Canseco, 1986,
VG 1.25

Topps, #207, Sandy Koufax, 1961,
VG 275.00

Topps, #21, Bob Bonner, 1982, EX/
NM 10.00

Topps, #212, Hank Aaron, 1959,
VG 5.00

Topps, #217, Carl Erskine, 1959,
EX/NM 3.00

Topps, #22, Bill Skowron, 1955, EX/
NM 7.00

Topps, #227, Joe Garagiola, 1952,
VG 17.50

Topps, #228, Bob Bailey, 1963,
VG 3.50

Topps, #234, Rich Beck, 1966, EX/
NM 2.00

Topps, #237, Bud Bodbielan, 1953,
VG 8.00

Topps, #238, Art Houtteman, 1952,
VG 4.50

Topps, #24, Vince Coleman, 1985,
EX/NM 4.00

Topps, #242, Bob Clemente, 1975,
EX/NM 2.50

Topps, #243, Carlos Bernier, 1953,
VG 8.00

Topps, #249, Bobby Adams, 1952,
VG 4.50

Topps, #264, Roy Hartsfield, 1952,
VG 10.00

Topps, #271, Foster Castleman,
1956, EX/NM 3.50

Topps, #273, Jim Davis, 1957, EX/
NM 8.00

Topps, #29, Whitey Herzog, 1957,
VG 2.25

Topps, #294, Rocky Bridges, 1957,
EX/NM 8.00

Topps, #301, Sam Esposito, 1957,
VG 2.00

Topps, #303, Harry Dorish, 1953,
VG 10.00

Topps, #303, Indians team, 1966,
EX/NM 1.75

Topps, #308, Luis Aloma, 1952,
VG 10.00

Topps, #314, Ed Bouchee, 1957,
VG 2.00

Topps, #318, Hal Gregg, 1952,
VG 40.00

Topps, #326, Connie Johnson, 1956,
EX/NM 3.50

Topps, #341, Steve Garvey, 1971,
EX/NM 55.00

Topps, #342, Jim Brosnan, 1958,
EX/NM 2.00

Topps, #346, Dick Littlefield, 1957,
VG 2.00

Topps, #4, Johnny Callison, 1965,
EX/NM' 2.50

Topps, #400, Gaylord Perry, 1973,
EX/NM 2.25

Topps, #401, Bob Schultz, 1952,
VG 40.00

Topps, #44, Con Dempsey, 1952,
VG 12.50

Topps, #45, Roger Maris, 1967,
VG 4.00

Topps, #463, Bobby Bragan, 1960,
EX/NM 2.25

Topps, #467, Phil Ortega, 1963, EX/
NM 4.00

Topps, #470, Ellis Clary, 1960, EX/NM **2.25**

Topps, #472, Terry Fox, 1966, EX/NM **1.25**

Topps, #499, JC Martin, 1963, EX/NM **4.00**

Topps, #503, Braves team, 1963, EX/NM **7.50**

Topps, #510, Ken McBride, 1963, EX/NM **2.00**

Topps, #52, Coot Veal, 1959, EX/NM **1.75**

Topps, #52, Ted Gray, 1953, EX/VG **2.50**

Topps, #520, Orlando Cepeda, 1963, EX/NM **10.00**

Topps, #524, Ollie Brown, 1966, VG **4.00**

Topps, #526, Paul Giel, 1960, EX/NM **4.00**

Topps, #528, Dave Duncan, 1964, EX/NM **2.50**

Topps, #528, Jesse Gonder, 1966, VG **4.00**

Topps, #528, Turk Lown, 1962, EX/NM **6.50**

Topps, #532, Dick Stigman, 1962, VG **2.50**

Topps, #532, Steve Boros, 1963, EX/NM **2.00**

Topps, #535, Willie Davis, 1966, VG **4.00**

Topps, #539, Gary Blaylock, 1959, EX/NM **5.00**

Topps, #542, Steve Hamilton, 1960, EX/NM **4.00**

Topps, #544, Duke Carmel, 1963, EX/NM **25.00**

Topps, #547, Bill Rohr, 1967, EX/NM **3.00**

Topps, #557, Bob Anderson, 1962, EX/NM **6.50**

Topps, #560, Ernie Banks, 1960, VG **5.00**

Topps, #562, Bill Monbouquette, 1961, VG **5.00**

Topps, #568, Phil Gagliano, 1964, EX/NM **2.00**

Topps, #569, Hank Allen, 1967, EX/NM **125.00**

Topps, #571, Billy Klaus, 1962, EX/NM **6.50**

Topps, #58, Jim O'Toole, 1962, EX/NM **1.25**

Topps, #581, Tony Perez, 1965, VG **12.00**

Topps, #584, Frank Fernandez, 1966, EX/NM **7.50**

Topps, #59, Jose Santiago, 1956, EX/NM **2.50**

Topps, #591, Ron Nischwitz, 1962, VG **8.00**

Topps, #593, Jack Hamilton, 1962, EX/NM **12.50**

Topps, #597, Amado Samuel, 1962, VG **5.00**

Topps, #597, Mickey Rivers, 1973, EX/NM **1.00**

Topps, #60, Luis Aparicio, 1967, EX/NM **3.25**

Topps, #616, Dave Augustine, 1975, VG **8.50**

Topps, #63, Jim Kaat, 1961, EX/NM **6.00**

Topps, #630, Steve Carlton, 1981, EX/NM **1.00**

Topps, #648, Rich Folkers, 1971, EX/NM **5.00**

Topps, #65, Frank Howard, 1971, EX/NM **1.50**

Topps, #692, Duffy Dyer, 1970, EX/NM **1.20**

Topps, #699, Jim Britton, 1971, EX/NM **1.25**

Topps, #70, Mike Cuellar, 1970, EX/NM **1.00**

Topps, #703, Mickey Mahler, 1978, VG **1.50**

Topps, #738, Jim Merritt, 1972, EX/NM **1.25**

Topps, #741, Skip Guinn, 1971, EX/NM **1.25**

Topps, #76, Bobby Richardson, 1959, VG **1.35**

Topps, #761, Ron Cey, 1972, EX/NM **9.00**

Topps, #773, Ron Brand, 1972, EX/NM **1.25**

Topps, #786, Chuck Brinkman, 1972, EX/NM **1.25**

Topps, #84, Moe Drabrowsky, 1957,
EX/NM **2.00**
Topps, #84, Rollie Fingers, 1973,
EX/NM **1.00**

Baskets

Hand-crafted baskets made from
1860 until around the turn of the
century are commanding good prices
on today's collectibles market, and
early factory-made baskets are gaining
in interest. Most valued are the
Nantucket Lighthouse baskets and
Shaker miniatures. Those designed
for specific use — cheese baskets,
herb baskets, and egg baskets, for
example — are preferred over the
general-purpose type.

See also Indian Artifacts.

Berry, child's, oak splint, walnut-
shell color, 1900, 7x6" ..**28.00**
Buttocks, half round, splint, single
back handle, 8x6x10" .**175.00**

Buttocks, splint, bentwood handle,
5½x9" diameter **65.00**
Cotton picking, splint, 19" ..**75.00**
Drying, splint, open rim handles,
openwork on base, 6x11x15",
EX **70.00**
Egg, oak splint, Shenandoah
County, VA, ca 1885, 12½x
11½" **90.00**
Egg, splint, bentwood handle,
5½x10" diameter **55.00**
Fruit, black ash, Maine, ca 1895, 7"
square bottom, 13½" ...**45.00**
Garden, chestnut splint, Blue Ridge
Mtns, ca 1890, 13½" ...**60.00**
Garden, oak splint, melon shaped,
ca 1895, 11½" **78.00**
Garden, oak splint, oval top & bot-
tom, from PA, ca 1910,
16x8x12" **43.00**
Gizzard, oak splint, TN, 1890,
12½" **150.00**
Herb gathering, oak, reinforced with
cleats, PA, ca 1895, 13" .**46.00**
Laundry, splint, 19½x30½" .**65.00**
Market, miniature, 3x3" ...**75.00**

Splint basket, 14" tall, 12" diameter, $70.00.

Miniature Nantucket basket, swing handle, initialed, early 20th century, 2¾" tall, $1,300.00.

Market, oak splint, ca 1890,
14x14x14" **75.00**
Market, splint, rectangle base, oval
top, ca 1880, 11", EX .. **40.00**
Melon, miniature, 5x7" **65.00**
Mussel gathering, oak splint, melon
shape, ca 1890, 10½" .. **30.00**
Picnic, factory made, oak splint,
tacked-on rim, with lid, ca
1900 .... **20.00**
Picnic, tin lined, ash & willow
handles, 20x15x15" ... **70.00**
Pigeon, ash splint, with hinged
double lid, carved handle, ca
1900 .... **80.00**
Rye straw, 4½x11" diameter...**25.00**
Table, oval with splayed sides,
handles at each end, ca 1880,
7" **33.00**
Utility, white oak, round, ca 1880,
7½x15½" **45.00**
Wall, oak splint, larger at top, ca
1900, 11½" **37.00**
Willow, with 2 handles, old green
paint, 16x17" **50.00**

Bauer

The Bauer Company moved from

Kentucky to California in 1909, producing crocks, gardenware, and vases until after the Depression when they introduced their first line of dinnerware. From 1932 until the early 1960s, they successfully marketed several lines of solid-color wares that are today very collectible. Some of their most popular lines are Ring, Plain Ware, and Monterey Modern.

Batter bowl, Ring, orange-red,
#37 .... **45.00**
Bread plate, LaLinda, ivory, 6"
diameter **5.00**
Butter dish, Monterey, white, ob-
long **45.00**
Butter dish, Ring, round with lid,
orange-red, #96 .... **62.00**
Cactus jar, orange, M Carlton,
4½" **45.00**
Cereal bowl, Ring, orange, 4½" di-
ameter **12.50**
Cookie jar, Ring, black ... **200.00**

Ringware pitcher, $40.00.

Lazy susan set, Al Fresco, green or
gray, complete **45.00**
Mixing bowl, Ring, black, #12, 2-
quart **60.00**
Mug, Ring, barrel, orange .. **20.00**
Nappy, Ring, green, 8" **22.50**
Planter, swan, green, 10" .. **30.00**
Plate, Ring, light blue, #61, 9" di-
ameter **12.00**
Salad bowl, Ring, green, 14". **30.00**

Shakers, Ring, barrel shape, green,
  pair **16.00**
Sherbet, Ring, yellow **40.00**
Teapot, Contempo, 6-cup . . .**20.00**
Tumbler, Ring, blue, 6-ounce**10.00**
Vase, fan shape, yellow, signed,
  4¼x5½" **28.00**

Beatles

Beatles memorabilia is becoming
increasingly popular with those who
grew up in the '60s. Almost any item
that could be produced with their
pictures or logos were manufactured
and sold by the thousands in department stores. Some have such a
high collector value that they have
been reproduced, beware!

Banjo, plastic, Mastro . . . **225.00**
Blanket, England **155.00**
Card set, Hard Day's Night **45.00**
Coat hanger, Yellow Submarine,
  1968 . . . .**25.00**
Colorforms, Yellow Submarine,
  1968 . . . .**100.00**
Cup & saucer, ceramic, made in
  England **175.00**
Curtains, England, 1964 . .**150.00**
Hairbrush **25.00**
Lamp shade, made in England,
  1964 . . . .**100.00**
Paperback book, Cellarful of Noise,
  1964, 127 pages **10.00**
Pillow, blue suits & red ties, signa-
  tures, 12" **68.00**
Pin-back button, I'm an Official
  Beatles Fan, 4" **15.00**
Pin-back button with photo, The
  Beatles, 1964 . . . .**8.00**
Pin-back flasher button, I Love
  Ringo, 2½" **15.00**
Record charm **3.00**
Record player, 1964, EX . .**255.00**
Scarf, 1964, marked Nems .**27.50**
Talcum powder, tin, made in Eng-
  land, 1964 . . . .**100.00**
Tennis shoes, 1964, unworn, mint
  in box **75.00**

Wallet, complete with all inserts,
  1964 . . . .**30.00**
Wig, 1964, mint in package .**35.00**

Beer Cans

The earliest beer cans, the flat
tops, were introduced in 1934 and
came with instructions on how to
use the punch opener. Cone tops,
patented in 1935, are rare today
and usually bring the highest prices.
From 1960 on, these were replaced
by the pull-tab type which is still in
use. Condition is very important.
Rust, dents, scratches, or other such
defects lessen the value considerably.

**Old German Brand, patented 1934,
Queen City Brewing Co, $45.00.**

ABC, flat top, 12-oz **20.00**
Adler Brau, flat top, 12-oz . .**14.00**
Alpine, flat top, 12-oz **42.00**
Bantam Ale, flat top, 7-oz . .**20.00**
Billy Carter, Billy Beer, unopened
  case **35.00**
Burgemeister Pilsner, flat top, 12-
  oz **8.00**

Cardinal, flat top, 12-oz **7.00**
Carling Red Cap Ale, flat top, 12-oz **15.00**
Colorado Gold Label, flat top, 12-oz **5.00**
Cook's, pull top, red & white, 12-oz **1.00**
Coors, flat top, 12-oz **10.00**
Drewrys, flat top, 16-oz **12.00**
Drewrys Malt Liquor , flat top, 12-oz **200.00**
Duke, pull top, Duke on label, gold, 12-oz **5.00**
El Rancho, pull top, 12-oz . . **20.00**
Falls City, flat top, 12-oz . . . **15.00**
Falstaff Draft, pull top, 16-oz **10.00**
Grace Bros Bavarian, pull top, 16-oz **15.00**
Hedrick, pull top, red & gold, 12-oz **5.00**
Heidelberg, pull top, 12-oz . . **8.00**
Home Ale, flat top, green & white, 12-oz **42.00**
Horton, flat top, orange, 12-oz **70.00**
Jax, pull top, gold & white, 10-oz **12.00**
Kingsbury, cone top, 12-oz . **30.00**
Malt Duck, pull top, 12-oz . . **30.00**
Olympia Light, pull top, 7-oz. **10.00**
Schlitz Malt Liquor, paper label, flat top, 1963, 8-oz **12.00**
Stroh's, flat top, 12-oz **5.00**
Winchester, pull top, 16-oz . . **5.00**

Beer Collectibles

Beer can collectors and antique advertising buffs as well enjoy looking for beer-related memorabilia such as tap knobs, beer trays, coasters, signs, and the like. While the smaller items of a more recent vintage are quite affordable, signs and trays from defunct breweries often bring three-digit prices. Condition is important in evaluating early advertising items of any type.

Yuengling's Beer, change tray, 4", $95.00.

Blotter, Silver Spring Brewery, paper, 16" diameter . . . **18.00**
Bottle, Jeffrey's Sparkling Edinburgh Ale Heriot Brewery, 8½" **10.00**
Calendar, Bradbury Dyer Wines & Liquors, 1884 . . . . **40.00**
Corkscrew, Anheuser Busch, brass, 3" **45.00**
Corkscrew, C Birkhofer Brewery Co, wood handle **38.00**
Corkscrew-opener, Eldredge Brewery Co, bottle shape . . . **35.00**
Cup, Old Man River Pure Rye Whiskey, collapsible, aluminum **42.00**
Dice holder, with 4 carved bone dice, Feigenspan's Ale, 1½" . . **34.00**
Foam scraper, Early Quandt Brewery Co, Troy, NY; red lettering **35.00**
Glass tumbler, American Brewery Co, Rochester, NY; eagle on shield, EX **45.00**
Glass tumbler, Buffalo Cooperative Brewery, buffalo head with flags **45.00**
Glass tumbler, Germania Brewery Co, Buffalo, NY; frosted lettering, EX **35.00**
Glass tumbler, West End Brewery, Miss Liberty wrapped in flag, EX **45.00**

Lithograph, They All Line Up for Pabst, circa 1920, EX ..**25.00**

Match holder & striker, American Brewery, stoneware ...**65.00**

Match safe, Anheuser Busch Association, St Louis **43.00**

Match safe, Rochester Brewery Co, diamond logo, EX **47.00**

Mug, Krugerbier, portrait of man drinking beer, 4½" **20.00**

Mug, Rochester Brewery Co, salt glaze **95.00**

Mug, South Bend Brewing Association, with factory scene, Mettlach **125.00**

Opener, celluloid handle, Molson's Ale, EX **15.00**

Opener, East India Ale, white label, scimitar shape **25.00**

Opener, Maltop Malt & Hops Buffalo, nude figural **25.00**

Photo, men drinking & smoking in bar, cardboard, 5x7" ...**30.00**

Poster, Jacob Hoffmann Brewing Co, NY; 31x21" **22.00**

Radio, Old Crow Whiskey, battery operated **75.00**

Sign, Carling's Ale, Nine Pints for the Law, tin **70.00**

Sign, Carling's Ale, reverse-painted glass in red/black/gold .**40.00**

Sign, corner; Hudepohl Brewing, Cincinnati; EX **12.00**

Sign, For Prosperity Legalize Beer & Wine, prohibition ...**78.00**

Sign, Grain Belt Beer, wood plaque & cast metal, 16x11" ..**18.00**

Statue, Schmidts of Philadelphia, bartender holding glass, 13" **28.00**

Tray, Budweiser, fox hunt scene, 10½x13" **30.00**

Wine glass, etched 'Canadaigua Wine & Liquor Co,' Buffalo, NY **35.00**

Bells

Of the many types of bells available to the collector today, perhaps the most popular are the brass figurals. School bells, sleigh bells, and dinner bells are also of interest. Bells have been made from a variety of materials — even glass and wood.

Figural lady, brass, 4½", $65.00.

Colonial lady with tiered skirt, figural, brass, 6½x3¼" ...**110.00**

Cow, tin with original leather neck strap, late 1800s **24.00**

Dutch girl with jug, figural, bronze, 4½" **125.00**

Geisha, figural handle, brass, English, 6" **60.00**

Lucy Locket, figural lady, brass, 3⅜" **75.00**

Napoleon, figural handle, brass, 6¾x3⅜" **65.00**

Old woman, figural, brass, heavy, 5¾x2¾" **115.00**

Peasant girl with jug, figural handle, brass, 6x3" **75.00**

Sheep, brass, strap handle .**40.00**

Sleigh, 10 on original leather neck strap **65.00**

Sleigh, 19 small brass bells on leather strap, 37" **85.00**

Wedding, Nailsea, clear with white
loopings, 10" **340.00**

**Call bell, New Departure Bell Co.,
Bristol, Conn., $45.00.**

Bennington

Bennington, Vermont, was the
location of two important potteries
that operated there from the late
1700s until the close of the next
century. The Norton Company made
redware and salt-glazed stoneware
for more than one hundred years.
The Fenton pottery (1847-1858)
produced much the same type of
ware but in addition also made
several lines of a more artistic nature. Their most famous product
was Rockingham, a brown-mottled
ware; and, though it was manufactured by many other firms until
well into the 20th century, it's not
unusual to hear an especially good
piece referred to as 'Bennington.'
Fenton also made scroddled ware,
graniteware, parian, and flint-
enameled ware. Possibly only one
in five Fenton pieces were marked,
either with a variation of the '1848'
impressed mark or the 'USP/United
States Pottery Company' backstamp, as the firm was known for
the last six years of its existence.
See also Stoneware.

Book flask, flint enamel, Departed
Spirits, 5½" **600.00**
Bottle, Coachman, 1849 mark, 11",
M **850.00**
Candlestick, Rockingham, 7⅛",
pair **600.00**
Chamber pot, flint enamel, 1849
mark, 8¾" , EX **250.00**
Creamer, Rockingham, cow form,
impressed N in base, 5½",
EX **495.00**
Cuspidor, Rockingham, impressed,
1849 mark, 9½" **200.00**
Inkwell, child sleeps with hat in
hand, brown glaze . . . **150.00**
Pitcher, Rockingham, plain, 9½",
NM **500.00**
Snuff jar, toby figure , non-flint,
4½" **575.00**
Soap dish, flint enamel, open, 1849
mark **225.00**
Soap dish, Rockingham, marked
1849, 5⅜" **35.00**
Tieback, flint enamel, 10-pointed
form, 4½", NM **300.00**
Tile, flint enamel, square with di-
agonal gridwork, marked, 7",
EX **400.00**
Tobacco jar, flint enamel, cylindri-
cal, tab handles, 7½" . **400.00**
Vase, flint enamel, tulip form, 10",
NM **600.00**
Vase, Heron, flint enamel . **575.00**

Rockingham pitcher, 9½", $500.00.

Vase, parian, boy with sheaf of wheat figural, 7", NM **100.00**
Wash bowl, flint enamel, paneled, 1849 mark, 13½", VG .**500.00**

Big Little Books

Probably everyone who is now forty to sixty years of age owned a few Big Little Books as a child. Today these thick hand-sized adventures bring prices from $10.00 to $75.00 and upwards. The first was published in 1933 by Whitman Publishing Company. Dick Tracy was the featured character. Kids of the early fifties preferred the format of the comic book, and Big Little Books were gradually phased out. Stories about super heroes and Disney characters bring the highest prices, especially those with an early copyright.

Andy Burnett on Trial, WD, 1958, VG **7.00**
Apple Mary & Dennie Foil Swindlers, 1936, EX **15.00**
Apple Mary & Dennie's Lucky Apples, 1939, EX **12.00**
Barny Google, 1935 ....**35.00**
Betty Boop, Snow White, Whitman, 1934 ....**35.00**

Big Chief Wahoo & the Great Gusto, 1938, EX **12.00**
Big Chief Wahoo & the Lost Pioneers, 1942, VG **12.00**
Blondie, Bouncing Baby Dumpling, 1940, NM **18.00**
Blondie & Dagwood in Hot Water, 1944-45, EX **12.00**
Bronco Peeler, Lone Cowboy, 1937, VG **14.00**
Buck Jones, City Below the Sea, 1934 ....**50.00**
Buck Rogers, Moons of Saturn, 1934, VG **65.00**
Buck Rogers, 25th Century AD, 1933, VG **55.00**
Bugs Bunny, 1943, VG **25.00**
Captain Midnight & Moon Woman, 1943 ....**28.00**
Chuck Mallory Railroad Detective, 1938, VG **18.00**
Cowboy Stories, 1933, EX ..**12.00**
Danger Trails in Africa, 1935, VG **25.00**
Donald Duck, Herald for Trouble, 1942, G **35.00**
Farmyard Symphony, Walt Disney, 1930 ....**25.00**
Fighting Heroes Battle for Freedom, 1943, NM **15.00**
Freckles & His Friends in the North Woods, 1935, NM **15.00**
G-Man in Action, 1940, EX .**20.00**

See listings for specific values.

Gulliver's Travels, 1939, VG.**18.00**
Jackie Cooper, Gangster's Boy, 1935, VG **18.00**
Jimmie Allen in Air Mail Robbery, 1936, NM **15.00**
Junior G-Men & the Counterfeiters, 1937, EX **15.00**
Kit Carson, 1933, EX **25.00**
Lil' Abner in New York, 1936, NM **35.00**
Little Orphan Annie, Mysterious Shoemaker, EX **22.00**
Little Orphan Annie, Thieves' Den, 1944, EX **25.00**
Lone Ranger, Secret of Somber Cavern **12.50**
Mandrake the Magician, Flame Pearls, 1946, EX **25.00**
Mickey Mouse in the Foreign Legion, EX **45.00**
Napoleon, Uncle Elby & Little Mary, 1939, EX **10.00**
Once Upon a Time, 1933 ...**50.00**
Pinocchio & Jiminy Cricket, 1940, VG **42.00**
Plainsman, 1936 ....**35.00**
Popeye, Quest of the Rainbird, 1943, EX **25.00**
Radio Patrol, Trailing the Safe Blowers **25.00**
Red Ryder, Code of the Range, 1941, VG **15.00**
Red Ryder, Secret Canyon, 1947-1948, EX **20.00**
Roy Rogers at Crossed Feather Ranch, 1945, EX **25.00**
Shirley Temple, Story of; 1930s, EX **25.00**
Smitty, Going Native, 1938 .**18.00**
Speed Douglas, Mole Gang, 1941, NM **15.00**
Spike Kelly of the Commandos, VG **15.00**
Sybil Jason, Little Big Shot, movie edition, 1935, EX **18.00**
Tailspin Tommy, Hooded Flyer, 1937, EX **20.00**
Tailspin Tommy, Hunting for Gold, 1935, G **20.00**

Tarzan, Lost Empire, 1933-48, EX **40.00**
Tarzan of the Apes, 1933 ...**60.00**
Tarzan of the Screen **22.00**
Terry & the Pirates, Giant's Vengeance, 1939, EX **20.00**
Texas Kid, 1937, EX **12.00**
Tim Tyler's Luck & Plot, 1939, EX **15.00**
Timid Elmer, Disney, 1939 .**30.00**
Tom Beatty, Ace of the Service, 1934, VG **15.00**
Treasure Island, 1943, VG .**15.00**
Uncle Don's Strange Adventure, 1936, EX **12.00**
Wash Tubbs, Pandemonia, 1934, EX **30.00**
We 3 Barrymores, 1935, G .**22.00**
Will Rogers, 1935, VG **16.00**
Zip Saunders, King of the Speedway, 1939, EX **15.00**

Black Americana

This is a wide and varied field of collector interest. Advertising, toys, banks, sheet music, kitchenware items, movie items, and even the fine arts are areas that offers Black Americana buffs many opportunities to add to their collections.

Ad card, Washburn's Best Hungarian Process, ca 1925, 5x3½", NM **7.50**
Advertising tin, Hancock Old Black Joe Axle Grease, 4½x3". **18.00**
Bell, Mammy & chef, painted ceramic, polychromed, Japan, ca 1925, pair **40.00**
Book, Bones, His Gags & Stump Speeches, New York, 1879, EX **15.00**
Book, Little Black Sambo, Rand McNally, 1934, 7x5½" ..**35.00**
Book, Little Brown Koko, illustrated by D Wagstaff, 1940 ...**42.00**

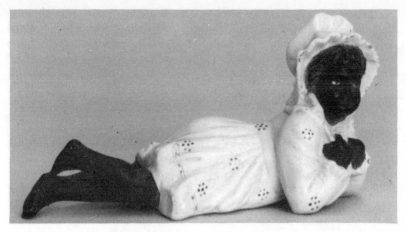

Bisque figurine, 6" long, $85.00

Book, Mammy's White Folks, 1919, NM **10.00**

Book, Uncle Wash, His Stories, 1910, NM **8.00**

Calendar, Smiling Through, lady's portrait, 1937, 20x11" . **18.00**

Cookbook, Diamond Cookbook, Cream of Wheat Co, ca 1920, NM **15.00**

Doll, Golliwog, felt, 3" **30.00**

Game, In Dixie Land **30.00**

Game, Little Black Sambo-Who Gets the 169 Pancakes, 1934 .... **57.00**

Game, Snap Cards, comical pictures, copyright 1892 .... **50.00**

Honey pot, chef with open mouth for ladle, Japan, 4¼" **30.00**

Magazine, Jet, 1963, May ... **5.00**

Mug, Japan, 4½", $32.00.

Mug, ceramic, Ooo! There Is a Difference, caricature of boy & girl, 4" **20.00**

Pin-back button, Black Is Beautiful, ca 1960, 1⅝" **7.50**

Pin-back button, Black Panther Party, ca 1965, 1¾" **10.00**

Post card, Some Folks Make Me Tir'd, ca 1912, 5½x3½" . **12.00**

Poster, Our Fight Is Here, Muhammed Ali, 1970, 22x17" . . **37.00**

Print, Colored Man Is No Slacker, WWI, 12x16" **100.00**

Salt & pepper, Mammy & chef, Japan, ca 1930 .... **27.00**

Sign, Armour, The Ham What Am & Bacon Too, 13x19" . . **50.00**

Sign, Colored Served in Rear, ca 1930, 12x3" **38.00**

Spoon rest, ceramic chef's head, Lefton, ca 1930, 4¼" . . . **32.00**

Stamp, 15¢ postal; Martin Luther King, block of 4, 1979 . . . **5.00**

Statue, seated boy, painted chalkware, 12x5x7" **30.00**

Stereoview card, Down in Dixie, ca 1920, 3½x7" **7.00**

String holder, Mammy, white apron, ca 1930 .... **65.00**

Tea towel, Mammy serving pies to children, ca 1935 ..... **22.50**

Teapot, brown face, marked Japan, ca 1935, 3¾x5⅛" **40.00**

Tin, Mammy's Favorite Brand Coffee, 4-pound, 10½" ...**125.00**
Toothpick, boy with cello, ceramic, Japan, 4" **25.00**
Toy, Tip Tap Joe, jigger dancer, in original box **85.00**
Tumbler, Old Folks at Home, on clear glass **15.00**
Valentine, linen post card, Where Is Dat Valentine...? **12.50**
Valentine, mechanical, children on donkey, large **25.00**

Black Cat

This line of fancy felines was produced mainly by the Shafford Company, although black cat lovers accept similarly-modeled, shiny glazed kitties of other manufacturers into their collections as well. Some of the more plentiful items may be purchased for $6.00 to $10.00, while the Napco bank is worth around $85.00 and the nine-piece spice set in a wooden rack usually sells for $75.00.

Ash tray, face only, flat, green eyes, red bow & ears, 3" **12.00**
Ash tray, full body, flat form, green eyes, gold trim, 3¼x4" ..**6.00**
Bookends, seated on book, fluffy look, 5½", pair **30.00**
Card caddy, long body, back holds cards, 4½x8" **35.00**
Cruet, seated, kitten forms handle, head removes, 8½" **18.00**
Cruet, seated, tail handle, red bow tie, 7½" **14.00**
Desk caddy, pen forms tail, spring body holds letters, 6½" .**10.00**
Figurine, slender, arched back, green eyes, red ears, 4⅜" **8.00**
Napkin ring, ring forms body, 2⅜" **2.50**
Pitcher, seated with milk bottle, tail handle , 8" **14.00**

Planter, seated, green emerald eyes, Alco-Japan label, 6" ...**12.00**
Shakers, on back legs, red bow, gold trim, 5", pair **12.00**
Shakers, seated, green eyes, IL label, 4", pair **16.00**
Shakers, voice boxes in base, Souvenir of...., 3⅛", pair ...**10.00**
Sugar bowl, cat's head, 3 paws, wire handle, with lid, 4¼" ..**25.00**
Tea set, 5" pot with creamer & sugar bowl **35.00**
Teapot, double spout **22.00**
Teapot, paw spout, 8½" **33.00**
Wall pocket, green eyes, red bow, pocket in back, 5½" **45.00**

Shakers, 4", $16.00 for the pair.

Blue and White Stoneware

Collectors who appreciate the 'country look' especially enjoy decorating their homes with this attractive utility ware that was made by many American potteries from around the turn of the century until the mid-thirties. Examples with good mold lines and strong color fetch the highest prices. Condition is important, but bear in mind that this ware was used daily in busy households, and signs of normal wear are to be expected.

Mug, Flying Birds, 4", $135.00.

Batter jar, Wildflower, with cover,
8x7" diameter **150.00**
Bowl, Apricots with Honeycomb,
light blue, 10" **50.00**
Bowl, berry; Flying Bird ... **95.00**
Butter crock, Cow, printed, with
bail **105.00**
Butter crock, Daisy on Snowflake,
NM **150.00**
Butter crock, Scroll, with original
lid **110.00**
Canister, Basketweave, Raisins,
original lid **195.00**
Canister, Snowflake, Rice .. **95.00**
Grease jar, Flying Bird, with origi-
nal lid **250.00**
Meat tenderizer, Wildflower, wood
handle **125.00**
Mug, Bow Tie **135.00**
Pitcher, Apricot, 8" **150.00**
Pitcher, Butterfly, 9x7" ... **165.00**
Pitcher, Cosmos **195.00**
Pitcher, Wild Rose **275.00**
Roaster, Wildflower **135.00**
Rolling pin, Wildflower, with ad-
vertising **225.00**
Salt crock, Butterfly with original
lid **185.00**

Salt crock, Eagle with Arrow, with
original lid **325.00**
Salt crock, Oak Leaf, with original
lid **125.00**
Salt crock, Peacock, with original
lid **300.00**
Soap dish, Cat **165.00**
Spittoon, floral decal **95.00**
Teapot, Swirl **450.00**
Toothbrush holder, Bow Tie. **45.00**
Vase, Swirl, cone shape ... **300.00**
Wash bowl & pitcher, Rose &
Fishscale, 2-piece set . **275.00**

Pitcher, Cattails, 7½", $160.00.

47

Water cooler, Apple Blossom, 17",
  NM **500.00**
Water cooler, Polar Bear ..**500.00**

Blue Ridge

One of the newest and most exciting collectibles on the scene today is American dinnerware. Some of the most attractive is Blue Ridge, produced by Southern Potteries of Erwin, Tennessee, from the late 1930s until 1956. More than four hundred patterns were hand painted on eight basic shapes. The Quimper-like peasant-decorated line is one of the most treasured and is valued at double the values listed below. For the very simple lines, subtract 25% to 50%.

Pitcher, Rebecca, 8¾", $85.00

Bowl, fruit; 5" **2.50**
Bowl, mixing; 8½" **18.00**
Bowl, round, 8" **9.00**
Butter pat **10.00**
Cake lifter **17.00**
Casserole, with lid **25.00**
Child's cereal **15.00**
Child's dish, feeding **17.50**
Child's mug **12.00**
Child's plate **10.00**
Creamer, demitasse **20.00**
Cup & saucer, demitasse ...**17.00**

Cup & saucer, demitasse;
  china **25.00**
Cup & saucer, jumbo **20.00**
Cup & saucer, regular **7.00**
Egg cup, double **15.00**
Gravy boat **12.00**
Gravy tray **10.00**
Lamp, china **50.00**
Plate, cake; 10½" **18.00**
Plate, dinner; 10" **12.00**
Plate, party; with cup well ..**7.50**
Plate, salad; 8½" **5.00**
Plate, snack; 3-part **15.00**
Plate, square, 7½" **7.50**
Platter, 11" **7.00**
Platter, 15" **17.00**
Platter, 9" **7.00**
Relish, heart shape, small ..**25.00**
Salad fork **25.00**
Shakers, Apple, pair **10.00**
Shakers, Chickens, pair ...**30.00**
Shakers, Range, pair **20.00**
Sugar bowl, demitasse **15.00**
Vase, bud **25.00**

Bottle Openers

Figural bottle openers are figures designed for the sole purpose of removing a bottle cap. To qualify as an example, the cap lifter must be part of the figure itself. Among the major producers of openers of this type were Wilton Products; John Wright, Inc.; L & L Favors; and Gadzik Sales. These and advertising openers are very collectible.

Alligator with head down, cast iron,
  worn paint, Wilton, 6" .**35.00**
Auto jack, chrome, 1920s ..**25.00**
Baseball cap, NY Mets, cast iron, 2-
  color paint **32.00**
Bull's head, tail handle, 6" .**28.00**
Clown head, brass **35.00**
Clown head with bow tie, cast iron,
  original paint, 4½" **75.00**
Crayfish, cast iron **40.00**

Dartmoor Pixie, brass, 6", $25.00.

Donkey, cast iron, with original paint, 3" **10.00**

Drunk at lamppost, top hat/tails, legs down, cast iron, EX paint, 4" **20.00**

Drunk at sign post, St Petersburg, FL, cast iron **15.00**

Drunk with top hat & bottle, wall mount **35.00**

Duck with head up, cast iron with worn paint, 3", EX **45.00**

Elephant, walking, trunk looped overhead, cast iron, worn paint, 2½" **25.00**

Fish, stainless steel & wood, 9½" long **10.00**

Goat, opener below beard, cast iron with worn paint, 4¼" . .**80.00**

Goat, sitting, horns curl back, cast iron with worn paint . .**40.00**

Indian, Iroquois Beer, aluminum, NM **30.00**

Lady's hand, brass, 5½" **20.00**

Lamb with ewe, recumbent, cast iron with gold & silver repaint, 4" **30.00**

Nude stands with arms raised, gilt metal, 4½" **15.00**

Palm tree, cast iron, worn multicolor paint, 4½" **105.00**

Parrot, with can punch, cast iron, worn original paint, 5" .**45.00**

Pelican, cast iron with EX paint, 3½" **30.00**

Rooster, cast iron with EX paint, John Wright, 3¼" **45.00**

Shark, aluminum **15.00**

Turtle, corkscrew tail, pot metal, EX **25.00**

4-Eyed man, painted cast iron, Wilton, G **35.00**

Bottles

Bottles have been used as containers for commercial products since the late 1800s. Specimens from as early as 1845 may be occasionally found today (watch for a rough pontil to indicate this early production date). Some of the most collectible are bitters bottles, used for 'medicine' that was mostly alcohol, a ploy to avoid paying the stiff tax levied on liquor sales. Spirit flasks from the 1800s were blown in the mold and were often designed to convey a historic, political, or symbolic message. Even bottles from the 1900s are collectible, especially beer or pop bottles and commercial containers from defunct bottlers.

Bitters, Abbott's Bitters, colorful label, round, amber . . .**55.00**

Bitters, African Stomach Bitters, round, amber **75.00**

Bitters, Atwood's Jaundice Bitters, screw top threading . . .**10.00**

Bitters, Bokers Stomach Bitters, round, amber **95.00**

Bitters, Brown's Iron Bitters, square, amber **35.00**

Bitters, Burdock Blood Bitters, rectangular, aqua **17.00**

Bitters, Dr J Hostetter's Stomach Bitters, square, amber .**12.00**

John Wyeth & Bro., medicine bottle, measuring cup top, patented 1899, cobalt, 6½", $24.00.

Bitters, Dr Whitney's Anti-Costive Bitters, oval, aqua 25.00
Bitters, Dr Wilson's Herbine Bitters, oval, clear 40.00
Bitters, Electric Bitters, amber, 9" 17.00
Bitters, Home Bitters, square, amber 75.00
Bitters, Iron Bitters, bubbles in glass, square, amber ...35.00
Bitters, Lash's Bitters, square, amber 25.00
Bitters, Lash's Kidney & Liver Bitters, square, 9¼" 12.50
Bitters, Malt Bitters Co, round, green 30.00
Bitters, Old Dr Warren's Quaker Bitters, rectangular, aquamarine 65.00
Bitters, Peychaud's American Aromatic Bitter Cordial, medium amber 50.00
Bitters, SO Richardson Bitters, rectangular, aqua 55.00

Bitters, ST Drakes, 1860, Plantation X Bitters, golden amber 55.00
Bitters, Wampoo Bitters, square, amber 35.00
Figural, bell, sheared refined lip, clear, 4¼x3½" 5.50
Ink, Carters # 5, amber, 2½" .5.50
Ink, Caw's, NY, aqua, 2½" ...2.50
Ink, Cross Pen Co, bell shaped, aqua, 2¾" 4.50
Ink, Diamond Ink Co, clear, 2½x 2½" 2.00
Ink, unembossed cylinder with many bubbles, aqua, 6" .6.50
Malt, Henry K Wampole, amber, 9" 4.00
Medicine, Bayer Aspirin, clear, 3" 2.00
Medicine, Dr Dickey's Eye Water, clear, 4" 4.50
Medicine, Dr WB Caldwell's Laxative Senna, clear, 7" 3.00
Medicine, Dr WH Alexander Healing Oil, with cork, 6" ...4.50

John Graf, address, brown, 8", $25.00.

Medicine, Jaynes & Co, golden amber, 9½" 3.50
Medicine, Rawleigh's, 8" 3.00
Medicine, S Grover Graham Dyspepsia Remedy, square bottom, 8" 2.50
Medicine, Uptight of Delight, with cork 5.00
Medicine, WB Schultz & Co Pharmaceutic, with cork, 4" .. 5.00
Medicine, Whitehall, amber, 3" diameter 3.00
Milk, Anchorage, quart 40.00
Milk, Anselmo Dairy Farm, painted front, square quart 14.00
Milk, Borges Sanitary Dairy, California 28.00
Milk, Carnation Co, clear square quart 10.00
Milk, Cloyed's Dairy Farm, round painted half-gallon 25.00
Milk, Corbin Dairy Fresh Milk, painted 5.00
Milk, Dutch Maid Dairy, embossed front, square quart 10.00
Milk, Golden State, cream top, embossed front, quart . 35.00
Milk, Harpains Dairy Farm, round painted half-gallon 4.00
Milk, Home Dairy, painted . 22.00
Milk, Hunt's Dairy, half-pint . 3.50
Milk, Lescoulie Dairy, round painted half-gallon 28.00
Milk, Matanuska Maid, round quart 40.00
Milk, Miller's Dairy, painted front & back 20.00
Milk, Morlen, embossed baby face on front, square quart . 45.00
Milk, People's San Francisco, round pint 25.00
Milk, Producer's Dairy Delivery Inc, round pint 10.00
Milk, Roosevelt Dairy, round painted half-gallon 38.00
Milk, Sun Valley Dairy, round half-pint 3.00
Milk, Union Dairy Sacramento, round half-pint 10.00

Indianapolis Brewing Co., winged lady on wheel with wreath, aqua, $95.00.

Milk, Valley Dairy, clear round pint 15.00
Milk, Valley Milk Distributors Assoc, painted front 20.00
Milk, Wharton's Dairies Inc, round half-pint 5.00
Milk, Woodbury Dairy, round pint 14.00
Nursing, dog, embossed, graduated, clear, 8-ounce, 7" 6.50
Perfume, Zonobia, oval, emerald green, 3" 4.50
Poison, embossed, 6-sided, ribs on 2 sides, cobalt blue, 6" ... 12.50
Poison, Sharp & Dohme, 6-sided, amber, 2½" 2.00
Poison, triangle with rounded back, embossed 2 sides, 3½" .. 3.00
Sarsaparilla, Dana's Sarsaparilla, Belfast, ME, 9" 4.00
Soda, Belfast Club, painted blue & white, 7-ounce 2.50
Soda, Big Chief, embossed Indian head on front and back, green 18.00

Soda, Bottle-O, painted label . 3.00
Soda, Circle A Beverage, clear with
    white paint, 9-ounce 6.50
Soda, Dream, painted label . . 3.00
Soda, Gleeola 8.00
Soda, Good Guy, painted red &
    white, EX 10.00
Soda, Grapette, painted label. 3.00
Soda, Green Spot 8.00
Soda, Hanford, 6½-ounce 6.00
Soda, King Kist, painted red & white
    on clear, 10-ounce 7.00
Soda, Mason's Root Beer, painted
    red & yellow on amber . 10.00
Soda, Polly Pop, painted label. 5.00
Soda, Royal Crown, 1936 . . . 8.00
Soda, Shara Soda, painted label,
    EX 5.00
Soda, Teaco, painted label . . . 5.00
Soda, Whistle, embossed front &
    back, ribbed, clear 8.00
Soda, White Rose Beverages,
    painted blue & white . . . 3.50
Soda, 7-Up, green with lady, white
    & orange logo, 7-ounce . . 6.50

Brass

    Brass, a non-rusting alloy of copper and zinc, was used as far back in civilization as the first century A.D. Items most often found today are from the 19th century, although even 20th-century examples are collectible due to the simple fact that most are now obsolete. Even decorative brass from the 1950s has collector value.

Ash tray, rounded base, 2 side holders, lid atop, ca 1950 . . . 17.50
Blowtorch, 7" 20.00
Bookends, English, unicorn & lion,
    6x5½" 40.00
Bowl, engraved floral design,
    marked China, 10" 55.00
Chestnut roaster, marked Made in
    England, 18" 43.00

Chisel, red brass, marked Beryl Co,
    S108, 7½" 52.00
Coal miner head lamp, marked
    Justrite, 4½" 35.00
Crumber, wood handle 15.00
Curtain tie-back, hook with screw-
    on backplate wall mount,
    pair 40.00
Curtain tie-back, pineapple finial
    with screw, large 22.00
Door knocker, lion's head with ring
    through nose, 6" 18.00
Doorknob, plain 15.00
Flashlight, marked TL-122-A, 7"
    long 5.00
Hair-straightening comb, metal
    spring-form handle, 10½"
    long 15.00
Horse brass, pierced-work . . 15.00
Horse brass, plain, for ear . . . 5.00
Inkwell, ca 1950, 3½", with 6" square
    tray 40.00
Jamb hook, 4" 45.00
Jardiniere, English, grapes in relief, footed, ca 1950, 8".. 30.00
Lighter, marked Made in Austria,
    2½" 18.50
Mail box, envelope style, lion's head
    ring opener, ca 1950 . . . 25.00
Match safe, engraved eagle design
    on front 12.00
Pull, plain, for cabinet 5.00
Pull, red brass, ring handle, for
    cabinet 5.00
Pull, with backplate, ornate, for
    chest or cabinet 6.00
Set: mortar, 3¼x5½" diameter; pestal, 7" 75.00
Shell, ca 1915, 6½" long, 2" diameter 12.00
Shoe mold, red brass, 11x9".. 20.00
Teaspoon, American, 19th century,
    worn 10.00
Thimble 3.50
Tray, divided fruit shape, marked
    Hong Kong, 1950s, 9" . . 45.00
Trouble light, 8" 24.00
Vase holder, ornate cutwork, ca
    1950, 13½" 25.00

Kettle with spider, 10" diameter, $75.00.

Wall pocket, resembles bed warmer, embossed fruit **15.00**

Water carafe, marked Maxwell Phillips, NY, 1950s, 8" . **30.00**

Watering can, European, hinged lid on oval body, 8x11" **52.00**

Brayton and Brayton Laguna

Located in Laguna Beach, California, this small pottery is especially noted for their amusing Disney figurines and their children's series which were made from the 1930s to the early 1950s.

Figurine, Ann **30.00**
Figurine, Butch **30.00**
Figurine, Dorothy **32.00**
Figurine, Ellen **32.00**
Figurine, Emily **32.00**
Figurine, Ethel **32.00**
Figurine, Eugene **32.00**

Figurine, Julia Ray **32.00**
Figurine, Miranda **32.00**
Figurine, panther, stalking, red, 13" long **130.00**
Figurine, Petunia **75.00**
Figurine, Pluto, head down, back legs straightened, Disney, 6" long **100.00**
Figurine, Sambo **75.00**
Flower frog, pouter pigeon, blue, white, and green, incising, 5½x6" **30.00**
Lamp, Hansel & Gretel **65.00**
Lamp, Priscilla, 10" **65.00**
Planter, Baby **25.00**
Planter, Frances **25.00**
Planter, Sally **25.00**
Shakers, peasant couple, white & brown crackle, marked, 5½", pair **45.00**
Vase, sunbonnet shape **15.00**

Bread Plates

Bread Plates were very popular

during the last part of the 1800s. They were produced by various companies, many of whom sold their wares at the 1876 Philadelphia Centennial Exposition. Though they were also made in earthenware and metal, the most popular with collectors are the glass plates with embossed designs that convey a historical, political, or symbolic message.

Martyrs, 12½", $100.00; Mitchell, 10¾", $250.00.

American Flag, 38 stars, frosted
center **225.00**
Balky Mule **70.00**
Bible, L-200, 10½" **55.00**
California Bear, 1894 Exposition,
L-104 ....**135.00**
Classic Warrior **170.00**
Constitution, L-43 ....**25.00**
Diagonal Band **25.00**
Do Unto Others **45.00**
Eagle & Constitution, Give Us This
Day **100.00**
Heroes of Bunker Hill **45.00**
Implement, L-101 ....**55.00**
Jewel Band, Bread Is the Staff of
Life **40.00**
Knights of Labor, L-512 ..**125.00**
Lattice, Waste Not Want Not,
11½x8" **32.00**
Liberty Bell, Signers **125.00**
McKinley, It Is God's Way, 10½"
long **60.00**
Railroad, Union Pacific **90.00**
Scroll with Flowers, 12" ...**35.00**
Ulysses Grant, square **45.00**

3 Graces, Faith, Hope, Charity,
dated 1875 ....**45.00**

Brownies

The Brownie characters — The London Bobby, The Bellhop, Uncle Sam, and others — were strange little creatures with potbellies and long spindle legs who emerged in the night to do wondrous deeds for children to delight in discovering the next morning. They were the progeny of Palmer Cox, who in 1883 introduced them to the world in the poem called *The Brownies Ride*. Books, toys, napkin rings, and advertising items are just a few of the items available to today's Brownie collectors.

Basket, silverplate, Brownies with
chocolate ad, Tufts ...**140.00**
Book, Brownie Primer, 1905.**35.00**
Book, Brownie Yearbook, McLoughlin, 1895, VG **55.00**
Book, Brownies, Their Book, 1897,
EX **175.00**
Book, Queer People, NM ...**75.00**
Book, The Second Brownie Book,
1911 ....**25.00**
Candlestick, Uncle Sam & Brownies, majolica **175.00**
Cup & saucer, silverplate .**100.00**
Doll, stuffed **95.00**

Mug, ironstone with gold trim, East Liverpool, 3", $65.00.

Game, Ring Toss **35.00**
Knife & fork, child size **20.00**
Napkin ring, Brownie climbs up side
of ring **145.00**
Puzzle, Scroll, McLoughlin. **125.00**
Ruler **20.00**
Spoon, demitasse; twist handle,
silverplate **35.00**
Stamps, miniature, set of 6 . **25.00**
Tin container, Brownie Ointment,
1924, mint in box **40.00**

Butter Molds

Butter molds were once used to decorate and identify butter made by the farmer's wife who often sold her extra churnings at the market. Because the early molds were hand carved, none were exactly alike, and endless variation resulted. The ones most highly treasured today are those with animals or birds or those with unusual shape or construction.

Acorn & flower, square case, 1-
pound **45.00**
Beet & radish, EX carving . **45.00**
Box, rectangular, initials CW carved
in 2 sections, 4x7" **25.00**
Cow, bell shape, pointed plunger,
3½" **215.00**
Geometric, round case, quarter-
pound **55.00**
Geometric floral, turned inserted
handle, round, 3½" **45.00**

Heart, deep carving, round, ca 1800,
3½", EX **260.00**
Horse, 3½x5½" **85.00**
House design, peaked roof, 2 chim-
neys, 4-part, 5x6x7" . . **215.00**
Rosette center, 1-pound **95.00**
Sheaf, cased sides, round case,
3⅝" **55.00**
Stalks of wheat, box style . . **55.00**
Star, individual pat, 1½" . . . **25.00**
Strawberry with leaf, cased sides,
round, 5" **65.00**
Swan, round case, 4½" **80.00**
Tulip, stylized, dovetailed, 5x6⅝"
long, VG **185.00**
Wheat, dated 1866 . . . . **85.00**
2-star pattern, 3x3½x5" **18.00**

Butter Stamps

Butter stamps differ from molds in that the mold is dimensional while the stamp is flat and was used not to shape the butter but merely to decorate the top.

Cow & tree, 1-piece handle, 4⅜"
diameter **155.00**
Eagle, turned handle, 3½" diam-
eter **230.00**
Eagle & star, inserted handle, 6¾"
long **140.00**
Flower, stylized, dated 1839, 3¾"
diameter **150.00**
Flower, stylized, turned handle,
4¼" diameter **65.00**

Two-part molds: Pineapple and floral, 4", $90.00; Pineapple and leaf, 4", $130.00; Sheaf of wheat, 4", $90.00

Butter stamps with turned handle: Leaf, 2¾x4" diameter, $70.00; Thistle, 3x4½" diameter, $90.00; Eagle, 3x4¼" diameter, $230.00.

Fruit & foliage, stylized, 3⅜" diameter 165.00

Geometric, stylized, square with inserted handle 90.00

Heart-shaped flower & foliage, turned handle, 4⅞" diameter 165.00

Pineapple, turned handle, 3¾" diameter 75.00

Pineapple, turned handle, 4¼" diameter 145.00

Pomegranate, turned handle, 4" diameter 155.00

Sheaf, deep hand carving, turned handle, 4½" diameter ..85.00

Star, turned handle, 4" diameter, EX 55.00

Star & flowers, deep carving, wide handle, 4¼" diameter ..75.00

Star flower, turned handle, 3⅝" diameter 75.00

Thistle, 1-piece, with handle, 3⅜" diameter 85.00

Tulip & hex designs, oval, 4x6⅝", EX 325.00

Cambridge

Organized in 1901 in Cambridge, Ohio, the Cambridge Glass Co. initially manufactured clear glass dinnerware and accessory pieces. In the 1920s they began to concentrate on color and soon became recognized as the largest producers of this type of glassware in the world. The company used various marks, the most common of which is the 'C in triangle.' The factory closed in 1958.

See also Carnival Glass.

Animal, Scottie, frosted 75.00

Apple Blossom, colors; creamer, footed 17.50

Apple Blossom, crystal; bowl, cereal; 6" 40.00

Apple Blossom, crystal; tumbler, #3135, footed, 10-oz. ...13.00

Bird, eagle, bookend 75.00

Bird, pouter pigeon, bookend.30.00

Bird, sea gull 45.00

Bird, swan, ebony, 4½" 85.00

Bird, swan, milk glass, 3½" .60.00

Bird, turkey, amber, w/lid .450.00

Caprice, blue; pickle bowl, #102, 9" 32.50

Caprice, blue; plate, dinner; #24, 9½" 115.00

Caprice, crystal; candlestick, #646, 2-light, 5" 14.00

Chantilly, crystal; pitcher, ball form, water size 110.00

Chantilly, crystal; salt & pepper shakers, pair 27.50

Cleo, all colors; platter, 15" .55.00

Crown Tuscan, candy dish, #3500/57, 3-part, with lid 65.00

Crown Tuscan, flower holder, seashell 58.00

Decagon, cobalt; sugar bowl, footed, open 20.00

Caprice, blue; individual creamer and sugar bowl, $32.50.

Decagon, red; compote, tall, 7", red or cobalt **30.00**
Diane, crystal; platter, 14" .**45.00**
Diane, crystal; soup bowl, #3400, with liner **23.00**
Elaine, crystal; cocktail, #3121, 3-ounce **22.00**
Elaine, crystal; tumbler, water; #1402, footed, 9-ounce .**17.00**
Flower Frog, Bashful Charlotte, pink, 6½" **125.00**
Flower Frog, Draped Lady, crystal, 8½" **95.00**
Flower Frog, Mandolin Lady, pink **225.00**
Flower Frog, Rose Lady, light green **65.00**
Gloria, colors; cup **25.00**
Gloria, crystal; butter dish, with lid, 2-handled **90.00**
Imperial Hunt Scene, colors; ice bucket **57.50**
MtVernon, amber; ice bucket, #92, with tongs **30.00**
MtVernon, amber; sherbet, #42, low, 4½-ounce **7.50**
Mt Vernon, crystal; relish tray, #200, 3-part, 11" **22.50**
Portia, crystal; cup, footed .**18.00**
Portia, crystal; puff box, ball form, with lid, 3½" **50.00**
Rosalie, colors; candlestick, keyhole, 5" **25.00**
Rosalie, colors; tray, center handle, 11" **30.00**

Rose Point, crystal; vase, #6004, footed, 5" **50.00**
Valencia, crystal; creamer, #3500/14 ....**15.00**
Valencia, crystal; sherbet, #1402, low **12.50**
Wildflower, crystal; pitcher, ball form **95.00**
Wildflower, crystal; vase, footed, 6" **30.00**

Campaign Collectibles

Pennants, buttons, posters — in general, anything related to presidential campaigns — are being sought by collectors who have an interest in the political history of our country. Most valued are items from a particularly eventful period or those things having to do with an especially colorful personality. Pinback buttons, popular campaign tools since 1896, are particularly appealing.

Bumper sticker, Wallace For President, blue & orange **2.00**
Button, All You Can Get from Wilkie Is Buttons, 1¼" **12.50**
Button, Carry On with Roosevelt, photo in center, 1" **6.00**
Button, Frank Knox For Governor, ½" **5.00**
Button, Goldwater/Miller, 2¾". **2.50**

Bandana, Our Next President, Maj. Gen. Winfield Scott Hancock, 1880, minor fading, 23x25", $300.00.

Button, Harding & Coolidge, ¾" **8.00**

Button, Harding For President, ⅝" diameter **7.00**

Button, Hoover For President, ⅞" **7.00**

Button, I'm For Nixon, photo of Nixon, 2½" **8.00**

Button, Landon, outline of sunflower & Landon in center, ¾" .**5.00**

Button, Landon & Knox, ½" .**6.00**

Button, LBJ For the USA, shows photo, with ribbon, 2½" .**6.00**

Button, Stevenson, photo in center, 1¾" **2.50**

Button, Vote No on Woman Suffrage, ¾" **5.00**

Button, Warren G Harding For President, with photo, ¾".**6.00**

Button, Wilkie & McNary, red, white, & blue,¾" **5.00**

Button, Wilkie For President, ¾" **10.00**

Clock, Roosevelt, FDR-The Man of the Hour, 15" **100.00**

Election token, Richard Nixon, A Profile of Integrity, 1½" .**3.00**

Freedom dollar, Barry Goldwater For President, 1964, 1½". **3.00**

Inaugural program, Richard Nixon, 1969 ....**7.50**

License plate, I Like Ike, blue & white letters, 4½x12" ...**6.50**

Liquor bottle, 1953 Presidential Inauguration, 11¼" **12.00**

Medal, Jimmy Carter, 1977 Inaugural, sterling, 1¼" **6.00**

Medallion, Franklin Roosevelt, Little White House, Warm Springs **7.00**

Medallion, Harry S Truman, brass, dated, 1¼" **15.00**

Newspaper, Nixon Resigns, Reno Evening Gazette **20.00**

Parade torch, nickel plated, 28", EX **42.00**

Pin, Ike, rhinestone studded, silver finish **6.00**

Salt & pepper, Lyndon Johnson, EX, pair **20.00**

Telephone directory, 1976 National Democrat Convention ..**15.00**

Toy, Tricky Dick, plastic figural, Poynter, Japan **23.00**

Wrist watch, Spiro Agnew, photo on 1½" face **28.00**

Mug, Teddy Roosevelt, New Deal, ceramic, 4", $45.00.

Candlewick

Candlewick was one of the all-time best-selling lines of The Imperial Glass Company of Bellaire, Ohio. It was produced from 1936 until the company closed in 1982. More than 741 items were made over the years; and, though many are still easy to find today, some (such as the desk calendar, the chip and dip set, and the dresser set) are a challenge to collect. Candlewick is easily identified by the beaded stems, handles, and rims characteristic of the tufted needlework of our pioneer women for which it was named.

Ash tray, eagle form, 6½" . . **35.00**
Ash tray, heart, 4½" **15.00**
Basket, beaded handle, 5" . **110.00**
Basket, handled, 11" **95.00**
Bell, 5" **35.00**
Bottle, bitters; w/tube, 4-oz . **40.00**
Bowl, baked apple; rolled edge, 6" **15.00**
Bowl, cntrpiece; flared, 11" . **35.00**
Bowl, cupped edge, 10" **40.00**
Bowl, fruit; 2-handle, 4¾" . . **12.00**
Bowl, heart, handled, 9" . . . **45.00**
Bowl, mint; handled, 6" **15.00**
Bowl, relish; 5-part, 13½" . . **32.50**
Candle holder, bowled-up base, handled, 5" **35.00**
Candle holder, floral, beaded stem, 4½" **25.00**
Candle holder, heart, 5" . . . **25.00**

Candy box, with lid, 7" **25.00**
Claret, #3400, 5-ounce **17.50**
Cocktail, #400/190, 4-ounce. **18.00**
Compote, beaded stem, 8" . . **22.50**
Creamer, beaded handle **7.50**
Creamer, domed foot **35.00**
Egg cup, beaded foot **30.00**
Plate, crimped edge, with handles, 12" **28.00**
Plate, dinner; 10" **22.00**
Sugar bowl, ind; bridge **7.50**
Tray, fruit; center handle . . **14.00**
Tumbler, beaded foot, #400, 10-ounce **12.50**
Vase, crimped edge, flat, 6" . **20.00**

Candy Containers

From 1876 until the 1940s, figural glass candy containers of every shape and description have been manufactured for the use of candy companies who filled them with tiny colored candy beads. When the candy was gone, kids used the containers as banks or toys. While many are common, some (such as Charlie Chaplin by L. E. Smith, Barney

Basket, 6", $35.00.

Google by the Barrel, Felix on the Pedestal, or the Rabbit Family) are hard to find and command prices in the $450.00 to $700.00 range.

Papier-mache figurals, usually relating to a specific holiday, are also very collectible. Many will be marked 'Made in Germany.'

Airplane, Spirit of St Louis, glass, #321 . . . .**300.00**
Army Bomber, glass, #328 . **25.00**
Basket, composition, paper trim & flowers, Germany, 6" . . **20.00**
Basket, glass, grape design, #223, NM **45.00**
Bear on Circus Tub, with blades, glass, #1, NM **300.00**
Boy on lemon, papier-mache, red shirt, green pants, 3½" . **90.00**

Tank, black paint details, $30.00.

Bureau, glass, #125 . . . . . . **115.00**
Bus, Rapid Transit, glass, #345, VG **400.00**
Charlie Chaplin by Barrel, Borgfeldt, glass, original paint, #83 . . . . **125.00**
Chicken in Sagging Basket, closure, glass, #8, NM **75.00**
Chinaman sits on log, papier-mache, Germany, 4" **245.00**
Cruet, glass, #615 . . . . **50.00**
Dog with Umbrella, glass, #19, NM **20.00**
Duckling, glass, closure, original paint, #30 . . . . **100.00**
Fire Engine, Large Boiler; glass, closure, #380 . . . . **125.00**
Flossie Fisher, Bed, glass, #127, NM **675.00**

Helicopter, glass, double blades, #330 . . . . **125.00**
Hippo, papier-mache, tan/brown, neck closure, 4", EX . . . **60.00**
Horn, 3-valve, with mouthpiece, glass, #281 . . . . **175.00**
Lamp, Hurricane; miniature, glass, #211 . . . . **100.00**
Lamp, ribbed base, glass, #208, NM **125.00**
Lantern, ruby flashed, glass, #575, NM **30.00**
Lantern, Twins on Anchor, glass, #186 . . . . **25.00**
Locomotive, Stough's #5, glass, #428 . . . . **35.00**
Man in egg, papier-mache, red, white, & blue, 4½" . . . **225.00**
Pipe, glass, #628 . . . . **60.00**
Potato, papier-mache, brown with green shamrock, 2x3" . **100.00**
Rabbit in Tree Trunk, glass, #485, NM **675.00**
Ram, papier-mache, Germany, 3½" long **175.00**
Soda Pop Bottle, glass **125.00**
Submarine, glass, #338 . . . **350.00**
Telescope, glass, #270 . . . . **825.00**
Turkey, papier-mache, multicolor, Germany, 6" **95.00**
Windmill, glass with pewter top, #443 . . . . **400.00**

Carnival Chalkware

Chalkware statues of Kewpies, glamour girls, assorted dogs, and horses were given to winners of carnival games from about 1910 until the 1950s. Today's collectors especially value those representing well-known personalities such as Disney characters and comic book heroes.

Alice the Goon, King Features Syndicate, 1940s, 10" **65.00**
Betty Boop, Max Fleischer Studios, 1930s, 14½" **190.00**

The Lone Ranger, 14½", $40.00
(Photo courtesy of Thomas G.
Morris, author of Carnival Chalk
Prizes.)

Boy & horse, no marks, ca 1935-
   1945, 11½" 15.00
Dog ash tray, no marks, ca 1940,
   5½" 10.00
Donald Duck's nephew on snow-
   ball, 1930s, 6½" 15.00
English saddle horse, 11" . .12.00
Fan Dancer, Portland Statuary Co,
   ca 1935-1945, 16" 55.00
Felix the Cat, no marks, ca 1922,
   12½" 75.00
Kewpie, sitting, hand painted, pink
   chalk, with mohair wig, 1915,
   6" 45.00
Lone Ranger, 14½" 40.00
Mae West, copyrighted by Wm Rain-
   water, 1936, 10½" 75.00
Majorette, El Segundo Novelty Co,
   1949, 12" 25.00
Miss Mailbu, copyrighted by JY
   Jenkins, 1933, 25½" . . .95.00
Scottie dog, no marks, ca 1940,
   10¼" 10.00

Sheba, mohair tufts, copyrighted as
   'Marie' by Jenkins, 1923,
   13½" 65.00
Ship lamp, glows from within, ca
   1940, 14¾" 70.00
Spaniel, pink chalk, hand painted,
   sad, 1920s, 12½" 95.00

Carnival Glass

From about 1905 until the late
1920s, carnival glass was manufactured by several major American
glass houses in hundreds of designs
and patterns. Its characteristic iridescent lustre was the result of
coating the pressed glassware with
a sodium solution before the final
firing. Marigold, blue, green, and
purple are the most common colors,
though pastels were also used.
Because it was mass-produced at
reasonable prices, much of it was
given away at carnivals. As a result,
it came to be known as carnival
glass.

Acanthus, bowl, green, Imperial,
   9½" 95.00
Acorn, bowl, amethyst, Fenton,
   7" 55.00
Acorn, bowl, marigold, Fenton,
   7" 35.00
African Shield, toothpick holder,
   marigold, English 45.00
Apple & Pear Intaglio, bowl, mari-
   gold, Northwood, 5" . . .30.00
Apple Blossom Twigs, bowl, mari-
   gold, Dugan 40.00
Apple Panels, creamer, marigold,
   English 30.00
April Showers, vase, blue, Fen-
   ton 50.00
Arcs, bowl, marigold, Imperial,
   8½" 30.00
Art Deco, bowl, marigold, English,
   4" 32.00

61

Australian Swan, bowl, marigold, Crystal, 5" **38.00**

Autumn Acorns, bowl, blue, Fenton, 8¾" **40.00**

Ball & Swirl, mug, marigold. **90.00**

Balloons, compote, marigold, Imperial **55.00**

Banded Diamonds, bowl, amethyst, Crystal, 5" **65.00**

Beaded Bull's Eye, vase, marigold, Imperial, 14" **45.00**

Beaded Cable, candy dish, amethyst, Northwood **60.00**

Beaded Shell, bowl, amethyst, footed, Dugan, 9" **95.00**

Bells & Beads, bowl, green, Dugan, 7½" **50.00**

Bells & Beads, bowl, marigold, Dugan, 7½" **35.00**

Birds & Cherries, compote, blue, Fenton **60.00**

Blackberry, bowl, marigold, footed, Northwood, 9" **47.00**

Bouquet, tumbler, blue **50.00**

Bouquet, tumbler, white, .. **65.00**

Brocaded Summer Gardens, bonbon, pastel **42.00**

Broken Arches, bowl, amethyst, Imperial, 10" **50.00**

Broken Arches, bowl, marigold, Imperial, 8½" **42.00**

Butterflies, tray, card; blue, Fenton **60.00**

Butterfly & Berry, bowl, footed, amethyst, Fenton, 5" .. **40.00**

Cane, bowl, marigold, Imperial, 7½" **30.00**

Cane, wine, pastel, Imperial. **60.00**

Cathedral, bowl, blue, 10" .. **50.00**

Cathedral, creamer, footed, marigold **45.00**

Checkers, bowl, 4" **18.00**

Cherry, bowl, flat, amethyst, Dugan, 8" **60.00**

Cherry, bowl, green, rare, Millersburg, 7" **75.00**

Circle Scroll, bowl, amethyst, Dugan, 5" **45.00**

Circle Scroll, bowl, marigold, Dugan, 10" **57.00**

Bernheimner bowl, $1,100.00.

Cobblestones, bowl, marigold, Dugan, 9" **55.00**
Coin Dot, bowl, green, 10" ..**40.00**
Columbia, vase, marigold ..**38.00**
Concord, bowl, amber, scarce, Fenton, 9" **95.00**
Crab Claw, bowl, green, Imperial, 5" **35.00**
Crackle, bowl, marigold, Imperial, 9" **18.00**
Crackle, wall vase, marigold, Imperial **35.00**
Cut Arcs, compote, blue **45.00**
Daisy & Plume, candy dish, green, Northwood **60.00**
Dandelion, tumbler, amethyst, Northwood **50.00**
Diamond Checkerboard, bowl, marigold, 9" **35.00**
Diamond Daisy, plate, marigold, 8" **75.00**
Diamond Star, vase, marigold, 8" **60.00**
Dotted Daisies, plate, marigold, 8" **65.00**
Double Loop, creamer, amethyst, Northwood **65.00**
Dutch Twins, ash tray **45.00**
Elegance, bowl, 8¼" **90.00**
Emu, bowl, marigold, rare, Crystal, 10" **80.00**
English Hob & Button, bowl, blue, English, 7" **60.00**
Engraved Grapes, tumbler, marigold, Fenton **20.00**
Fashion, punch cup, marigold, Imperial **22.00**
Feathered Serpent, bowl, blue, Fenton, 10" **60.00**
Fentonia, bowl, footed, 9½" .**70.00**
Field Thistle, spooner, marigold, US Glass **70.00**
Fine Cut Rings, butter dish, marigold, English **70.00**
Fishscale & Beads, plate, marigold, Dugan, 7" **40.00**
Frosty, bottle, marigold **25.00**
Fruit Salad, cup, marigold, rare, Westmoreland **30.00**

Brocaded Palms, large handled cake plate, $90.00.

Garden Path, bowl, amethyst, Dugan, 8½" **70.00**
Garden Path, bowl, peach opalescent, Dugan, 5" **47.00**
Golden Oxen, mug **48.00**
Grape, bowl, fruit; marigold, Imperial, 8¾" **36.00**
Grape, bowl, Imperial, 10" ..**50.00**
Grape Arbor, tumbler, marigold, Northwood **45.00**
Hobstar Panels, creamer, marigold, English **45.00**
Holly, goblet, pastel, Fenton.**58.00**
Intaglio Ovals, plate, pastel, US Glass, 7½" **80.00**
Interior Panels, mug **75.00**
Inverted Strawberry, creamer, marigold **90.00**
Jewelled Heart, plate, marigold, Dugan, 6" **125.00**
Lattice & Daisy, bowl, marigold, Dugan, 9" **60.00**
Lattice & Daisy, tumbler, blue, Dugan **48.00**
Leaf Chain, plate, blue, Fenton, 7½" **90.00**
Leaf Tiers, tumbler, footed, amethyst, rare, Fenton **90.00**
Little Beads, bowl, peach opalescent, 8" **45.00**
Lustre Rose, bowl, marigold, flat, Imperial, 7" **35.00**
Lustre Rose, creamer, marigold, Imperial **42.00**
Lustre Rose, pitcher, marigold, Imperial **85.00**

Dolphins, compote, green, radium finish, $975.00

Maple Leaf, creamer, blue, Dugan **62.00**

Melon Rib, candy jar, marigold, Imperial **30.00**

Melon Rib, tumbler, marigold, Imperial **24.00**

Moxie, bottle, pastel, rare .. **78.00**

Nell, mug, marigold, Higbee. **65.00**

Octagon, bowl, marigold, Imperial, 8½" **38.00**

Octagon, sugar bowl, marigold, Imperial **58.00**

Octet, bowl, marigold, Northwood, 8½" **48.00**

Optic Flute, bowl, marigold, Imperial, 5" **25.00**

Orange Tree, bowl, green, footed, Fenton, 5½" **30.00**

Oriental Poppy, tumbler, marigold, Northwood **38.00**

Oval & Round, bowl, amethyst, Imperial, 7" **30.00**

Oval & Round, bowl, marigold, Imperial, 4" **20.00**

Pansy, bowl, Imperial, 8¾" . **65.00**

Peacock & Urn, bowl, blue, Fenton, 8½" **70.00**

Peacock at the Fountain, bowl, blue, Northwood, 5" **45.00**

Peacock Tail, bowl, blue, Fenton, 10" **32.00**

Persian Medallion, bowl, green, Fenton, 5" **36.00**

Pigeon, paperweight **80.00**

Pleats & Hearts, shade **70.00**

Polo, ash tray, marigold ... **40.00**

Pony, bowl, marigold, Dugan, 8½" **70.00**

Question Marks, compote, marigold, Dugan **40.00**

Ranger, creamer, marigold, Imperial **40.00**

Ribbon & Fern, atomizer, marigold, 7" **75.00**

Rococo, bowl, marigold, Imperial, 5" **26.00**

Sailboats, bowl, Fenton, 6" . **60.00**

Shell, plate, marigold, 8½" . **80.00**

Six Petals, bowl, marigold, Dugan, 8½" **38.00**

Ski-Star, bowl, Dugan, 5" .. **50.00**

Ski-Star, bowl, Dugan, 5" .. **50.00**

Small Thumbprint, creamer, marigold **60.00**

Smooth Panels, vase, marigold, Imperial **36.00**

Smooth Rays, bowl, amethyst, Northwood-Dugan, 6" .. **48.00**

Snow Fancy, creamer, marigold, McKee **47.00**

Soda Gold, tumbler, marigold, Imperial **40.00**

Soda Gold Spears, bowl, marigold, Dugan, 8½" **38.00**

Star Center, bowl, amethyst, Imperial, 8½" **36.00**

Star Spray, bowl, marigold, Imperial, 7" **28.00**

Star Spray, bowl, pastel, Imperial, 7" **30.00**

Stippled Flower, bowl, peach opalescent, Dugan, 8½" **80.00**

Stork & Rushes, bowl, marigold, Dugan, 5" **25.00**

Strawberry, bonbon, amethyst, Fenton **45.00**

Studs, pitcher, milk; marigold, Imperial **70.00**

Thin Rib, candlestick, marigold, Fenton, pair **60.00**

Three Fruits, bowl, blue, Northwood, 9" **56.00**

Three Fruits, bowl, marigold, Northwood, 5" **22.00**

Thunderbird, bowl, amethyst, Australian, 5" **45.00**

Tree Bark, pickle jar, marigold, Imperial, 7½" **35.00**

Tree of Life, pitcher, marigold, Imperial **60.00**

Triplets, bowl, green, Northwood, 6" **42.00**

Twins, bowl, marigold, Imperial, 5" **24.00**

Two Flowers, bowl, marigold, footed, Fenton, 5" **28.00**

Urn, vase, marigold, 9" **40.00**

Vineyard, pitcher, marigold, Dugan **85.00**

Waffle Block, creamer, marigold, Imperial **60.00**

Washboard, creamer, marigold, 5½" **42.00**

Whirling Star, compote, marigold, Imperial **55.00**

Windflower, bowl, pastel, Dugan, 8½" **85.00**

Windmill, tumbler, amethyst, Imperial **58.00**

Wishbone, bowl, marigold, flat, Northwood, 10" **50.00**

Wishbone, tumbler, marigold, scarce, Northwood **75.00**

Stippled Acorns, covered candy dish, marigold, $75.00.

Catalogs

Vintage catalogs are an excellent source of reference for collectors as well as being quite collectible in their own right. While some collectors specialize in trying to accumulate a particular company's catalogs in sequence, others prefer to look for those specializing in only one area of interest — knives, lighting fixtures, or farm machinery, for instance. Original catalogs are often hard to find, and several companies have reprinted some of their earlier editions.

Aladdin Homes Catalog #32, 2nd edition, 1920, 116 pages .**6.00**

Altman's Women's, Men's, & Kid's Clothes, 1928 . . . .**7.00**

American Sawmill Machinery Co #14, 1906, 109 pages . . .**5.00**

Atlantic Tea Co, ca 1900 . . .**15.00**

China & Artware by Hubert Mills, 1937 ....4.00
De Laval Cream Separators, 1927, illustrated 15.00
Eastman Kodak, 1939, illustrated, 35 pages 6.00
Edison Phonographs, 1906, illustrated 15.00
Enderes, 1930 ....12.00
Firestone Tire & Rubber Co, 1914, 32 pages 20.00
FW Woolworth Co, 1940, Christmas, 39 pages 10.00
Gearhart's Improved Knitter, 1906, 12 pages 12.50
Hardbound Red Jacket Pumps, 1915 ....30.00
J Galef, sporting equipment, 1939, 62 pages 20.00
Kirsh Co, 1929, 32 pages ...12.00
Knitting Instruction Book for Gearheart Machine, 1925 ..10.00
Landers Household Appliances, 1931 ....10.00
Lionel Trains, 1947, 31 pgs .18.00
Martha Lane, ladies' and children's clothing, 1924, 134 pgs .15.00

Matco Mechanics' Tools Catalog #7980, 1979, 318 pages .5.00
Montgomery Ward, March and April Sale of Home Furnishings, 1911 ....12.50
Oak Lawn Farm, 1906 ....12.00
Rock Island Line Coal & Wood Ranges, 1936, colored illustrations 7.00
Sandler Shoes of Boston, 1959, hard cover, 120 pages 6.50
Sanico Ranges, ca 1930, colored pictures 10.00
Victor Records, 1929 ......10.00
Washington Stoves & Ranges, ca 1930 ....7.00
Welch Laboratory Apparatus, 1959, 840 pages 10.00
Western Trap & Skeet, 1936, illustrated, 67 pages 10.00
Wilmarth Fishing, 1937 ...16.00

Ceramic Arts Studio

Whether you're a collector of American pottery or not, chances are you'll like the distinctive styling of the figurines, salt and pepper shakers, and other novelty items made by the Ceramic Arts Studio of Madison, Wisconsin, from about 1938 until about 1952. They're among the newest collectibles on the market, and a trip to any good flea market will usually produce one or several good buys of their shelf sitters or wall-hanging pairs. They're easily spotted, once you've seen a few examples; but, if you're not sure, check for the trademark: the name of the company and its location.

Bowl, Bonita 28.00
Candle holder, Bedtime Boy & Girl, 4¾", pr 45.00
Figurine, Bali Gong, 5½" ...35.00
Figurine, Colonel Jackson, Southern gentleman 35.00

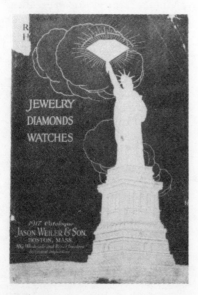

**Jason Weiler & Son, 1917, 7x10",
$18.00.**

Bench sitters, 4", $35.00.

Figurine, Egyptian man & woman,
pair **120.00**
Figurine, Lu Tang **25.00**
Figurine, Pixie/snail, 2¾" .. **17.50**
Figurine, rooster, pink & black, B-
481, 7" **45.00**
Figurine, Summer Bell, dinner bell,
5¼" **65.00**
Jug, ballerina, 2" **20.00**
Planter, Lorelei/seashell, 6". **45.00**
Plaque, Attitude & Arabesque, red,
pair **55.00**
Plaque, Mary Contrary, 5" . **50.00**
Shakers, chair & boy, pr ... **25.00**
Shakers, fish on tail, 4", pr . **22.00**
Shakers, Penguins, pr **25.00**
Shelf sitter, Chinese boy and girl,
pr **35.00**
Shelf sitter, girl with cat, 4". **22.00**
Vase, man with gong, 6¼" .. **15.00**

Character Collectibles

One of the most popular areas of
collecting today and one with the
most available memorabilia is the
field of character collectibles. Flea
markets usually yield some of the
more common examples — toys,
books, lunch boxes, children's
dishes, and sheet music are for the
most part quite readily found. Trade
papers are also an excellent source.
Often you will find even the rare
and hard-to-find listed for sale.
Disney characters, movie stars, television personalities, comic book
heroes, and sports greats are the
most sought after.

Admiral Dewey, spoon **8.00**
Alice in Wonderland, ceramic fig-
ure, 5" **15.00**
Annie Oakley, hat, red felt Western
with hat cord **18.00**
Annie Oakley, lunch box, ca 1955,
EX/NM **18.00**
Barney Google, sheet music.. **20.00**
Batman, bicycle horn, battery oper-
ated in original box **15.00**
Batman & Robin, puzzle, Whitman,
ca 1966, 11½x14½" **15.00**
Batman & Robin, thermos . **18.00**
Betty Lou, spoon **10.00**
Bing Crosby, record duster . **18.50**
Bordon's Elsie, cookbook ... **15.00**
Bozo the Clown, sewing kit, 1959,
NM **12.00**
Bullwinkle, View Master reel set,
1962, complete **10.00**
Buster Brown, box camera & 30-
page booklet **25.00**
Buster Brown, camping set, 5-piece,
each with logo stamped on bot-
tom **16.00**
Buster Brown, dictionary, 1923,
EX **16.00**
Buster Brown, growth-recorder
chart **28.00**
Buster Brown, hose supporter but-
tons, pin-back, pr **6.00**
Buster Brown, mug, white porce-
lain gold trim, 3½" **25.00**

**Disney characters scatter rug,
1950s, 45x59", $75.00.**

Buster Brown, reverse-painted stand-up sign **18.00**

Buster Brown, ring, heavy embossed brass, marked **18.00**

Buster Brown, shoe brush, 8½", EX/NM **20.00**

Buster Brown, shoe stretchers, pr **16.00**

Campbell Boy, spoon **10.00**

Campbell Kids, book, Campbell Kids at Home **15.00**

Captain Gallant, coloring book, 1956, 128-page **12.00**

Captain Marvel, paper horn, Fawcett Publications ..**12.00**

Captain Midnight, airline map, EX/NM **15.00**

Captain Ray-o-Vac, flashlight, red with decal, 1950s **15.00**

Casper, Magic Color paint set, EX/NM **18.00**

Casper, punch-out book, 1960, unused **25.00**

Charles Lindbergh, coin, Lucky Lindbergh on back **12.00**

Charles Lindbergh, pendant, NY to Paris Non-Stop, brass-color metal **15.00**

Charlie Chaplin, pencil case, tin, 8" **45.00**

Charlie McCarthy, Rummy card game, dated 1939, 5x7". **25.00**

Charlie McCarthy, spoon ..**10.00**

Cinderella, standing ceramic figure, 5" **15.00**

Colonel Sanders, bank **20.00**

Davy Crockett, cereal bowl, red on white glass **8.00**

Davy Crockett, flashlight, ca 1950, in original box **20.00**

Davy Crockett, flashlight, plastic body with paper label ..**10.00**

Davy Crockett, mug **7.50**

Davy Crockett, picture ring, brass-color plastic with photo .**9.00**

Davy Crockett, scarf, Pioneer of the West, silk, 4x28" **15.00**

Dick Tracy, coloring book, dated 1946, 9x11" **25.00**

Dick Tracy, pen-lite, EX ...**22.00**

Dick Tracy, sub-machine gun, Top Plastics Incorporated, 12", EX/NM **27.00**

Donald Duck, bank, painted tin, marked Chein, 3x6x3" .**50.00**

Donald Duck, charm **3.00**

Hopalong Cassidy wrist watch, U.S. Time, in original box, $85.00.

Donald Duck, Christmas card, 1945, unused **5.00**

Donald Duck, pencil sharpener, red celluloid, decal, 1½" ... **35.00**

Dopey, painted hard rubber, Disney, 6" **20.00**

Douglas Fairbanks, spoon ... **8.00**

Dr Kildare, stethoscope, Richard Chamberlain pictured, 1963, EX/NM **12.00**

Ducky Daddles, fork **6.00**

Dumbo, 10¢ coloring book .. **15.00**

Orphan Annie mug, made for Ovaltine, 3", $42.00.

Elvis Presley, flasher pin, Love Me Tender, 1956, 2½" **7.00**

Elvis Presley, photo button, Fan Club, ca 1950, 1¾" **9.00**

Elvis Presley, pocket calendar, 1969, 4x2" **8.00**

Flash Gordon, space compass, EX/NM **20.00**

Fred Flintstone, camera, British Hong Kong, complete in original box **25.00**

Gene Autry, button, Gene Autry Club Badge, 1¼" **8.00**

Gloria Swanson, spoon **8.00**

Green Hornet, book, Case of Disappearing Doctor, 1966 . **6.00**

Green Hornet, playing cards, 1966, complete deck, NM **8.00**

Gumby, figurine, 1965, Lakeside Toys, factory sealed on original card **12.00**

Hopalong Cassidy, cup, milk glass, ca 1950, 3" **15.00**

Hopalong Cassidy, pencil case, EX/NM **22.00**

Hopalong Cassidy, pin-back button, NM **8.50**

Hopalong Cassidy, thermos, metal & plastic, 6½ **15.00**

Howdy Doody, bank, plastic with fuzzy flocking, 8½" **20.00**

Howdy Doody, card game, Russell Co, original box **20.00**

Howdy Doody, earmuffs, ca 1950, NM **22.00**

Howdy Doody, mug, ceramic, colorful **20.00**

Howdy Doody, night light, marked Nor'East Nauticals, 7" . **42.00**

Howdy Doody, record, It's Howdy Doody Time, 78 rpm **6.00**

Mickey Mouse Bagatelle, 24x12", NM, $275.00.

Howdy Doody, shoe polish, in original box **18.00**
Huckleberry Hound, game . **12.00**
Katzenjammer Kids, Hockey Game, complete **25.00**
Kiss, backpack, 1977 . . . . . . **10.00**
Kit Carson, neckerchief, Coca Cola issue, ca 1950, 22" **18.00**
Lassie, game, Adventures of Lassie, complete, ca 1955 . . . . **15.00**
Little Abner, puppet, in original box, EX **25.00**
Little Orphan Annie, knitting spool, ca 1935, 3½" **35.00**
Little Orphan Annie, mug . . **38.00**
Little Orphan Annie, sheet music, Ovaltine issue, 1931 . . . **12.00**
Lone Ranger, badge, Safety Scout, pin-back **12.00**
Lone Ranger, hairbrush, 1939, 2½x3" **18.00**
Lone Ranger, picture printing set, ca 1939 . . . . **32.00**
Lone Ranger, silver bullet pencil sharpener, 1¼" **16.00**
Lone Ranger, Target Game, Louis Marx & Co, 1938 . . . . . . **30.00**
Lucky, dalmation pup squeeze toy, Dell, 7" **10.00**
Maggie, chalk statue, 12" . . **55.00**
Maggie & Jiggs, paperweight, glass, early **35.00**
Magilla Gorilla, puppet **22.00**
Mickey & Minnie Mouse, parasol, Walt Disney, 1933 . . . . **30.00**
Mickey & Minnie Mouse, valentine, Walt Disney, '39, 5x4½". **27.00**
Mickey Mouse, ceramic planter, colorful **20.00**
Mickey Mouse, standing figure, bisque, Made in Japan, Walt Disney, 3" **30.00**
Mickey Mouse, gloves **15.00**
Mickey Mouse, hot water bottle, marked Disney Productions, 12" **24.00**
Mickey Mouse, Mousegetar, Mattel, ca 1950 . . . . **25.00**
Mickey Mouse, puzzle, marked 1933, Walt Disney **37.00**

Mickey Mouse, sew-on button for coat, domed glass over enamel motif **6.00**
Mickey Mouse Club, Official Duncan Yo-Yo, ca 1950 . . . . **12.00**
Mighty Mouse, cut-out book, 1959, unused **30.00**
Monkees, thermos, 1967 . . . . **9.00**
Munsters, thermos **10.00**
Orphan Annie, Pep pin **10.00**

Thumper, American Potteries, 4½", **$30.00.**

Pendant, gold-colored metal hangs from neck chain **35.00**
Pinky Lee, coloring book, Health & Safety, 80-page **25.00**
Pinocchio, lunch box, marked copyright WDP, ca 1940, 4" . **35.00**
Pinocchio, paperweight/thermometer, Plastic Novelties . . **27.00**
Pinocchio, valentine, mechanical, ca 1940 . . . . **8.00**
Popeye, Bubble Set, 1936 . . **25.00**
Popeye, lunch box **20.00**
Popeye, paints, American Crayon Company, ca 1933 . . . . **20.00**
Popeye, Skill game, 1929 . . **65.00**
Popeye, vinyl doll, marked Cameo KFS on back, 13" **45.00**
Popeye, xylophone mechanical-action pull toy, Metal Masters, EX/NM **45.00**
Puss 'N Boots, spoon **10.00**

Quick Draw McGraw, bank **12.00**
Raggedy Ann & Andy, Nite Lite
Radio **35.00**
Ranger Joe, mug, blue transfer on
white milk glass **4.00**
Red Ranger, tin gun, marked Wyan-
dotte Toys, 8" **16.00**
Red Riding Hood, coloring box #544,
American Crayon Company,
11½x8" **9.00**
Red Riding Hood, warming dish,
Excello, 7" **20.00**
Red Ryder, target game, Whitman
Publishing, dated 1939 **42.00**
Rin Tin Tin, puzzle, Tinny & Tusty,
EX **12.50**
Rootie Kazootie, cards **25.00**
Roy Rogers, bubble gum cards, set
of 24 .... **25.00**
Roy Rogers, camera, plastic box with
carrying strap **25.00**
Roy Rogers, double holsters & gun-
belt **10.00**
Roy Rogers, harmonica **20.00**
Roy Rogers, pin-back button, photo
in center, 1¼" **7.00**
Roy Rogers, plastic mug, 4" . **18.00**
Roy Rogers, post card **7.00**
Roy Rogers, puzzle, dated 1952,
complete **20.00**
Roy Rogers, thermos **25.00**
Roy Rogers & Trigger, binoculars,
NM **15.00**
Roy Rogers & Trigger, drinking
glass, 4¾" **15.00**
Shmoo, salt & pepper shakers, plas-
tic, pair **8.00**
Sky King, poster, He Flies! He Rides!
He Battles!, ca 1960 ... **18.00**
Snow White, looking glass ca 1940,
9½" **20.00**
Snow White, planter, marked Leeds
China, 6½" **20.00**
Snow White & Seven Dwarfs, tea
set, 1937, 9-piece **57.00**
Star Trek, View Master reel set,
copyright 1968 .... **10.00**
Starsky & Hutch, board game,
complete **15.00**

Steve Canyon, space goggles, ca
1950 .... **30.00**
Superman, Pep pin, Kellogg's,
1940 .... **20.00**
Superman, plaster, 16" **32.00**
Tarzan, board game **25.00**
Tennessee Jed, ink blotter, ca 1940,
4x7" **6.00**
Thumper, ceramic figure, Ameri-
can Pottery, 4" **32.00**
Tinker Belle, Tiddly Winks game,
EX **45.00**
Tom Mix, decoder badge ... **35.00**
Tom Mix, spy ring **39.00**
Tony the Tiger, spoon **10.00**
Underdog, bank, colorful plastic
figure, 7½" **10.00**
Wendy, hand puppet, Walt Disney
Productions, ca 1950 ... **8.00**
Willie & Millie, salt and pepper,
pr **20.00**
Wonder Woman, watch, Super Hero,
1977 .... **20.00**
Woody Woodpecker, spoon, marked
WLP, 6" long **10.00**
Yogi Bear, spoon **10.00**
Zorro, game, Whitman, ca 1965,
complete **12.00**
007, game, Enter the Dangerous
World James Bond, '65 . **25.00**
007, pistol ring **6.00**

Children's Books

Books were popular gifts for children in the latter 1800s; many were
beautifully illustrated, some by
notable artists such as Frances
Brundage and Maxfield Parrish.
From this century, tales of Tarzan
by Burroughs are fast becoming very
collectible — *Tarzan of the Apes*,
1914, McClurg first edition, in very
good condition, is worth about
$650.00.

Adventures of Tom Sawyer, Harper,
illustrated, 1917 ...... **10.00**

Alice in Story Land, Worthington Co., NY, copyright 1888, $15.00.

Bird's Christmas Carol, Houghton Mifflin, illustrated, 1929, EX/NM 20.00

Buttercup's Visit to Little Stay At Home, illustrated, 1881. 50.00

Child's Garden of Verses, Eulalie illustrated, 1932 ......20.00

Childhood, Duff, color illustrated, 1907 ....80.00

Children of Dickens, Jessie W Smith illustrated, 1942 ......30.00

Father Bear, Harper, 1932, 12-page, EX/NM 7.00

Gulliver's Travels, RG Mossa illustrated, ca 1940 ......20.00

Hitty, MacMillan, D Lathrop illustrated, 1930 ....15.00

Jack Sprat, Little Mother Goose Series, ca 1898 ......15.00

Joan of Arc, McKay, 1918 ..30.00

Little Goody Two-Shoes, Grosset & Dunlap, color illustrated, 1944, EX/NM 15.00

Little Lame Prince, Whitman, illustrated, 1916 ....38.00

N By E, New York, 1st trade edition, illustrated, 1930 ..35.00

Overall Boys, 1924 ....40.00

Parachute Pup, Lippincott, watercolor illustrated, 1941 .15.00

Peter Rabbit the Magician, illustrated, 1942 ....24.00

Phronsie Pepper, 1st ed, illustrated, 1897 ....20.00

Pied Piper of Hamelin, Wessels Co, VanDyck illustrated, 1900, EX/NM 20.00

Pinocchio, Whitman, Alice Carsey illustrated, 1916 ......38.00

Poems of Childhood, Maxfield Parrish illustrated, 1904 ..45.00

Puss in Boots, McLoughlin, 1888, linen pages 100.00

Ring-A-Round, MacMillan, 1st edition, 1930 ....8.00

Snow Fight, Bavaria, illustrated, 12-page 12.00

Snow White & Rose Red, illustrated, 1929 ....20.00

Story of a Mother, Christensen, illustrated, 1929 ......30.00

Tale of Peter Rabbit, 1943 ..18.00

Through the Looking Glass, 50 illustrations, 1899 ......22.00

Tom Thumb & Other Old-Time Fairy Tales, Rand McNally, 1926 ....25.00

Tortoise & the Hare, Whitman, Disney illustrated, 1935, EX/NM 35.00

Tragedy of Pudd'n Head Wilson, Hartford, CT, color illustrated, 1904 ....175.00

Wonder Book, color llustrated, 1893 ....17.00

Children's Dishes

In the late 1900s, glass companies introduced sets of small-scaled pressed glass dinnerware, many in the same pattern as their regular lines, others designed specifically for the little folks. Many were of clear glass, but milk glass, opalescent glass, and colors were also used. Not to be outdone, English ceramic firms as well as American potteries made both tea sets and fully-accessorized dinnerware sets decorated with decals of nursery rhymes, animals, or characters from children's stories. Though popularly collected for some time, your favorite flea market may still yield some very nice examples of both types.

China and Pottery

Bowl, Barnyard Scenes, Royal Windsor, England, 5⅜" . **12.00**
Bowl, Children Fishing, Noritake, 5⅞" **15.00**
Bowl, Little Miss Muffet, 6" . **8.00**
Bowl, yellow ware **30.00**
Cake plate, Blue Willow, Made in Japan, 5¼" **30.00**
Creamer, Merry Christmas, Leuchtenberg, Germany, 3". **22.50**
Creamer, Nippon, 2¼" **7.00**
Creamer, Otter Cocoa, Noritake, 2" **45.00**
Creamer, tan and grey lustre, Phoenix China, Made in Japan, 2¼" **8.00**
Crock, blue & white, with wire bail handle **45.00**
Crock, green, 2¼" **25.00**
Cup, Bluebird Dinner Set, Noritake, 1¼" **7.00**
Cup, Boy with Doll, Geisha Girl, 2" **10.00**

Cup, Floral Medallion, Made in Japan, 1¾" **2.00**
Cup, Gaudy Ironstone, marked England, 1⅞" **22.00**
Cup, Mickey Mouse, Occupied Japan, 1¼" **8.00**
Mug, Mary Had a Little Lamb, 2⅝" **6.00**
Plate, Davy Crockett, 7¼" ...**5.00**
Plate, Dutch Children, Made in Japan **3.00**
Plate, Water Hen, Staffordshire, 5½" **8.00**
Platter, Bears, marked Made in Japan, 6¼" **6.00**
Stein, shield front, marked Bavaria, 1⅞" **4.00**
Sugar bowl, Elephant Lustre, Made in Japan, 2⅜" **12.00**
Teapot, Butterfly, Made in Japan, 3⅜" **8.00**

Pattern Glass

Acorn, spooner, clear, 3⅛" .. **90.00**
Alabama, sugar bowl with lid, clear, 4" **80.00**
Amazon Variant, creamer, clear, 2⅞" **30.00**
Bead & Scroll, creamer, 3" .**65.00**
Beaded Swirl Variation, sugar bowl, clear, 3¾" **30.00**
Block & Rosette, spooner, clear, 2⅜" **50.00**

Bridesmaid pattern, Germany, 6-place setting, $250.00.

Braided Belt, creamer, light green, 2⅝" **85.00**

Button Panel 44, sugar with lid, clear, George Duncan's Sons, 3" **90.00**

Buzz Saw, punch cup, clear, United States Glass, 4¼" **6.00**

Chimo, spooner, clear, 2⅛" . **40.00**

Cloud Band, spooner, milk glass, Gillinder & Sons, 2⅜" . . **75.00**

Colonial, pitcher, clear, 3⅜". **30.00**

Dewdrop, spooner, amber, Columbia Glass, 2⅝" **50.00**

Doyle 500, mug, clear, Doyle & Co, 2" **40.00**

Dutch Boudoir, pitcher, blue milk glass, 2¼" **55.00**

Euclid, sugar bowl with lid, clear, Higbee, 2¾" **25.00**

Fine Cut Star & Fan, creamer, clear, Higbee, 2⅜" **18.00**

Flute, bowl, clear, 2" **30.00**

Galloway, pitcher, clear, United States Glass, 4" **30.00**

Grapevine with Ovals, butter with lid, clear, McKee, 1¾" . . **75.00**

Hawaiian Lei, creamer, clear, Bryce Higbee, 3⅛" **30.00**

Hobnail with Thumbprint base No 150, sugar bowl, 4" **70.00**

Horizontal Threads, spooner, clear, ca 1910, 2⅛" **40.00**

Lacy Daisy, berry, mint green, United States Glass, 1". **15.00**

Large Block, spooner, blue milk glass, 3⅛" **70.00**

Liberty Bell, mug, clear, Gillinder & Sons, 1⅞" **90.00**

Mardi Gras, rose bowl, clear, Duncan & Miller, 2⅛" **75.00**

Northwood Hobnail, creamer, clear, 3" **60.00**

Ornamental Hobnail, cup & saucer set, clear **30.00**

Oval Star No 300, tumbler, clear, Indiana Glass, 2⅜" **10.00**

Pattee Cross, pitcher, clear, United States Glass, 4¼" **40.00**

Pennsylvania No 15048, butter, clear, 3½" **65.00**

Pert, sugar bowl with lid, clear, 5⅛" **65.00**

Petite Hobnail, tumbler, clear, 2¼" **35.00**

Plain Pattern No 13, sugar bowl, King Glass, 3⅜" **55.00**

Pointed Jewel, spooner, United States Glass, 2½" **80.00**

Sawtooth, butter, clear, 3⅛". **35.00**

Stippled Vine & Beads, sugar bowl, clear, 2⅛" **80.00**

Style, spooner, Higbee, 2¼" . **18.00**

Children's Furnishings

Just about anything made for adults has been reduced to children's size. Early handmade items

Twin Snowshoes table set, U.S. Glass Co., $265.00.

may be as primitive or as elaborate as their creator was proficient. Even later factory-made pieces are collectible. Baby rattles, highchairs, strollers, wagons, and sleds from the 1800s are especially treasured.

Bed, brass, half tester frame with ball finials, 28x32" . . . **175.00**
Blanket, cowboy design **15.00**
Crumbcake skillet, brass, 3½" diameter **20.00**
Cupboard, pine, single door with wavy glass, 12½" **195.00**
Egg beater, blue & white painted handle **8.00**
Funnel, blue & white graniteware, EX/NM **10.00**
Ironing board, wood **20.00**
Mug, blue graniteware **10.00**
Potato masher, wood, 6½" . . **15.00**
Rolling pin, wood **20.00**
Salt box, tin, 2½" **75.00**
Set: dustpan & wastebasket; blue & white tin litho **32.00**
Sewing machine, Kayanee, Germany **75.00**
Sewing machine, Little Miss Lindstrom, with box **45.00**
Sewing machine, Singer, in box, with booklet copyright 1955 . **27.00**
Shovel, wood, 24¼" **65.00**
Sleigh, wood with iron runners, red repaint, 26½" **110.00**
Stove, Royal Gas, 4¼x3¼" . . **35.00**
Stove, tin, with cast iron pots & pans, painted, VG **45.00**
Sugar bucket, with lid **45.00**
Teakettle, cast iron, porcelain knob, Wagner, 3¾" **50.00**
Umbrella, black silk with fringe, wood handle, 19" **55.00**
Washboard, ca 1850 . . . . **55.00**
Washing machine, Sunny Suzy , ca 1914 . . . . **35.00**
Washing machine, Wee Washer, ca 1914 . . . . **75.00**
Writing box, Dennison Manufacturing Co **25.00**

Chair, mahogany, 22½", $110.00.

Christmas

No other holiday season is celebrated to the extravagant extent as Christmas, and vintage decorations provide a warmth and charm that none from today can match. Ornaments from before 1870 were imported from Dresden, Germany — usually made of cardboard and sparkled with tinsel trim. Later, blown glass ornaments were made there in literally thousands of shapes such as fruits and vegetables, clowns, Santas, angels, and animals. Kugles, heavy glass balls (though fruit and vegetable forms are found occasionally) were made from about 1820 to late in the century in sizes from very small up to 14". Early Santa figures are treasured, especially those in robes other than red. Figural bulbs from the '20s and '30s are popular, those that are character related in particular.

Bookmark, Welcome to Merry Christmas, cardboard ...**2.50**

Bulb, baby in red stocking, milk glass, EX **45.00**

Bulb, bell **10.00**

Bulb, bird **10.00**

Bulb, cross, VG red paint on clear glass **25.00**

Bulb, house, green with snow on roof, milk glass, C-6 Japan, EX/NM **25.00**

Bulb, Humpty Dumpty, VG paint, milk glass, 3" **65.00**

Bulb, Japanese lantern, C-6 Japan, small **16.00**

Bulb, lantern, VG paint, milk glass, Japan, large **22.00**

Bulb, Matchless Star, green with red center, 2" **10.00**

Bulb, rose, milk glass, C-6 Japan, EX/NM **20.00**

Bulb, rose, open, VG red paint, milk glass **35.00**

Bulb, Santa, 2-faced, red paint, milk glass, 3" **28.00**

Candy container Santa, cardboard with paper bag, dated 1926, 10", $35.00.

Bulb, snowman with pack on back, milk glass, Japan **22.50**

Bulb, woman in shoe, multicolor paint, milk glass, NM ..**75.00**

Candy container, boot, celluloid, 4", NM **7.50**

Candy container, boot, red papier-mache with flannel trim, 4½" **12.00**

Candy container, cornucopia, red foil **5.00**

Candy container, Father Christmas, ca 1925, glass, 4½" **80.00**

Candy container, house, glass, red brick, green roof, 3" ...**75.00**

Candy container, Santa, paint on clear glass, 5½" **65.00**

Candy container, Santa, red cotton, plaster face, 3½" **55.00**

Candy container, Santa in basket, plaster hands, Japan, 5", EX/NM **80.00**

Candy container, snowman with top hat & pipe, celluloid, 6". **10.00**

Candy container, straw basket, pink with handle, 2¼x3" **12.00**

Candy container, wreath, Dresden, 4¼" **135.00**

Card, May Your Christmas Be Merry, Prang, 3½" **15.00**

Garland, blown glass beads, ca 1900, 132" **80.00**

Garland, red paper rope ...**20.00**

Garland, silver, gold, green, & red beads, ca 1920, 168" ...**65.00**

Kugel, ball, cobalt, Baroque cap, 2½" **45.00**

Kugel, grapes, silver, embossed brass hanger, 7" **285.00**

Kugel, pear, emerald green, Baroque brass hanger, 3¾" **250.00**

Lights, birds, plastic on string, boxed **30.00**

Lights, icicles, plastic on string, boxed **30.00**

Lights, snowman, eight on string, boxed **20.00**

Ornament, angel, plastic **5.00**

Ornament, hand-blown fruit in Victorian basket, 4", $40.00.

Ornament, angel diecut praying in tinsel frame, 4" **30.00**

Ornament, apple, pressed cotton, ca 1910 . . . .**35.00**

Ornament, baby diecut in cotton dress with crepe paper trim, 5½" **45.00**

Ornament, bell, blue glass, floral trim, ca 1920, 1½" **20.00**

Ornament, bell, plastic, large. **2.50**

Ornament, bell, red, white, & blue blown glass, 2¼" **25.00**

Ornament, berry, unsilvered pink blown glass, 1910, 2" . .**20.00**

Ornament, bird on nest, blown glass, clip-on, ca 1890 . . . . . .**50.00**

Ornament, bird with spun glass tail, ca 1910, 5¼" **35.00**

Ornament, choir boy, bottle brush type **6.00**

Ornament, Christmas tree, blown glass, clip-on, ca 1920 . .**40.00**

Ornament, clown head on ruffle, blown glass, 2¼" **22.00**

Ornament, cockatoo with spun glass tail, early **35.00**

Ornament, Father Christmas diecut on flat cotton star, 5" . .**42.00**

Ornament, flower basket, honeycomb paper, Germany, 3⅞", EX/NM **20.00**

Ornament, house, paper, pink with silver beads, Japan, ca 1930, EX/NM **15.00**

Ornament, pine cone, red blown glass, 2" **12.00**

Ornament, pine cone elf, plastic face, cotton & chenille body . **12.50**

Ornament, Santa paper scrap in oval, tinsel trim, 3½x2¼", EX/NM **12.00**

Ornament, saxophone **2.00**

Ornament, skier, cotton figure, paper skis, 5" **45.00**

Ornament, snowflake, double-sided Dresden type, ca 1900 . **35.00**

Ornament, snowman, cotton, Germany, 3" **85.00**

Ornament, table lamp, painted blown glass, 1930, 3¼" . **18.00**

Ornament, teapot, cobalt blown glass, 3" **30.00**

Ornament, teapot, frosted pink blown glass with mica flecks, 5" **26.00**

Reindeer, celluloid, large . . .**17.50**

Santa, composition, made in Japan, 6", $60.00.

Reindeer, celluloid, small ..**12.50**
Santa, cotton with black cotton legs,
3" **40.00**
Santa, plaster figure, made in Japan, cardboard base, 9". **75.00**
Santa, straw body, rubber face, fabric clothing, 15" **35.00**
Santa, stuffed, figure in red flannel suit, electric blinking eyes, 26" **45.00**
Trade card, Eldridge & Co, Santa with tree & toys, 1887 .**30.00**
Tree, bottle brush with natural wood base, 3½" **4.00**
Tree, cellophane, 1950, 51" .**80.00**
Tree, green paper rope with beads, 3½" **10.00**
Tree, tinsel branches, tin base, Germany, 12" **75.00**
Tree, white Glolite, colored candles, 110V bulb, 17" **35.00**
Tree stand, cast iron, tree stump form **45.00**
Tree top, angel, plastic, Paramount, original box **30.00**
Wreath, aluminum foil **7.00**
Wreath, bottle brush with green glass beads, 4" **8.00**
Wreath, bottle brush with red composition berries, 9" **15.00**
Wreath, red paper rope with pine cones, 5" **12.00**

Civil War Collectibles

Mementos from the great Civil War represent many things to many people — the downfall of the antebellum grandeur of the South, the resulting freedom of the Black race, and the conflict itself that was the most personal tragedy America has ever known. In this context, collectors of Civil War memorabilia regard their artifacts with a softness of heart perhaps not present in those whose interests lie in militaria of the 20th century.

Massachusetts 37th Regiment guidon, ca 1862-64, names of survivors inked in on reverse in 1928, 29" long, VG, $250.00.

Belt buckle, brass, eagle on rectangle **85.00**
Binoculars, brass, ca 1864 ..**32.50**
Book, Personal History of Ulysses S Grant, 1st, 1868 ......**17.50**
Bottle, medical; glass with stopper, dated 1862, 9" **23.50**
Broadside, Reunion of Veterans, Batesville, VA, 1916, 8x6½", EX **25.00**
Bullet mold, 2-cavity **15.00**
Button, eagle with C in center, cuff size **4.00**
Cap box, Union Army **27.50**
Carbine cartridge box, dated 1850, EX **55.00**
Check, dated 1861 ....**8.00**
Comb, folding, opens to 6" ..**22.50**
Compass, brass **23.50**
Crutch, oak with hand-stitched padded top **21.00**
Document, letter on Treasury Department stationery, 1864, 1-page **10.00**
Eyeglasses, steel frame **10.00**
Flag, parade; 1864, 18x11" .**35.00**

Harness buckle, 6x3" **15.00**
Hat emblem, large horn with brass
   trim, ca 1861 . . . . **21.00**
Invalid feeder, ceramic, marked
   Germany **45.00**
Map, Gettysburg & Appomatox
   Court House, 20x25" . . **12.00**
Newspaper, Boston Daily Adver-
   tiser, May 5, 1862 . . . . . **25.00**
Newspaper, New York Tribune, July
   12, 1864 . . . . **20.00**
Newspaper, The Liberator, July
   1865 . . . . **9.50**
Note, Confederate $10 bill, dated
   1864 . . . . **8.00**
Note, Confederate $2 bill, dated
   1864 . . . . **12.00**
Note, Confederate $20 bill, dated
   September 2, 1861 . . . . **25.00**
Pamphlet, Prison Life During the
   Rebellion , dated 1869, 48-
   page **17.50**
Spoon, folding **21.00**
Telegram, military, 1864 . . . . **5.00**
Token, Indian head, 1863 . . . **4.00**
Token, Peace Forever & Washing-
   ton 1863 on sides **9.00**

Cleminson

Hand-decorated Cleminson ware
is one type of the California-made
novelty pottery that collectors have
recently taken an interest in.
Though nearly always marked,
these items have a style that you'll
easily become acquainted with; and
their distinctive glaze colors will be
easy to spot. It was produced from
the early 1940s until 1963.

Ash tray, boat shaped, for 6 ciga-
   rettes, marked **15.00**
Butter dish , Distlefink, bird form
   6½x4¾" **25.00**
Butter dish, lady figural . . . **30.00**
Canister, cherries on branch.**25.00**
Darner, 5" **15.00**

Gravy boat, Distlefink, 6x7½", with
   ladle **20.00**
Hair receiver, girl with hands folded,
   2-piece **20.00**
Pitcher, Distlefink, 9½" **25.00**
Plaque, kitten in basket . . . **12.00**
Razor blade bank, man's head and
   shoulders **12.00**
Shakers, Distlefink, pair . . . **10.00**
Sprinkler bottle, girl, 6½" . . **18.00**
String holder, apple with butterfly,
   marked **35.00**
Tray, sandwich; Deco fruit, center
   handle, marked **25.00**
Wall pocket, clock, 'Time' . . **12.50**
Wall pocket, coffeepot **15.00**

**Distlefink gravy boat and ladle,
$20.00.**

Clocks

Because many of the early clocks
have handmade works, condition is
important when you are considering a purchase. Repairs may be
costly. Today's collectors prefer
pendulum-regulated movements
from the 18th and 19th centuries
and clocks from the larger manufacturers such as Sessions, Ithica,
Ingraham, Seth Thomas, Ansonia,
and Waterbury.

Alarm, brass plaque, Kroeber Clock
   Company, 1890s, 12" . **100.00**
Alarm, Erie Canal, oak case, 30-
   hour, 1900, 6¼" **125.00**

Ansonia bank clock, 8-day, time only, runs only when a nickel is deposited every 24 hours, 6", $200.00.

Anniversary, brass with glass dome, 11" **90.00**

Ansonia, French Empire, figurines of hunter & fisherman, 21½" **325.00**

Ansonia, Lucia, crystal regulator **900.00**

Ansonia, Peep-O-Day, 30-hour, 8" **100.00**

Aulding,carriage, brass & enamel face, leather case, 6½"..**450.00**

Birge & Fuller, Empire, 8-day, time & strike, 33" **425.00**

Brewster & Ingraham, steeple, 30-hour, 1850, 19¾" **125.00**

Burroughs, shelf, Gothic, ca 1940, 7" **75.00**

Carriage, brass, ca 1930, 4" **90.00**

Deer, novelty, eye moves, ceramic figural **45.00**

French, mantel, works marked H Mclle, Paris, 14¼" **175.00**

Germany, novelty, boy with pecking goose, ca 1970 .....**50.00**

Gilbert, Lake #4, kitchen, oak, 8-day **175.00**

Ingraham, mantel, pillar front, ca 1890 ....**60.00**

Ingraham, school regulator, oak case, EX **150.00**

Keebler, novelty, bulldog with kitten, EX **30.00**

Lux, novelty, showboat, paddle turns, 1950 ....**90.00**

Lux, novelty, spinning wheel, alarm on top **125.00**

New Haven, beehive, rosewood & mahogany, 30-hour, 1850, 19½" **200.00**

New Haven, office regulator, calendar, oak case, 43" **400.00**

New Haven, porcelain, floral trim, 30-hour, 1900, 5½" **60.00**

New Haven, tambour mantel, 30-hour, 1910, 6¾" **35.00**

Seikosha, shelf, oak, Japan .**65.00**

Sessions, mantel, black paint, metal columns, 30-hour, 5¾" .**70.00**

Sessions, mantel, Gothic, 3-day movement, 9" **60.00**

Sessions, mantel, mahogany with inlay, 30-hour, porcelain dial, 8" **80.00**

E.N. Welch shelf clock, weight driven, strikes hour and half-hour, thirty hour, brass works, rosewood case, 26", $200.00.

Sessions, tambour mantel, 30-hour, 1930, 5½" **25.00**

Seth Thomas, alarm, tin case, ca 1900, 9" **40.00**

Seth Thomas, banjo, sailing ships, eagle atop, 1920, 20" . .**150.00**

Seth Thomas, shelf, green marbleized trim, ebony-finished case, 11½" **115.00**

Seth Thomas, shelf, rosewood veneer, 1875, 15" **175.00**

Seth Thomas, 8-day, rosewood, ca 1850, 14½" **65.00**

Smith, novelty, boxing dog & bear, arms move, 1960s **105.00**

Standard, office, oak, round top, 3 ringers, electric, 60" . . .**60.00**

Telechron, Bakelite, electric. **48.00**

Waterbury, kitchen, golden oak, elaborate case **150.00**

Westclox, Tom Thumb, ca 1920, 8½" **100.00**

World, novelty, figural, 3" diameter, NM **50.00**

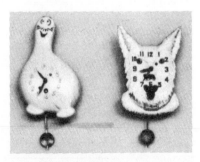

Lux novelties: Shmoo, 6", $100.00; Scottie, 5", $75.00.

Cloisonne

Several types of cloisonne (a method of decorating metal with enameling) have been developed since it was introduced in the 16th century — plique a jour (transparent enamel work); foil cloisonne; wireless cloisonne; or cloisonne on ceramic, wood, or lacquer. The type you are most likely to encounter at flea markets has the pattern outlined with fine metal wires, filled in with colored enamels. The finest examples date from 1865 until 1900, though excellent work is still being produced in China and Taiwan.

Belt buckle, lotus blossoms on black, 2¾x1⅛" **50.00**

Bird, removable head, floral motif 4", pair **220.00**

Bottle, snuff; multicolor flowers & butterfly on blue, 3" . . .**90.00**

Bowl, dragon, 1880, 5x5" . . .**75.00**

Box, double T-fret, multicolor flowers on foliage on red, ball feet, 1¼x3¼" **55.00**

Box, floral, 1800s, 4" **110.00**

Box, snuff; Wall of China, oval, 2" long **20.00**

Bracelet, bangle; multicolor branch on blue, 1⅜" wide **65.00**

Charger, floral branches & butterflies on blue, 12" **125.00**

Cigarette case, 3 colorful dragons on green **125.00**

Vase, birds and flowers on green, 7", $265.00.

Crumber, flowers, animals, & people, marked China . **60.00**
Figure, Guanyin, multicolor/turquoise robe, sits on oval base, 12" **300.00**
Incense burner, dragon's-head foot, 6" **125.00**
Jar, dragon, yellow on black, with cover, late, 6¼", NM ...**90.00**
Napkin ring, multicolor floral, 2" diameter **25.00**
Salt cellar, florals on blue, footed, pair **18.00**
Sheath, 1800s, 42" **600.00**
Teapot, florals with foil centers on cobalt, Japan, 5¾" ...**225.00**
Teapot, multicolor swastikas on white, 1800s **175.00**
Tray, flowers on blue, bronze sides & feet, 8" **90.00**
Vase, birds, fish nets, & waves, Meiji Period, 7" **1,000.00**
Vase, multicolor birds & florals on turquoise, abstract bands, Japan, 11" **250.00**
Vase, dragon, 1890, 10" ...**125.00**
Vase, flowers & foliage, blue on yellow, 8" **65.00**
Vase, florals on brick red, teakwood base, 8¾" **250.00**
Vase, Thousand Flower, multicolor on white, double gourd shape, 9½" .... **295.00** .
Vase, tiger lilies, orange on green, silverplated rim & base, Japan, 10" **600.00**

Clothing and Accessories

Here's one collection you can enjoy wearing, and many do! Victorian whites, vintage furs, sequined gowns, designer fashions — whatever look you prefer is yours at only a fraction of today's prices for modern copies. Alterations are possible, but unless done with tenderness and care may lessen the value.

Fabrics may have become more delicate with the passing of the years, so very gentle cleaning methods are a must. Accessories are fun; and hats, fur boas, belts, and shoes from the era of your outfit finish it off with smashing authenticity.

Dress, white with lace and eyelet trim, ca 1900, $135.00.

Apron, child's full body, cotton print, back tie, 1930, EX **5.00**
Bathing slippers, black & white canvas **10.00**
Bathing suit, wool, green & wine, Bradley, 1920s **26.00**
Bathing tunic, black cotton sateen, 1910 .... **22.00**
Blouse, elaborate embroidery & tucks, Victorian **22.00**
Bolero, ivory wool, ¾-sleeves, ca 1920s, VG **35.00**
Bonnet, child's, calico **22.00**

Bonnet, silk, hand-crochet edging, ca 1895 . . . . **35.00**

Bonnet, sleep; pink sateen with machine-made lace front, pink bow **22.00**

Camisole, ivory, embroidered lace net with flower fillet insert, EX **20.00**

Capelet, elaborate black beading, Victorian **75.00**

Coat, baby's, 1890s styling . **35.00**

Coat, man's, beige linen, MOP buttons, Victorian, EX **75.00**

Collar, ecru lace with jabot, Victorian **25.00**

Corset, white **20.00**

Dress, beige with beads & sequins, sleeveless, mini, with jacket, 1950 . . . . **35.00**

Dress, christening; white cotton, eyelet bodice, lace trim, 34", EX **50.00**

Dress, evening; black lace with deep V neckline & full skirt, 1930s, EX **85.00**

Dress, flapper's, rhinestones & beadwork on green chiffon with girdle **75.00**

Dress, girl's, white lawn, elaborate lace & tucks **27.00**

Dress, white dimity lawn, shirt-waist/long sleeves, 1910. **75.00**

Dress, white organdy, eyelet trim, street length, 1920 . . . . **75.00**

Fur boa, mink **35.00**

Fur cape, white ermine **75.00**

Fur coat, muskrat, full-length, late 1930s, VG **75.00**

Fur muff, child's, white, neck strap, 5" diameter, EX **12.00**

Gloves, kid leather **16.00**

Gloves, leather, opera-length style **15.00**

Gown yoke, crochet fillet, Diamond Spoke pattern, open front/ armholes **15.00**

Hat, black felt, Amish, old . **40.00**

Hat, black velvet, WWI **25.00**

Hat, light blue organdy, 4" brim, ca 1940, EX **15.00**

Hat, man's, top hat, beaver, MA label, original box **95.00**

Hat, toque, black silk with velvet ties, 1870s, EX **35.00**

Jacket, peach & white satin, long sleeves, frogs, peplum, 1930s, EX **22.00**

Muffler, black lace, 1940s . . **25.00**

Nightgown, white dimity, Edwardian **55.00**

Child's shoes, leather with wooden soles and brass nails, ca 1780s, $110.00.

Pants, Capri style, lemon yellow, side zipper, 1958, EX . . **10.00**

Parasol, black lace **65.00**

Petticoat, white cotton & crochet, gathered waist, ca 1925, EX **22.00**

Scarf, silk, elaborate embroidery, ca 1985 . . . . **45.00**

Sheath, black sateen with embroidered roses, ankle length, 1920s, NM **80.00**

Shoes, baby's, black leather, 4-button style **22.00**

Shoes, pumps, lavender satin, ca 1920s, EX **20.00**

Shoes, pumps, white satin, 1950s, EX **10.00**

Skirt, linen, gored, 1900 . . . **25.00**

Skirt, felt, 1950s **23.00**

Slip, child's, wool, prairie style, EX **15.00**

Spats, wool, pair **18.00**

Suit, man's, gray pin-stripe wool worsted, 3-piece, 1930 . **75.00**

Sweater, mohair, button front, ¾-sleeves, 1950s **45.00**

Swim suit, green faille, halter style, designer label, 1940s . . **40.00**

Trousers, drop front, wool . . **50.00**

Waist, navy silk, puffy long sleeves, stays, bustle-back, 1890s, EX **40.00**

Coca-Cola

Since it was established in 1891, the Coca-Cola Company has issued a wide and varied scope of advertising memorabilia, creating what may well be the most popular field of specific product-related collectibles on today's market. Probably their best-known item is the rectangular Coke tray, issued since 1910. In excellent condition, some of the earlier examples may bring prices up to $500.00. Before 1910, trays were round or oval. The 1908 'Topless' tray is valued at $1,800.00.

Most Coca-Cola buffs prefer to limit their collections to items made before 1970.

Apron, canvas, with logo, different styles, 1950s, EX **15.00**

Blotter, 1905, Drink a Bottle of Coca-Cola, rare, NM . . **115.00**

Blotter, 1926, Refresh Yourself, Drink Coca-Cola, NM . . **30.00**

Blotter, 1929, Pause That Refreshes, man & lady, EX **60.00**

Blotter, 1930, Off to a Fresh Start, NM **65.00**

Blotter, 1940, clown drinking Coke, EX **40.00**

Book, The Truth About Coca-Cola, 1912 . . . . **20.00**

Book, 14th Anniversary Coca-Cola Bottler, 1949, NM **28.50**

Bottle, Big Chief, embossed Indian head, light green **6.00**

Bottle, Royal Wedding, United Kingdom, 1981, M **20.00**

Bottle, seltzer; Bradford, PA, script Coca-Cola, blue, EX . . . **95.00**

Bottle, Westminster, MD, Coca-Cola in block, dark green . . . **85.00**

Bottle, Wyanode Brand, script logo, light green **150.00**

Bowl, green glass, 1930s . . **175.00**

Calculator, pocket; Coke Is It, EX/NM **10.00**

Calendar, 1944, lady with Coke, 2 rows of pads, EX **70.00**

Calendar, 1957, Pause That Refreshes, complete, NM . **35.00**

Cigarette lighter, can shape, logo in diamond, mini, 1960 . . . . **8.00**

Clock, Drink Coca-Cola, metal frame, glass front, 1942, 16", NM **325.00**

Clock, Drink Coca-Cola, wood frame, 1939, 16" square **450.00**

Clock, neon, 1941, octagonal, 18", NM **750.00**

Cooler, Things Go Better with Coke, vinyl, 1963 . . . . **25.00**

Tin sign, ca 1950s, 20x28", $65.00.

Cup holder, Drink Coca-Cola Iced, wooden, NM **70.00**

Earrings, Coke can shape, metal, ca 1960 .... **10.00**

Fan, cardboard, triple fold, 1950s, EX **20.00**

Flashlight, bottle shape, ca 1950s, in original box, 3" **15.00**

Ice pick/ bottle opener, with wood handle, 1920-1930, NM. **15.00**

Menu board, reverse-painted glass, metal frame, NM **75.00**

Menu board, tin, '70s, NM .**10.00**

Music box, Coke cooler figural, plastic, 1950s, NM **60.00**

Necktie, Coke Adds Life, M .**10.00**

Pencil, mechanical; Have a Coke, M **18.00**

Pencil, mechanical; with bottle-shaped clip **15.00**

Pencil sharpener, shaped like bottle with top open, 1930 ...**24.00**

Playing cards, 1928, lady with bottle, EX **175.00**

Playing cards, 1943, lady in stewardess hat, unopened ..**40.00**

Playing cards, 1956, lady with ice skates, unopened **30.00**

Pop gun, cardboard, Christmas scenes both sides, 1954 .**6.00**

Post card, Coca-Cola Bottling Co, St Petersburg, FL, NM **8.00**

Post card, Coca-Cola Relieves Fatique, picture of Ocean Park fire, NM **16.00**

Radio, vending machine shape, 1970s, NM **70.00**

Ring puzzle, Drink Coca-Cola, metal, 1920s, M **150.00**

Ruler, Work Refreshed, Play Refreshed, EX **3.00**

Sheet music, Rum & Coca-Cola, Andrews Sisters, ca 1940, EX/ NM **18.00**

Sign, embossed tin, 1922, 4x8", NM **225.00**

Stock certificate, 10 shares in Coca-Cola, 1929, NM **75.00**

Thermometer, bottle shape, tin, 1930s, 17", NM **100.00**

Thimble, Coca-Cola in Bottles, aluminum with red enamel lettering, 1930s **30.00**

Tie tack, Coke bottle, MIB .**10.00**

Toy, truck, Jumbo Trailer, Japan, 1970s, 16" long, M **75.00**

Toy, truck, Metalcraft, 10 bottles, rubber tires, 1930, EX. **325.00**

Tray, 1922, summer girl, 10½x 13¼", NM **425.00**

Tray, 1926, Coke sports couple, 10½x13¼", NM **350.00**

Tray, 1932, girl in yellow bathing suit, 10½x13¼", NM . .**250.00**

Tray, 1957, sandwiches & Cokes, Canada, 10½x13", NM .**75.00**

Tumbler, modified flare **75.00**

Visor brim, Have a Coke, VG .**5.00**

Tray, 1937, NM, $80.00.

Coffee Grinders

In the days before packaged ground coffee was available, coffee beans were either ground at the local grocery or in the home. Now gone the way of the pickle barrel and Grandma's washboard, coffee grinders are collected by those to whom visions of warm kitchens, rocking chairs, fresh-baked bread, and the wonderful aroma of fresh-ground coffee are treasures worth preserving.

American Beauty, canister, with original cup & papers . .**40.00**

Arcade, Imperial, table, wood & cast iron, 1-pound, 13" **75.00**

Arcade No 700, lap, with dust cover, Sears, ca 1908 . . . .**90.00**

Brighton, Wrights Hdwe, table, 1-pound, 8" **75.00**

Coles Mfg No 7, counter, cast iron, pat 1887, 16" wheels, 27" overall **475.00**

De Ve, Holland, lap, 1950s, 4¾x 5⅛x8⅛" **45.00**

Elgin National No 44, original cast iron with eagle, 15" wheels, 24" overall **325.00**

Elma, counter, cast iron with wooden drawer, 11" single wheel, 17" **85.00**

Enterprise, table, cast iron, brass hopper, patented 1873, 6" wheels **375.00**

Favorite #7, side mill, cast iron hopper with lid **65.00**

Golden Rule, canister, cast iron with glass front, wood box .**225.00**

Grand Union Tea, table, cast iron, square base with round hopper **95.00**

J Fisher, Warranted, lap, dovetailed walnut, brass hopper .**145.00**

Enterprise No. 3, 2 wheels, original decals, 1873, $500.00. (Photo courtesy of Terry Friend, author of book on coffee mills.)

Landers, Frary, and Clark, Regal
No 44, canister, tin & cast
iron **80.00**
Lil Tot, original drawer, miniature,
4" **80.00**
Logan & Strobridge, Franco American, lap, cast iron and
wood **85.00**
New Model, lap, cast iron, cast iron
drawer, 5½x4½x5½" ...**65.00**
Parker, side, cast iron, grind ad-
justment on front, patented
1876 ....**60.00**
Primitive, lap, cherry, dovetailed,
brass hopper, 4x4" ...**155.00**
Sun Mfg, table, 1-lb, 12" ...**75.00**
Universal #0012, black tin with red
decal, 13" **55.00**

Comic Books

The 'Golden Age' is a term refer-
ring to the period from 1930 until
1950, during which today's most-
prized comic books were published.
First editions or those that feature
the first appearance of a popular
character are the most valuable and
may bring prices of several hundred
dollars—some even more. The original Batman comic, issued in the
spring of 1940, is today worth
$7,000.00 in excellent condition.
Most early comics, however, are
valued at less than $5.00 to $30.00.
Remember—rarity, age, condition,
and quality of the art work are factors to consider when determining
value.

Ace Comics, #2, 1937, G ...**30.00**
Adventure Comics, #282,VG.**18.00**
Air Boy Comics, V8 #3, VG .**11.00**
Andy Panda, #25, 1943, G ..**19.00**
Annie Oakley & Tagg, #4 ..**18.00**
Archie Comics, #11, G **12.00**
Archie's Pals & Gals, #16, EC Giant,
VG **18.00**
Archie's Rival Reggie, #11 ...**8.00**

Batman #99, EX, $30.00.

Atomic Rabbit, #6, 1957, VG .**7.50**
Baffling Mysteries, #25 .....**7.00**
Best of Dennis the Menace, #3, 1960,
NM **6.00**
Blinky's Buddies, #1, EX **2.00**
Blonde Phantom, #16, G ...**10.00**
Boy Comics, #46, EX **10.00**
Buster Brown, #7, NM **15.00**
Captain Marvel, #52, EX ...**25.00**
Circus Comics, #2, EX **5.00**
Crimefighters, #2, NM **7.50**
Dandy Comics, #3, VG **17.00**
Davy Crockett, #8, Charlton, VG/
EX **4.00**
Defenders, #2, EX **3.00**
Dennis the Menace, #82 ....**5.00**
Detective, #183, EX **42.00**
Dick Tracy, #51 ....**20.00**
Dizzy Dames, #3, EX **2.00**
Donald Duck, Beach Party, #6, EX/
NM **15.00**
Dr Solar, #1, EX **7.00**
Exciting, #49, EX **17.00**
Falling in Love, #25, EX **4.00**
Felix the Cat, #39, March 1953,
VG **6.50**
Fighting Yank, #14, NM ...**52.00**
Four Color, #353, M **10.00**

Foxy Grandpa, #1905, G ...**10.00**
Frankenstein, #3, EX **1.50**
Frisky Animals, #44 ......**10.00**
Funnyman, #5, NM **30.00**
Gabby, #7, NM **7.00**
Gang Busters, #9 ....**20.00**
GI Joe, #11, VG **7.00**
Girl's Life, #2 ....**5.00**
Gomer Pyle, #2, NM **7.00**
Heckle & Jeckle, #2, VG **5.00**
House of Mystery, #185, NM .**8.50**
Howdy Doody, #29, ' 54, NM.**18.00**
Huckleberry Hound, #10, Hanna
   Barbera cartoon, EX **3.50**
Jetson's, #2, NM **5.00**
Junie Prom, #2, EX **4.00**
Kid Cowboy, #2, EX **6.00**
Koko & Kola, #5, VG **2.50**
Lassie, #10, EX **2.50**
Little Lulu, #84, VG **9.00**
Lone Ranger, #21 ....**30.00**
Lone Ranger, #28, Dell, EX .**31.00**
Magic Comics, #33, EX **32.00**
Man from UNCLE, #2, photo cover,
   EX **6.00**
March of Comics, #78, Gene Autry,
   EX **45.00**
Mickey Finn, #1, EX **37.50**
Mickey Mouse, #36, EX **8.00**
Mighty Mouse, #6, second series,
   EX **10.00**
More Fun, #121, EX **20.00**
Nickel Comics, #6, VG **75.00**
Peter Cotton Tail, #2, EX ..**11.00**
Puppet Comics, #2, VG **5.00**
Raggedy Ann & Andy, #6,NM.**4.00**
Rin Tin Tin, #15, NM **3.00**
Snagglepuss, #3, VG **1.50**
Space Squadron, #4, VG ...**20.00**
Superior Stories, #2, VG **4.00**
Superman's Girlfriend, #21, EX/
   NM **5.00**
Tales of the Unexpected, #4, EX/
   NM **16.00**
Tomb of Dracula, #27, EX ...**5.00**
Vampirella, #2, EX **4.00**
Wedding Bells, #2, VG **5.00**
Yogi Bear Jellystone Jollies, #10,
   NM **6.00**

Cookbooks

Advertising cookbooks, those by well-known personalities, and figural diecuts are among the more readily-available examples on today's market. Cookbooks written prior to 1874 are the most valuable; they often sell for $200.00 and up.

Best Chocolate and Coca Recipes, dated 1931, 5x7", $12.00.

Aunt Jane's Cookbook, ca 1933,
   McCannon & Co **10.00**
Baker's Chocolate Recipe Book,
   copyrighted 1923 .....**18.00**
Betty Crocker Picture Cookbook, 1st
   edition **20.00**
Fannie Farmer Cookbook, 1965,
   544-page **10.00**
Good Housekeeping Book of Meals,
   3rd edition, 1930, 256-page, EX/
   NM **5.00**
Home Baked Delicacies, 1929.**5.00**
Kerr Home Canning, 1941 ..**5.00**
Let's Eat Cookbook, 1931 ...**8.00**
Mary Dunbar's New Cookbook,
   1933, EX **5.00**
Metropolitan Life, 1922, 64-page,
   EX **6.00**

New American Cookbook, 1946, EX/
NM 10.00
New Delineator Recipes, 1930, EX/
NM 9.00
New Orleans Restaurant Cookbook,
1967 ....8.00
Pillsbury 21 Successful Little Din-
ners, 1942 ....5.00
Prairie Farmer WLS Cookbook,
Centennial ed, 1941 ...12.50
Recipes To Match Your Sugar Ra-
tion, 1942 ....5.00
Royal Cookbook, 1932 ......5.00
The Bread Basket, 1942 ....5.00
Treasury of Great Recipes, by Vin-
cent Price, 1965 ......22.00

Cookie Jars

The Nelson McCoy Pottery Co.,
Robinson Ransbottom Pottery Co.,
and the American Bisque Pottery
Co., are three of the largest producers of cookie jars in the country.
Many firms made them to a lesser
extent. Today, cookie jars are one of
the most popular of modern collectibles. Figural jars are the most
common, made in an endless variety of subjects. Early jars from the
1920s and '30s were often decorated
in 'cold paint' over the glaze. This
type of color is easily removed —
take care that you use very gentle
cleaning methods. A damp cloth and
a light touch is the safest approach.
See also McCoy.

After School Cookies, marked 741
USA, American Bisque . 20.00
Albert Apple, Pee Dee Co ..40.00
Alice in Wonderland, cream, pump-
kin knob, Walt Disney .55.00
Atlantic Owl 10.00
Barefoot Boy 185.00
Baseball Boy with Bat, marked 875
USA 40.00
Bear, Avon promotion 45.00

Bear, eyes open, unmarked Ameri-
can Bisque 20.00
Boots, American Bisque ...30.00
Captain, Robinson Ransbottom
Company 45.00
Casper, cookie in hand, Harvey
Productions Inc 130.00
Cat in Basket 20.00
Cat on Beehive, USA, American
Bisque 25.00
Chef, Pearl China 150.00
Clown, pastel blue & red, marked
USA, American Bisque 15.00
Cookie Monster 30.00
Cookies, nut on lid 30.00
Cup of Hot Chocolate, American
Bisque 20.00
Dog in Basket, manufacturer un-
known 25.00
Dove, FAP Company 17.50
Dutch Boy, USA, American
Bisque 30.00
Ee-Yore, Walt Disney 50.00
Elephant, American Bisque. 25.00
Farmer Pig, marked USA, Ameri-
can Bisque 30.00

**Metlox, squirrel on pine cone,
$38.00.**

Fire Chief, hat with #1 in front, Robinson Ransbottom .**40.00**
Flasher Clown, USA, American Bisque **40.00**
Granny, American Bisque ..**35.00**
Howdy Doody **200.00**
Ice Cream Cone, USA **45.00**

Maurice of California, chef, copyright 1976, $45.00.

Jukebox, Wurlitzer 1015 Bubbler, unmarked **80.00**
Lamb, brown, Twin Winton. **25.00**
Lion, Twin Winton **25.00**
Mammy, Pearl China **200.00**
Morton Twins, USA, American Bisque **45.00**
Oscar the Grouch, from Sesame Street **35.00**
Pig, boy or girl, unmarked American Bisque **25.00**
Pine Cones Coffeepot, USA, American Bisque **25.00**
Poodle, behind counter, Twin Winton **25.00**
Porky Pig, Warner Bros ...**30.00**
Preacher, black hat, square glasses, Robinson Ransbottom .**40.00**
Rooster, American Bisque ..**30.00**
Train, Sierra Vista **45.00**
Tug Boat, California **25.00**
Winnie the Pooh, marked Walt Disney **35.00**

Yogi Bear, Hanna Barbera Productions **75.00**

Coors

Though they made a line of commercial artware as well, the Coors Pottery is best represented at today's flea markets and dinnerware shows by their popular dinnerware line, Rosebud. Rosebud was made in solid colors accented only by small contrasting floral elements; the line is extensive and includes kitchen and baking ware as well as table settings.

Baking pan, Rosebud, 11" ..**17.50**
Bowl, mixing; Rosebud, handled, 3½-cup **15.00**
Bowl, pudding; Rosebud ...**12.50**
Cake plate, Rosebud, 11" ...**16.00**
Cup, custard; Rosebud, 4" ...**7.50**
Egg cup, Rosebud, 3" dia ...**14.00**
Muffin set, Rosebud, 8" plate with 5½" domed lid **40.00**
Pitcher, Rosebud, with cover, 14-ounce **36.00**

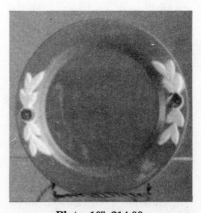

Plate, 10", $14.00.

Plate, dinner; Rosebud, 9" ..**10.00**
Shakers, Rosebud, straight sides, 4½", pair **12.00**
Teapot, Rosebud, 2-cup **30.00**

Tumbler, Rosebud, low foot, 12-
ounce **22.00**

Copper

Early copper items are popular
with those who enjoy primitives,
and occasionally fine examples can
still be found at flea markets. Check
construction to help you determine
the age of your piece. Dovetailed
joints indicate 18th-century work;
handmade seamed items are usually from the 19th century. Tea-
kettles and small stills are especially collectible.

Ash tray, cowboy hat, souvenir,
recent **5.00**
Basin, tin lined, side handle, 5x14",
G **80.00**
Boiler, fits inside top of wood stove,
polished & coated **75.00**
Candle snuffer, wrought iron
handle, 12" long **30.00**
Coffeepot, brass lid, wood handle,
engraved design, 10" . . **45.00**

Cow bell, 7" **15.00**
Desk set, blotter, inkwell, pen tray,
hammered/stippled **45.00**
Dust pan, embossed design, 9x8¼",
EX **35.00**
Flashlight, Ray-O-Vac, 8" . . **25.00**
Funnel with brass plunger, 8½
x6" **40.00**
Kettle, wood & iron handle, wood
finial, Majestic, 10" **50.00**
Measure, cup shape with handle,
marked ½, 2½" **20.00**
Measure, cup shape with handle,
marked ⅓, 2" **15.00**
Measure, pitcher shape with handle,
tin lined, Kreamer, 8" . . **60.00**
Measure, 1-quart, G **49.00**
Mold, crown shape, hammered,
Germany, 1920, 3" **28.00**
Oil can, hinged spout **30.00**
Planter, 10 grooved panel sides,
flared top, China, 5x4" . **15.00**
Plaque, embossed chrysanthe-
mums, 1950, 12x8½" . . . **37.50**
Rug beater, wood handle, 30" long,
EX **30.00**
Shoe buckle, worn silverplate, 2¾"
long **25.00**

Teapot, Manning Bowman, #41432, $85.00.

Spray pump, copper base, brass pump, 14" **32.50**
Tankard, English, traces of silver-plate, marked ½ Pint, 3⅞", EX **10.00**
Tip tray, hammered surface, scalloped edges, 7¼x5" **10.00**
Tray, butler type, wood sides, engraved bottom, 16" **42.50**
Tray, for restaurant, ca 1950, 12" diameter **20.00**
Wash boiler, Canco, no lid, 14" high, 27" long **62.50**

Copper Lustre

Small pitchers and bowls in the copper lustre glaze made by many of the Staffordshire potteries in the 1800s are still very much in evidence at even the smaller flea markets. They may be had for around $30.00 to $50.00 in excellent condition, often even for less. Larger items are harder to find and, depending on the type of decoration, may bring prices of $100.00 or more. Hand-painted scenes and examples with historical transfers are the most valuable.

Mug, lustre band with house, 3½", **$65.00.**

Bowl, wide blue band, 6" . . .**25.00**
Goblet, flowered band, 4" . .**45.00**
Mug, agate band, 2¾" **75.00**
Mug, white reserves with flowers, canary lustre band, 3". **100.00**

Pitcher, amber band, 6" . . .**45.00**
Pitcher, embossed multicolor flowers, 8" **100.00**
Pitcher, gilt band, 3" **37.50**
Pitcher, purple lustre, cream bands, 5¾" **35.00**
Tea set, flowers on white band, purple lustre, 3-piece .**120.00**
Tumbler, green band, 3¼" . .**50.00**

Coverlets

After the introduction of the Jacquard loom in America in the 1820s, weavers began to make the elaborate florals, pictorials, and medallion patterns that in years previous were so tediously handwoven that they were reserved just for the rich. Dark blue and natural or white were colors most often used, but red and green were used with white, or several colors were used in combination. They were sometimes signed and dated in one corner; the name was either that of the weaver or the owner-to-be. Condition is very important; those with intricate patterns, dates, and signatures are most valuable. The following listings refer to blue and white coverlets unless otherwise described.

Chains, squares, & snowflakes, 2-piece double, 68x80" .**275.00**
Floral, gold/blue/white/maroon, dated 1854, 1-piece single, 72x87" **250.00**
Floral, vintage border, 1-piece single, 76x84" **245.00**
Floral, 3-color, Mfg by Fehr & Keck, 1845 woven in corners, 1-piece **525.00**
Floral bars in 3 colors alternate with white, building and eagle in border **375.00**
Floral medallions, flowers & bird-in-tree border, 2-piece double, EX **200.00**

Central star medallion, 1-piece single weave jacquard, 4-color, $200.00.

Floral/foliage, fruit 4-color, signed/ 1846 . . . . **675.00**
Floral/grapes center, eagle spandrels, bird corners, 4-color, 1-piece **500.00**
Medallions, double building border, 4-color, signed/1865, 1-piece, VG **350.00**
Oak leaf center, angel spandrels, 5-color, EX **425.00**
Overshot, geometrics, red/dark blue/ natural, 70x80" **275.00**
Overshot, optic geometrics, 2-piece, 62x89" **175.00**
Overshot, optical, red/white, 2-piece, 74x84", NM **210.00**
Overshot, optical geometrics, 4-color, sewn-on fringe, 2-piece, 76x94", NM **350.00**
Rose medallions/birds, 3-color, 1-piece single, NM **350.00**
Snowflake, pine tree border, ca 1840, 82x82" **375.00**
Star medallion, eagle corners, 4-color, 1-piece, EX **375.00**
Starflower with bird border, 4-color, 1-piece double, 82x90". **500.00**
Sunburst medallion, shield-bodied eagle corners, 3-color . **400.00**

Cracker Jack

The sugar-coated popcorn confection created by the Ruekeim brothers in 1893 has continued to the present day to delight boys and girls with its crunchy goodness, and each 'toy inside every box' since 1916 has become a prized adult treasure. More than 10,000 different prizes have been distributed. The older ones, depending on scarcity, are usually worth in the $15.00 to $40.00 range, though some (the 2½" cast metal horse and wagon for example) may fetch as high as $110.00. Early advertising and packages are also collectible. 'CJ' in the listings indicates pieces that are marked Cracker Jack.

Animal, stand-up, plastic, alphabet letter on back **3.50**
Badge, cast metal, Police, CJ, 1¼" **22.00**
Badge, shield, Jr Detective, silver, 1¼" **22.00**
Baseball score counter, paper, CJ, NM **40.00**
Book, Animals (or Birds), to color, CJ, each **30.00**
Booklet, Angelus Recipes by CJ, 1930s **16.00**
Bookmark, tin, bulldog, CJ . **12.50**
Cart, tin & wood, CJ **28.00**
Clicker, Noisy CJ, tear shape, CJ, 2" **18.00**
Dollhouse candlestick, cast metal, NM **6.50**
Fortune Wheel, tin **30.00**
Halloween mask, paper, CJ, 10", NM **12.00**
Harmonica, tin, early premium, CJ, NM **185.00**
Pistol, cast metal, inked, rare, CJ, NM **180.00**
Pocket watch, gold painted tin, CJ, NM **30.00**

Pocket watch, silver or gold paint on tin, CJ, 1½" **33.00**
Post card, bear series, paper, 1907, CJ **14.00**
Railroad car, plastic, CJ **6.00**
Riddle card, paper, CJ, from series of 20 . . . . **7.00**
Sled, plated tin, CJ, 2" **31.00**
Top, cardboard, rainbow design on string, CJ **25.00**
Whistle, plated tin, 2-tone, CJ, EX/NM **13.00**

Charge coin, Lit Brothers, Philadelphia, PA, $10.00.

Tin litho train car, 2¼" long, $25.00; Ambulance, 1½" long, $35.00.

Credit Cards and Charge Coins

Charge coins, first used in the late 1800s, were the forerunners of our modern-day credit cards. Although the earliest cards were introduced in the early 1900s, it wasn't until 1940 that they became commonplace.

Card, ARCO, Atlantic Richfield Co, 1975 . . . . **2.00**
Card, BankAmericard, no magnetic stripe, account number in tan area **8.00**
Card, Hertz, drawing of 2-door Ford on back, 1969 . . . . **6.00**
Card, Lit Bros, metal plate . **3.00**
Card, MasterCard, pre-hologram type **3.00**
Card, Phillips Petroleum, Lifetime Executive Courtesy Card. **7.00**

Card, TWA, swimsuited couple, 1972 . . . . **7.00**
Card, Visa, pre-hologram . . . **2.50**
Coin, Gimble Bros, Phila, PA, white metal, lion shield with GB **8.00**
Coin, Jordan Marsh, Boston, white metal, J over M Co **8.00**
Coin, L Bambergher & Co, Newark, NJ, celluloid **30.00**
Coin, Strawbridge & Clothier, Phila, PA, arrowhead shape . . **10.00**

Cruets

Used to serve vinegar, cruets were made during the 1800s through the early 20th century in virtually every type of plain and art glass available. Nearly every early American pressed glass tableware line contained at least one style. Nice examples are still relatively easy to find, though some of the scarce art glass cruets are often valued at well over $300.00.

Alaska, blue opalescent with hand-painted flowers **275.00**
Amber, blue handle and stopper, 8¼x4" **135.00**
Amberina, reed handle, footed, hollow stopper **300.00**
Argonaut Shell, blue opal . **350.00**
Beaded Swirl with lens, ruby stained **110.00**

Blazing Cornucopia, purple stain
with gold **65.00**
Buckingham **55.00**
Butterfly & Daisy, Pairpoint Mfg
Co, 7" **135.00**
Coin Spot, amberina with hand-
painted florals, amber stopper,
4½" **350.00**
Coin Spot, blue opalescent. **200.00**
Daisy & Button with Crossbars,
vaseline, large **160.00**
Dewey, amber **110.00**
Double Circle, blue **175.00**
Esther, green with gold trim,
large **250.00**
Feather **65.00**
Flora, emerald green with original
flower stopper **195.00**
Guttate, pink satin **325.00**
Herringbone, green **110.00**
Intaglio, clear opalescent . **125.00**
Ivy Scroll, blue **135.00**
Leaf Bracket, chocolate ... **185.00**
Leaf Mold, cranberry with white
inner casing **335.00**
Manhattan, small **60.00**

Medallion Sprig, green shaded to
clear **235.00**
Nestor, amethyst **175.00**
Panelled Daisy & Button . . **45.00**
Portland **45.00**
Prize, green **175.00**
Royal Ivy, rubena **335.00**
Shoshone, green **95.00**
Stars & Bars, amber **90.00**
Swag with Brackets, vaseline opal-
escent **385.00**
Tiny Optic, emerald with decora-
tion **250.00**
Wild Bouquet, opalescent . **200.00**
Wild Rose & Bow Knot, clear &
frosted **115.00**
Wing Scroll, custard **235.00**

Cup Plates

It was the custom in the early
1800s to pour hot beverages into a
deep saucer to cool. The cup plate
was used under the cup in the same
manner as we use coasters today.
While Sandwich was the largest
manufacturer, mid-western glass
houses also made many styles.
Condition is always an important
factor; but, because of the lacy nature of the patterns, it is common to
find minor edge chips. Occasionally
you may find an example where the
mold did not completely fill out —
this was due to the primitive manufacturing methods used and the
intricacy of the designs.

Collectors identify their cup plates
by code numbers suggested in
American Glass Cup Plates by Ruth
Webb Lee and James A. Rose, a
standard reference.

Keystone, McKee, ca 1901, $40.00.

R-11, VG **35.00**
R-148, VG **32.00**
R-172B, EX **37.00**
R-176A, VG **30.00**
R-22, VG **30.00**

Thistle, R-133, VG, $50.00; Sunburst, opalescent, R-538, EX, $50.00.

R-246, VG 34.00
R-29, EX 32.00
R-333, VG 15.00
R-343-A, rare, VG 48.00
R-37, scarce, EX 42.00
R-391, VG 13.00
R-40, VG 25.00
R-465-F, VG 16.00
R-479, VG 18.00
R-48 . . . . 40.00
R-593, scarce, EX 55.00
R-619A, VG 30.00
R-65, scarce, EX 50.00
R-680 . . . . 26.00
R-891, EX 15.00
R-98, VG 70.00

Czecholslovakian Collectibles

Items marked Czechoslovakia are popular modern collectibles. Pottery, glassware, jewelry, etc., were produced there in abundance.

Atomizer, amethyst glass, gold trim, tall slim foot, 7" 110.00
Basket, aqua glass with black handle & trim, 12½" . . . 35.00
Basket, candy; blue glass, yellow ruffled top with black handle 110.00
Basket, candy; mottled glass with thorn handle, 6½" 125.00
Bottle, scent; black opaque with applied jewels, clear floral stopper, 4⅛" 105.00

Bottle, scent; cut glass, blue, clear cut stopper, signed, 9" . 525.00
Bottle, scent; etched flowers, floral intaglio stopper, 4" 55.00
Lamp, beaded crystal basket filled with blue flowers, 9" . . 395.00
Lamp, perfume; hand-painted florals, yellow/frost, 4" . . 135.00
Lamp, student; acid-cut clear glass shade, slender brass standard, 21" 395.00
Napkin, white with pink stripe, label, 12" 5.00
Necklace, metal chain with blue stones, 18" 35.00

Glassware vase, red with applied blue and clear flower, 8", $58.00.

Pitcher, amber glass with yellow overlay, 11½" 125.00
Shakers, talcum; pink with cut decor, rare, 4¾", pr . . . 250.00
Vase, jack-in-pulpit; yellow glass, 6" 75.00
Vase, pottery, colorful Egyptian decor, 9¼" 200.00
Vase, red glass with green aventurine, fan form, 7½" 150.00

Ceramic perfume bottles, gold trim, 3½", $75.00 for the pair.

Vase, white cased glass, applied blue
leaf at waist, 8½" **65.00**
Wall pocket, woodpecker, ceramic
figural **42.00**

Decanters

The James Beam Distilling Company produced its first ceramic whiskey decanter in 1953 and remained the only major producer of these decanters throughout the decade. By the late 1960s, other companies such as Ezra Brooks, Lionstone, and Cyrus Noble were also becoming involved in their production. Today these fancy liquor containers are attracting many collectors.

ASI, Oldsmobile **75.00**
Beam, Apaloosa **10.00**
Beam, Baggage Car **55.00**
Beam, Bing Crosby 30th, Sports
Series, 1971 ....**10.00**
Beam, Bluejay **9.00**
Beam, Cable Car, 1958 ..... **7.50**
Beam, Dining Car **60.00**
Beam, Doe **20.00**

Beam, Ducks Unlimited #2, Wood
Duck **45.00**
Beam, Ducks Unlimited #4, Mallard Head **35.00**
Beam, Great Dane **10.00**
Beam, Harold's Club Covered
Wagon, 1974 ....**25.00**
Beam, Horses, Trophy Series,
1962 ....**18.00**
Beam, Jewel Tea Wagon ...**78.00**
Beam, Kentucky Derby, 1971.**6.00**
Beam, Lumber Car **30.00**
Beam, Mare & Foal **50.00**
Beam, Mortimer Snerd, '76 .**20.00**
Beam, Olsonite Eagle Racer,
1975 ....**50.00**
Beam, Pennsylvania, 1967 ..**8.00**
Beam, Pheasant **15.00**
Beam, Presidential, Executive Series, 1968 ....**8.00**
Beam, Red Cardinal **30.00**
Beam, Unser Olsonite Eagle Racecar **60.00**
Beam, Volkswagen **38.00**
Beam, 1913 Model T Ford ..**45.00**
Beam, 1957 Chevy Bel Air .**60.00**
Brooks, African Lion **30.00**
Brooks, Bengal Tiger **30.00**
Brooks, Corvette Mako Shark, Auto
Transportation Series .**22.00**

Brooks, Cuddles, Clown Series #5, 1980 . . . . **22.00**

Brooks, Man O'War, Animal Series, 1969 . . . . **12.00**

Brooks, Minuteman, People Series, 1975 . . . . **18.00**

Brooks, Pagliacci, Clown Series #3, 1979 . . . . **22.00**

Brooks, Phoenix Bird, 1971 . **25.00**

Brooks, Phonograph, Heritage China Series, 1970 . . . . **22.00**

Brooks, Razorback Hog, '69 **25.00**

Brooks, Snow Egret **30.00**

Cyrus Noble, Bull Elk **45.00**

Cyrus Noble, Dancers South of the Border, 1978 . . . . **32.00**

Cyrus Noble, Walruses Family, 1978 . . . . **50.00**

Famous Firsts, Panda Bear **50.00**

Grenadier, Arabian Horse . . **20.00**

Hoffman, Barber, Mr Lucky Series, 1980 . . . . **35.00**

Hoffman, Big Red Machine, Sport Series, 1973 . . . . **32.00**

Hoffman, Cat **12.00**

Hoffman, Golden Eye, Duck Decoy Series, miniature, pair . **18.00**

Hoffman, Railroad Engineer, Mr Lucky Series, 1980 . . . . **35.00**

Lionstone, Canadian Goose . **50.00**

Lionstone, Circus Series #1 through #6, mini, each **35.00**

Lionstone, Football or Basketball Players, 1974, each **25.00**

Lionstone, Gambler, Old West Series, 1970 . . . . **15.00**

Lionstone, Pheasant **50.00**

Lionstone, Roadrunner, Bird Series, 1969 . . . . **27.00**

Lionstone, Western Bluebird, 1972 . . . . **25.00**

McCormick, Benjamin Franklin, 1975 . . . . **25.00**

McCormick, Elvis, Karate, miniature **50.00**

McCormick, Elvis #1 . . . . . . **75.00**

McCormick, Elvis #2 . . . . . **40.00**

McCormick, Elvis #2, mini . **20.00**

McCormick, Hank Wms, Jr . **90.00**

McCormick, Hank Wms, Sr **45.00**

McCormick, Lancelot, 1979 . **22.00**

Old Bardstown, Citation . . **125.00**

Old Bardstown, Stanley Steamer, 1978 . . . . **40.00**

Beam Jewel Tea Wagon, $78.00.

Old Bardstown, Surf Miner **20.00**
Old Bardstown, Tiger **28.00**
Old Commonwealth, Elusive Lep-
  rechaun, 1980 . . . . **35.00**
Old Commonwealth, Firefighter #1,
  Modern Hero **35.00**
Old Commonwealth, Firefighter #4,
  Fallen Comrade **40.00**
Old Commonwealth, Miner #5,
  miniature **20.00**
Old Commonwealth, Miner with
  Lump of Coal #3 . . . . . . **35.00**
Old Commonwealth, Miner with
  Pick #2 . . . . **50.00**
Old Commonwealth, Octoberfest,
  1983 . . . . **45.00**
Old Commonwealth, Tennessee
  Walking Horse **28.00**
Pacesetter, Ford Tractor #4. **60.00**
Ski Country, Bassett Hound. **50.00**
Ski Country, Chucker Partridge,
  1979 . . . . **30.00**
Ski Country, Dove **45.00**
Ski Country, Eagle Dancer, Indian
  Series, 1979 . . . . **175.00**
Ski Country, Gyrafalcon . . . **40.00**
Ski Country, Idaho Snake River
  Stampede **65.00**
Ski Country, Mrs Cratchit . **48.00**
Ski Country, Palomino Horse,
  1975 . . . . **45.00**
Ski Country, Pheasant in the
  Corn **55.00**
Ski Country, Pintail Duck . . **70.00**
Ski Country, Redtail Hawk . **60.00**
Ski Country, Rocky Mountain
  Sheep **60.00**
Ski Country, Skunk Family. **55.00**
Ski Country, Deer **85.00**
Ski Country, Widgeon Duck. **35.00**
Wild Turkey, Series I, #1 through
  #4, miniature, each **10.00**
Wild Turkey, Series I, #5 . . **30.00**
Wild Turkey, Series I, #5 through
  #8, miniature, each **16.00**
Wild Turkey, Turkey & Bobcat,
  1983 . . . . **100.00**
Wild Turkey, Turkey & Fox, mini-
  ature, 1985 . . . . **35.00**

Wild Turkey, Turkey in Flight,
  1984, miniature **35.00**

Decoys

Although ducks are the most commonly encountered type, nearly every species of bird has been imitated through decoys. The earliest were carved from wood by the Indians and used to lure game birds into the hunting areas. Among those most valued by collectors today are those carved by well-known artists, commercial decoys produced by factories such as Mason and Dodge, and well-carved examples or rare species. Many reproductions are on the market today that were produced for ornamental purposes only. Buyer beware!

Black Duck, hollow, carved eyes,
  Harry Boice **300.00**
Black Duck, repainted, Mason
  Challenge **95.00**
Black Duck, turned head, original
  paint, Canada **60.00**
Black Duck, working repaint, re-
  pair, AE Crowell **550.00**
Black Duck, working repaint, Strat-
  ford, CT **40.00**
Blackbellied Plover, sleeping, signed
  Bob White, 1967 . . . . . **100.00**
Bluebill, hollow, repainted with
  flaking & wear, age split, Bill
  Brown **75.00**
Bluebill Drake, original paint,
  Mason Standard, EX . . **70.00**
Bluebill Drake, premier head,
  Mason Challenge, EX . . **80.00**
Bluebill Drake, working repaint,
  Stevens Co **70.00**
Broadbill Hen, working repaint,
  Houghton Lake, MI . . . **60.00**
Canada Goose, painted stylized body
  on driftwood base, 7¼" . **55.00**
Canada Goose, 2-piece hollow body,
  repaint, New Jersey . . **190.00**

Canvasback Drake, cork body, working repaint, MD **40.00**
Canvasback Drake, repaint, Taylor Boyd, Perryville, MA .**300.00**
Canvasback Drake, working repaint, MA **120.00**
Canvasback Drake, working repaint, Stevens Co **110.00**
Canvasback Drake, working repaint, Susquahana Flats, early, EX **125.00**
Coot, hollow with carved wing tips, EX, Ed Clark **60.00**
Coot, original paint, Gus Melow, Oshkosh, WI **75.00**
Coot, original paint, Wildfowler Co **110.00**
Crow, turned head, hollow body, original paint, Charles Perdew, EX **150.00**
Curlew, hollow body, original paint, Sandbridge, VA **75.00**
Dove, original condition, Herter's Factory **140.00**
Duck, hollow body, marked CW, 18" long **155.00**
Eider Drake, original paint, Herter's Factory **50.00**
Goldeneye Drake, detailed feather carving, original paint, Wm Cooper **160.00**
Goldeneye Drake, original paint, Ogdensburg, NY **50.00**
Goldeneye Drake, working repaint, Stevens Co **65.00**
Goose, canvas-covered slat, old paint with average wear, Fred Bailey, EX **400.00**
Greenwinged Teal Hen, working repaint, Ivy Landry ...**75.00**
Hooded Merganser Hen, head turned right, signed/dated 1975, A Carney **70.00**
Mallard, flying, half-size, signed/ 1983, Judson Budd ...**150.00**
Mallard, glass eyes, signed Ken Harris 1962, 7x17x7" .**100.00**
Mallard Drake, original paint, Joliet, IL, worn **125.00**

Mallard Drake, original paint, Mason Standard **130.00**
Mallard Drake, original paint, signed WRG, CA **100.00**
Mallard Drake, painted tin, hollow body, 14" long **115.00**
Mallard Hen, working repaint, replaced eyes, Verne Cheesman, EX **110.00**
Mallards, original paint, William E Pratt Co, pair **130.00**
Merganser Hen, hollow, original paint, Henry Grant ..**185.00**
Owl, contemporary, stamped Bundick, EX **160.00**
Pintail Drake, hollow body, original weight & paint, IL ...**100.00**
Pintail Drake, original paint, Wildfowler Co, NJ **105.00**
Pintail Hen, original paint, signed Larry Zalesky, 1975 ...**50.00**
Redbreasted Merganser, Frank Finney, Virginia **80.00**
Redbreasted Merganser Drake, original paint, Charles Spiron, NM **195.00**
Redhead Drake, original paint, Bob McGaw, MD **120.00**
Ringbill Drake, original paint, Ski Rogers, EX **150.00**
Ringbill Drake, original paint, Willy Comardelle **85.00**
Ruddy Turnstone, detailed carving, signed Bob White, EX. **105.00**
Scoter, contemporary, original paint shows wear, ME **100.00**
Sea gull, hollow body, original paint, CA, EX **130.00**
Widgeon Drake, original paint, Evans McKenney, MA. **140.00**
Widgeon Drake, original paint, Herter's, EX **65.00**
Widgeon Drake, working repaint, Bob McGaw, Havre de Grace, MD **170.00**
Willet, original paint, heavy wear & flaking, Lou Barkelow. **175.00**
Wood Duck Drake, original paint, Herter's, EX **125.00**

Yellowlegs, original paint, South Westport, MA **175.00**

Degenhart

The 'D' in heart trademark indicates the product of the Crystal Art Glass factory, which operated in Cambridge, Ohio, from 1947 until the mid-1970s. It was operated by John and Elizabeth Degenhart who developed more than 145 distinctive colors to use in making their toothpick holders, figurines, bells, and other novelties.

Priscilla, Green Lavender Slag, $100.00.

Beaded Toothpick, Sapphire.**12.00**
Buzz Saw Wine, Cobalt **40.00**
Centennial Bell, Slag **15.00**
Daisy and Button Toothpick, Lime Ice **20.00**
Dog, April Green **15.00**
Dog, Gun Metal **20.00**
Elephant Toothpick, Sapphire Blue **25.00**

Forget-Me-Not Toothpick, Cobalt Carnival, unsigned **8.00**
Gypsy Pot, Honey Amber ..**20.00**
Heart Toothpick, Bernard Boyd's Ebony **35.00**
Hobo Shoe,Custard Slag ...**20.00**
Owl, Blue-Green **72.50**
Owl, Crystal **10.00**
Pooche, Royal Violet **20.00**
Priscilla, Crystal **75.00**
Priscilla, Smokey Blue **95.00**
Seal of Ohio Cup Plate, Colored Crystals **10.00**
Wildflower Candy Dish, Twilight Blue **25.00**

Depression Glass

Depression Glass, named for the era when it sold through dime stores or was given away as premiums, can be found in such varied colors as amber, green, pink, blue, red, yellow, white, and crystal. Mass-produced by many different companies in hundreds of patterns, Depression Glass is one of the most sought-after collectibles in the United States today.

Adam, bowl, dessert; pink or green, 4¾" **10.00**
Adam, bowl , with cover, green, 9" **65.00**
Adam, coaster, green, 3¼" ..**13.00**
Adam, creamer, pink **13.00**
Adam, lamp, pink **225.00**
Adam, plate, salad; pink, square, 7¾" **8.00**
Adam, sherbet, green, 3" ...**28.00**
American Pioneer, bowl, console; pink, 10⅜" **40.00**
American Pioneer, candlestick, green, 6½", pair **65.00**
American Pioneer, goblet, wine; green, 3-ounce, 4" **40.00**
American Pioneer, plate, green handles, 6" **10.00**

American Pioneer, plate, handles, green, 11½" 14.00
American Pioneer, sugar bowl, pink, 3½" 16.00
American Pioneer, whiskey, green, 2-ounce, 2¼" 65.00
American Sweetheart, bowl, soup; flat, pink, 9½" 29.00
American Sweetheart, cup & saucer, pink 9.50
American Sweetheart, plate, luncheon; monax, 9" 8.00
American Sweetheart, sherbet, footed, pink, 3¾" 12.00
Anniversary, bowl, fruit; pink, 9" 14.00
Anniversary, cake plate, with cover, crystal 10.00
Anniversary, plate, dinner; pink, 9" 5.50
Aunt Polly, bowl, large berry; blue, 7⅞" 22.00
Aunt Polly, creamer, blue . .33.00
Aunt Polly, pitcher, blue, 48-ounce, 8" 135.00
Aunt Polly, sherbet, blue 8.50
Avocado, bowl, 2-handled, green, 5¼" 23.00

Avocado, bowl, oval, 2-handled, green, 8" 20.00
Avocado, pitcher, pink 425.00
Avocado, sherbet, pink, 6¾". 40.00
Beaded Block, bowl, deep, opalescent, 6" 15.00
Beaded Block, bowl, lily; opalescent, 4½" 15.00
Beaded Block, vase, bouquet; green, 6" 10.00
Bubble, bowl, cereal; blue, 5¼" 8.00
Bubble, bowl, large berry; crystal, 8½" 4.00
Bubble, plate, blue, 9⅜" 5.00
Bubble, tumbler, water; red or blue, 9-ounce 6.00
Cameo, bowl, cream soup; green, 4¾" 45.00
Cameo, butter dish, green .150.00
Cameo, cookie jar, green ...37.50
Cameo, cup, green 11.00
Cameo, cup, yellow 6.50
Cameo, pitcher, water; green, 56-ounce, 8½" 37.50
Cameo, plate, green, 9½" ...12.00
Cameo, saucer (sherbet plate), green, 6" 2.00

Green Bowknot, sherbet, $8.00; berry bowl, $8.00; tumbler, 10-oz, 5", $11.00; tumbler, footed, 5", $11.00; plate, $7.50.

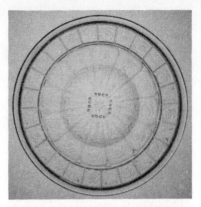

Doric & Pansy, plate,teal, $17.50.

Cameo, tumbler, flat, green, 10-ounce, 4³/₄" **20.00**
Cameo, tumbler, green, 15-ounce, 5¼" **45.00**
Cameo, tumbler, water; green, 9-ounce, 4" **18.00**
Cherry Blossom, bowl, fruit; 3-leg, green, 10½" **42.00**
Cherry Blossom, child's creamer, pink **27.50**
Cherry Blossom, child's set, 14-piece, pink **195.00**
Cherry Blossom, cup, green . **16.00**
Cherry Blossom, platter, divided, green, 13" **40.00**
Cherry Blossom, tumbler, with allover pattern, footed, pink, 3¾" **11.00**
Circle, goblet, wine; green or pink, 4½" **5.00**
Circle, tumbler, water; green or pink, 8-ounce **5.00**
Cloverleaf bowl, dessert; yellow, 4" **17.50**
Cloverleaf, plate, luncheon; yellow, 8" **10.50**
Cloverleaf, sherbet, footed, green, 3" **4.50**
Colonial, bowl, cream soup, green, 4½" **42.00**
Colonial, creamer, pink, 8-ounce, 5" **13.50**
Colonial, tumbler, footed, green, 5-ounce, 4" **22.50**

Colonial Fluted, bowl, berry; green, 4" **4.00**
Columbia, cup, crystal **4.50**
Columbia, cup, pink **12.00**
Columbia, plate, pink, 6" **7.50**
Coronation, bowl, pink, 6½" . **3.50**
Coronation, plate, luncheon; pink, 8½" **3.50**
Cube, bowl, salad, 6½" **7.00**
Cube, butter dish, pink **40.00**
Cube, plate, green, 6" **2.50**
Cube, salt & pepper shakers, green, pair **28.00**
Cupid, bowl, console; pink or green, 11" **35.00**
Cupid, ice bucket, 6" **50.00**
Cupid, sugar bowl, footed, pink or green, 5" **32.50**
Cupid, vase, elliptical, any color, 8¼" **75.00**
Daisy, plate, amber, 7⅜" . . . **6.00**
Daisy, platter, green, 10¾" . . **5.00**
Diamond Quilted, cup, blue . **8.00**
Diamond Quilted, pitcher, green, 64-ounce **40.00**
Diana, bowl, cream soup; amber, 5½" **6.00**
Dogwood, bowl, berry; green, 8½" **75.00**
Dogwood, bowl, pink, 5½" . . **16.00**

Fire-King Dinnerware, "Philbe", cookie jar with cover, $400.00.

Floragold, "Louisa," 10- & 11- oz tumbler, iridescent, footed, $10.00 ea.

Dogwood, pitcher, American Sweetheart style, pink, 8" . . **450.00**

Dogwood, plate, luncheon; green, 8" **5.00**

Dogwood, plate, salver, monax, 12" **18.00**

Dogwood, sherbet, pink . . . **20.00**

Dogwood, tumbler, decorated, green, 5" **75.00**

Doric, bowl, large berry; pink, 8¼" **9.50**

Doric, cake plate, green **12.50**

Doric, plate, salad; pink, 7" . **12.50**

Doric & Pansy, butter dish, ultramarine **400.00**

Doric & Pansy, creamer, ultramarine **15.00**

Doric & Pansy, plate, child's, ultramarine **7.00**

Doric & Pansy, sugar bowl, child's, ultramarine **30.00**

Doric & Pansy, tray, handled, ultramarine, 10" **15.00**

English Hobnail, bowl, pink or green, 8" **22.00**

English Hobnail, celery dish, pink or green, 9" **20.00**

English Hobnail, plate, round or square, pink or green, 8". **7.50**

Fire King, Alice, cup, jadeite . **1.25**

Fire King, Alice, plate, jadeite, 8½" **5.00**

Fire King, Jane Ray, creamer, jadeite **2.25**

Fire King, Philbe, bowl, cereal; all colors, 5½" **50.00**

Fire King, Philbe, plate, luncheon; all colors, 8" **25.00**

Fire King, Square, cup & saucer, all colors **2.75**

Fire King Oven Glass, bowl, utility; blue, 8⅜" **10.00**

Fire King Oven Glass, coffee mug, blue, 7-oz **17.50**

Fire King Oven Glass, custard cup, blue, 5-ounce **2.50**

Fire King Oven Glass, pie plate, blue, 9" **8.00**

Floragold, bowl, cereal; iridescent, 5½" **20.00**

Floragold, candy dish, iridescent, 6¾" **35.00**

Floragold, plate, dinner; iridescent, 8½" **18.00**

Floral, bowl, pink, 7½" **10.00**

Floral, sherbet, green, 6" . . . **12.00**

Floral & Diamond Band, pitcher, green, 42-ounce, 8" **80.00**

Florentine No 1, ash tray, crystal, 5½" **17.00**

Florentine No 1, creamer, ruffled, pink **25.00**

Florentine No 1, sherbet, footed, yellow, 3-ounce **8.50**

Florentine No 2, bowl, cereal; yellow, 6" **17.00**

Florentine No 2, cup, green . . **6.00**

Florentine No 2, pitcher, green, 76-ounce, 8" **77.50**

Florentine No 2, plate, salad; yellow, 8½" **7.00**

Florentine No 2, salt & pepper, green, pair **35.00**

Florentine No 2, tumbler, water; yellow, 9-ounce **16.00**

Forest Green, bowl, batter . . **8.00**

Forest Green, punch cup **2.00**

Fortune, bowl, rolled edge, pink, 5¼" **4.50**

Fortune, cup & saucer, pink . **5.00**

Fortune, sherbet, crystal, 6" .2.00
Fruits, cup & saucer, green . .7.00
Fruits, pitcher, flat bottom, green,
7" 45.00
Georgian, butter dish with cover,
green 67.50
Harp, coaster, crystal 2.00
Harp, cup, crystal 5.50
Harp, vase, crystal, 6" 10.00
Heritage, bowl, large berry; crystal,
8½" 20.00
Hex Optic, bowl, berry; pink or
green, 7½" 5.00
Hex Optic, bowl, mixing; pink or
green, 9" 15.00
Hex Optic, sherbet, footed, pink or
green, 5-ounce 3.50
Hobnail, decanter & stopper, crys-
tal, 7" 20.00
Hobnail, pitcher, milk; crystal, 18-
ounce 13.00
Holiday, butter dish, pink . .30.00
Holiday, plate, pink, 9" 9.50
Holiday, sugar bowl, pink . .5.00
Holiday, sugar lid, pink 8.50
Holiday, tumbler, flat, pink, 10-
ounce, 4" 15.00

Homespun, butter dish, pink or
crystal 40.00
Homespun, sugar bowl, footed, pink
or crystal 6.50
Homespun, tumbler, footed, pink or
crystal, 15-ounce, 6½" . .20.00
Horseshoe, creamer, yellow. 12.50
Indiana Custard, bowl, cereal; ivory,
5¾" 15.00
Indiana Custard, plate, luncheon;
ivory, 8⅞" 8.50
Iris & Herringbone, bowl, soup;
crystal, 7½" 80.00
Iris & Herringbone, butter dish,
crystal 27.50
Iris & Herringbone, cup & saucer,
iridescent 11.50
Iris & Herringbone, goblet, wine;
crystal, 4½" 13.00
Iris & Herringbone, plate, dinner;
iridescent, 9" 20.00
Iris & Herringbone, sherbet, footed,
iridescent, 2½" 10.00
Jubilee, cheese & cracker set, topaz, pair 65.00
Jubilee, plate, luncheon; yellow,
8¾" 9.00

Fortune, pink; candy dish & cover, $15.00; salad bowl, $8.00; small bowls, $4.00; tumbler, $4.50.

"Parrot," Sylvan, sherbet, blue, $75.00.

Jubilee, plate, sandwich; topaz, 13" 25.00
Lace Edge, bowl, plain or ribbed; pink, 9½" 14.00
Lace Edge, butter dish with cover, pink 45.00
Lace Edge, creamer, pink ..16.00
Lace Edge, saucer, pink 7.50
Lace Edge, vase, pink, 7" .245.00
Lake Como, cup & saucer, white with blue scene 17.50
Lake Como, plate, salad; white with blue scene, 7¼" 7.50
Laurel, bowl, berry; green, 5". 4.00
Laurel, bowl, blue, 6" 10.00
Laurel, plate, ivory, 9⅛" 7.50
Lincoln Inn, cup, blue 14.00
Lincoln Inn, sherbet, red or blue, 4¾" 15.00
Lincoln Inn, tumbler, footed, red, 5-ounce 15.00
Lorain, bowl, oval vegetable; yellow, 9¾" 37.50
Lorain, platter, crystal, 12" .18.00
Lorain, saucer, yellow 4.50
Madrid, bowl, large berry; amber, 9⅜" 14.50
Madrid, bowl, cream soup; amber, 4¾" 10.00
Madrid, butter dish, green .70.00
Madrid, cookie jar, amber ..32.50
Madrid, pitcher, juice; amber, 5½" 30.00
Manhattan, plate, salad; crystal, 8½" 7.50

Manhattan, vase, crystal, 8".11.50
Mayfair, bowl, cream soup; pink, 5" 34.00
Mayfair, candy dish, pink ..37.50
Mayfair, cookie jar, pink ...32.50
Mayfair, cup, blue 35.00
Mayfair, cup, pink 13.00
Mayfair, pitcher, pink, 6" ..32.00
Mayfair, plate, blue, 9½" ..45.00
Mayfair, tumbler, water; pink, 9-ounce 22.00
Mayfair Federal, platter, oval, amber, 12" 20.00
Miss America, bowl, berry; pink, 6¼" 12.50
Miss America, creamer, footed, pink 13.00
Miss America, cup, pink ...16.00
Miss America, goblet, juice; crystal, 5-ounce, 4¾" 16.00
Miss America, pitcher, with ice lip, pink, 65-ounce, 8½" ...97.50
Miss America, plate, pink, 8½" 14.00
Moderntone, butter dish, metal cover, cobalt 65.00
Moderntone, plate, dinner; cobalt, 8⅞" 10.00
Moderntone, sugar bowl, open, cobalt 7.50
Moondrops, bottle, scent 8.00
Moondrops, cup & saucer, blue or red 18.00

Swirl, "Petal Swirl," pitcher, ultramarine, $850.00.

106

"Thumbprint," Pear Optic, green, sherbet, $4.00; plate, $2.00; cup, $2.50; saucer, $1.00.

Moondrops, sugar bowl, red or blue, 2¾" **13.50**

Moonstone, bonbon, heart shape, 1-handle, opalescent **8.50**

Moonstone, cigarette jar, with cover, opalescent **14.50**

Moonstone, cup, opalescent ..**6.00**

Mt Pleasant, bowl, fruit; square, footed, black, 4" **15.00**

Mt Pleasant, creamer, scalloped, black **12.50**

Mt Pleasant , plate, grill; black, 9" **9.00**

New Century, butter dish with cover, green **48.00**

New Century, plate, grill; crystal, 10" **8.00**

New Century, plate, salad; green, 8½" **6.00**

New Century, tumbler, pink, 5-ounce, 3½" **7.00**

Newport, cup, cobalt **7.50**

No 610, sugar bowl, crystal .**17.00**

No 612, cup, green **7.00**

No 612, plate , luncheon; green, 9⅜" **8.00**

Normandie, bowl, cereal; amber, 6½" **9.00**

Normandie, pitcher, amber, 80-ounce, 8" **50.00**

Normandie, plate, amber, 8". .**6.00**

Old Cafe, tumbler, red, 3" ..**7.50**

Old English, tumbler, footed, green, 4½" **13.00**

Oyster & Pearl, bowl, fruit; deep, pink, 10½" **16.00**

Oyster & Pearl, candle holder, ruby, 3½", pair **32.50**

Oyster & Pearl, relish dish, oblong, pink, 10¼" **7.00**

Parrot, bowl, green, 5" **13.00**

Parrot, plate, amber, 9" ...**25.00**

Patrician, cookie jar, with cover, amber **65.00**

Patrician, cup, amber **8.00**

Patrician, salt & pepper shakers, green, pair **45.00**

Patrician, tumbler, amber, 14-ounce, 5½" **28.00**

Peacock Reverse, creamer, flat, all colors, 2¾" **48.00**

Peacock Reverse, cup, red ..**25.00**

Petalware, sherbet, monax ..**4.50**

Pineapple & Floral, bowl, cereal; crystal, 6" **18.00**

Pineapple & Floral, tumbler, crystal, 12-ounce, 5" **30.00**

Princess, bowl, pink, 5" ...**14.00**

Princess, candy dish, with cover, green **35.00**

Princess, cookie jar, pink . . **40.00**
Princess, plate, dinner; pink. **13.00**
Princess, salt & pepper, pink, 4½",
pair **33.00**
Princess, tray, relish; divided, pink,
7½" **13.00**
Pyramid, bowl, pink, 4¾" . . **12.50**
Pyramid, tumbler, footed, yellow, 8-
ounce **40.00**
Queen Mary, ash tray, round, crys-
tal, 3½" **2.00**
Queen Mary, sherbet, pink . **4.00**
Queen Mary, tray, relish; 4-part,
crystal, 14" **8.50**
Queen Mary, tumbler, water; pink,
9-ounce, 4" **6.00**
Raindrops, sherbet, green . . . **5.00**
Raindrops, tumbler, green, 10-
ounce, 5" **8.00**
Ribbon, cup & saucer, green . **4.00**
Ring, creamer, footed, green . **4.00**
Ring, sherbet, footed, green with
decoration, 4¾" **7.50**
Ring, vase, crystal, 8" **13.00**
Rock Crystal, bowl, salad; scalloped
edge, red, 8" **45.00**

Rock Crystal, candelabra, 2-light,
pink, pair **50.00**
Rock Crystal, compote, footed crystal, 7" **28.00**
Rock Crystal, plate, salad; crystal,
7½" or 8½" **6.50**
Rock Crystal, tumbler, pink, 9-
ounce **20.00**
Rosemary, bowl, oval vegetable;
green, 10" **20.00**
Roulette, plate, luncheon; crystal,
8½" **4.00**
Royal Lace, bowl, cream soup; pink,
4¾" **12.00**
Royal Lace, pitcher, green, 68-ounce,
8" **75.00**
Royal Lace, tumbler, pink, 9-ounce,
4⅛" **1.00**
Royal Ruby, bowl, vegetable; oval,
red, 8" **27.50**
Royal Ruby, plate, luncheon; red,
7¾" **4.00**
Royal Ruby, tumbler, water; red, 9-
ounce **5.00**
S Pattern, bowl, cereal; crystal,
5½" **2.50**

Waterford, "Waffle," ash tray, crystal, 4", $5.00.

S Pattern, cup, amber **3.50**
S Pattern, plate, luncheon; amber,
   8" **2.50**
Sandwich (Hocking), bowl, berry;
   crystal, 4⅞" **4.00**
Sandwich (Hocking), creamer, crystal **4.50**
Sandwich (Hocking), pitcher, ice lip,
   crystal, ½-gallon **45.00**
Sandwich (Indiana), bowl, berry;
   crystal, 4¼" **3.00**
Sandwich (Indiana), butter dish,
   crystal **65.00**
Sandwich (Indiana), sugar bowl,
   pink **6.00**
Sharon, bowl, cream soup;
   amber, 5" **17.50**
Sharon, sherbet, amber **9.00**
Sharon, tumbler, thick or thin, pink,
   12-ounce, 5¼" **32.50**
Sierra, bowl, pink, 5½" **7.00**
Sierra, butter dish, green ..**50.00**
Sierra, cup, pink **7.50**
Sierra, salt & pepper, green,
   pair **30.00**
Spiral, sandwich server, center
   handle, green **17.50**
Spiral, sugar bowl, pink **5.00**
Starlight, creamer, white ...**3.00**
Starlight, plate, luncheon; crystal,
   8½" **2.50**
Starlight, sugar bowl, white .**3.00**
Strawberry, creamer, pink or green,
   4⅝" **17.50**
Strawberry, tumbler, iridescent, 9-
   ounce, 3⅝" **14.00**
Sunflower, cake plate, green .**9.00**
Sunflower, plate, pink, 9" ...**9.00**
Swirl, bowl, footed, closed handles,
   ultramarine, 10" **22.50**
Swirl, cup, ultramarine **8.50**
Swirl, sugar bowl, pink **6.50**
Swirl, tumbler, footed, ultramarine,
   9-ounce **18.00**
Tea Room, bowl, vegetable; oval,
   pink, 9½" **40.00**
Tea Room, cup, green **27.50**
Tea Room, sugar bowl,open, pink,
   4" **10.00**

Tea Room, tumbler, footed, pink,
   11-ounce **35.00**
Twisted Optic, bowl, cereal; all colors, 5" **3.00**
Twisted Optic, plate, luncheon; pink
   or green, 8" **2.00**
Vitrock, berry bowl, white, 4". **3.50**
Vitrock, plate, white, 8¾" ...**2.00**
Vitrock, plate, white, 7¼" ...**2.00**
Vitrock, sugar bowl, white ..**3.00**
Waterford, pitcher, juice; tilted,
   crystal, 42-ounce **17.50**
Waterford, salt & pepper, crystal,
   pair **8.00**
Windsor, bowl, 3-legged, pink,
   7⅛" **15.00**
Windsor, tray, green, 4⅛x9" .**8.00**

Doll Furniture

Every little girl has her favorite
doll and, like all good mothers, wants
her loved one to have all the 'necessities' of life! Thus a vast array of
doll-size furniture can be found,
ranging from the most elaborate to
those homemade items of simple
design.

Bed, poster, cherry, 21" ...**125.00**
Bed, rope & poster, cherry & oak,
   husk mattress, 19½" ...**75.00**
Cabinet, 2-drawer with 2 doors
   above, dated 1909, 9½" .**75.00**
Carriage, black-painted wire & wire
   mesh, 23" **135.00**
Chair, Adirondack, worn black paint
   over red, 7¾" **145.00**
Chair, red paint, turned legs, cane
   seat, 9¼" **115.00**
Chest, oak, 10½x7x6½" **50.00**
Chest, 5-drawer, pine, square nails,
   porcelain pulls, 22¾" .**650.00**
Couch, rosewood, paint and upholstery, scroll back, 1910,
   11½" **90.00**
Cradle, pine, original red paint with
   yellow striping, 16" ...**500.00**

Dresser with mirror and three drawers, 12x10", $65.00.

Cradle, pine & poplar, dated 1886, 15¾" long **95.00**
Cradle, poplar with worn dark finish, primitive, 12¾" . . .**35.00**
Cradle, walnut, dovetailed, well-shaped rockers, curved crest, EX **175.00**
Cradle, walnut, gold trim, good detail, 22¼" **135.00**
Dresser, painted floral, carved detail, 12" **95.00**
Dresser, 3 drawers, mirror top, scalloped detail, 11¾" . .**95.00**
Highchair, Mission oak **45.00**
Ironing board, oak, 13x17" .**26.00**
Linen press, mahogany with inlay, bone pulls, 12x10" **95.00**
Rocker, Adirondack, 12" . . .**55.00**
Rocker, bentwood, 15" **37.00**
Rocker, plank seat, 23x14" .**40.00**
Washstand, green paint, with accessories, 1900, 13" . . .**145.00**

Dollhouse Furnishings

Collecting antique dollhouses and building new ones is a popular hobby with many today, and all who collect houses delight in furnishing them right down to the vase on the table and the scarf on the piano! Flea markets are a good source of dollhouse furnishings, especially those from the 1940s through the '60s made by Strombecker, Renwal, or the Petite Princess line by Ideal.

Armchair, Tootsie Toy **12.00**
Bathtub, Germany, tin . . .**150.00**
Bathtub, Tootsie Toy **12.00**
Bedroom set, Tootsie Toy, 6-piece, EX/NM **55.00**
Birdcage, silver **185.00**
Cedar chest, Strombecker, lid lifts up **12.00**
Chair, German Biedermeier, stenciled gold on black **65.00**
Chair, oak, padded seat, 5" . .**8.50**
Chair, Renwal, overstuffed . .**8.00**
Chair, wing-back; Petite Princess, in original box **10.00**
Chifferobe, Mattel **4.00**
Coal skuttle, tin, handmade. **40.00**
Couch & chair, Strombecker.**22.00**
Cupboard, kitchen; Petite Princess, EX/NM **45.00**
Dining table, gate-leg, mahogany stained, 5¼x5" **18.00**
Dressing table, Petite Princess, in original box **15.00**
Grand piano, Petite Princess, in original box **20.00**
Grandfather clock, Petite Princess, EX/NM **28.00**

Petite Princess, host dining chairs, #4413-1, in original box, $17.50.

Porcelain bathroom fixtures, in box marked 'Made in Japan,' $35.00.

Ice box, tin 145.00
Kitchen range, Tootsie Toy, black,
   EX/NM 20.00
Kitchen sink, with accessories,
   Petite Princess 50.00
Living room set, Tootsie Toy, 5-piece,
   EX/NM 55.00
Ottoman, Schoenhut 12.50
Phonograph, Renwal 8.00
Piano, Tootsie Toy 20.00
Playpen, Renwal 8.00
Rug, hooked, 3" diameter ...4.50
Sewing machine, Renwal ..15.00
Sofa, German Biedermeier, sten-
   ciled gold on black ...300.00
Sofa, Petite Princess, green, in origi-
   nal box 17.00
Table, dining; Petite Princess, in
   original box 18.00
Table & chair, porcelain ...75.00
Television, Petite Princess .60.00
Twin bed, Renwal, brown frame with
   white stencil spread 8.00
Vanity, Renwal 7.00
Victrola 20.00

Dolls

Doll collecting is no doubt one of
the most popular fields today. Antique as well as modern dolls are
treasured, and limited edition or
artist's dolls often bring prices in
excess of several hundred dollars.
Investment potential is considered
excellent in all areas. Dolls have
been made from many materials —
early to middle 19th-century dolls
were carved of wood, poured in wax,
and molded in bisque or china.
Primitive cloth dolls were sewn at
home for the enjoyment of little girls
when fancier dolls were unavail-
able. In this century from 1925 to
about 1945, composition was used.
Made of a mixture of sawdust, clay,
fiber, and a binding agent, it was
tough and durable. Modern dolls are
usually made of vinyl or molded
plastic.

Learn to check your intended
purchases for damage which could
jeopardize your investment. Bisque
dolls may have breaks, hairlines, or
eye chips; composition dolls may
sometimes become crazed or
cracked. Watch for ink or crayon
marks on vinyl dolls. Original clothing is important, although on bisque
dolls replacement costumes are

acceptable as long as they are appropriately styled.

In the listings, values are for mint or mint-in-box dolls in these categories: American Character, Ideal, Mattel, and Trolls. Played-with, soiled dolls are worth from 50% to 75% less, depending on condition.

Cloth doll, glued-on wig, eyes to the side, all original, Primrose Doll Co. of Chicago, ca 1930s, 15½", $75.00.

American Character

Annie Oakley, 17"	165.00
Baby Chuckles, 18"	100.00
Baby Toodles, 14"	70.00
Ben Cartwright, 8"	65.00
Betsy McCall, 8"	100.00
Butterball, 19"	165.00
Cricket, 9"	20.00
Dream Baby, composition, molded hair, sleep eyes, 11"	90.00
Ricky Jr, 20"	95.00
Sally Says, plastic/vinyl, 19"	95.00
Sweet Sue, plastic, lavender jumper, marked AC, 15"	110.00
Tiny Tears, plastic/vinyl, 9"	50.00
Tiny Tears, vinyl, 8"	30.00

Toodle-Loo, 18"	145.00
Whimette, 7½"	25.00

Armand Marseille

#326, 10"	250.00
#327, on toddler body, 10"	350.00
#329, 14"	350.00
#390, socket head, fully jointed, 10"	145.00
#390, socket head, fully jointed, 18"	325.00
Baby Betty, 1890s, 16"	425.00
Baby Betty, 1890s, 20"	545.00
Floradora, 1890s, 9"	165.00
Floradora, 1890s, 14"	225.00
Floradora, 1890s, 25"	525.00
My Dream Baby, Kiddie Joy, #345, black bisque, 9"	265.00
My Dream Baby, Kiddie Joy, #345, 6"	165.00
My Dream Baby, Kiddie Joy, #351, black bisque, 16"	525.00
My Dream Baby, Kiddie Joy, open mouth, ca 1924, 9"	225.00
My Dream Baby, Our Pet, #341, brown bisque, 9"	265.00
My Dream Baby, Our Pet, with open mouth, ca 1924, 7"	165.00
Painted bisque, 11"	125.00

Armand Marseille, 12" marked: A.M. 345, painted eyes & jointed body, $1,000.00.

Painted bisque, 14" **165.00**
Queen Louise, 18" **400.00**
Rosebud, open mouth, incised name,
   1898, 16" **225.00**
Shoulder head with kid body,
   15" **225.00**
Shoulder head with kid body,
   21" **325.00**
Shoulder head with kid body,
   26" **475.00**
Socket head on good quality fully-
   jointed body, 10" **145.00**
Socket head on good quality fully-
   jointed body, 14" **200.00**
Socket head with crude 5-piece body,
   10" **135.00**
1914, kid body, 40" **1,600.00**

Effanbee

Baby Cuddleup, vinyl on cloth body,
   2 lower teeth, 1953, 20". **60.00**
Baby Dainty, composition and
   cloth, 15" **150.00**
Baby Evelyn, composition and cloth,
   17" **165.00**
Baby Tinyette, compo, 8" .**165.00**
Babyette, composition and cloth,
   12½" **165.00**
Babykin, vinyl, 10" **45.00**
Betty Brite, composition, fur wig,
   sleep eyes, 16" **225.00**
Bright Eyes, composition and
   cloth, flirty eyes, 18" ..**200.00**
Bubbles, Ltd Ed, 1984 .....**85.00**
Button nose, compo, 8" ...**165.00**
Button nose, vinyl/cloth, 18"..**50.00**
Candy Kid, composition, Black,
   12" **285.00**
Candy Kid, compo, 12" ...**225.00**
Carolina, Made for Smithsonian,
   1980, 12" **65.00**
Charlie McCarthy, composition and
   cloth, 19" **250.00**
Crowning Glory, Limited Edition,
   1978 ....**200.00**
Currier & Ives, plastic and vinyl,
   12" **50.00**

16" "Patsy Joan" marked: Effanbee
Patsy Joan, on body. $300.00.

Dewees Cochran, Limited Edition,
   1977 ....**175.00**
Fluffy, vinyl, 10" **35.00**
Grumpy, composition and cloth,
   12" **165.00**
Honey, composition, 20" ..**245.00**
Honey, plastic, 14" **150.00**
Ice Queen, composition, open mouth,
   skating outfit, 17" **675.00**
Lovums, composition and cloth,
   16" **200.00**
Mary Ann, 20" **225.00**
Mary Jane, plastic/vinyl, walker,
   freckles, 31" **165.00**
Mickey, composition with flirty eyes,
   22" **265.00**
Mickey, vinyl wearing molded hat,
   11" **95.00**
Patricia, composition, 14" .**250.00**
Patsy Ann, 19" **300.00**
Patsy Joan, 16" **300.00**
Patsy Lou, 22" **375.00**
Patsy Mae, 30" **500.00**
Patsyette, 9" **190.00**
Polka-Dottie, 21" **150.00**
Precious Baby, Limited Edition,
   1975 ....**450.00**

Prince Charming, 16" **225.00**
Rootie Kazootie, 21" **165.00**
Rosemary, cloth and compositon,
14" **165.00**
Sherlock Holmes, Limited Edition,
1983 ....**145.00**
Skippy, composition, 14" ..**300.00**
Sugar Baby, composition and
cloth, sleep eyes, molded hair,
16" **200.00**
Sunny Toddler, plastic and vinyl,
18" **65.00**
Susan B Anthony, Limited Edition,
1980 ....**150.00**
Suzanne, composition, 14". **200.00**
Tommy Tucker, composition and
cloth, flirty eyes, 18" ..**200.00**
WC Fields, composition and cloth,
22" **695.00**
WC Fields , plastic and vinyl,
15" **250.00**

Half Dolls

Black ribbon on neck, rose in hair,
Schneider, 5¼" **185.00**
Carmen, Germany, 4" **45.00**
Child, jointed shoulders, 3" .**55.00**
Cleopatra, Germany, #14291 on
base, 4¼" **150.00**

**Half doll, 3½" tall. Marks: Germany.
$60.00.**

Dancer, arms away, necklace/ear-
rings, eyeshadow, #17039 on
base, 4" **80.00**
Dog's head, Japan, 2¼" **20.00**
Flapper, fur collar, #155 on base,
5" **265.00**
Flapper, holds compact, #4737 on
base, 4½" **175.00**
Flapper, with umbrella, 4". **110.00**
Hands to shoulder, yellow dress,
blue trim, #6644, 2¼" ..**30.00**
Hands touch body, papier-mache,
3" **12.00**
Holds book at waist, pastel bodice,
Germany, 1⅞" **30.00**
Jointed shoulders, 12" **125.00**
Lady with animal, 5" **75.00**

Heubach

#6692, smiling, shoulder head, in-
taglio eyes, 15" **450.00**
#6736, laughing, open/close mouth,
molded teeth, 10" **800.00**
#6896, pouting, jointed composition
body, 19" **795.00**

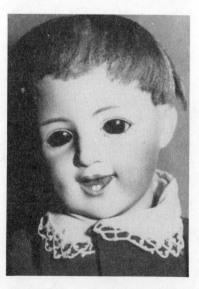

**19" Marked: 6½ Heubach; Sunburst
mark, DEP. Germany. $1,700.00.**

#7604, laughing, intaglio eyes, jointed body, 12" **400.00**
#7622, boy, closed mouth, molded hair, intaglio eyes, 12". **650.00**
#7634, crying with squinted eyes, 14" **850.00**
#7644, laughing, socket head, intaglio eyes, 14"' **500.00**
#7711, open mouth, jointed body, 12" **325.00**
#8191, smiling, fully jointed body, 12" **750.00**
#8420, pouting expression, glass eyes, 14" **525.00**

Heubach-Koppelsdorf

Black, #1900, 13" **450.00**
Black, #399, celluloid, 12" . **250.00**
Black, #399, 9" **350.00**
Black, #444, 10" **500.00**
Child, jointed composition body, with open mouth and sleep eyes, 14" **245.00**
Child, jointed composition body, with open mouth and sleep eyes, 8" **125.00**
Infant, #340, cloth body, sleep eyes, closed mouth, 12" **525.00**
Infant, #350, cloth body, sleep eyes, closed mouth, 14" **600.00**

Ideal

Baby Belly Button, plastic and vinyl, Black, 9" **15.00**
Baby Belly Button, plastic and vinyl, 9" **8.00**
Baby Crissy, 24" **40.00**
Betsy Wetsy, composition head, rubber body, 14" **120.00**
Bonnie Walker, plastic, pin-jointed hips, W-25, 23" **60.00**
Cinnamon, 12" **50.00**
Dina, 15" **50.00**
Flossie Flirt, composition and cloth, flirty eyes, 22" **95.00**
Goody Two Shoes, walking and talking, 27" **125.00**

19" "Princess Mary" of 1954, hard plastic with vinyl head, $75.00.

King Little, composition and wood, 14" **175.00**
Little Lost Baby, 3 different faces, 22" **45.00**
Look Around Cricket, 18" . . **30.00**
Magic Lips, vinyl coated cloth and vinyl, lower teeth, 24" . **65.00**
Miss Revlon, 10½" **65.00**
Pebbles, plastic and vinyl, 8". **12.00**
Penny Playpal, 32" **125.00**
Pinocchio, composition and wood, 11" **200.00**
Sandy McCall, boy, 36" . . . **350.00**
Sara Ann, plastic, marked P-90, 14" **150.00**
Snow White, compo, 12" . . **400.00**
Snow White, with molded hair, 14" **175.00**
Sparkle Plenty, 15" **45.00**

Kestner

A, shoulder head, open mouth, MIG/Kestner, 19" **550.00**

E/9, shoulder head, open mouth, MIG, 26" **850.00**

G/8, turned shoulder head, open mouth, MI/JDK, 19" . . **500.00**

Grace Putnam, bisque, 1-pc, painted eyes, 10/10/COPR, 6" . **650.00**

145, shoulder head, kid open/close mouth, 15" **1,200.00**

145, socket head, closed mouth, MI/O/G/18, 14" **1,100.00**

257, socket head, 5-piece baby, open mouth, G/JDK, 10" . . . **400.00**

257, socket head, 5-piece baby, open mouth, G/JDK, 24" . **1,200.00**

Madame Alexander

African, hard plastic, 1966-1971, 8" **350.00**

Alexander-kin #500, hard plastic, 1956-1964, 8", complete with wardrobe **150.00**

Alice in Wonderland, composition, 9", M **200.00**

Annabelle, plastic, 15" **350.00**

Baby Genius, all cloth, 1930s, 11", M **450.00**

Baby Jane, compo, 16" **700.00**

Baby McGuffey, compo, 20" **175.00**

Ballerina, plastic, 14" **285.00**

Barbara Jane, plastic and vinyl, 29" **325.00**

Binnie Walker, plastic, 15". **175.00**

Bunny, Melinda, plastic and vinyl, 1962, 18" **365.00**

Carmen, composition, 1936, all original, 7½" **125.00**

Chatterbox, hard plastic, vinyl head, rooted hair, 1962, 24" . **285.00**

Cissette, hard plastic, 1957, in sunsuit & purse, 10" **175.00**

Cissy, hard plastic with vinyl arms, 1957, all original, 21" . **245.00**

Clarabelle clown, cloth, 19".**185.00**

Cookie, composition, 19" . . **265.00**

Dilly Dally Sally, Tiny Betty, composition, 1937, 7" **175.00**

21" 1957 "Cissy," hard plastic with vinyl arms jointed at elbows. $245.00.

Dog, cloth **300.00**

Edith the Lonely Doll, plastic and vinyl, 1958, 16" **325.00**

Egyptian, Tiny Betty, composition, 1936, 7" **175.00**

Elise, plastic, original ballgown, 16½" **350.00**

Elise Ballerina, hard plastic and vinyl, jointed, 1957, 17" .**350.00**

Elise Ballerina, vinyl and plastic, 1974, 17", M **125.00**

Gainsborough, Portrait, 1961 on head, 1978, 21" **350.00**

Genius, vinyl, flirty eyes, all original, 21" **150.00**

Gidget, plastic/ vinyl, 14" .**500.00**

Gretel, Tiny Betty, composition, 1938, 9" **175.00**

Hawaiian **450.00**

Honeybun, vinyl, 23" **150.00**

Jeannie Walker, composition, all original, 13" **325.00**

Kate Greenaway, Princess Elizabeth, composition, 14". **400.00**

Kathy, all vinyl, 1954-1956, molded hair, sleep eyes, 11" . . . **85.00**

Kathy, vinyl, 19" **150.00**

Kelly, Lissy, hard plastic, 1959, 12" **425.00**

Kelly, Marbel, vinyl with rooted hair, sleep eyes, 1959, 22" . . **325.00**

Kelly, plastic, 12" **450.00**

Little Genius, composition on cloth, all original, 17" **185.00**

Little Genius, 8" **165.00**

Maggie, plastic, 15" **350.00**

Maggie Walker, hard plastic, sleep eyes, tagged outfit . . . **425.00**

Margaret Rose, Princess, plastic, 14" **425.00**

Marme, Margaret, hard plastic, 1948, 15", EX **285.00**

Mary Muslin, cloth, pansy eyes, 1951, 19" **400.00**

McGuffey Baby, composition, all original, 11" **125.00**

Muffin, cloth, 14" **95.00**

Peruvian Boy, hard plastic, 1965-1966, bend knee walker, all original, 8" **500.00**

Peter Pan, plastic, 15" **500.00**

Pinky, composition, 23" . . . **175.00**

Princess Elizabeth, closed mouth, composition, 13" **350.00**

Rusty, cloth and vinyl, 20". **450.00**

Sleeping Beauty, plastic, all original, 16¼" **450.00**

Slumbermate, composition, all original, 21" **400.00**

Sonja Henie, composition, jointed waist, 14" **375.00**

Sunbeam, vinyl, 16" **165.00**

Sunbonnet Sue, Little Betty, composition, 1937, 9" **200.00**

Sweet Tears, vinyl, 9" **100.00**

Tiny Tim, cloth **450.00**

Wendy Ann, composition, sleep eyes, all original, 11" **325.00**

Yugoslavia, Wendy Ann, hard plastic, bend knees, 1968-1972, all original, 8" **125.00**

Mattel

Barbie, Beautiful Bride, bendable knees, 1976 . . . . **75.00**

Barbie Beauty Secrets, 1980. **20.00**

Barbie, Ponytail Swirl, no curly bangs, 1964 . . . . **125.00**

Barbie, Sun Valley, ski accessories, 1974 . . . . **60.00**

Brad, talking, Black, 1975 . **75.00**

Casper the Ghost, 16" **32.00**

Christie, Golden Dream, 2nd issue, 1980 . . . . **30.00**

Clothes, Barbie Fancy Free, #943, dress only **5.00**

Clothes, Barbie in Switzerland, #0822, dress & apron . . . **6.00**

Clothes, Barbie Peachy Fleecy Coat, #915, coat only **5.00**

Clothes, Barbie swimsuit, pink & green striped **3.00**

Clothes, Barbie Tennis Anyone?, #941, sweater only **4.00**

Mattel's Barbie #1, holes in feet, MIB, $1,500.00.

Clothes, Barbie Winter Holiday, #975, coat, no belt 5.00
Clothes, Fashion Fantasy . . 15.00
Clothes, Ken beach set, red & white jacket, red trunks 7.00
Clothes, Ken Campus Hero, #770, sweater only 5.00
Clothes, Ken Graduation, #795, no diploma 9.00
Clothes, Ken Play Ball, #792, all original 30.00
Clothes, Ken Sports Shorts, #783, complete, no shoes 10.00
Dancerina, 24" 30.00
Francie, knees bend, 1966 . . 60.00
Grandma Beans, 11" 17.50

Bend knee Barbie in "American School Girl" haircut, $150.00.

Herman Munster, 16" 25.00
Hush Lil' Baby, 15" 15.00
Julia, Twist'N Turn, 2-piece nurse's uniform, MIB 125.00
Ken, All Star, 1982 . . . . . . 20.00
Ken, flocked hair, movable head, arms, & legs, 1961 . . . . 70.00
Ken, Super Star, including free gift, 1977 . . . . 65.00
Ken, Walk Lively, with painted hair, 1972 . . . . 85.00
Midge, bouffant hair, bendable legs, 1965 . . . . 100.00
Moon Mystic, 11½" 12.50
Mother Goose, 20" 40.00
Randy Ready, 19" 25.00
Rockflowers, 6½" 14.00
Sister Belle, 17" 32.00
Skipper, Funtime, blonde, bendable knees, 1967 . . . . 40.00
Skipper, Super Teen, 1979 . 25.00
Skooter, straight legs, 1965 . 40.00
Stacey, talking, 1968 . . . . . . 75.00
Stand, #1, two-prong 55.00
Swingy, 20" 25.00
Tatters, 10" 25.00
Tinkerbelle, 19" 15.00
Truly Scrumptious, talking, bendable legs, 1969 . . . . . . 185.00
Twiggy, blonde, bendable knees, mini dress, 1967 . . . . . 100.00

SFBJ

226, composition, inset eyes, 16" 1,700.00
227, closed dome, open mouth, inset eyes, 15" 1,700.00
233, comp, inset eyes, 14" . 1,600.00
236, laughing Jumeau, open mouth, open/close eyes, 12" . 1,200.00
237, compo, with sleep eyes, 16" 1,800.00
60, Kiss-Blower, cryer-walker, 22" 1,200.00

Shirley Temple

Bisque, Japan, 7½" 245.00

22" Shirley in rare aviator outfit from movie "Bright Eyes," $625.00.

Composition, cowboy outfit, original pin, 11", EX 650.00
Composition, flirty eyes, original clothes, 27", EX 900.00
Composition, original clothes, 18", EX 585.00
Composition, sailor suit, 20", EX/ NM 750.00
Composition, tagged blue & white dress, pin, 1930s, all original, 13" 575.00
Vinyl, Ideal, green & white dress, slip, 1957, 12", MIB ..150.00
Vinyl, Ideal, replaced clothes, 15" EX/NM 245.00
Vinyl, Ideal, with 4 outfits, 1957, 12", MIB 250.00
Vinyl, Ideal Stowaway, 1982, 8", EX/NM 45.00
Vinyl, Stand Up & Cheer dress, 1973, 16", MIB 245.00

Trolls

Cow 20.00
Dam Things, 16" 30.00
Dam Things, 6" 20.00
Donkey 65.00
Giraffe 65.00
Grandma & Grandpa, 1977, 13", each 25.00
Horse 65.00
Monkey, M 55.00
Turtle, Dam 1964, 5" 55.00
Unmarked, 12" 12.00
Unmarked, 6" 8.00

Uneeda

Anniversary Doll, 25", M ...55.00
Baby Dollikins, 21" 35.00
Baby Trix, 16" 20.00
Ballerina, vinyl, 14" 22.50
Blabby, 18" 22.50
Dollikins, 11" 20.00
Fairy Princess, 32" 70.00
Freckles, 32" 70.00
Lucky Linda, compo, 14" ..245.00
Pollyanna, 10½" 32.50
Pollyanna, 31" 90.00
Pri-thilla, 12" 20.00
Rita Hayworth, compo, 14" .22.00
Serenade, battery-operated talker, 21" 40.00
Suzette, sleep eyes, 11½" ...32.00
Suzette, 10½" 28.00
Tiny Teens, 5" 10.00

Vogue

Baby Dear, 1961, 12" 45.00
Ballerina, Frolicking Fables Series, painted lashes, 1952 ..200.00
Brickette, 22" 80.00
Bride, strung doll, painted lashes, 1952 ....250.00
Hug-A-Bye Baby, 16" 22.00
Jill, 10" 45.00
Love Me Linda, 15" 30.00
Miss Ginny, 15" 50.00
Star Bright, 18" 40.00
Tiny Miss Series #41, painted lashes, red caracul wig, 1952 .275.00
Welcome Home Baby Turns Two, 24" 65.00

Cowboy Toddles, ca 1943, M, $400.00;
EX, $325.00; VG, $100.00.

Rooster, painted cast iron,
ca 1940s, 4¾x3" **150.00**
Woodpecker, tree backplate, painted
cast iron **55.00**

Parrot in oval, painted cast iron, 4",
$45.00.

Door Knockers

Figural door knockers were made
in cast iron, often with painted-
on colors, or brass — they're not
easy to find and often bring high
prices on today's market.

Butterfly, painted cast iron, oval
back **145.00**
Cherub, cast iron with mother-of-
pearl, for interior door .**40.00**
Eagle, bronze, heavy, 7½" ..**35.00**
Gargoyle, brass, large **30.00**
Girl knocking at door, painted cast
iron, 3½" **125.00**
Heart shape, wrought iron .**85.00**
Kissing couple with roses, brass,
5½" **50.00**
Lady's hand, cast iron with worn
repaint, 4½" **20.00**
Masonic emblem, brass, old. **32.00**
Owl, painted cast iron, oval back,
4½" **125.00**

Doorstops

Doorstops, once called door por-
ters, were popular from the Civil
War period until after 1930. They
were used to prop the doors open
during the hot summer months so
that the cooler air could circulate.
Though some were made of brass,
wood, and chalk, cast iron was by
far the most preferred material,
usually molded in amusing figurals
— dogs, flower baskets, frogs, etc.
Hubley was one of the largest producers.

Aunt Jemima, polychrome painted
cast iron, 8¾", NM ...**175.00**
Aunt Jemima, traces of paint on
cast iron, 8¾" **75.00**
Camel, full-figure, oval base, black
painted cast iron, 5⅝" ..**45.00**

Cat, black & white painted cast iron, blue eyes, 10x6" **65.00**

Cat, brown painted cast iron, blue eyes, 7x8" **85.00**

Cat, seated, gold repainted cast iron, dated 1925, 7" **65.00**

Chicken, white painted cast iron with red trim, 8½x5½" . **85.00**

Colonial woman with purse & bonnet, Littco, 10¼" **75.00**

Conestoga wagon, yellow top, red wheels, 8x11" **75.00**

Doe with fawn, full-figure, painted cast iron, marked USA . **45.00**

Dog, Boston bulldog, standing painted metal, 10" **65.00**

Dog, German Shepherd, copper painted cast metal, 6" . . **40.00**

Dog, Greyhound, worn bronze finish on cast iron, 6⅝" . . . **70.00**

Dog, pointer; white & brown painted cast iron, 14½x9" **80.00**

Dog, Terrier, black & white painted cast iron, 5" **75.00**

Fireplace with lady at wheel, Eastern Specialty, 6¼x8" . . **150.00**

Fisherman, in rain wear with net, painted cast iron **75.00**

Flower basket, painted cast iron, 1-sided, 5x9" **50.00**

Flower bouquet on plinth, polychrome, cast iron, 6½" . **45.00**

Grapes & leaves, purple fruit & vines, Albany Foundry, 7¾x 6½" **150.00**

Horse, full-figure, original paint on cast iron, 10¾" **85.00**

Indian, Trail's End **150.00**

Lion, full-figure, original black painted cast iron, 7" . . . **70.00**

Little boy with bear, full-figure, Albany Co, 5¼x3½" . . . **100.00**

Little girl, painted cast iron, 7½", EX **70.00**

Pirate, cast metal, 5½" **40.00**

Pirate, seated on treasure chest, cast iron, 5½" **40.00**

Ram, worn white painted cast iron, 7¼" **185.00**

Sailor, polychrome painted cast iron, 8½" **145.00**

Ship, red, black, green, & white painted cast iron, 12" . . **35.00**

Southern belle, repainted cast iron, 6¾" **130.00**

Sunbonnet Baby, repainted cast iron, 6¼" **85.00**

Windmill with red roof, National Foundry, 6¾" **75.00**

Egg Cups

The variety of egg cups available in the marketplace today offers interesting possibilites to the collector, and their small size allows for an extensive, yet space-conserving collection. They were made by manufacturers of both fine china and novelty ware.

Beswick, blue, double, 4x5" . **45.00**

Crown Staffordshire, Rangoon, red dragon on white **10.00**

French, porcelain, white with blue flowers **8.00**

Angora cat, marked Hubley, painted cast iron, 9", $125.00.

Japan, Moss Rose pattern . . . **5.00**
Japan, violets on white **4.00**
Nippon, yellow floral on blue back-
ground **18.00**
Occupied Japan, white, plain. **7.50**
Rosenthal, white w/gold . . **12.50**
Royal Worchester, Palissy, bucket
shape **5.00**
Spode, bird & fruit on white. **15.00**

Erphila

Well-modeled novelty items as
well as household necessities were
made for a short time in Czechslo-
vakia and Germany. These are
stamped 'Erphila' with the country
of origin.

Cracker jar, orange poppy . . **35.00**
Figurine, nude child on goat, marked
Germany **85.00**
Figurine, English Setter, standing,
9¾" **45.00**
Jar, serpents on cobalt, 7" . . **75.00**
Platter, iris & rose garlands at rim,
bouquet in center, 11" . **25.00**
Wall pocket, desert scene, gold &
black, marked Czechoslovakia,
5½" **35.00**
Wall pocket, pottery, Art Deco flow-
ers, 7" **45.00**

Farm Collectibles

Farming memorabilia is a specialized area of primitives that is of
particular interest to those wishing
to preserve the memory of farm life
when horses drew the plow and
steam engines ran the thrashers,
when 'hands' were called to noon-
time 'dinner' by the ringing of the
dinner bell, and work days began at
three in the morning. Today, cast
iron implement seats make stools
for the family room bar; and scythes,
wagon wheels, and oxen yokes are

almost commonplace on restaurant
walls.

**Horse windmill weight, 16½",
$250.00.**

Apple butter stirrer, 36" . . . **12.50**
Barrel spigot, wood, 8" **4.50**
Calf weaner, iron, with spikes,
5" **28.00**
Chick feeder, pine, handmade &
primitive **14.00**
Corn dryer, 10-prong wrought
iron **10.50**
Corn sheller, hand crank, leather
strap, marked Patented July
30, 1973 . . . . **30.00**
Cow kickers, iron with chain links,
used for milking **8.00**
Egg basket, wire, non-collapsible
type, 9" **18.00**
Fly sprayer, tin, marked Rawleigh
Co **8.00**
Grain measure, brass, marked
Howe, 8½x4½" **125.00**
Grain measure, handmade, half-
gallon **50.00**
Grain scoop, carved wood, 1-piece,
7½x14" **75.00**
Hames, brass ends, 26" **15.00**
Hog ringer, iron, marked Hill's
Hog Ringer, Patented August
1872 . . . . **18.00**
Hog scraper, iron with wood handle,
7½" **15.00**
Horse rein holder, smithy wrought
iron **22.00**
Maple sap funnel, carved maple
wood, 1-piece **95.00**

Grain measures, maker and owner initialed, New England, 4½" to 8", $50.00 to $75.00.

Meat hook, 2-pronged iron with V-shaped top **12.50**

Mole trap, wire, marked Patented October 1916 . . . . **11.00**

Nose ring, polished copper, used for bull **6.50**

Ox yoke key, wrought iron, 6".**8.50**

Rake, wood, 24" long **35.00**

Sap spigot, carved wood **4.50**

Sap spigot, cast iron **6.50**

Sausage press, cast iron, original paint, stenciled name . . **35.00**

Seed sack, Wild Bill Cody Alfalfa, burlap, 16x28", EX **20.00**

Shucking peg, on original signed leather strap **15.00**

Sugar cane cutter, cast iron, wood case/legs, original paint. **45.00**

Tool box, John Deere **20.00**

Fenton

The Fenton glass company, organized in 1906 in Martin's Ferry, Ohio, is noted for their fine art glass. Over 130 patterns of carnival glass were made in their earlier years (see Carnival Glass), but even items from the past 25 years of production (Hobnail, Burmese, and the various colored 'crest' lines) have collector value.

Aqua Crest, compote, 7" . . . **30.00**

Aqua Crest, plate, 8½" **22.00**

Aqua Crest, vase, 4½" **17.50**

Basketweave, basket, ruby opalescent, cupped bowl, 6" . . **20.00**

Beaded Melon, creamer, gold overlay, #11 . . . . **35.00**

Burmese, vase, jack-in-the-pulpit; 11" **65.00**

Coin Dot, bowl, French opalescent, 6½" **20.00**

Coin Dot, jug, cranberry, 5" **55.00**

Crystal Crest, plate, 8½" . . . **24.00**

Diamond Lace, epergne, French opalescent, #1948 . . . . . **95.00**

Diamond Optic, shakers, amber, pair **40.00**

Diamond Optic, vase, lime opalescent, 12" **45.00**

Hobnail basket in cranberry opal, 7", $65.00.

Dolphin, compote, footed, ruby, #1533, 6" **45.00**
Emerald Crest, cake plate . .**75.00**
Emerald Crest, flowerpot . .**75.00**
Emerald Crest, vase, fan form, #3635, 6¼" **28.00**
Georgian, tumbler, ruby, flat 8-ounce **10.00**
Hobnail, cruet, cranberry opalescent, small **35.00**
Hobnail, goblet, wine; blue opalescent **15.00**
Hobnail, pitcher, French opalescent, water size **60.00**
Hobnail, rose bowl, topaz opalescent, 4½" **45.00**
Ivory Crest, candle holder, cornucopia form, 6¼" **30.00**
Jade Green, rose bowl, cupped, footed, 4" **35.00**
Lincoln Inn, cup, ruby **14.00**
Melon Rib, bottle, scent; pink overlay, with stopper, 7" . . .**25.00**
Ming, bowl, pink, deep, 3-legged, 7" **30.00**
Ming, tumbler, green, flat, water size **10.00**
Peach Crest, basket, milk glass handle, #203, 7" **75.00**

Peach Crest, vase, #7254 . . .**30.00**
Rosalene, basket, threaded . **55.00**
Rosalene, bell **42.50**
Rosalene, compote, with lid. **60.00**
Ruby Overlay, bowl, 9" **50.00**
Ruby Overlay, shakers, #2206, 2¾", pair **35.00**
September Morn, flower frog, crystal **90.00**
September Morn, flower frog, red transparent **175.00**
Silver Crest, cake plate, high footed, 13" **30.00**
Silver Crest, cup & saucer . **25.00**
Silver Crest, plate, 11½" . . .**25.00**
Silver Crest, powder jar . . .**22.00**
Silvertone, pitcher, iced tea; etched #1352, ca 1937 . . . . . .**65.00**
Spiral Optic, vase, cranberry opalescent, 5½" **35.00**
Thumbprint, compote, pink **15.00**
Thumbprint, wine, footed, Colonial blue **10.00**
Vasa Murrhina, vase, green with blue aventurine, 4" **35.00**

Fiesta

Since it was discontinued by Homer Laughlin in 1973, Fiesta has become one of the most popular collectibles on the market. Values have continued to climb until some of the more hard-to-find items now sell for several hundred dollars each. In 1986, HLC re-introduced a line of new Fiesta that buyers should be aware of. To date, these colors have been used: cobalt (darker than the original), rose (a strong pink), black, white, apricot (very pale tan-peach), yellow (a light creamy tone), and some turquoise. When old molds were used, the mark will be the same. The ink stamp differs from the old — all the letters are upper case.

'Original color' in the listings

indicates values for four of the original six colors — ivory, light green, turquoise, and yellow.

Ash tray, '50s colors **38.00**
Ash tray, original colors . . . **22.00**
Ash tray, red or cobalt **28.00**
Bowl, cream soup; '50s colors, with handles **28.00**
Bowl, cream soup; original colors, with handles **18.00**
Bowl, cream soup; red or cobalt, with handles **24.00**
Bowl, dessert; 6", '50s colors **22.00**
Bowl, dessert; 6", orig colors **14.00**
Bowl, fruit; 4¾",'50s colors . **13.50**
Bowl, fruit; 4¾", orig colors . . **9.00**
Bowl, fruit; 4¾", red **15.00**
Bowl, fruit; 5½", '50s colors . **15.00**
Bowl, fruit; 5½", orig colors . **11.00**
Bowl, fruit; 5½", red **14.00**
Bowl, individual salad; 7½", yellow **35.00**
Cake plate, Kitchen Kraft, red or cobalt **35.00**
Candle holders, bulb; original colors **30.00**
Candle holders, bulb; red or cobalt **40.00**

Carafe, original colors, $75.00.

Casserole, original colors . . **50.00**
Casserole, 7½", Kitchen Kraft, yellow or light green **55.00**
Casserole, 8½", Kitchen Kraft, red or cobalt **70.00**
Coffeepot, original colors . . . **68.00**
Coffeepot, red or cobalt **80.00**
Comport, sweets; original colors, footed **22.00**
Comport, sweets; red or cobalt, footed **30.00**
Creamer, '50s colors **12.00**
Creamer, individual; yellow. **28.00**
Creamer, original colors **9.00**
Creamer, red or cobalt **12.00**
Creamer, stick handle; original colors **12.00**
Cup, demitasse; original colors, stick handle **18.00**
Cup, medium green and '50s colors **19.00**
Cup, original colors **13.00**
Egg cup, original colors **23.00**
Fork, Kitchen Kraft, red . . . **35.00**
Fork, Kitchen Kraft, yellow or light green **30.00**
Gravy boat, '50s colors **30.00**
Gravy boat, medium green . **30.00**
Gravy boat, original colors . **18.00**
Mixing bowl, #1, nested, original colors **35.00**
Mixing bowl, #2, nested, original colors **25.00**
Mixing bowl, #3 nested, original colors **27.00**
Mixing bowl, #4 nested, original colors **32.00**
Mug, Tom & Jerry **22.00**
Nappy, 8½", original colors . **12.00**
Nappy, 8½", red or cobalt . . **25.00**
Nappy, 9½", original colors . **17.00**
Nappy, 9½", red or cobalt . . **28.00**
Pie plate, 10", Kitchen Kraft, yellow or light green **30.00**
Pie plate, 9", Kitchen Kraft, yellow or light green **25.00**
Pitcher, disk juice; yellow . . **18.00**
Pitcher, disk water; original colors **31.00**

13" oval platter, Harlequin spruce green. $125.00-150.00.

Pitcher, 2-pint; orig colors . **37.00**
Plate, calendar; 10", 1954 . . **27.00**
Plate, chop; 13", '50s colors . **31.00**
Plate, chop; 13", orig colors . **16.00**
Plate, chop; 15", orig colors . **18.00**
Plate, compartment; 10½", '50s colors **20.00**
Plate, compartment; 10½", original colors **11.00**
Plate, compartment; 10½", red or cobalt **17.00**
Plate, compartment; 12", original colors **14.00**
Plate, deep; original colors . **14.00**
Plate, deep; red, cobalt, or '50s colors **21.00**
Plate, 10", '50s colors **23.00**
Plate, 10", original colors . . **12.00**
Plate, 6", '50s colors **4.00**
Plate, 6", medium green **5.00**
Plate, 6", original colors **3.00**
Plate, 6", red or cobalt **4.00**
Plate, 7", '50s colors **7.00**
Plate, 7", medium green **8.00**
Plate, 7", original colors **4.00**
Plate, 9", '50s colors **10.00**
Plate, 9", medium green . . . **12.00**
Plate, 9", original colors **5.00**
Plate, 9", red or cobalt **10.00**
Platter, '50s colors **22.00**
Platter, original colors **12.00**
Salt & pepper shakers, medium green, pair **18.00**

Salt & pepper shakers, original colors, pair **17.00**
Salt & pepper shakers, red or cobalt, pair **13.00**
Saucer, '50s colors **3.00**
Saucer, demitasse; orig colors. **6.00**
Saucer, medium green **4.00**
Saucer, original colors **1.50**
Saucer, red or cobalt **2.00**
Sugar, w/lid, '50s colors **22.00**
Sugar, w/lid, original colors . **17.00**
Tray, figure-8; cobalt **32.00**
Tray, utility; original colors. . **15.00**
Tray, utility; red or cobalt . . **20.00**
Tumbler, juice; orig colors . . **14.00**
Tumbler, juice; cobalt **20.00**
Tumbler, original colors . . . **22.00**
Vase, bud; ivory **22.00**
Vase, bud; original colors . . **27.00**

Finch, Kay

From 1939 until 1963, Kay Finch and her husband, Braden, operated a small pottery in Corona Del Mar, California, where they produced figurines of animals, birds, and exotic couples as well as some dinnerware. Most items are marked.

Ash tray, shell form, pink lustre & white **12.00**

Bank, Panda figural, 9" 35.00
Cookie jar, Puppy, pink with hand-
painted details, 12¾" . 150.00
Figurine, camel, hand-painted de-
tails, 5" 50.00
Figurine, elephant, 7" 45.00
Figurine, Mitzi, Pomeranian, hand-
painted details, 10" . . 200.00
Figurine, peasant girl, plate above
head, hand painted 20.00
Figurine, pig, standing, pink, with
hand painting, 4" 25.00
Planter, monkey 25.00
Wall mask, Grecian man & lady,
pink lustre with gold trim, 10",
pair 100.00

Rooster, 11", $130.00.

Fire Fighting Collectibles

Fire fighting squads from the early 19th century were made up of volunteers; their only pay was reward money donated by the homeowner whose property they had saved. By 1860, cities began to organize municipal fire departments.

Much pomp and ceremony was displayed by the brigade during parade festivities. Fancy belts, silver trumpets, and brightly-colored jackets were the uniform of the day. Today these are treasured by collectors who also search for fire marks, posters, photographs of engines and water wagons, and equipment of all types.

Axe, hickory handle, 35" . . . 35.00
Badge, Hudson NY/shield . . 65.00
Bell, engine; bronze, with eagle,
LaFrance, EX 425.00
Blotter, Northwestern Mutual In-
surance Agency 17.50
Book, Handbook of Fire Protection,
9th edition 25.00
Bucket, leather, 11¼" 55.00
Bucket, leather, worn repaint, dated
1835, 12" 200.00
Calendar, Needham Mass Fire Dept,
1973 . . . . 3.00
Card holder, leather embossed gilt
motif, Niagara Fire Insur-
ance 30.00
Carte-de-visite, torch boy, parade
attire 50.00
Clock, metal, Pennsylvania Fire
Insurance, 6½" 100.00
Extinguisher, foam type, marked
American La France . . . 20.00
Hat, white plastic top, black visor,
gilt metal cap badge . . . 10.00
Helmet, brass with leather chin
strap & liner 70.00
Magazine, Emergency!, September
1976 . . . . 2.00
Nozzle, brass, with control, marked
Colt, 9½" 85.00
Nozzle, fog; brass, early, 5" . 24.00
Photograph, firefighters in front of
station, 1890 . . . . 25.00
Pin, 20 Years Service, 10K . 35.00
Rattle, wooden alarm, with original
paint 75.00
Sheet music, The Firemen's Polka,
by William Dressler . . . 32.00

Tool box, Dover-1, painted black
& red with gold letters,
10x10x36" **145.00**

**Fire mark of the Guardian
Assurance Co. of London, copper
with good paint, $125.00.**

Fireplace Accessories

From the primitive cooking utensils of the early years of our country
to the elegant Federal brass andirons, fireplace accessories (while
rarely collected in that particular
context) are purchased for reasons
as varied as the items themselves.
Screens, fire fenders, bellows, and
the like may be needed to furnish a
period room, while simple items such
as gypsy pots, trivets, and firebacks
may be put to a decorative use for
which they were never intended.

Andiron, black painted cast iron,
scroll feet, 14", pair ...**50.00**
Andiron, brass, cannonball, double
spur leg, American, 18½",
pair **87.50**
Andiron, brass, Corinthian design,
36¼", pair **80.00**
Andiron, dolphin figural, cast iron,
B&H, 14¼", pair **95.00**
Bellows, leather with brass nozzle,
original paint, 18¾" ..**150.00**

Bellows, fruit & foliage design, brass
nozzle, 17½" **60.00**
Coal bucket, brass, English, cone
shaped, 13" **85.00**
Coal bucket, brass, English, 8" high,
14" diameter **165.00**
Coal tongs, brass, 10½" **35.00**
Fender, brass with urn finials,
14x43" **90.00**
Fender, copper with brass trim,
13x46" **85.00**
Fireback, cast iron, scrollwork, ca
1875, 20½x21½" **110.00**
Kettle shelf, brass & iron, ca 1880s,
5½x7" **35.00**
Posnet, cast iron, 3 feet, side handle,
7" diameter **28.00**
Pot pusher, wrought, twisted feet,
crimped, 7" wide **78.00**
Spider pan, wrought iron, 3 legs,
6x7", with 14" handle .**165.00**
Toaster, wire with brass ferrule,
long wood handle **50.00**
Tool stand, brass, with ship finial &
5 tools, 55" **125.00**
Trammel, wrought iron, adjustable,
with chain & hook, 22" .**85.00**

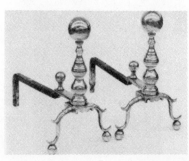

**Federal brass cannonball andirons,
20", $225.00.**

Fishing Collectibles

Very much in evidence at flea markets these days, old fishing gear is
becoming a popular collectible.
Because the hobby is newly established, there are some very good

buys to be found. Early 20th-century plugs were almost entirely carved from wood, sprayed with several layers of enamel, and finished off with glass eyes. Molded plastics were of a later origin. Some of the more collectible manufacturers are James Heddon, Shakespeare, Rhodes, and Pfueger.

Button, pin-back; New York Hunting, Trapping, & Fishing, 1939 ....6.00
Button, pin-back; Pennsylvania, 1943, 1¾" 6.50
Button, pin-back; PA Fishing License, 1957, 1¾" 6.00
Catalog, Creek Chub, 1948 .30.00
Counter sign, Pfueger, colorful cardboard 35.00
Lure, Creek Chub, Skipper, glass eyes, wood 25.00
Lure, Halik, mechanical frog, rubber 30.00
Lure, Heddon, deep diving wiggler, green with yellow & black details 40.00
Lure, Heddon, Meadow Mouse, bead eyes, wood 12.00

Lure, Heddon Gamefisher, no eyes, wood 20.00
Lure, Helga Devil, no eyes, plastic, EX/NM 10.00
Lure, Jim Dandy, no eyes, wood, EX/NM 35.00
Lure, Martin, 4½" 8.00
Lure, Miller's Reversible Minnow, no eyes, wood 500.00
Lure, Paw Paw Bullhead, tack eyes, wood 80.00
Lure, Pflueger Popright, carved eyes, wood 15.00
Lure, S Pike Oreno, tack eyes, wood 10.00
Lure, Scatback, painted eyes, plastic 10.00
Lure, Shakespeare, Revolution, no eyes, metal 150.00
Lure, South Bend Bass-Oreno, EX/NM 10.00
Lure, Wilson Wobbler 12.00
Lure, Winchester, 2-hook model, glass eyes, wood 150.00
Minnow trap, Camp, glass .65.00
Reel, brass, marked Kelly & Son, Doublin, 2⅜" diameter .60.00
Reel, Pflueger Spinkast #1953, EX/NM 10.00

Fishing creel, leather bound, measurements indicated on top, 12½" long, $30.00.

Reel, Shakespeare, Wonderreel,
level wind **6.00**
Rod, Heddon Black Beauty, bamboo, 108" **75.00**
Tackle box, Outing, metal ..**20.00**

Florence Ceramics

Produced in California during the 1940s and '50s, these lovely figurines of beautiful ladies and handsome men have recently become items of much collector interest. Boxes, lamps, planters, and plaques were also made. Values are based on size, rarity, and intricacy of design.

Ann, 6" **75.00**
Ballerina, 7" **95.00**
Chinese Girl, white with green, planter, 7½" **30.00**
Choir Boy, 6" **45.00**
Delia, 7½" **95.00**
Her Majesty, 7¼" **75.00**
Jim, gray suit, 6¼" **75.00**
Marie Antoinette, white with gold, lace, & roses, 10" **175.00**
May, planter, 5½" **30.00**
Plaque, lady with parasol, P-4, 9x 6½" **65.00**
Priscilla, pink, 8" **95.00**
Roberta, pink, 9" **85.00**
Tess, 7" **95.00**
Victor, white & black, 9½" .**100.00**

Girl with muff, 6", $60.00; Joy, 6", $65.00.

Vivian, with umbrella, 9" .**125.00**

Folk Art

Examples of folk art represent various aspects of our cultural heritage. Adirondac smoking stands, tramp art, shellwork frames, whirligigs, baskets, and samplers are only a few subtypes within this broad field of collectibles.

Box, stylized carved horse, sliding lid, 1-piece, 4¼" **35.00**
Box, worn polychrome paint, applied fruit, 7¾" **55.00**
Calligraphy, Act of Faith, Hope, & Charity..., 3¾x3¾" **40.00**
Cane, man's hand carved as handle, 33½" **105.00**
Cane, carved winding snake, woodburned detail, 38" **85.00**
Cane, relief-carved design with figures & animals, 35" ...**40.00**
Cat, stuffed woven wool, whiskers, eyes, 15¾" **275.00**
Corner shelves, cut-out sides with chip carving, 19x63¼". **105.00**
Cutting, concentric snowflake type, signed/1849, 16x16" ..**445.00**
Drawing, pencil, sailboats, signed/ dated 1891, original frame, 26x21" **350.00**
Footstool, 1-board top, 4 cone-turned feet, old, 11" **205.00**
Gourd, painted as man with cap & tie wearing white suit, ca 1900, 7x5½" **135.00**
Marionette, carved wood, man in evening clothes, painted facial features **45.00**
Noisemaker, wood, ratchet style, intricately painted, 1900, 7x5x1" **45.00**
Painting, wagon train, oil on board, ca 1900, 18x28" **125.00**
Rocking horse, carved with tack eyes and plank seat, 1900, 11x27x19" **185.00**

Box, carved inscription, dated 1922, bk: 'From Father,' 6x5x7", $145.00.

Snake, jointed wood, worn original paint, with rhinestone eyes & hide tongue **10.00**

Stand, pine, 3 legs, red & yellow striping, 28¼x19¾" **65.00**

Theorem on velvet, fruit basket, fine color, period mahogany frame, 8x10" **400.00**

Toy, train engine, wood & tin, wheels, 13" **110.00**

Tray, turkey shaped cutout, painted both sides, 30x41" **50.00**

Whirligig, Black man with sad expression, painted wood, 1900s, small **85.00**

Whirligig, flying duck, paddle wings, tack eyes, 1900, 25" ... **95.00**

Whirligig, Indian with paddles, bright paint, 15½" **800.00**

Whirligig, sailor, arms with paddles pivot, carved & painted, 1700s, 8" **375.00**

Whirligig, soldier, worn polychrome paint, 16½" **125.00**

Wood carving, eagle with 2-headed dog on cylinder base, unsigned, 6" **155.00**

Wood carving, horse with applied mane, free standing, 1890s, 9½x3x10" **225.00**

Wood carving, parrot, painted, glass eyes, 18½" **75.00**

Wood carving, wart hog, unsigned, 8½", long **45.00**

Wood carving, woman with 2 birds, signed, 7½" **95.00**

Fostoria

Fostoria has been called the largest producers of handmade glassware in the world. One of their most famous lines was their American pattern, which was introduced in

1915 and continued in production until the plant closed in 1986. They also produced lamps and figures of animals and birds.

Coin Glass candy jar, electric blue, 6½", $50.00.

American, bowl, handle, 4½" . **8.00**
American, creamer, individual, 4¾-ounce **7.50**
American, handkerchief box, with lid, 5⅛x4⅝" **125.00**
American, plate, 9½" **15.00**
Animal, horse, bookend **16.00**
Animal, seal **85.00**
Animal, squirrel, frosted . . . **20.00**
Animal, whale **20.00**
Baroque, blue; candelabrum, 3-light, 24-lustre, 9½" . . . **60.00**
Baroque, blue; tumbler, water; 9-ounce **26.00**
Baroque, yellow; candlestick, 4", pair **12.50**
Colony, crystal; ice bucket . . **45.00**
Colony, crystal; salt & pepper shakers, 3⅝", pair **12.50**
Fairfax, amber; creamer . . . **10.00**

Fairfax, green; bowl, centerpiece; oval, 13" **22.50**
Fairfax, orchid; mayonnaise. **12.00**
Fairfax, rose; plate, bread & butter; 6" **2.00**
June, blue; creamer, footed . **20.00**
June, crystal; decanter . . . **150.00**
June, crystal; tumbler, footed, 9-ounce **15.00**
June, rose; platter, 12" **40.00**
June, topaz; candy dish, with lid, 3-part **90.00**
June, topaz; sherbet, high standard, 6-ounce **25.00**
Kashmir, green; pitcher, water; footed **350.00**
Kashmir, yellow; ash tray . . **25.00**
Kashmir, yellow; plate, 9" . . . **9.00**
Trojan, rose; cup, footed . . . **16.00**
Trojan, rose; sweetmeat . . . **13.50**
Trojan, topaz; ice dish **30.00**
Trojan, topaz; salt & pepper shakers, footed, pair **70.00**
Versailles, blue; grapefruit . **60.00**
Versailles, blue; tray, center handle, 11" **35.00**
Versailles, green; goblet, claret; 4-ounce **40.00**
Versailles, green; plate, bread & butter; 6" **4.00**
Versailles, green; vase, fan form, footed, 8½" **85.00**
Versailles, pink; bowl, 7" . . **25.00**
Versailles, pink; tumbler, footed, 5-ounce **20.00**
Versailles, yellow; comport, footed, 7" **30.00**
Versailles, yellow; plate, grill; divided, 10" **25.00**
Vesper, amber; creamer . . . **20.00**
Vesper, amber; plate, 8½" . . . **8.50**
Vesper, blue; candlestick, 3". **30.00**
Vesper, green; ash tray **25.00**
Vesper, green; sugar bowl . . **15.00**

Fountain Pens

Fountain pens have been manufactured commercially since the 1880s. Today's collectors value those made by well-known companies such as Waterman, Parker, and Sheaffer's, or those made of gold or set with jewels. Various types of pumping mechanisms were employed.

Bicks, 1914, black hard rubber, eyedropper filler **20.00**
E Pen Co, Art Deco, black body with gold stars & moon, 4¾" .**15.00**
Eversharp, 1936 Coronet, gold-filled metal/black pyralin ..**350.00**
Parker, #45 ....**10.00**
Parker, Deluxe Challenger Art Deco, black body, marked, 5" .**15.00**
Parker, 1912 Lucky Curve, black hard rubber, eyedropper filler, EX **115.00**
Parker, 1925 Duofold Jr, black, button filler, EX **50.00**
Parker, 1926 Duofold Jr, red, button filler, EX **52.00**
Parker, 1945 Blue Diamond Duofold, silver stripe, lever filler **30.00**
Parker, 1947 Blue Diamond, #51, with gold trim, vacuumatic filler **30.00**
Redipoint, 1928, gold-filled metal with logo on cap, EX ...**25.00**
Sheaffer's, black body with 14K gold marked tip, ca 1940, 5" .**12.00**
Sheaffer's, 1925 Lifetime, black, EX **100.00**
Sheaffer's, 1935 Wasp Clipper, black, lever filler, EX ..**35.00**
Sheaffer's, 1938 Lifetime, red striped, lever filler **52.00**
Sheaffer's, 1939 Feather Touch, black, lever filler, EX ..**35.00**
Sheaffer's, 1939 Lifetime, gold striped, lever filler, M .**95.00**
Sheaffer's, 1941 Lifetime, #875, black, G **25.00**
Sheaffer's, 1948 Statesman, #875, blue, EX **42.00**

Sheaffer's, 1959 Craftsman, brown, M **25.00**
Swan, 1928 Swallow, black marbled, EX **45.00**
Wahl, black & blue speckled body, 5th Avenue, ca 1940 ...**12.00**
Wahl-Eversharp, 1932 Bantam, emerald marbled, aeromatic filler, EX **35.00**
Waterman's Citation Taperite, black, EX **65.00**
Waterman's Ideal, 1905, #12, black hard rubber, eyedropper filler, EX **59.00**
Waterman's Ideal, 1922, #52V, black chased hard rubber ...**59.00**
Waterman's Ideal, 1926, #52V, blue-green ripple, lever filler. **95.00**
Waterman's Ideal, 1932, #94, marbled green & gold, lever filler **95.00**

Franciscan

Dinnerware has been made by Gladding McBean and Company from 1934 until the present day. Their earlier lines have become popular collectibles, especially Coronado (Swirl) which was made in more than sixty shapes and fifteen solid colors; and Apple, the ivory line with the red apple on the branch whose design was purchased from the Weller Pottery. During the 1930s the ware was marked with a large 'F' in a double-walled square; a two-line mark was used in the 1940s, and after 1947 a circular mark identified their product.

Apple, bowl, vegetable; sm .**12.00**
Apple, chop plate, 14" **50.00**
Apple, coffeepot **45.00**
Apple, mug **18.00**
Apple, plate, 10½" **18.00**
Apple, plate, 6½" **10.00**
Coronado, bowl, cereal **10.50**

Apple, nested bowl set, 6", 7¼", 8¾", $80.00.

Coronado, bowl, cream soup. **12.00**
Coronado, candlestick, pair . **25.00**
Coronado, candy dish, round, with
cover **45.00**
Coronado, coffeepot, demitasse,
(after dinner) **45.00**
Coronado, cup & saucer **10.00**
Coronado, gravy boat with attached
tray **25.00**
Coronado, nut cup, footed .. **14.00**
Coronado, plate, chop; 12" .. **15.00**
Coronado, plate, 6½" **5.50**
Coronado, teapot **35.00**
Desert Rose, ash tray **10.00**
Desert Rose, bowl, vegetable; with
cover **35.00**
Desert Rose, egg cup **14.00**
Desert Rose, goblet **22.00**
Desert Rose, pitcher, 1-pint **16.00**
Desert Rose, plate, 8½" **14.00**
Desert Rose, plate, 9½" **18.00**
Desert Rose, platter, 19½" .. **95.00**
El Patio, bowl, fruit **9.00**
El Patio, butter dish **28.00**
El Patio, creamer **8.00**
El Patio, cup, jumbo **15.00**
El Patio, plate, 8½" **10.00**
El Patio, saucer **3.00**
El Patio, teapot, with cover, 6-cup
capacity **35.00**
Fine China, cup **15.00**
Fine China, plate, dinner .. **25.00**
Fine China, saucer **10.00**

Frankoma

Since 1933, the Frankoma Pot-

tery Company has been producing
dinnerware, novelty items, vases,
etc. In 1965 they became the first
American company to produce a line
of collector plates. The body of the
ware prior to 1954 was a honey tan
color. A brick-red clay was used from
then on, and this and the colors of
the glazes help determine the period of production.

Ash tray, Texas **6.00**
Bank, dog, 7½" **35.00**
Bean pot, Wagon Wheel, with
warmer **20.00**
Bookend, charger horse **75.00**
Bowl, black, #220, 6" **12.00**
Bowl, Gracetone, Pine Cone. **20.00**

**Figure of a horse, brown glaze, 7",
$42.00.**

Candle holder, Oral Roberts, 1971 .... 10.00
Candle holder, square, #307, 1042, pair 30.00
Casserole, #946, 1948-1954, individual 25.00
Christmas card, 1947 ..... 75.00
Christmas card, 1976 ..... 20.00
Christmas card, 1979, Grace Lee & Milton Smith, signed .. 35.00
Compote, shell form, #214, 1942-1950, 6" 8.00
Cornucopia, Desert Gold ... 25.00
Cornucopia, Prairie Green, #222, 12" 25.00
Donkey mug, 1975 .... 15.00
Donkey mug, 1976 .... 18.00
Elephant mug, 1968 ..... 85.00
Elephant mug, 1970 ..... 55.00
Honey jar, Beehive, #803, with lid, 12-oz 5.00
Lamp base, Wagon Wheel, Ada clay 25.00
Mask, Peter Pan, Flame ... 40.00
Miniature, swan 30.00
Pitcher, Aztec, green, #551 .. 7.50
Pitcher, Eagle, #555, 1942-1964 2⅜" 8.00
Planter, swan, Redbud 20.00
Plate, Bicentennial, 1975 .. 15.00
Plate, Christmas, Laid in Manger, 1969 .... 30.00
Plate, Easter, 1972 ...... 15.00
Plate, 50th Anniversary ... 15.00
Sculpture, charger horse, Prairie Green, red clay 35.00
Sculpture, Coati-Mundi ... 300.00
Sculpture, prancing colt .. 250.00
Shakers, black puma, pair . 35.00
Swan, #228, open tail, 7½" . 25.00
Trivet, Will Rogers 15.00
Tumbler, juice; #90-C, 2½" .. 3.00
Vase, bud; #28 .... 7.00
Vase, Cactus, Red Bud 45.00
Vase, cross, white, #804 ... 15.00
Wall pocket, acorn, Desert Gold, 5½" 15.00
Wall pocket, boot, green, Ada clay, 7" 15.00

Wall pocket, Wagon Wheel, Prairie Green, #94Y 20.00

Collector vase, V-8, Freedom Red and white, 1976, $55.00.

Fruit Jars

Some of the earliest glass jars used for food preservation were blown, and corks were used for seals. During the 19th century, hundreds of manufacturers designed over 4,000 styles of fruit jars. Lids were held in place either by a wax seal, wire bail, or the later screw-on band. Jars were usually made in aqua or clear, though other colors were also used. Amber jars are popular with collectors, milk glass jars are rare, and cobalt and black glass jars often bring $3,000.00 and up, if they can be found! Condition, age, scarcity and unusual features are also to be considered when evaluating old fruit jars.

Acme (on shield with stars & stripes), clear, quart 2.00

J&B (within octagon)/Fruit Jar/ Patd June 14th 1889, aqua pint, with hard-to-find original lid, $95.00.

Ohio Quality Mason, quart . **12.00**
Pacific Mason, clear, quart . **12.00**
Pansey, paneled, clear **200.00**
Pearl, aqua, quart **30.00**
Queen, aqua, quart **15.00**
Root Mason, aqua, quart **5.00**
Root Mason, olive green, half-gallon **48.00**
Sealfast, base: Foster, clear, half-pint **8.00**
Texas Mason, zinc lid, clear, quart **15.00**
Trade Mark Lightning, amber, half-gallon **45.00**
Trademark Mason CFJ Co Improved, aqua, midget . . **15.00**
Woodbury, aqua, quart **25.00**

Amazon Swift Seal, blue **8.00**
Atlas, E-Z Seal, amber **28.00**
Atlas, Mason Fruit Jar, aqua **6.00**
Ball, block letters, aqua . . . **10.00**
Ball Eclipse Wide Mouth, clear, quart **1.00**
Ball Sure Seal, blue **8.00**
Beaver, embossed, clear . . . **30.00**
Best Amber, clear, quart . . **350.00**
Canton Domestic Fruit Jar, clear, pint **125.00**
Chattanooga Mason, clear . . . **6.00**
Clark's Peerless, aqua, pint **12.00**
Crystal Jar, clear, quart . . . **30.00**
Dexter, aqua, half-gallon . . . **35.00**
Eagle, aqua, half-gallon . . . **95.00**
Fruit Commonwealth Jar . **100.00**
Globe, aqua, quart **15.00**
Globe, clear, half-gallon . . . **25.00**
Hero, name above cross, wire bail, aqua, pint **35.00**
Ideal Imperial, aqua, quart . **25.00**
Mason, script, underlined, clear, quart **6.00**
Mason Jar of 1872, quart . . **35.00**
Mason's CFJ Co Improved, amber, half-gallon **150.00**

Lyon & Bossard's/Jar/East Stroudsburg/PA, aqua quart, original glass lid (repro yoke clamp), rare, NM, $130.00.

Furniture

Golden oak continues to be a favorite of furniture collectors; Victorian, Country, and Mission Oak are also popular, and flea markets are a good source for all these styles. After the industrial revolution, mail-order furniture companies began to favor the lighter weight oak over the massive rosewood and walnut pieces, simply because shipping oak was less costly. This type of furniture retained its popularity throughout several decades of the 20th century. Mission was a style developed during the Arts and Crafts movement of the late 1900s. It was squarely built of heavy oak, with extremely simple lines. Two of its leading designers were Elbert Hubbard and Gustav Stickley. Country furniture is simply styled, often handmade, and generally primitive in nature. Recently, good examples have been featured in magazine articles on home decorating.

Painted maple ladderback child's armchair, New England, early 18th century, 30½", $550.00.

Armchair, ice cream; white painted metal, padded seat **55.00**

Armchair, walnut, Victorian, red velvet, ca 1875 . . . . . . **100.00**

Bed, rope; curly maple posts, poplar headboard, 44x51x72". **250.00**

Bed, rope; pine, old red stain, ¾-size **150.00**

Bed, sleigh; walnut, original rails, 44¾x51½x44¾" **145.00**

Bench, bootjack ends, primitive, weathered, 18x18x72" . **30.00**

Bench, bootjack ends, 1-board 15x54" top **65.00**

Bench, French Empire black with gilt, 32" long **165.00**

Bench, pine, cut-out feet, worn paint, square nails, 16x10x112" **100.00**

Bench, pine, shoe feet mortised through plank top, painted, 22" **95.00**

Bench, pine, square nails, refinished, 22x8x28" **85.00**

Bin, poplar, square nails, divided interior, 31x42x21" . . . **175.00**

Bookcase, Mission oak, gallery & slat sides, 5-shelf, no mark/unsigned **300.00**

Candle stand, curly maple, turned column on 3 feet . . . **1,000.00**

Candle stand, mahogany, tilt top, 3-footed base, 28¼" . . . **1,000.00**

Candlestand, birch, shaped tilt top, turned column, 19" . . . **150.00**

Candlestand, mahog, Chippendale style, 21x16" tilt top . **275.00**

Chair, side; Country Queen Anne, rush seat, vase splat . . **260.00**

Chair, side; Sheraton Hitchcock, original paint **175.00**

Chair, side; walnut, Victorian, velvet seat, American **95.00**

Chair, side; Windsor, 9-spindle hoop back **900.00**

Chair, side; Windsor bowback, shaped seat, 7-spindle. **400.00**

Chest, blanket; dovetailed pine/poplar bracket feet, 22" . . **325.00**

Fruitwood tavern table, 19th century, 37" long, $800.00.

Chest, blanket; pine, smoke marbleizing, 13¾" long ...**375.00**

Chest, blanket; pine, wrought iron hardware, ca 1830 ...**250.00**

Chest, blanket; pine, 6-board, scrolled front apron, old gray paint **300.00**

Chest, immigrant's; pine, dome top, iron hardware, old black paint **65.00**

Chest, mule; pine, 6-board, 2 cut-out feet, 2-drawer, 41 x 44 x 18½" **650.00**

Chest, pine, 4-drawer, porcelain pulls, ca 1875 ......**230.00**

Chest, Sheraton, bow front, mahogany veneer on birch ..**600.00**

Chest, Sheraton, pine, 4-drawer, scalloped apron, 39½" .**675.00**

Cupboard, jelly; poplar, country style, primitive red paint traces, 63x44" **650.00**

Cupboard, jelly; poplar, paneled doors, some gray paint remains, 59" **340.00**

Cupboard, pine, 2-piece, 6 dovetailed drawers, 2 panel doors, 87" **550.00**

Desk, lap; mahogany, brass bound, 6¾x20" **150.00**

Desk, lap; poplar, dovetailed case & drawer, slant lid **115.00**

Dry sink, poplar, brown & yellow grainpaint, paneled door, 35x42" **350.00**

Dry sink, poplar, cut-out feet, 2-panel door, 43x42x18" .**450.00**

Footstool, beveled edge, original brown paint, 6x8x12" ..**55.00**

Footstool, pine, cut-out legs mortised through top, 15" ..**75.00**

Footstool, pine, primitive, 6½x9x 17½" **65.00**

Highchair, arrow back, original stencil, 1840s **70.00**

Piano stool, oak & cast iron, needlepoint seat **45.00**

Pie safe, poplar, 6 star-&-circle punched tins, 1-drawer, primitive, 54" **375.00**

Rocker, armchair; ladderback Shaker style, woven tape seat, EX **200.00**

Rocker, Boston; maple, only partially painted, American, ca 1840 ....**110.00**

Rocker, child's armchair; sausage, turnings, 3-slat back .**450.00**

Rocker, Lincoln; mahogany, velvet upholstery, 1840 .....**110.00**

Rocker, sewing; bird's eye maple, caned seat & back **150.00**

Rocker, slipper; walnut, Victorian, American, ca 1865 ....**70.00**

Shelf, Adirondac; twist-roots with sapling posts, painted white, 44x48" **120.00**

Shelf, poplar, scrolled bracket, square nails, 12½x10" .**40.00**

Shelf, jigsaw-work dogs & scrolls, 13x19½" **150.00**

Shelf, walnut, jigsaw cut-out ends, scrollwork, 30x20" ...**150.00**

Shelf, walnut, 3-tier, American, 1900, 35x25" **400.00**

Stand, cherry, Country Hepplewhite, dovetailed drawer, 28¾" **250.00**

Stand, cherry/pine, Hepplewhite, dovetailed drawer **850.00**

Stand, curly maple, dovetailed drawer, 30½" **550.00**

Stand, poplar, turned legs, single board top, 28¼" **180.00**

Stand, walnut, dovetailed drawer, 29x17¼x21" **175.00**

Table, card; mahogany, Victorian, American, ca 1850 . . . **120.00**

Table, ice cream; red painted wood top, with 4 chairs **105.00**

Table, pembroke; walnut, Hepplewhite, 1-drawer, 2 leaves, 27", EX **325.00**

Table, sewing; walnut veneered top, Victorian, 1865 . . . . . **160.00**

Table, work; turned legs, dovetailed drawer, 29x31x65" . . . **125.00**

Utensil rack, pine, carved starflowers and initials, 7-hook, 10x36" **275.00**

Washstand, cherry, dovetailed drawer, turned legs 18½x21x29" **315.00**

Washstand, pine, Country Sheraton **150.00**

Gambling Devices

Though Lady Luck still attracts her share of eager partakers at the games of chance, today those interested in vintage gambling devices can be confident of gaining, rather than losing, by making wise selections on their investments. Especially valued are cheating devices, layouts, and items that can be authenticated as having been used in the 'Floating Palace' riverboats or in the early days of the famous casinos of the West.

Ash tray, A Friend in Need, dogs playing cards, Homer Laughlin **15.00**

Book, Fools of Fortune, copyright 1891, 640 pages **70.00**

Book, Gambling, by James H Romain, 1st ed, 1891 . . . . **40.00**

Book, Hoyle's Games, Phila, copyright 1845, 269 pages . . **28.00**

Book, If You Must Gamble, 1st edition, 1946, 127 pages . . **10.00**

Bowie knife, double-edged blade, Gambler's Companion, Germany **95.00**

Broadside, Texas Mutual Benefit Association Lottery, 1874, 8x 5½" **45.00**

Card holdout, Monarch, patent applied for, 3", EX **50.00**

Card holdout, Wizard Card Clip, patent date June 16, 1903, EX **130.00**

Catalog, KC Card Company, 1961, 79 pages **66.00**

Catalog, Mason & Co Blue Book, 1932, 108 pages **95.00**

Catalog, Manufacturers & Designers of Casino Clubroom Equipment, 9x6" **100.00**

Dice cage with bell, celluloid dice, 18" **165.00**

Dice cup, carved wood, ca 1810, hand-carved, 3" **50.00**

Dice cup, embossed leather reads Pour la Roblesse, 4" . . . **40.00**

Money changer, black painted metal, CL Downey Company, ca 1917 . . . . **90.00**

Paperweight, glass, black & white Saratoga Race Track photo on base **15.00**

Paperweight, slate die, 2" sq. **15.00**

Photo, silver, interior of saloon, 8x10" **12.00**

Photo, tintype, 3 men drinking & playing cards, 2¼x3½" . **22.00**

Playing cards, Triplicate Playing Cards, A Dougherty, New York **100.00**

Poker chip set, 300 in wood case, 5x12x8" **275.00**

Poker dice, celluloid, Segram VO Canadian Whiskey **37.00**

Roulette wheel, Bakelite with aluminum, stamped ES Lowe, boxed **75.00**

Roulette wheel, felt, ball & directions **45.00**

Roulette wheel, silver spinner, solid wood, France, 8" **77.00**

Roulette wheel, tabletop; brass &
wood, 11½" **42.00**
Spittoon, brass, marked Rochester
Stamping Co, 4½x7½" ..**17.00**

Games

Before the turn of the century,
several large companies began to
produce parlor games; among them
were Milton Bradley and Parker
Brothers, both of whom still exist
and continue to distribute games
that delight young and old alike.
These early games make wonderful
collectibles; especially valuable are
those dealing with a popular character, transportation theme, Black
theme, or other areas of special
interest. Condition of both game
pieces and the box is important.

Authors, Parker Bros, in original
box **12.00**
Authors, 48 cards, McLoughlin
Brothers, NY **40.00**
Courtship & Marriage, 50 cards with
instructions, 1864 .....**50.00**
Flip M Up, Northwestern Mail Box
Co Works, 7x5x½" **12.00**

Game of India, Milton Bradley,
original box **18.00**
Game of US History, Parker Bros,
lithographed box **12.50**
Gang Way, board game, 1964, in
original box **22.00**
Pollyanna Glad Game, 1915, in
original box **10.00**
Puzzle, Gunsmoke, Whitman Co,
1958, 11x14" **10.00**
Raffles-The Sophisticated Game of
Chance, Corey Game Company,
1939 ....**14.00**
Rook, Parker Brothers, 1951 .**6.00**
Space 1999, in original box .**15.00**
Tiddly Winks, Disney, 1963 .**6.00**
Touring, Parker Brothers ..**20.00**
Trolley Card, Snyder Brothers,
1904, in original box ...**20.00**

Gas Globes and Panels

Globes that once crowned gaso-
line pumps are today being collected
as a unique form of advertising
memorabilia. There are basically
four types: plastic frames with glass
inserts from the 1940s and '50s;
glass frames with glass inserts from
the '30s and '40s; metal frames with

Picture Lotto, Loughlin Bros., U.S.A., paper litho, with box, $35.00.

glass inserts from the '20s and '30s; and one-piece glass globes (no inserts) with the oil company name etched, raised, or enameled onto the face from 1914 to 1931. There are variations.

American, glass frame, glass inserts,
1920s-1940s **185.00**
California Richfield, metal frame,
glass inserts, ca 1925 .**325.00**
Champlin Presto, glass frame &
inserts, 1930s-1940s ..**150.00**
Clark Brand, plastic body, glass
insert, 1940s-1950s ...**85.00**
DX-Boron, plastic body, glass inserts, 1930s-1950s **85.00**
Essolene, metal frame, glass inserts,
1920s-1930s **190.00**
Gold Crown Standard, 1-piece globe,
with company name ..**200.00**
Imperial, plastic body, glass inserts,
1930s-1950s **100.00**
Mobil, plastic body, glass inserts,
1940s-1950s **50.00**
Mobil Ethyl, with flying horse, metal
band, 1920s-1930s ...**225.00**
Mobilgas Pegasus, metal frame with
glass inserts, 15", 1915-
1930s **250.00**
Pure, plastic body, glass inserts,
1930s-1950s **90.00**
Red Crown, 1-piece, company name,
1914-1931 ....**200.00**
Shell, 1-piece glass, shell shape,
1914-1931 ....**175.00**
Skelly, glass frame, glass inserts,
1920s-1940s **150.00**
Skelly Regular, glass frame & inserts, 1930s-1940s ...**150.00**
Spartan, glass frame & inserts,
1920s-1940s **210.00**
Standard, metal body & frame, glass
inserts, 1915-1940s ..**250.00**
Standard Red Crown, glass frame,
inserts, 1920s-1940s ..**185.00**
Sunoco, metal frame, glass insert,
1920s-1930s **225.00**

Texaco Sky Chief, plastic body &
globe, 1940s-1950s **80.00**
Tidex, metal frame, glass inserts,
16", 1915-1930s **250.00**
Wood River, plastic body, glass inserts, 1930s-1950s ...**110.00**

Geisha Girl China

More than sixty-five different patterns of tea services were exported from Japan around the turn of the century, each depicting geishas going about the everyday activities of Japanese life. Mt. Fuji is often featured in the background. The generic term for these sets is 'Geisha Girl China.'

Berry set, Chinese Coin, 1 master &
5 individual **150.00**
Biscuit jar, Garden Bench H, 5 reserves on cobalt **55.00**
Bonbon dish, Bamboo Trellis, red
with gold **45.00**
Bowl, Cat, raised foot, 9-lobed, green
with gold, 2¾x8¾" **75.00**
Bread tray, Boat Dance, jagged edge,
red-brown with gold ...**45.00**
Celery dish, Boat Festival, orange,
gold lacing, 13x5½" **28.00**
Cocoa pot, Battledore, conical body,
yellow-green, 8" **55.00**
Creamer, Chrysanthemum Garden,
red, toy size **10.00**
Cup & saucer, AD; Bamboo Trellis,
red with gold buds **10.00**
Pancake server, So Big, floral design on rim, red with gold lacing, 9½" **150.00**
Plate, Lantern B, cobalt with gold,
6" **12.00**
Sauce dish, Baskets of Mums, 4-
lobed, cut-out handle, green
with gold **8.00**
Shakers, Cloud B, square body with
round tops, pair **12.00**

Footed bowl, 4½" diameter, $18.00; Plate, 8½", $18.00.

Teacup/ saucer, Bamboo Tree. **7.00**
Teapot, Boy with Scythe, cobalt with
    gold, #20 ....**30.00**
Toothpick holder **18.00**
Tray, jewel; footed **15.00**

Goofus Glass

Produced in the early part of the
20th century, 'goofus' glassware was
pressed with designs in very high
relief and painted on the reverse
with metallic lustres. Lamps, pickle
jars, vases, and trays are easy to
find. Flea markets are often a good
source, but watch for flaking paint.
Careful cleaning is a must to pre-
vent paint loss.

Bottle, scent; tulips, original stop-
    per, 3½", VG **15.00**

Bottle, water; basketweave, ame-
    thyst, 10" **27.00**
Bowl, butterfly, original paint, 4x8"
    diameter **42.00**
Bowl, roses, 5-sided, rare, 3½x9"
    diameter **60.00**
Cake plate, acorns & leaves, ame-
    thyst, 12" **20.00**
Cake plate, La Belle, original paint,
    11" **40.00**
Coaster, flowers, rare, 3" ...**10.00**
Compote & saucer, poppies, crackle
    glass, original paint, 4" .**25.00**
Fairy lamp, flash-fired green rose
    cluster, 7" **30.00**
Lamp, cabbage roses, with chim-
    ney, miniature, 12" **32.00**
Lamp, Poppy, Gone-with-the-Wind
    base, 15" **55.00**
Nut dish, cluster of cherries, ring
    handle, original paint, scalloped
    rim **37.50**

Cabbage Rose salt and pepper shakers, 3½", $40.00.

Plate, Gibson Cameo, original paint, 8½" 37.50

Plate, full-blown roses, original paint, 8½" 35.00

Plate, strawberries, 11", M .40.00

Salt & pepper shakers, cabbage roses, original paint & top, 3½", pair 37.00

Sugar shaker, grapes, milk glass, 4½" 30.00

Syrup, cabbage roses, paint scaled away, 5½" 35.00

Syrup, grape cluster on clear, original lid 50.00

Syrup, strawberries, original paint, no top, 6½" 40.00

Tray, cabbage roses, amethyst, 7x11" 35.00

Tray, dresser; roses, heart shaped, amethyst, rare, 6" 50.00

Vase, grapes, crackle glass, turned amethyst, 9" 15.00

Vase, roses, crackle glass, straight sides, paint, 9" 15.00

Vase, 3 clusters of grapes, original paint, 10" 17.00

Water bottle, basketweave, original white paint, 10" ...40.00

Water bottle, grapes on crackle glass, with stopper, 7½". **42.00**

Graniteware

A collectible very much in demand by those who enjoy the 'Country' look in antiques, graniteware (also called enameled ware) comes in a variety of colors, and color is one of the most important considerations when it comes to evaluating worth. Purple, brown, or green swirl pieces are generally higher than gray, white, or blue — though blues and blue-swirled examples are popular. Decorated pieces are unusual, as are salesman's samples and miniatures; and these also bring top prices.

Bowl, mixing; brown swirl, 10½", NM 85.00

Bowl, mixing; robin's egg blue mottle, medium, NM ..40.00

Bowl, soup; gray 18.00

Bucket, berry; blue & white marbleized, 8" **75.00**

Can, cream; red, with lid & bail, 1-quart **55.00**

Can, milk; blue & white swirl, matching lid, 9" **110.00**

Can, milk; white, Dutch girl. **75.00**

Candlestick, blue & white swirl, NM **145.00**

Candlestick, dark green . . . **95.00**

Candlestick, white, with handle, NM **30.00**

Chamber pot, blue swirl, with lid, NM **95.00**

Chamber pot, turquoise swirl, with bail & lid, tall, EX **95.00**

Choppette, white, with wood chopping bowl, Rochester, NY, 2-piece **50.00**

Coffeepot, gray, teardrop form, ring on back, VG **215.00**

Colander, blue & white speckled, footed **35.00**

Colander, brown & white swirl, white interior **175.00**

Creamer, white with red trim, 6", NM **55.00**

Cuspidor, brown, 2-piece . . . **25.00**

Dipper, gray mottle **23.00**

Dipper, white with red **21.00**

Funnel, blue & white swirl, 3" diameter **85.00**

Kettle, gray, with wooden bail, large, NM **32.00**

Measure, gray mottled, with handle, 1-cup **85.00**

Measure, powder blue mottle, marked Elite, 4-cup . . . **65.00**

Mold, gray, melon shaped, loop handle, 8½" long **65.00**

Mold, gray, turban shaped with center tube **65.00**

Mold, octagonal, cobalt, M . **85.00**

Mug, blue & white mottle . . **23.00**

Mug, child's; brown **35.00**

Mug, cobalt & white large swirl, NM **60.00**

Mug, gray, 3½" diameter . . **20.00**

Mug, solid blue, white interior, fluted, miniature **65.00**

Crown mold, light blue with white interior, 6" long, $95.00.

144

Pan, pie; blue & white swirl, 9½"
VG 35.00
Pan, pudding; green & white marbleized, 7", EX 75.00
Pan, sauce; blue, miniature, 2¼"
diameter 55.00
Pan, sauce; teal blue speckled, with
lid, miniature 50.00
Pan, sauce; white with blue trim, 8"
diameter 22.00
Pitcher, gray & white mottle, water
size 85.00
Pitcher, white with navy trim, 6",
NM 29.00
Plate, dinner; cobalt 22.00
Plate, dinner; teal swirl 35.00
Platter, gray, oval, 16" 65.00
Roaster, blue & white mottle with
lid 85.00
Scoop, gray, with wood handle, large,
NM 100.00
Skillet, gray, 8½" 65.00
Skimmer-ladle, blue with white
interior 35.00
Soap dish, gray swirl, EX ..30.00
Spatula, white, M 35.00
Spoon, cooking; white with black
trim 10.00
Teakettle, solid red, with matching
lid 45.00
Teakettle, white with red trim, with
matching lid 45.00
Teapot, blue & white speckled,
squatty with metal lid, 8-cup,
NM 75.00
Teapot, blue & white with eagle
design 38.00
Thermometer, oven; white, green
base, marked Taylor ...35.00
Tray, cobalt, oval, shell shaped,
1¼x10x8¼" 50.00
Tumbler, white with navy blue rim,
marked KER Sweden ..20.00
Wash basin, gray, handles, 15" diameter 30.00
Washboard, blue & white mottle
design 85.00
Washboard, cobalt, marked Imperial 70.00

Dust cloth bin, Dutch inscription,
9½x6", $42.00.

Green and Ivory

Green and ivory stoneware is
identical in design to the more
familiar blue and white ware. It
was produced from about 1910 until
1935 by many manufacturers,
though it is never marked.

Bowl, Apricot, 9½" 65.00
Bowl, Wedding Ring, 10" ...40.00
Butter crock, Daisy & Waffle, with
lid 95.00
Pitcher, Apricot, 8" 125.00
Pitcher, Cow, 7½" 125.00
Pitcher, Grape 85.00
Pitcher, Pine Cone, 9" 135.00
Spittoon, Cosmos, 6" 75.00
Spittoon, Waffle & Grape, salesman's sample, 2" 75.00
Toothpick holder, Swan 25.00
Umbrella stand, Iris, 20" ..250.00

Griswold

During the latter part of the 19th

century, the Griswold company began to manufacture the finest cast iron kitchenware items available at that time. Soon after they became established, they introduced a line of lightweight, cast aluminum ware that revolutionized the industry. The company enjoyed many prosperous years until its closing in the late 1950s. Look for these marks: Seldon Griswold, Griswold Mfg. Co., and Erie.

Ash tray, cowboy hat, 5" . . .**47.00**
Ash tray, kettle shape, 3" . .**32.00**
Ash tray, skillet shape **15.00**
Cake mold #866, rabbit . . .**125.00**
Corn stick pan #183 . . . .**28.00**
Corn stick pan #22 . . . .**24.00**
Corn stick pan #282, with wheat kernels **70.00**
Dutch oven #9, later version, with lid **40.00**
Egg poacher, holds 7 eggs . .**30.00**
Griddle #616, round, with bail handle **20.00**
Griddle skillet #107 . . . .**35.00**
Muffin pan, makes 11, round, 7½x11" **38.00**

Cast iron Santa mold, $250.00.

Popover pan #10 . . . .**35.00**
Skillet #10, with lid **25.00**
Skillet #12, smoke ring **65.00**
Skillet #3, with lid **20.00**
Skillet #42, snack size **52.00**
Skillet #8 . . . .**12.00**
Skillet rack **100.00**
Teakettle, 6-quart **45.00**
Trivet, hexagonal, small . . .**15.00**
Waffle iron #11, square **45.00**
Waffle iron #8 . . . .**40.00**

Hall

Most famous for their extensive lines of teapots and colorful dinnerwares, the Hall China Company still operates in East Liverpool, Ohio, where they were established in 1903. For listings of their most popular dinnerware line, see Autumn Leaf.

Acacia, casserole, Radiance .**28.00**
Ash tray, Palmer House, with match holder, turquoise **15.00**
Blue Blossom, creamer **22.00**
Blue Blossom, jug, batter .**125.00**
Blue Bouquet, bowl, salad; 9" diameter **12.00**
Blue Garden, casserole, Sundial, #4, with lid **24.00**
Blue Garden, creamer, Morning style **20.00**
Bowl, Radiance, red, 3½" **4.00**
Cactus, batter bowl, 5-Band. **35.00**
Cameo Rose, butter dish with lid, ¼-lb **40.00**
Cameo Rose, creamer **8.00**
Canister, Radiance, ivory, with lid 2-quart **20.00**
Canister, sugar; brown **45.00**
Classic, cup, Zeizel **6.50**
Classic, sugar bowl, Zeizel .**12.00**
Clover, casserole, Radiance .**28.00**
Coffeepot, Amory, emerald .**24.00**
Coffeepot, Cathedral, dripolator, large **18.00**
Colonial, sugar bowl, lettuce.**14.00**
Crest, dripolator **28.00**

Football teapot, cobalt with gold trim, $400.00.

Crocus, cake plate **18.00**
Crocus, creamer, Colonial . . **14.00**
Garden Wall, syrup **35.00**
Heather Rose, bowl, vegetable; with
    lid **14.00**
Heather Rose, pie plate **12.00**
Heather Rose, sugar bowl . . . **8.00**
Monticello, bowl, fruit; small. **3.50**
Mt Vernon, creamer **5.00**
Mt Vernon, flat soup **8.50**
Mt Vernon, platter, 16" **15.00**
Orange Poppy, baker, fluted sides,
    3-pint **18.00**
Orange Poppy, bowl, vegetable; 9¼"
    diameter **18.00**
Orange Poppy, casserole, oval, with
    lid **32.00**
Orange Poppy, custard **4.00**
Pastel Morning Glory, bowl, salad;
    9" **15.00**
Pastel Morning Glory, jug, #3, ball
    type **25.00**
Pastel Morning Glory, teapot, Alad-
    din **50.00**
Piggly Wiggly, casserole . . . **34.00**
Red Poppy, bowl, fruit; 5½" . . **3.00**
Red Poppy, bowl, soup **10.00**

Red Poppy, cake plate **12.00**
Red Poppy, casserole **20.00**
Richmond, bowl, cereal **6.00**
Richmond, jug **12.00**
Rose Parade, baker **16.00**
Rose Parade, creamer **8.00**
Rose White, casserole **20.00**
Rose White, custard **12.00**
Rose White, jug, 7½" **20.00**
Rose White, sugar bowl **7.50**
Royal Rose, bowl, 8½" **15.00**
Sani-Grid, jug, red & white, me-
    dium **18.00**
Silhouette, bowl, salad; 9" . . **14.00**
Springtime, bowl, vegetable; 9"
    diameter **16.00**
Springtime, creamer, modern
    style **6.00**
Springtime, teapot, French . **45.00**
Tea tile, cobalt with gold decora-
    tion, 6" **30.00**
Teapot, Airflow, cobalt blue, 8-
    cup **27.00**
Teapot, Boston, green with gold, 2-
    cup **28.00**
Teapot, Cleveland, emerald green
    with gold **28.00**

Teapot, Cozy Cover, black matt glaze **25.00**
Teapot, Globe, cobalt **75.00**
Teapot, Parade, canary **14.00**
Teapot, Philadelphia, cobalt with gold, 4-cup **35.00**
Teapot, Surfside, medium green with gold **55.00**
Tom & Jerry, punch set, black, 7-piece **65.00**
Tulip, bowl, oval **14.00**
Tulip, bowl, salad **15.00**
Tulip, plate, 9" **10.00**
Wild Poppy, baker, oval ...**24.00**
Wild Poppy, creamer, Hollywood style **15.00**
Wild Rose, casserole **22.00**
Wildfire, baker, French **12.00**
Wildfire, drip jar **16.00**
Wildfire, jug, Radiance, #5 .**24.00**
Wildflower, bowl, oval **18.00**
Yellow Rose, bowl, cereal; 6" .**5.00**
Yellow Rose, cup **5.00**
Yellow Rose, drip jar **16.00**
Yellow Rose, stack set **45.00**

"Zephyr" water bottles. $65.00.

Halloween

Halloween items are fast becoming the most popular holiday-related collectibles among today's flea marketers. Although originally linked to pagan rituals and superstitions, Halloween has long since evolved into a fun-filled event; and the masks, noisemakers, and jack-o'-lanterns of earlier years are great fun to look for.

Candy container, black cat atop pumpkin, composition, Germany, 5" **120.00**

Lantern, tin with molded glass pumpkin face, battery operated, ca 1950, 5½", $25.00.

Candy container, skull, 6"..**165.00**
Decoration, black cat, papier-mache, 4" **85.00**
Decoration, Dracula, pressed cardboard, Japan, 1950s ...**45.00**
Decoration, owl, papier-mache, orange, 3½" **45.00**
Decoration, owl with wings wide, diecut, Germany, 15" ..**45.00**
Decoration, witch, cardboard with tissue fold-out wings, Germany, 8" **35.00**
Decoration, witch & moon, diecut, Germany, 10" **28.00**
Figurine, pumpkin man & witch, papier-mache, Germany, 4", pair **70.00**
Horn, green cucumber, wood mouthpiece, working, 7½" ...**125.00**
Jack-O'-Lantern, papier-mache, eyelashes & mustache, 3x4" diameter **85.00**
Jack-O'-Lantern, papier-mache, faces both sides, 10½" ..**70.00**
Jack-O'-Lantern, tin litho, owl, moon & bats, 1930s, 5" **45.00**

Noisemaker, orange & black tin litho, Chein, 5½" diameter, 11" long **40.00**
Nut cup, pumpkin, papier-mache, small **12.00**
Rattle, witches & cats on tin litho, Gotham, 6x4" diameter. **35.00**
Skeleton, glass lantern, battery op, 1950s, 3" **45.00**
Toy, skeleton, spring limbs, Germany, 5" **40.00**

Harlequin

Made by the Homer Laughlin China Company who also produced the popular Fiesta, Harlequin was a lightweight dinnerware line made in several solid glaze colors. It was introduced in 1938 and was marketed mainly through Woolworth stores. During the early forties, the company made a line of Harlequin animals: a fish, lamb, cat, duck, penguin, and donkey. Values designated 'low' in the listings that follow are for these colors: mauve blue, turquoise, and yellow. 'High' values are for maroon, gray, medium green, spruce green, chartreuse, dark green, rose, red, and light green.

Animal, maverick **23.00**
Ashtray, basketweave, high **27.00**
Bowl, cream soup; high **13.00**
Bowl, fruit; high, 5½" **7.00**
Bowl, nappy; high, 9" **12.00**
Bowl, oval baker, high **18.00**
Butter dish, low, ½-pound .. **53.00**
Candle holder, high, pair .. **65.00**
Casserole, with lid, high ... **55.00**
Creamer, novelty, high **15.00**
Cup, demitasse; high **32.00**
Egg cup, dark blue, high ... **16.00**
Gravy boat, high **16.00**
Plate, deep; high **12.00**
Plate, high, 10" **13.00**
Platter, high, 11" **11.00**

Saucer, low **2.00**
Sugar bowl, with lid, high .. **13.00**
Teapot, high **50.00**
Tray, relish; mixed colors . **120.00**
Tumbler, low **23.00**

Ash tray saucer, $23.00 to $28.00; Basketweave ash tray, $23.00 to $27.00; Regular ash tray, $21.00 to $24.00.

Hatpin Holders

Made from many materials, hatpin holders are most often encountered in china decorated by hand painting or floral decals. Glass hatpin holders are rare, especially those of slag or carnival glass.

Austria, hand-painted florals, saucer type **65.00**
Carnival, Orange Tree, blue iridescent **195.00**
Daisy & Button, clear, silver top, rare, 8" **300.00**
Goss, souvenir, City of York crest, 3½" **85.00**
Japan, desert scene **35.00**
Nippon, gold moriage butterflies, gold top & base, 5" **65.00**
Nippon, scenic, gold trim, open top, green wreath mark **65.00**
Royal Bayreuth, country scenes, with saucer base, blue mark, 5" **250.00**
Royal Bayreuth, penguin figural, blue mark, 5" **450.00**

Hanging hatpin holder with florals and gold beading, 7", $110.00.

RS Germany, floral, 6" **60.00**

RS Prussia, hand-painted roses, drape mold, attached tray, with lid **200.00**

Schaffer & Vater, 2 faces, white & pink Jasper, 5½" **135.00**

Suhl Prussia, florals, gold border, 5" **80.00**

Unmarked china, Flow Blue, Victorian scenes, marked Watteau, 6" **125.00**

Unmarked china, red roses, 2-handle **65.00**

Hatpins

Hatpins range in length from about 4" to as long as 12", depending upon the fashion of the day. The longer type was required to secure the large bonnets that were in style from 1890 to 1914. Many beautiful examples exist — some with genuine or manufactured stones, some in silver or brass with relief-molded Art Nouveau motifs, others of hand-painted porcelains, and 'nodder' types.

Amethyst glass **18.00**

Bakelite, black with rhinestones, 6" **25.00**

Brass, sunflower **24.00**

Brass & amethyst, 1¼" tilt top with hook to hang on back .**195.00**

Carnival glass, bat figural, near-black with gold lustre ..**95.00**

Emerald glass bead, ¾", on 7⅞" steel pin **35.00**

Jet glass, riveted wand, 3¾", 12" pin **195.00**

Mosaic, intricate colors, designs, or flowers, 1½", each **125.00**

Rhinestone with amethyst stones, lacy design, 1½" **55.00**

Seashell, wired to pin, 8" ..**28.00**

Sterling, Art Nouveau lady's head embossing **35.00**

Sterling, golf club, 8" **95.00**

Sterling, heart with Nouveau lady's head, 1", 7¼" steel pin .**55.00**

Vanity, vinaigrette, enamel top, ½", 8" pin **195.00**

Wire, twisted openwork, black rhinestones, 10¾" **38.00**

Head Vases

Many of them Japanese imports, head vases were made primarily for the florist trade. They were styled as children, teenagers, clowns, and famous people. There are heads of religious figures, Blacks, Orientals, and even some animals. Among the most common are ladies wearing pearl earrings and necklaces.

African lady, earrings, Relpo, #6673, 6½" **25.00**

Baby, ruffled bonnet, EO Brody, #A987, 6½" **12.50**

Blond lady, black hat, gloved hand to her face, Napcoware, #C348, 7" **15.00**

Child praying, eyes closed, Inarco, #E778, 5" **10.00**

Clown, polka-dot hat, red nose, gold trim, Napco, 6¼" **15.00**

Dutch Girl, hand toward chin, Inarco, #E1611, 5½" . . . **15.00**

Fireman, #5 on hat, hose in hands, Inarco (paper label), 5" . **10.00**

Geisha girl, gilt trim, unmarked, #3237, 7½" **20.00**

Girl, bow in long frosted hair, 1 pearl earring, Napcoware, #C8494, 7" **20.00**

Girl, 2 braids, bow at bangs, unmarked, #4796, 5¾" . . . **10.00**

Jackie Onassis, scarf over hair, Inarco, #1852, 5½" **65.00**

Lady, flat hat, polka-dot bow, bristle lashes, Napco, 5½" **12.50**

Lady, flowers on hat, winking, bow at neck, unmarked, 5" . **10.00**

Lady, poinsettia at neck, Napcoware, #CX5409, 4½" . . . **10.00**

Lady, ruffled collar, hand to face, Sampson Import, 6" . . . **15.00**

Lady, scarf over hair, hand to face, Inarco, #E1904, 6½" . . . **15.00**

Lady, short frosted hair, pearls & earrings, Napcoware, #C7473, 7½" **14.00**

Lady with fan, curls on neck, earrings, Inarco, 6" **15.00**

Mammy, green scarf at neck, Lefton's, #542, 7½" **20.00**

Mary & Child, Napcoware (paper label), #47076, 6½" **12.50**

Toddler with kitten, Enesco (paper label), 5½" **10.00**

Heisey

The Heisey glassware company operated in Ohio from 1896 until 1957, producing fine dinnerware lines, many of which were made in lovely colors and etched with intricate floral motifs. They also made animal and bird figures, some of which sell for more than $500.00 each. They signed their ware with an H in a diamond mark or with a paper label.

Animal, colt, kicking **190.00**

Animal, colt, standing, amber **550.00**

Animal, dolphin, candlestick, #110, pair **350.00**

Animal, elephant, large . . . **350.00**

Animal, elephant, small . . **195.00**

Animal, fish, bookend, ... **100.00**

Animal, frog, cheese plate, marigold **350.00**

Animal, giraffe, head back. **175.00**

Animal, horse head, bookend, clear, pair **250.00**

Lady with pearl earrings and necklace, Inarco, #E-2966, 11", $65.00.

Footed marigold tumbler, $35.00.

Animal, Plug horse **95.00**
Bird, Asiatic Pheasant . . . **375.00**
Bird, chick, head down **60.00**
Bird, duck, ash tray, flamingo **195.00**
Bird, goose, wings down . . **350.00**
Bird, Kingfisher, flower block, moongleam **250.00**
Bird, Mallard, wings half . **150.00**
Bird, rooster, stem cocktail . **55.00**
Bird, swan, individual nut dish, #1503 . . . . **45.00**

Dinnerware

Adam, crystal; wine, footed, #3376, 3-ounce **25.00**
Adam, flamingo; finger bowl. **15.00**
Albemarle, crystal; tumbler, footed, 10-ounce **10.00**
Albemarle, marigold; claret, #3368, 4½-ounce **20.00**
Carcasonne, flamingo; tumbler, iced tea; footed, 12-ounce . . . **25.00**
Carcasonne, sahara; finger bowl, footed, #3390 . . . . **25.00**

Coarse Rib, crystal; oil, #407, 6-ounce **40.00**
Coarse Rib, hawthorne; plate, #407, 8" **20.00**
Creole, alexandrite; finger bowl, footed, #3381 . . . . **85.00**
Creole, alexandrite; tumbler, footed, 10-ounce **100.00**
Empress, crystal; plate, square, #1402, 10½" **65.00**
Empress, moongleam; plate, 6" diameter **65.00**
Heisey Rose, crystal; cruet **160.00**
Kohinoor, crystal; bowl, salad; #4085, 11" **35.00**
Kohinoor, zircon; bowl, fruit; #1488, 15½" **125.00**
Octagon, hawthorne; plate, 14" diameter **45.00**
Octagon, moongleam; ice bucket, #500 . . . . **75.00**
Old Dominion, crystal; decanter, #1404, 1-pint **95.00**
Old Dominion, flamingo; parfait, #3380, 5-ounce **25.00**
Pleat & Panel, moongleam; goblet, #1170 . . . . **30.00**
Pleat & Panel, moongleam; sherbet, #1170, 5-ounce **20.00**
Ridgeleigh, crystal; plate, round, #1469, 8" **12.00**
Saturn, zircon; comport, #1485, 7" diameter **125.00**
Saturn, zircon; tumbler, #1485, 10-ounce **55.00**
Stanhope, crystal; cup & saucer, #1483 . . . . **25.00**
Stanhope, crystal; ice bucket, handled, #1483 . . . . . . **50.00**
Tudor, crystal; salt & pepper shakers, #411, pair **35.00**
Tudor, crystal; sherbet, footed 5-ounce **12.00**
Victorian, cobalt; vase, #1425, 4" **150.00**
Victorian, crystal; cruet, #1425, 3-ounce **47.50**
Yeoman, crystal; candy box, with lid, #1184, 6" **60.00**

Orchid, individual sugar and creamer, $65.00 for the set.

Historical Blue Ware

Made by many Staffordshire potteries from as early as 1820 for export to America, this type of transfer-printed earthenware was decorated with views of American landmarks to assure its acceptance in this country. Early wares were dark blue on white; later, light blue, green, black, red, and pink transfers were used, but these are not as valuable today. Some views are rarely found, and naturally these bring top prices. In addition to color, condition of the glaze and brilliance of the print are important.

Bowl, English Estate, dark blue, beaded rim, 7½", ...**110.00**
Creamer, Wadsworth Tower, dark blue, Wood, EX **165.00**
Cup plate, Fisherman, dark blue, double transfer, Clews, 3½", NM **115.00**
Dish, Ottoman Empire, dark blue, leaf form, EX **100.00**
Plate, Bamborough Castle, Northumberland, dark blue, Adams, 10" **95.00**
Plate, Boston State House, medium blue, Wood, 8¼", M ...**150.00**

Plate, Castle of Furstenfeld, dark blue, Henshall, 9" **65.00**
Plate, Columbus, landing scene, light blue, Adams, 10¾".**60.00**
Plate, Eashing Park, Surrey, dark blue, Hall's select views, 7⅜", M **50.00**
Plate, Faulkbourn Hall, dark blue, Stevenson, 8¾" **85.00**
Plate, Ibex, dark blue, Wood's Zoological series, 6½" **70.00**
Plate, Llanarth Court, dark blue, Hall, 10" **75.00**
Plate, Ludlow Castle Salop, dark blue, Adams, 7½" **75.00**
Plate, Pagoda, dark blue, Clews, 8¾", M **70.00**
Plate, Pains Hill, Surrey, dark blue, 10" **95.00**

Platter, Niagara Falls from the American Side, dark blue, Woods, 15", $600.00.

153

Plate, St Paul's School, dark blue, Adams, 7¾" **85.00**

Platter, Pagoda, medium-dark blue, 19", EX **145.00**

Sauce boat, Caribou, dark blue, Wood, EX **150.00**

Soup, Indian Temple on River, dark blue, 8½" **40.00**

Teapot, Washington, Scroll in Hand, dark blue, Wood **525.00**

Tray, Hyena, dark blue, Wood , 8", EX **55.00**

Homer Laughlin

Founded in 1871, the Homer Laughlin China Company continues today to be a leader in producing quality tablewares. Some of their earlier lines were produced in large quantity and are well marked with the company name or HLC logo; collectors find them fun to use as well as to collect, since none are as yet very expensive.

See also Fiesta; Harlequin; Riviera.

Amberstone, casserole **5.00**

Amberstone, pie plate **23.00**

Americana, creamer **5.00**

Americana, sugar bowl **9.00**

Casualstone, cup & saucer .. **6.00**

Casualstone, sugar bowl **5.00**

Conchita, bowl, fruit; 5" **5.50**

Conchita, platter, 11½" **11.00**

Epicure, coffeepot **25.00**

Epicure, plate, 6½" **3.00**

Hacienda, bowl, 8" **14.00**

Hacienda, sauce boat **12.00**

Jubilee, casserole **14.00**

Jubilee, sauce boat **12.00**

Laughlin Art China, pot, demitasse; Currant **135.00**

Laughlin Art China, vase, Currant, 16" **125.00**

Mexicana, creamer **5.00**

Mexicana, egg cup, rolled edge style **18.00**

Priscilla, plate, 8" **3.50**

Rhythm, bowl, mixing; Kitchen Kraft, 6" **55.00**

Rhythm, cup & saucer **7.00**

Rhythm Rose, bowl, nested, medium **11.00**

Rhythm Rose, plate, 9" **4.00**

Rhythm Rose, sugar bowl ... **6.00**

Serenade, shakers, pair **9.00**

Tango, bowl, nappy, 8¾" **6.00**

Tango, plate, 10" **7.00**

Virginia Rose, bowl, nested, small **9.00**

Virginia Rose, butter dish, half-pound **45.00**

Virginia Rose, pitcher, 5" ... **9.00**

Wells Art Glaze, nappy, 8" .. **6.00**

Wells Art Glaze, platter, 16" **11.00**

Wells Art Glaze, teapot **20.00**

Hull

Established in Zanesville, Ohio, in 1905, Hull manufactured stoneware, florist ware, art pottery, and tile until about 1935, when they began to produce the lines of pastel matt-glazed artware which is today very collectible. The pottery was destroyed by flood and fire in 1950. The factory was rebuilt and equipped with the most modern machinery which they soon discovered was not geared to duplicate the matt glazes. As a result, new lines — Parchment and Pine, and Ebb Tide, for example — were introduced in a glossy finish. During the forties and into the fifties, their Red Riding Hood kitchenware and novelty line was very successful. Collectors of character memorabilia, Hull collectors, and kitchenware collectors alike vie to own these endearing figural charmers — match safes, banks, canisters, salt and pepper shakers, etc. — dressed in the traditional red cape and hood and carrying a basket to Grandma's house.

Bow Knot cup and saucer wall pocket, $58.00.

Athena, cornucopia vase, #608, 8½" **15.00**
Basket, #79, embossed Brown-Eyed Susans, blue handle ... **18.00**
Blossom, bowl, mixing; 9½" . **30.00**
Blossom, pitcher, 16-ounce . **25.00**
Blossomflite, basket, T-2, 6" .**25.00**
Bow Knot, candle holder, B-17, 4", pair **60.00**
Bow Knot, vase, B-4, 6½" .. **50.00**
Bowl, #25, H in circle, 7" ... **12.00**
Butterfly, bowl, B-7, rectangular, 6x9" **20.00**
Butterfly, ewer, B-11, 8¾" .. **40.00**
Butterfly, pitcher, B-11, 9". . **40.00**
Calla Lily, vase, #504, 6" ... **36.00**
Calla Lily, vase, #505, handles, 6" **40.00**
Camellia, basket, hanging; #132, 7" **80.00**
Camellia, vase, swan, blue & pink, #118, 6½" **35.00**
Candy dish, gray froth on dark gray, gold trim, with lid, 9" .. **22.00**
Coronet, swan, white with green trim, #213 .... **20.00**
Debonair, cookie jar, 8¾" ... **30.00**
Dogwood, cornucopia vase, #522, 4" **25.00**

Dogwood, ewer, #505, 8½" . **55.00**
Early Art, vase, #80-6, H in circle, 8" **25.00**
Early Utility, stein, #498, American Legion, H in circle mark, 6½" **30.00**
Floral, pitcher, #46, 6" **25.00**
House & Garden, pitcher, brown, 9½" **12.00**
Imperial, ewer, #401, 13½" . **45.00**
Iris, vase, #403, 7" **50.00**
Iris, vase, #406, 8½" **60.00**
Magnolia, glossy; console bowl, H-23, pink floral, 13" **50.00**
Magnolia, glossy; cornucopia, pink floral, H-10, 8½" **22.50**
Magnolia, glossy; ewer, H-11, blue floral, 8½" **35.00**
Magnolia, glossy; vase, H-8, gold trim, 8½" **40.00**
Magnolia, matt; ewer, 4¾" . **24.00**
Mardi Gras, bowl, mixing; 10".**20.00**
Mardi Gras, matt; vase, #49, Deco, pink & blue, footed, 9" . **30.00**
Mirror Brown, butter dish ... **6.00**

Wildflower vase, 16", $175.00.

Mirror Brown, coffee server, with
lid **12.00**
Nuline, pitcher, Diamond Quilted,
blue, B-7, 1-quart **40.00**
Old Spice, mug, Friendship .**12.00**
Old Spice, mug, Grand Turk deco-
ration **12.00**
Orchid, bowl, #312, low, 7" .**45.00**
Orchid, vase, #301, beige & pink,
4¾" **25.00**
Parchment & Pine, basket, black &
green, S-3, 8" **42.00**
Parchment & Pine, cornucopia, S-6,
11¾" **40.00**
Parchment & Pine, teapot, 8".**60.00**
Planter, #154, light green, melon
rib, oval, 8½" **6.00**
Planter, #61, kitten, 6x8" . .**22.00**
Planter, #80, swan, bow tie, green &
pink, 7¼x6" **20.00**
Planter, parrot, #60, 9½" . . .**20.00**
Red Riding Hood, cookie jar, open-
end basket, with apron .**95.00**
Red Riding Hood, shakers, large,
pair **35.00**
Sueno Tulip, bud vase, 6" . .**35.00**
Sun Glow, ewer, #90, 5½" . .**15.00**
Thistle, vase, #53, 6½" **25.00**
Tokay, basket, #11, half-moon form,
10½" **50.00**
Water Lily, console bowl, L-21,
13½" **75.00**
Water Lily, vase, L-19, 8½" .**60.00**
Water Lily, vase, L-5, pink & green,
6½" **25.00**
Wildflower, vase, W-5, 6½" .**40.00**
Woodland, glossy; teapot . . .**45.00**

Hummel

Figurines, plates, and plaques
produced since 1935 by Franz Goebel of West Germany are today
highly collectible, often bringing
prices several times that of their
original retail value. They can generally be dated by their marks, each
variation of which can be attributed
a production period: (1) Crown

mark, 1935-1950 (2) Full Bee mark,
1950-1959 (3) Stylized Bee mark
with variations, 1957-1970 (4)
Three-Line mark, 1964-1972 (5)
Goebel Bee mark 1972-1979 (6)
Current mark, no bee, 1979 to the
present.

**Forest Shrine, Stylized Bee mark,
9½", $500.00.**

Angel with Birds, Crown mark, font,
#22/0, 2¾x3½" **90.00**
Angel with Birds, 3-Line mark, font,
#22/0, 2¾x3½" **25.00**
Baker, Stylized Bee mark, #128,
4¾" **225.00**
Bookworm, Stylized Bee mark, #3/
I, 5½" **225.00**
Bookworm, 3-Line mark, #8,
4" **140.00**
Chick Girl, Crown mark, #57/0,
3½" **395.00**
Child with Flowers, Stylized Bee
mark, font, #36/1, 3½". . .**100.00**
Chimney Sweep, Stylized Bee mark,
#12/2/0, 4" **60.00**
Christ Child, Full Bee mark, #18,
2x6" **110.00**
Congratulations, Crown mark, no
socks, #17/0, 6" **350.00**
Congratulations, Full Bee mark, no
socks, #17/0, 6" **225.00**

156

Doll Mother, Full Bee mark, #67, 4¾" **200.00**

Easter Greetings, 3-Line mark, #378, 5½" **340.00**

Farm Boy, Crown mark, #66, 5¼" **550.00**

Festival Harmony, Full Bee mark, angel with mandolin, #171/II, 10¾" **750.00**

Flower Madonna, Full Bee mark, #10/I (white), 9½" **150.00**

Going to Grandma's, Full Bee mark, #52/0, 4¾" **250.00**

Going to Grandma's, 3-Line mark, #52/0, 4¾" **150.00**

Good Shepherd, Stylized Bee mark, #42/0, 6¼" **90.00**

Good Shepherd, Stylized Bee mark, font, #35/1, 2¾x5¾" .. **100.00**

Goose Girl, Full Bee mark, #47/3/0, 4" **145.00**

Guardian Angel, Stylized Bee mark, font, #29, 2½x5⅝" ..**1,500.00**

Happy Pastime, Crown mark, #69, 3¼" **360.00**

Happy Traveler, Stylized Bee mark, #109/0, 5" **75.00**

Hear Ye Hear Ye, Full Bee mark, #15/0, 5" **180.00**

Heavenly Angel, Full Bee mark, #21/0, 4¼" **100.00**

Herald Angels, Crown mark, candle holder, #37, 2¼x4" ...**460.00**

Herald Angels, Stylized Bee mark, candle holder, #37, 4" .**130.00**

Infant of Krumbad, Stylized Bee mark, #78/VI, 10" **150.00**

Joyful, Full Bee mark, ash tray, #33, 3½x6" **160.00**

Joyful, Full Bee mark, candy box, #III/53, 6¼" **325.00**

Joyous News, Stylized Bee mark, #27/III, 4¾x4¼" **625.00**

Little Fiddler, #2/1, 7½" ..**270.00**

Little Gabriel, Crown mark, #32/1, 5" **300.00**

Little Hiker, Full Bee mark, #16/1, 5½" **185.00**

Little Hiker, Crown mark, #16/2/0, 4¼" **300.00**

St. George and the Dragon, 3-Line mark, 6½", $225.00.

Little Scholar, Stylized Bee mark, #80, 5½" **110.00**

Lullaby, Full Bee mark, candle holder, #24/I, 3¼x5" .. **155.00**

Madonna, Stylized Bee mark, plaque, #48/0, 3x4" **80.00**

March Winds, 3-Line mark, #43, 5" **85.00**

Meditation, Crown mark, #13/0, 5¼" **350.00**

Meditation, Full Bee mark, #13/2/0, 4¼" **150.00**

Not for You, 3-Line mark, #317, 6" **120.00**

Out of Danger, Stylized Bee mark, #56/B, 6¼" **160.00**

Out of Danger, Stylized Bee mark, table lamp, #44/B, 9½". **300.00**

Plate, annual; 1982, in box . **60.00**

Playmates, Full Bee mark, #58/0, 4" **140.00**

Playmates, 3-Line mark, #58/I, 4½" **160.00**

Postman, 3-Line mark, #119, 5¼" **125.00**

Puppy Love, Crown mark, #1, 5" **400.00**

Quartet, 3-Line mark, plaque, #134, 6x6" **225.00**

Sensitive Hunter, Crown mark, #6, 4¾" **500.00**

Shepherd's Boy, Stylized Bee mark, #64, 5½" **130.00**

Singing Lesson, Stylized Bee mark, #63, 2¾" **85.00**

Sister, 3-line mark, #98/0, 5¾" **100.00**

Skier, Full Bee mark, #59, 5¼" **260.00**

Skier, 3-Line mark, #59, 5¼" **145.00**

St George, Stylized Bee mark, #55, 6¾" **225.00**

Imperial Glass

The Imperial Glass Company became a well-known fixture in the glassmaking business in 1910, due to the large quantities of carnival glass they produced. During the next decade they employed the lustre process in the manufacture of another successful product, Imperial Jewels, today called stretch glass. In 1958 Imperial bought the old Heisey and Cambridge molds and reproduced some of their original lines; Imperial marked these items with the 'I' superimposed over a 'G' logo.

Animal, Champ Terrier, caramel slag **200.00**

Animal, elephant, pink carnival, marked Heisey, small .. **15.00**

Animal, rabbit, paperweight, milk glass, marked Heisey .. **10.00**

Animal, Scotty, Heisey **45.00**

Animal, tiger, jade, Heisey . **15.00**

Bird, Wood Duck, caramel slag **27.50**

Bottle, bar; Cape Cod, #244, with stopper **60.00**

Butter dish, Cape Cod **25.00**

Champagne, Cape Cod **6.00**

Compote, Cape Cod, footed, with lid, 6" **45.00**

Gravy boat, Cape Cod **55.00**

Hurricane lamp, Cape Cod, original chimney **85.00**

Pitcher, Cape Cod, milk size, 16-ounce **35.00**

Pitcher, Old Williamsburg, yellow, 32-ounce **25.00**

Ram's head bowl, iridescent cobalt, 10" wide, $87.00.

Relish, Cape Cod, 3-sectioned, 9½" 18.00
Sherbet, Cape Cod, high stem. 60.00
Vase, Dewdrop, amberina, hat shape 45.00
Vase, free-hand, blue & gold iridescent, flared, 5" 110.00
Vase, free-hand, butterscotch, orange lustre throat, 8½" .95.00
Whiskey, Cape Cod 10.00

Imperial Porcelain

From 1947 through 1960, the Imperial Porcelain Company of Zanesville, Ohio, produced a line of figurines, trays, bottles, etc., called Blue Ridge Mountain Boys, designed by Paul Webb. It is for this series that they are best known, although they also produced others: the Al Capp Dogpatch series and American Folklore miniatures, a line of twenty-three animals measuring one inch or less.

American Folklore miniature, cat, 1½" 40.00
American Folklore miniature, hound dogs 35.00

American Folklore miniature, sow 30.00
Ash tray, #105, baby, hound dog, & frog ·..............110.00
Ash tray, #92, 2 men by tree stump, for pipes 125.00
Decanter, #100, outhouse, man, & bird 75.00
Decanter, man, jug, snake, & stump, Hispch Inc, 1946 ......75.00
Figurine, man sitting, 3½". 85.00
Hot pad, Dutch boy with tulips, round, IP mark 30.00
Mug, #94, ma handle, 4¼" ..95.00
Mug, #94, man with yellow beard & red pants handle, 4¼" ..75.00
Pitcher, lemonade 200.00
Planter, #100, outhouse, man, & bird 75.00
Planter, #110, man, with jug & snake, 4½" 65.00
Planter, #81, Uncle Rafe, dog by washtub, IP mark, 4" ..75.00
Shakers, standing pigs, IP mark, 8", pair 95.00

Indian Artifacts

Anything made by or related to

Dog planter #81, 4x5½", $45.00.

the American Indian is of interest to collectors, whether it be a simple utilitarian tool or an object of art. Often each tribe exhibited certain characteristics in their work which help collectors determine the origin of their treasures. Some of the tribes are best known for their expertise in a particular craft. For instance, Navahos were weavers of rugs and blankets, the Zuni excelled in petit-point and inlay jewelry, and the Hopi made beautiful kachina dolls. Ceremonial items, fine beaded clothing and bags, and antique rugs are among the most valuable examples of Indian art.

Nez Perce twined cornhusk bag with false embroidery, native repair, 20x26", $475.00.

Amulet, Cheyenne, turtle shape, beaded, 3" **45.00**
Arrow head, middle Mississippian, tan colored, 3¼" **13.00**
Basket, Alaskan, sea grass, 6" diameter **55.00**
Basket, Chippewa, sweet grass with birch bark lid, 3x4½" .. **45.00**
Basket, mission, squat shape, painted decor, 4x6½" . **275.00**

Basket, Papago, willow & martynia, 2½x5½" **85.00**
Basket, Papago, yucca & martynia, with lid, 4x8" diameter . **30.00**
Bolo, Navaho, 4 turquoise & 1 coral on sterling silver, 4" .. **175.00**
Bowl, Cherokee, incised decoration on gray clay, 2x2½" **30.00**
Bowl, Maricopa, black on polished red clay, 2x3¾" **30.00**
Bowl, Santa Clara, buff on red slip, signed, 4x7½" **135.00**
Bowl, Santa Clara, polished redware, 4x6" **30.00**
Bracelet, Navaho, 5 webbed turquoise on silver **105.00**
Bridle, Navaho, silver **450.00**
Container, Algonquin, birch bark, 3x6½" diameter **30.00**
Container, laced birchbark, punched design, square base, 5" . **65.00**
Container, Plains, polychrome paint on rawhide, 7" **170.00**
Cuffs, Crow, floral bead on white, 8¼" **175.00**
Doll, Plains, cloth body with yarn hair, beaded dress, 5" .. **30.00**
Drill, flint, Texas, 2⅞" **27.00**
Drum, green painted hide over wood hoop with feathers & beads, 14" **55.00**
Fetish, umbilical cord; Plains, blue & white bead work turtle, 6½" **160.00**
Figurine, owl, Zuni, amber on cream, 5" **45.00**
Gauntlets, Yakima, floral bead work, 13", pair **105.00**
Gorget, Plains, shell, 2" **25.00**
Headdress, turkey & maribou feathers, bead work band, 52" long **95.00**
Jar, Hopi, umber & orange geometrics on orange slip, 8" .. **75.00**
Jar, San Ildefonso, double spout with handle, ca 1930, 6½" ... **30.00**
Moccasins, Chippewa, colorful bead work floral with wool cuff **125.00**

Laguna polychrome pottery jar, 1920s, 7x9", $475.00.

Moccasins, Iroquois, beaded floral design with velvet cuff . **70.00**

Moccasins, Sioux, red, white, & blue beads on green, 10¾" . **125.00**

Necklace, large treated turquoise nuggets, 29" **105.00**

Necklace, Navaho, bear claw with turquoise & mother of pearl, 14" **115.00**

Necklace, Navaho, silver squash blossom, early, 26" . . . **300.00**

Necklace, Zuni, bird fetish carved from green serpentine, 2-strand, 30" **75.00**

Necklace, Zuni, fetish with heshi, 3-strand, 30" **225.00**

Painting, Pueblo, gouache, signed Ma Ha Re **105.00**

Point, black flint, notched corners, 1½" **12.00**

Pouch, Chinook, beaded eagle on leather, 9½" **125.00**

Pouch, Woodlands, polychrome floral on black velvet **35.00**

Powder flask, Nez Perce, rawhide with wood stopper **55.00**

Purse, change; Iroquois, beaded, ca 1890, 4x2½" **15.00**

Purse, Iroquois, beaded, ca 1890, 7x7" **25.00**

Rug, Navaho, natural wool, tan, brown, & red, 33x54" . **125.00**

Rug, Navaho, optical design, black, gray, red, & tan wool, 40x 53" **175.00**

Saddle, Plains, sinew-sewn rawhide over wood, ca 1920 . . . **105.00**

Saddle blanket, Navaho, wool twill, red tassels, 30x40" **95.00**

Scraper, Plains, 13½" long . **75.00**

Snowshoes, Cree, wood, rawhide laces, 43" long, pair . . . **65.00**

Snowshoes, Fahlin, bear paw design, 21", pair **35.00**

Spade, flint, 7" long **55.00**

Spoon, Hupa, horn, 6" **20.00**

Tapestry, Navaho, Yeis with turquoise necklaces, 29x 38" **225.00**

Tray, Hopi, wicker, painted brown bird, 16" diameter **105.00**

Klagetoh/North Central Reservation rug, 55x96", M, $600.00.

Inkwells

Since about 1835 when ink was refined, there has been a market for inkwells. Today collectors appreciate them for their beauty, ingenuity, rarity, and styling. They are found in abundance in art glass of all types, brass, bronze, cast iron, wood with glass liners, natural stones, pottery, and pewter.

Apple, Bakelite **55.00**
Bear, carved wood figural, original insert, 8" **60.00**
Bear wearing neck tie, seated, metal, hinged lid, 4" **65.00**
Beehive, relief Orientals, bird atop, bronze, 2x1⅞" **75.00**
Blue glass, octagonal, 2⅜" . **135.00**
Boot, amber glass, with lid . **65.00**
Brass, Chinese, with blotter & letter holder, set **45.00**
Brass, English, 5x9" **48.00**
China, octagonal with floral, English, 2" **42.00**
Cobalt, diamond shape **15.00**
Crystal, plated hinged lid, square, 2¼" **25.00**
Cut glass, blue, pyramidal shape, 2⅞" **50.00**
Cut glass, hinged, bulbous cut top, 5" **200.00**
Cut glass, sapphire blue, hinged lid, 2x2⅝" **110.00**
Daisy & Button, amber, matching lid, 2" **115.00**
Dog, Scottish Terrier, hinged, glass, 3" **150.00**

Cast iron lion head, painted gold, 4", $175.00.

Dog, bow at neck, glass **60.00**
Elk, metal head & cover, glass well insert **50.00**
Flow blue, brass mounts, 6". **195.00**
Green glass, blown, paperweight base, hat-shaped lid ... **50.00**
Sylvanware, light green, English pottery **28.00**
Travel well, black leather .. **30.00**
Violin, brass figural **145.00**
Walrus head, brass figural with 2" tusks, hinged, 4¼" ... **185.00**

Insulators

After the telegraph was invented in 1844, insulators were used to attach the transmission wires to the poles. With the coming of the telephone, their usefullness increased, and it is estimated that over 3,000 types were developed. Collectors today value some of them very highly — the threadless type, for example, often brings prices of several hundred dollars. Color, rarity, and age are all important factors to consider when evaluating insulators. In the 1960s, N.R. Woodward developed a standard system of identification using numbers with a 'C.D.' prefix.

CD, #102, Brookfield, aqua .. **5.00**
CD, #102, California, blue ... **3.00**
CD, #102, Hemingray, aqua. **10.00**
CD,#102.2, Westinghouse ... **8.00**
CD, #106, Hemingray, aqua . **1.00**
CD, #112.5, No Name, deep olive green **10.00**
CD, #115, Armstrong, clear .. **1.00**
CD, #121, Agee, green-aqua . **10.00**
CD, #121, Canada, purple .. **13.50**
CD, #122, McLaughlin, apple green **30.00**
CD, #128, Kerr, clear **4.00**
CD, #131.4, LGT Co, aqua . **50.00**
CD, #133, California, aqua .. **4.00**

CD, #135, Chicago, blue ...**75.00**
CD, #143, Standard, purple. **15.00**
CD, #145, GTP, mauve **20.00**
CD, #145, Hawley, aqua **5.00**
CD, #154, Whital Tatum, pink.**2.00**
CD, #164, Lynchburg, green. **10.00**
CD, #164, Mclaughlin, emerald green **10.00**
CD, #197, Whitall Tatum, medium smoke **10.00**
CD, #233, Pyrex, carnival ..**35.00**
CD, #245, T-H, aqua **65.00**
CD, #252, No 2 Cable, aqua. **15.00**
CD, #262, Columbia, green **70.00**
CD, #287, Locke, aqua **10.00**

Irons

The iron gradually evolved from the smithy-made flatiron to the improved patented models of the 1870s (all of which had to be heated on the stove) to box irons (which held heated slugs), charcoal irons, gas irons, and finally to electric models. Fluting irons, pleating irons, and tailor's irons did little to make ironing day easier, but nevertheless performed specialized jobs efficiently.

Asbestos, sadiron, child's, 4".**25.00**
B&Co #7, sadiron **22.50**

Baby Betsy Ross, electric, in original box **20.00**
Charcoal, cast iron, figural lion finial **35.00**
Charcoal, cast iron, figural rooster finial **50.00**
Child's, Dover, sadiron **30.00**
Child's, Sandy Andy #22, sadiron, 4" **30.00**
Child's, swan figural, cast iron, 2½" **55.00**
Coleman, #609-A, black granite, gas burner **20.00**
Coleman, blue granite, with brass pump **35.00**
Diamond, simply styled, gas burner **22.50**
Fluter, Geneva, cast iron 1866, 2-piece **65.00**
Fluter, Shepherd Hdw, cast iron with 2 slugs **70.00**
Mrs Potts', sadiron with separate wood handle **20.00**
Ober #12 Pat Pend, open holes in handle **15.00**
Pleater, cast iron & brass ..**95.00**
Sadiron, wrought iron with scroll handle, 6½" **85.00**
Sleeve, Sensible #1, detachable handle **30.00**
Tailor's, Cannon, twist handle, 12-lb **38.00**
Tailor's, pressing, twisted/forged-on handle **45.00**

Ober #12 Pat. Pend., $15.00; Enterprise Mfg. Co., fluted handle, $40.00; Turkish-toe model, beaded handle, 2-piece casting, $45.00.

Ironstone

There are many types of decorated ironstone available today, but the most sought-after is the simple white dinnerware sometimes decorated in relief with fruit, grains, foliage, ribbing, and scallops. It was made by many English potters from the last quarter of the 18th century until well into the 1900s.

Baker, Atlantic, oval, no cover, Boote, 1858 .... **31.00**
Bowl, Fuchsia, oval vegetable, with cover, 9" long **60.00**
Bowl, soup; 9⅞" **12.00**
Bowl, vegetable; no pattern, round, Meakin, 5" **6.00**
Cake plate, Basketweave, handles, Shaw & Son, 8½x10½" . **25.00**
Coffeepot, Gothic, Edwards. **165.00**
Compote, Greenwood China Co, 5½" **35.00**
Compote, Haveloch, oval, 10½" **155.00**
Creamer, Grenade, T&R Boote, 1860s, 5½" **62.50**
Creamer, Wheat & Blackberry, Meakin **65.00**
Cup, handleless; Huron, 3¼" diameter **15.00**
Cup, handleless; Trent, 3⅝" diameter **25.00**
Gravy boat, Ceres, 5" **50.00**
Gravy boat, Fuchsia, 5¼" .. **35.00**
Honey dish, Laurel, marked Wedgwood **20.00**
Honey dish, Wheat, J&G Meakin, 4¼" **12.00**
Mold, crown, large **54.00**
Pitcher, brown floral, 10⅝".. **25.00**
Pitcher, Ceres, Elsmore & Forster, 10¾" **125.00**
Pitcher, Corn & Oats, bulbous, Wedgwood, 8½" **85.00**
Pitcher, fully ribbed, Pankhurst, 9¾" **80.00**

Plate, Sydenham, Boote, 9½" diameter **16.00**
Punch bowl, Sydenham, 6x8¾" diameter **85.00**
Sauce tureen, Laurel Wreath, with lid, Elsmore & Forster. . **150.00**
Shaving mug, Potomac, 4" . **75.00**
Soap dish, Octagon, with lid, T&R Boote **35.00**
Sugar bowl, Hyacinth, 7" ... **45.00**
Teapot, Columbia, 9" **125.00**
Toddy cup, Sydenham, low foot, 3¾" **25.00**
Wash bowl & ewer, Wheat, Elsmore & Forster **295.00**
Waste bowl, Columbia, 1850s, 4x 6½" **55.00**

Ivory

Ivory, through primarily thought of as the material composing the elephant's tusk, may also be from the tusks and teeth of other animals. Teeth of the sperm whale is also considered ivory. Much of what we are familiar with are Oriental carvings, but this substance was often used for more utilitarian objects by carvers in other parts of the world as well.

Baby rattle, amber & blue glass beads, 4" **150.00**
Corkscrew, metal with ivory handle, English, 2⅜" **55.00**
Cribbage board, carved openwork, brass feet, 7⅝" **65.00**
Cribbage board, tusk shape, with game pieces, 8¾" **175.00**
Glove stretcher **38.00**
Mallet, 4⅛" **65.00**
Napkin ring, beveled, 1½" .. **15.00**
Pie crimper, cut-out opening at handle top, 6⅜" **95.00**
Pie crimper, wood handle, 6". **75.00**
Rule, folding; with brass fittings, 12" **125.00**

Unmarked ivory thimbles with scrimshaw, $15.00 each.

Rule, folding; marked Made in London, 24" **175.00**
Rule, folding; nickel fittings, marked TM Nelson, 24" **175.00**
Scrimshaw tooth, ship with foliage, 4¾" **150.00**
Shaving brush, traveling; in ivory case, 4¾" **65.00**
Tooth, 4" **35.00**
Top, octagonal, 1¼" **65.00**
Tusk, flat, 41½" **150.00**
Wax seal, ivory handle, brass monogram **55.00**
Wax seal, elaborate carved handle, brass monogram, 2⅝" . **200.00**
Whistle, horn insert in mouthpiece, 2⅜" **115.00**

Jewelry

Today, anyone interested in buying gems will soon find out that the antique stones are the best values. Not only are prices from ⅓ to ½ less than on comparable new jewelry, but the craftsmanship and styling of modern-day pieces are lacking in comparison. Costume jewelry from all periods is popular, especially Art Nouveau and Art Deco examples. Signed pieces are particularly good, such as those by Miriam Haskell, Georg Jensen, David Anderson, and other well-known artists.

Bar pin, brass bird with blue enamel detail **12.50**

Bar pin, cut & faceted garnets, ca 1900 . . . . **85.00**
Bar pin, textured gold, with rubies & diamonds, 1860s **85.00**
Bar pin, 14k, pearl & amethyst sets, 2½" **225.00**
Beads, Bohemian jet, 1895. **100.00**
Beads, Venetian Peking glass, ca 1930 . . . . **75.00**
Bracelet, baby; silver, ¼" . . . **35.00**
Bracelet, bangle; apple-juice clear Catalin with floral back-carving **55.00**
Bracelet, bangle; uncarved Catalin, narrow **3.00**
Bracelet, sterling with 9 lava cameos **110.00**
Bracelet, stretch; original elastic, Catalin & metal **25.00**
Brooch, Art Nouveau embossing, silver, ca 1910 . . . . **85.00**
Brooch, French enamel rooster & marcasites, ca 1900 . . . **35.00**
Brooch, mourning; jet, set with marcasites, ca 1890 . . . **75.00**
Brooch, picture; 14k gold, bow at top, pin-back, 1½x¼" . . . **35.00**
Brooch, portrait; porcelain, miniature size **35.00**

Bracelet, Mexican, sterling silver, marked TaxCo, $135.00.

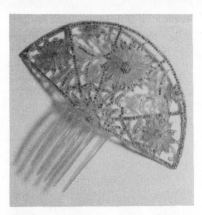

Comb, celluloid set with brilliants, 8" wide, $50.00.

Brooch, rhinestone & simulated pearl sets, marked, ca 1930, large **65.00**
Brooch, sterling, floral design, ca 1930, small **25.00**
Brooch, sterling, marcasite berries & leaves, 2" wide **75.00**
Brooch, sterling, marcasite flower & leaves, ¾x1½" **24.00**
Brooch, sterling silver filigree, ca 1940, small **25.00**
Buckle, Art Deco, set with red rhinestones **18.00**
Dress clip, Art Deco, emamel on gold wash, ca 1925 .... **15.00**
Dress clip, simulated aquamarines, white metal, ca 1935 .. **10.00**
Earrings, copper, marked Gert Barkin, ¾" **18.00**
Earrings, marcasites, small cluster mounting **10.00**
Earrings, rhinestone crescent with pearl, marked Hobe ... **75.00**
Earrings, stylized floral-carved Catalin, pair **6.00**
Hairpin, gilt filigree with wax bead pearls, ca 1930 .... **10.00**
Money clip, sterling, dollar sign set with marcasites **25.00**
Necklace, aurora borealis, blue, 2-strand **28.00**
Necklace, aurora borealis, clear 3-strand **30.00**

Necklace, carved Catalin animal figures on cellulose acetate chain **85.00**
Necklace, chain with attached tassel, marked Monet **16.00**
Necklace, gold color medallion on 30" chain, marked Lane. **72.00**
Necklace, green aventurine beads, 1-strand **25.00**
Pendant, butterscotch amber, 2" wide **65.00**
Pendant, 14k, carved carnelian set, 1½" **125.00**
Pin, multicolor Art Deco design, Catalin, small **20.00**
Pin, stylized floral-carved Catalin, large **25.00**
Pin, with danglers, novelty or patriotic, 1-color Catalin ... **60.00**
Ring, Art Deco, enamel on gold, ca 1925 .... **135.00**
Ring, 10k, oval opal with 4 small diamonds **50.00**

Pin, Norwegian, surrealistic design, sterling silver, 1930s, 2", $125.00.

Kentucky Derby Glasses

Souvenir glasses commemorating the Kentucky Derby have been produced since the 1940s. These have become popular collectibles, especially among race fans.

1940s, aluminum	**125.00**
1940s, plastic Beetleware	**250.00**
1945, short	**350.00**
1945, tall	**125.00**
1948	**45.00**
1949, He Has Seen ... All	**45.00**
1950	**150.00**
1951	**100.00**
1952, Gold Cup	**40.00**
1953	**35.00**
1954	**30.00**
1955	**27.00**
1956	**26.00**
1957	**25.00**
1958, Gold Bar	**24.00**
1958, Iron Liege	**37.50**
1959-1960, ea	**20.00**
1961	**18.00**
1962-1963, each	**16.00**
1964-1965, each	**15.00**
1966	**14.00**
1967-1968, each	**13.00**
1969	**12.00**
1970	**10.00**
1971	**9.00**
1972	**8.00**
1973	**7.00**
1974	**6.00**
1975	**5.00**
1976	**4.50**
1977-1978, each	**4.00**
1979-1980, each	**3.50**
1981-1982, each	**3.00**
1983	**2.50**
1984-1986, each	**2.00**
1987-1988, each	**1.50**

Kewpies

Since first introduced through the pages of *The Ladies' Home Journal*, Rose O'Neill's Kewpies have continued to work their charms on us all. Collectors today treasure dolls with the original O'Neill label. Anything decorated with Kewpies is considered very collectible.

Bell, brass, figural handle	**55.00**
Book, Cordially Yours	**18.00**
Book, Kewpies, by Ruggles	**45.00**
Bowl, 6 Kewpies, marked & signed, 7"	**110.00**
Card holder, metal figural	**50.00**
Dish, Kewpie sits on heart-shape lid, unmarked	**30.00**
Door knocker, brass, figural, 3"	**110.00**
Flannel, seashore, 1914	**22.00**
Kewpie, bisque, jointed arms, signed on foot, 5"	**155.00**
Kewpie, bisque, sitting, holding pencil, 3½"	**395.00**
Kewpie, brass, rare, 4"	**95.00**
Kewpie, celluloid, glass eyes, 8"	**125.00**
Kewpie, celluloid, jointed arms, blue wings, patent #, 2½"	**85.00**
Kewpie, pewter	**25.00**
Kewpie, plastic, jointed arms, 1950s, 8"	**60.00**
Kewpie, plush, Clown, O'Neill tag, EX	**50.00**
Kewpie, wooden, Santa, signed, dated 1913, 12"	**245.00**
Kewpie Cuddles, cloth, with wings, Krueger, Inc, 10"	**100.00**

Kewpie Huggers, Japan, 1920s, 2½", $85.00.

Kewpie Hot 'N Tot, black bisque, marked Germany, 5" . **350.00**
Kewpie Huggers, bisque, Germany, 3½" **125.00**
Kewpie Ragsy, vinyl, molded suit & cap, Cameo, 8" **50.00**
Lapel pin, Kewpie with straight arms **150.00**
Light bulb, Christmas tree . **45.00**
Note paper, signed **10.00**
Pincushion, bisque Kewpie half-doll, 2¾" **325.00**
Pitcher, Kewpies on blue jasper-ware, signed **285.00**
Plate, paper **5.00**
Post card, 2 Kewpies in a basket, signed **25.00**
Poster, dated 1973 .... **30.00**
Recipe book, Jell-O **30.00**
Shakers, Kewpies on tummies, old Japan, pair **45.00**
Thimble, metal, signed **39.00**
Thread holder, metal **69.00**
Tray, brass, Kewpie handle. **30.00**
Tray, pin; Kewpies, Royal Rudol-stadt **45.00**
Whistle, brass, figural **20.00**

Kitchen Collectibles

From the early patented apple peelers, cherry pitters, and food choppers to the gadgets of the twenties and the thirties, many collectors find special appeal in kitchen tools.

Apple peeler, Hudson, cast iron, 3-gear, dated 1882 ...... **55.00**
Apple peeler, Lockey Howland, cast iron, 1856 .... **60.00**
Apple peeler, White Mountain, Goodel, dated 1849 .... **50.00**
Apple peeler, White Mountain #3, Goodel, ca 1898 .... **38.00**
Bean pot, Wagner #8 ...... **30.00**
Bottle corker, Yankee Patent, cast iron & nickel plate ... **125.00**

Copper teakettle, dovetailed, ca 1800s, repaired bottom, replaced finial, $200.00.

Bowl, mixing; clambroth green, 8¾" **30.00**
Butter dish, Jennyware, pink, deep bottom **65.00**
Candy-making pan, brass, American, double handle, 16" diameter **110.00**
Cherry seeder, cast iron, dated 1896 .... **23.00**
Cherry seeder, Enterprise #16, cast iron **36.00**
Cherry seeder, Home, cast iron, dated 1917 .... **35.00**
Cherry seeder, Logan & Strobridge, New Brighton PA **32.00**
Churn, Dazey #20, dated February 14, 1922 .... **70.00**
Churn, Dazey #60, glass ... **60.00**
Churn, Lightening Butter Machine, glass, patent 1917 ..... **45.00**
Colander, brass with punched circles, iron handle **90.00**
Cracker biscuit pricker, carved wood, 4 prongs, 3" **150.00**
Dipper, brass, 4½" diameter bowl, 13" long **75.00**
Dipper, brass, 7½" diameter bowl, 26" long **125.00**
Egg basket, round bottom, heavy wire, folds, old, small .. **25.00**
Egg basket, standing, old wire, with handle **55.00**

Apple peeler, cast iron, mark indistinguishable, 8x6", $50.00.

Egg beater, Dover #11, very small
beaters **35.00**
Food grinder, Enterprise #22, cast
iron **20.00**
Griddle, Wagner, round **20.00**
Grinder, Enterprise #22 . . . **20.00**
Jar holder, wire **3.00**
Kettle, Wagner, bail handle, sales-
man's sample, 3" **24.00**
Kraut cutter, ash, dovetailed hop-
per, 13x44¼" **50.00**
Kraut cutter, butternut, heart cut-
out handle, 7½x20" . . . **150.00**
Lemon squeezer, metal, mechani-
cal, pliers type, EX **7.00**
Maple sugar mold, gingerbread boy,
carved wood . . . . ,**45.00**
Muffin pan, tin, 6 diamond-shaped
cups **14.00**
Pail, milk or water; brass, rolled
rim, brass bail, 9x10" . . **75.00**
Pastry cutter, made of horn, with
fork end, 8½" **40.00**
Pestle, maple, 9" **12.00**
Pie crimper, maple, 6" **20.00**
Pie lifter, patented May 18, 1875,
14½" **30.00**
Pitcher, milk; blue delphite, Py-
rex **30.00**
Popover pan, Wagner **36.00**

Potato masher, cast iron, lacy round
end **22.00**
Rolling pin, curly maple . . . **38.50**
Salt & pepper shakers, delphite,
pair **30.00**
Spatula, wrought iron & brass,
simple style, 7¾" **110.00**
Stew pot, Wagner, bail handle, 2-
quart **10.00**
Teakettle, brass, wood handle &
finial, ca 1920, 8" **45.00**
Wash board, wood frame with brass
rubbing surface **30.00**
Wire wisk, old **8.00**

Knives

Collectors of pocket knives look
for those with bone handles in mint,
unsharpened condition; those with
pearl handles; Case doctor's knives;
and large display models.

Case, #B100, marked Tested, black
composition handle, 1 blade,
3½" **160.00**
Case, #GS2027½, marked Tested,
gold stone handle, 2 blades,
2¾" **210.00**

Case, #M100, marked XX, Red Cracked Ice handle, 1 blade, 3¼" **120.00**

Case, #P249, marked Tested, mottled brown handle, 2 blades, 4" **360.00**

Case, #R1048, marked Tested, candy stripe handle, 1 blade, 4⅛" **260.00**

Case, #02245, Tested, slick black handle, 2 blades, 3¼" .**160.00**

Case, #22001R, Tested, slick black handle, 2 blades, 2⅝" .**110.00**

Case, #3124, marked Tested, yellow composition, 1 blade, 3".**120.00**

Case, #3200, marked Tested, yellow composition handle, 2 blades, 4" **460.00**

Case, #3224½, marked Tested, yellow composition handle, 2 blade, 3" **135.00**

Case, #5205RAZ, marked Tested, stag handle, 2 blades, 4" **335.00**

Case, #52052, marked Tested, stag handle, 2 blades, 3½" .**160.00**

Case, #5232, marked Tested, stag handle, 2 blades, 3⅝" .**160.00**

Case, #61048, Tested, green bone handle, 1 blade, 4⅛" ..**150.00**

Case, #61215½, marked Tested, 1 blade, 5" **675.00**

Case, #6151, marked Tested, green bone handle, 1 blade, 5¼" **500.00**

Case, #6185, marked XX, red bone handle, 1 blade, 5¼" ..**110.00**

Case, #6213, marked Tested, Rogers bone handle, 2 blades, 4" **600.00**

Case, #6220½, marked XX, bone handle, 2 blades, 2½" ..**50.00**

Case, #6233, marked 10 Dot, delrin handle, 2 blades, 2⅝" ..**40.00**

Case, #6235½, marked Tested, stag handle, 2 blades, 3¼" .**150.00**

Case, #81051, marked Tested, pearl handle, 1 blade, 3⅞" ..**400.00**

Kentucky Rifle commemorative knife by A.G. Russell, $75.00.

Case, #92042, marked XX, cracked ice handle, 2 blades, 3" . **28.00**

Case, #92210, marked Tested, cracked ice handle, 2 blades, 3⅜" **400.00**

Primble, #4984, bone handle, 2 blades, 3½" **55.00**

Primble, #900, brown bone handle, 2 blades, 3" **25.00**

Primble, #919, peachseed bone handle, 3 blades, 3⅛" . . **45.00**

Remington, #R1 handle, 1 blade, 3⅜" **70.00**

Remington, #R111, redwood handle, 3 blades, 3½" **100.00**

Remington, #R1128, cocobolo handle, 2 blades, 3⅜". **1350.00**

Remington, #R1284, pearl handle, 2 blades, 3" **190.00**

Remington, #R1325, pyremite handle, 1 blade, 3" . . . **130.00**

Remington, #R1437, ivory handle, 1 blade, 4¼" **140.00**

Remington, #R1572, black handle, 1 blade, 3" **100.00**

Remington, #R175, pyremite handle, 2 blades, 3¾" . **150.00**

Remington, #R1833, bone handle, 2 blades, 3⅝" **150.00**

Remington, #R22, black handle, 1 blade, 3⅜" **90.00**

Remington, #R252, black handle, 2 blades, 3⅝" **150.00**

Remington, #R328, cocobolo handle, 2 blades, 3⅞" **160.00**

Remington, #R3414, pearl handle, 3 blades, 3⅜" **290.00**

Remington, #R3520BU, buffalo horn handle, 3 blades, 3⅜" . **225.00**

Remington, #R3575, pyremite handle, 3 blades, 3⅞" . **200.00**

Remington, #R3933, stag handle, 2 blades, 3⅞" **400.00**

Remington, #R4200, buffalo horn handle, 3 blades, 3⅜" . **215.00**

Remington, #R4443, bone handle, 3 blades, 3¼" **200.00**

Remington, #R4548, cocobolo handle, 3 blades, 4" . . **150.00**

Remington, #R55, pyremite handle, 2 blades, 3⅜" **170.00**

Remington, #R590, buffalo horn handle, 2 blades, 3¼" . **250.00**

Remington, #R609, metal handle, 1 blade, 3⅜" **185.00**

Remington, #R983, bone handle, 2 blades, 2⅞" **130.00**

Russell & Co, hunting, black wood handle, 8½" **10.00**

Schrade Cutlery, #115S, bone handle, 1 blade, 3⅜" . . . **70.00**

Schrade Cutlery, #1152, ebony handle, 1 blade, 3⅜" . . . **35.00**

Schrade Cutlery, #1157¼, stained bone handle, 1 blade, 3⅜" **75.00**

Schrade Cutlery, #1251, cocobolo handle, 1 blade, 3¼" . . . **40.00**

Schrade Cutlery, #1354¼B, black celluloid handle, 1 blade, 4" **65.00**

Schrade Cutlery, #1514C, cocobolo handle, 1 blade, 4" . . . **150.00**

Schrade Cutlery, #2012, ebony, 2 blades, 3⅝" **70.00**

Schrade Cutlery, #2023, bone, 2 blades, 3⅝" **100.00**

Schrade Cutlery, #7086B, mother-of-pearl, 2 blades, 3" . . . **50.00**

Schrade Cutlery, #7118, buffalo horn, 2 blades, 3⅜" **55.00**

Winchester, #1608, cocobolo, 1 blade, 3⅜" **70.00**

Winchester, #1921, stag handle, 1 blade, 3⅜" **120.00**

Winchester, #2840, stag handle, 2 blades, 2" **100.00**

Winchester, #2992, stag handle, 2 blades, 3⅝" **140.00**

Winchester, #4910, stag handle, 4" **550.00**

Labels

The colorful lithographed labels that were once used on wooden packing crates are being collected for their artwork and advertising. Clever association between company name or location and depicted themes are common; particularly good examples of this are usually most desirable. For instance, Santa Paula lemon labels show a jolly Santa Claus, and Red Cat oranges have a cat mascot.

Brynhilda, tobacco, $9.00.

Blue and Gray Oranges and Grapefruit, 1920s, 9x9", $15.00.

Airline, globe with wings, stars, red, white, & blue **1.00**
Airport, Bourbon Whiskey, ca 1934, 3x5" **5.00**
American Tribute, Uncle Sam seated at his desk **20.00**
Anne Arundel Pride Tomatoes, field with farmer & wagon, 8x15" **16.00**
Bare Foot Boy Brand Tomatoes, 8x18" **12.00**
Big Wolf Cigars, green wolf with red lettering & gold trim . . **18.00**
Carefree, pretty laughing blond, blue **1.00**
Conewango, Indian in yellow canoe on lake **15.00**
El Arabe Imported Sumatra Wrapper-Long Filler, Arabian on horse **20.00**
First Cabinet Cigars, President Washington & his cabinet signing paper **100.00**

Gen Fitzhugh Lee, portrait & scenes with gold trim, 10x12" . .**40.00**
Gettysburg Commanders, portraits & flags, 11½x14½" . . .**165.00**
Golden Rod, spray of goldenrod, black **1.00**
Grey Bear Cigars, brown bear in field with pond, 1930 . .**15.00**
Lady in western garb smoking cigar, embossed, 9½x11" .**18.00**
Lone Eagle, ca 1930, 13x5" . .**6.00**
Magnolia, huge white magnolia blossom, navy blue **8.00**
Mark Antony, soldier in Roman helmet, maroon **2.00**
Mark Twain Cigars, ca 1910, 7x 9" **5.00**
Marquita, pretty brunette holding orange, blue & purple . . .**5.00**
Medal of Honor Cigars, ribbon & medal, embossed **15.00**
Old Black Joe Butter Beans, ca 1930, 5½x4" **4.00**

Boatmen's Bank Building, tobacco, $10.00.

Pure Gold, prospector & mule, gold
& blue **1.00**
Redlands Foothill, orchard scene
with Spanish mission ...**2.00**
Smoke New Cuba Cigars, faces of
Gomez & Garcia, 1897 .**15.00**
Snow Owl Apples, white owl, yellow
& white, fruit crate **15.00**
Upland Pride, red rose & bud on
navy blue **4.00**
Wake Up, colorful rooster, 1888,
10½" square **15.00**
Western Queen, pretty Indian
maiden, bright green & royal
blue **4.00**
Wide Awake, battleships on ocean,
Uncle Sam, 10½x13½" .**20.00**

Lace, Linens, and Needlework

Crocheted and tatted lace are
varieties of handwork most often
encountered at flea markets today;
and collectors can still appreciate
the tedium, expertise, and eyestrain
that went into their making. If your
treasured laces are yellowed or
stained, an instant tea bath can be
used to obtain a natural ecru look
and is far less damaging to the old
threads than using bleach to whiten
them. Doilies are often framed and
hung in groupings on bedroom walls
or used to top throw pillows. From
remnants of lace trims, you can
create your own Victorian 'waist' —
either trim a ready-made or sew one
up using a basic pattern. Machine
washing is not recommended.

Bedspread, crochet, Popcorn &
Diamond patterns, white,
95x108" **210.00**
Bedspread, all-over floral embroi-
dery on white, crochet edge,
77x90" **125.00**
Blanket, white & red woven wool,
62x77" **115.00**
Blanket, wool, white & brown plaid,
hand sewn, minor wear, 70x72",
EX **225.00**
Centerpiece, Battenburg lace, 11½"
square **29.00**
Centerpiece, Battenburg lace, 16½"
square **45.00**
Doily, Battenburg lace, flower pat-
tern, ecru, 10", M **85.00**
Doily, crochet, 'BREAD,' white 5x
12" **15.00**
Hankerchief, Battenburg lace edge,
white **18.00**
Pillowcase, Battenburg inserts,
31x19", pair, M **50.00**
Runner, overshot,11½x28".. **20.00**
Sheet, cotton with crochet insert &
trim, 84x90", EX **35.00**

Battenburg lace tablecloth, 68" diameter, $250.00.

Sheet, homespun linen, handsewn, 74x76" **45.00**

Sheet, homespun wool, handsewn, 67x78" **45.00**

Tablecloth, Battenburg lace, 70" diameter **275.00**

Tablecloth, elaborate crochet border, 50" diameter **125.00**

Tablecloth, hand crochet, white 60x66" **145.00**

Tablecloth, linen, red & white, 44x68" **65.00**

Tablecloth, linen, white, 72x104", with 12 napkins **130.00**

Tablecloth, overshot, brown & white, 40x60" **100.00**

Tablecloth, rayon, ivory, Daisy Lace, 1930s, 68x108", EX **85.00**

Vanity set, Tuscany lace, off-white, 3-piece, EX **45.00**

Lamps

From the primitive rush light holder and Betty lamp to Tiffany's elaborate stained glass lamps, lighting devices have evolved with the style of the times and the development of better lighting methods. Depending on the taste of the collector, there are many types that are especially desirable. Miniature figural and art glass lamps are popular and often bring prices of several hundred dollars.

Fairy lamps, Gone-with-the-Wind lamps, and pattern glass lamps of many types are also treasured. Aladdin lamps are the most popular kerosene lamps; they have been made since 1908 by the Mantle Lamps Company of America in over eighteen models and more than one hundred styles. Emeralite lamps, recognized by their green cased glass shades, are also highly collectible. They were made from about 1909 into the forties by the H.G. McFaddin Company in a variety of styles.

Student lamp, brass with green glass shade, 21", $395.00.

Aladdin, Alacite, G-230, regency lamp, electric, EX **22.00**

Aladdin, Beehive, B-81, green crystal, complete, EX **75.00**

Aladdin, Beehive, B-83, ruby crystal, with burner **280.00**

Aladdin, Cathedral, #107, clear, complete **80.00**

Aladdin, Cathedral, #107, clear, NM **80.00**

Aladdin, Corinthian, B-104, clear, black base **55.00**

Aladdin, hanging lamp, #8, original shade, EX **400.00**

Aladdin, hanging lamp, Model #3, with #203 shade, EX . **500.00**

Aladdin, hanging lamp, Model B, parchment shade, EX . **145.00**

Aladdin, Lincoln Drape, B-77, ruby, old, tall, NM **45.00**

Aladdin, Lincoln Drape, Short; B-62, ruby crystal, M . . . **400.00**

Aladdin, Orientale, B-131, green, EX **100.00**

Aladdin, Orientale, B-133, silver, EX **110.00**

Aladdin, Quilt, B-86, green moonstone, complete, EX . .**110.00**

Aladdin, Simplicity, B-29, green, VG **60.00**

Aladdin, table lamp, #12 . . .**65.00**

Aladdin, Venetian, #103, rose, NM . . . . :**115.00**

Aladdin, Venetian, #99 . . .**250.00**

Aladdin, Washington Drape, B-53, clear, no oil fill, plain stem, EX **85.00**

Argand, cast metal, brass decoration, cut & etched, EX. **550.00**

Betty, sheet iron, riveted, with hanger, 4½" **150.00**

Fairy, blue Diamond Quilt mother-of-pearl, clear Clarke base, 4⅝" **165.00**

Fairy, blue verre moire, ruffled Clarke base, 5½" **425.00**

Fairy, burmese with florals, clear marked base, 4" **250.00**

Fairy, green overshot, Clarke base, pyramid size, 3¾" **110.00**

Float, 1 clear bowl, gilt metal stand, slate base, 11½" **75.00**

Brass whale oil lamp with blown globe, 13", $175.00; Tin candle lantern, punch-decorated sliding door, three glass panels, 9", $175.00.

Gone-with-the-Wind, Grape & Leaf, red satin, 29" **650.00**

Gone-with-the-Wind, mums hand-painted on milk glass, 10" shade, 19" **350.00**

Gone-with-the-Wind, smokey satin, blown-out baby face, all original **750.00**

Hanging, hall, florals on clear, 13½" diameter **275.00**

Hanging, Rubena with optic opal stripes, 10" shade **375.00**

Hanging, Swirled Rib, cranberry shade, clear font, brass frame, 30" **375.00**

Kerosene, cobalt to white to clear with black amethyst foot, 9½", EX **150.00**

Kerosene, yellow cased satin with diamond motif, domed shade, 16" **950.00**

Lantern, candle, tin, 3-corner shape, turret top, 18½", VG . .**210.00**

Lantern, skater's, brass . . .**85.00**

Miniature, Acanthus, pink & white, NM **290.00**

Miniature, Cone, pink-cased satin, nutmeg burner, 8", . . .**325.00**

Miniature, Delft-style cherubs on porcelain, replaced burner, 6", EX **300.00**

Miniature, Octavia, green, original burner & chimney, EX. **125.00**

Miniature, ruby, melon ribs, 4⅝", EX **80.00**

Pattern glass, Apollo, blue with burner, 12" **275.00**

Pattern glass, Centennial, finger lamp, 8" **235.00**

Pattern glass, Daisy & Button, blue, finger lamp **155.00**

Pattern glass, Feather Duster, amber, 8" **140.00**

Pattern glass, Rosa, emerald green, M **70.00**

Pattern glass, Torpedo, flat, finger lamp **80.00**

Peg, pear-form, pressed in 2-part mold, applied stem, 4" .**30.00**

Peg, yellow overlay mushroom shade, brass candlestick, 15x 6½" **525.00**

Rush light, wrought iron & brass holder on boot foot ...**400.00**

Sconce, prisms & beads on gilt frame, electric, 14", pr. 350.00

Slag glass, reticulated motif, Art Nouveau bronze standard, 24" **525.00**

Student, green cased shade, nickel-plated frame, 21" **550.00**

Whale oil/burning fluid, Harp (Lyre), flint, Sandwich, 8", NM **150.00**

Letter Openers

Made from wood, ivory, glass, and metals, letter openers are fun to collect without being expensive. Generally the most valuable are advertising openers and figurals made of brass, bronze, copper or iron.

Bear's head, glass eyes, carved wood, 14¾" **45.00**

Dog's head, sterling with celluloid blade **35.00**

Fuller Brush, advertising tortoise shell plastic **7.50**

Gargoyle handle, brass, openwork blade, 10¼" **105.00**

Lone Star Bag & Bagging, copper, 12" **15.00**

Monkey, carved ivory **38.00**

Northern Waste Co **20.00**

Pacific States Fire Insurance Co, 8" **10.00**

Remington **15.00**

Scarab, brass, large **38.00**

Seashell, pewter **12.50**

Train engine, celluloid with steel blade, Roland Electric .**15.00**

Uneeda Biscuit, die-cut tin .**75.00**

Welsbach **65.00**

License Plates

Early porcelain license plates are treasured by collectors, and those in good shape often sell for more than $100 for the pair when found in excellent condition.

California, black, 1976 .....**3.00**

Illinois, 1923 ....**12.50**

Kansas, 1916, G **20.00**

Michigan, porcelain, 1914, G **140.00**

Nebraska, leather, pre-state.**125.00**

New Jersey, 1921 ....**22.50**

New York, porcelain, 1912 .**65.00**

North Dakota, 1970 ....**3.50**

Oregon, 1927 ....**16.50**

Pennsylvania, porcelain, the year 1906 ....**200.00**

For achievement in the Army/Navy, marked Doehler, Toledo, ca 1942, 8½", $20.00.

Pennsylvania, porcelain, the year
1915 ....**32.00**
Rhode Island, 1940 ....**10.75**
Wisconsin, 1915, G **10.00**

Locks

Among the most collectible locks on the market today are those made by Yale, Sargent, Winchester, and Keen Kutter. When evaluating the value of locks consider construction, condition, and rarity. Generally, brass and bronze locks outsell those made of steel or iron. Some railroad locks are included here, also see section on Railroadiana.

Internal Revenue with '$,' numbered, brass, 2½", $150.00.

Bull, iron lever tumbler, word Bull embossed on front, 2⅝" .**10.00**
Chicago Combination Lock Co, logo on front, brass, 2¾" **75.00**
Cleveland, 4-way, 8-lever ..**40.00**
Columbia, embossed Columbia 6-Lever, brass push-key type, 2¼" **30.00**
DM&Co, wrought iron lever type, barrel key, 4¼" **15.00**
Dragon, word Dragon & dragon embossed on front, 2⅞" .**12.00**
Eagle, brass pin-tumbler type, Eagle stamped on body, 2⅞" ..**15.00**
Edwards, iron, Edwards stamped on body **12.00**
Fraim, power lever, no key ..**5.00**
Goliath, steel, Goliath 8-Lever stamped on front **15.00**
Indian Head, iron lever tumbler, Indian head emblem on front, 3" **40.00**
Jackson's, brass lever tumbler, Jackson's stamped on front, 2½" **25.00**
Miller, steel, Miller 8-Lever stamped on front **12.00**
Number or letter combination with 3 disks, brass, 1¾" **65.00**
Pearl, brass pin-tumbler type, Pearl embossed on body, 2⅛" .**12.00**

Rex, steel case warded type, embossed letters, 2⅝" **15.00**
Ruby, brass lever tumbler, Ruby embossed in scroll, 2¾".**25.00**
Samson, brass, Samson 8-Lever stamped on front **15.00**
Segal, iron pin-tumbler type, Segal embossed on shackle, 3¾" **35.00**
Siberian, brass lever tumbler, Siberian embossed on shackle, 2½" **50.00**
Ten Star, embossed Ten Star 6-Lever, push key, 2¼" ..**40.00**
Unique, iron lever tumbler, word Unique embossed on front, 3¼" **35.00**
Winchester, brass lever tumbler, Winchester embossed on front, 3" **95.00**
Yale, Bi-Centric, 2 key holes, with key **50.00**
Yale, brass, 6-lever type, Yale embossed on front **10.00**

Lu Ray Pastels

Introduced in the 1940s by Taylor, Smith, and Taylor of East Liverpool, Ohio, Lu Ray Pastels is a line that has become popular with today's collectors of American dinnerware. It was made in solid colors: Windsor Blue, Gray, Persian Cream, and Sharon Pink.

Teapot, 5", $25.00.

Bowl, salad; large **30.00**
Bowl, tab handle, 6" **10.00**
Bowl, vegetable, 9" **8.50**
Casserole, with cover **55.00**
Creamer, demitasse; ovoid . **45.00**
Cup & saucer **7.50**
Pitcher, bulbous **30.00**
Pitcher, footed **35.00**
Plate, cake **40.00**
Plate, very rare, 8" **15.00**
Platter, oval, 11½" **8.00**
Sauce boat, fast stand **15.00**
Shakers, pair **8.50**
Sugar bowl, with cover **7.50**
Teapot, with cover **25.00**
Tray, pickle **10.00**
Tumbler, juice **10.00**
Tumbler, water **12.00**

Lunch Boxes

In the early years of this century, tobacco companies often packaged their products in tins that could later be used for lunch boxes. By the 1930s oval lunch boxes designed to appeal to school children were produced. The rectangular shape that is now popular was preferred in the 1950s. Character lunch boxes decorated with the faces of TV personalities, super heroes, Disney and cartoon characters are especially sought after by collectors today.

Addams Family, 1974, EX . **15.00**
Annie, with thermos, 1981 . **12.00**
Annie Oakley, 1955, EX ... **45.00**
Buck Rogers, with thermos, 1979, NM **30.00**
Campbell Soup Kids, with thermos, 1965, EX **35.00**
Charlie's Angels **13.00**
Daniel Boone, Aladdin, EX . **50.00**
Dukes of Hazzard, 1980 ... **12.00**
Empire Strikes Back, 1980 . **12.00**
Flintstones, 1971, EX **15.00**
Green Hornet, with thermos, 1966, EX **45.00**
Hee-Haw, 1970 .... **12.00**
Hopalong Cassidy, with thermos, NM **35.00**
Indiana Jones, w/thermos .. **13.00**
Lawman, w/thermos, 1961 . **85.00**

Clockwise from top: Sporting activities, marked Metal Package, ca 1920s, $60.00; Mickey Mouse, Geuder Mfg., ca 1935, VG, $150.00+; Circus scene, National Can Co., ca 1930, $45.00; Mother Goose characters, handle marked Kiddyland, ca 1930, $75.00; Girls jumping rope, no mark, $45.00.

Peanuts, Snoopy at piano . . **12.00**
Peter Pan, Disney, 1969 . . . **30.00**
Roy Rogers & Dale Evans, 1953,
    NM **50.00**
School Bus, Disney, dome top, 1962,
    EX **20.00**
Tom Corbett, with thermos, blue,
    1952 . . . . **110.00**
Trigger, ca 1950 . . . . **20.00**
Wild Bill Hickok & Jingles, 1955,
    EX **40.00**
Winnie the Poo, NM **20.00**
Yellow Submarine, 1968 . . **125.00**
Zorro, 1958, NM **48.00**

Magazines

Magazines are collected for both their contents and their covers, often signed by well-known illustrators. Their values hinge on the type and quality of the advertising they contain, their cover illustrations, age, rarity, and condition.

Ace, 1937, December Vol 1, No 3,
    NM **10.00**
American Builder, 1926 . . . **15.00**
Arizona Highways Magazine, 1927,
    March **5.00**
Atlantic, 1959, May **15.00**
Atlantic, 1960, July **25.00**
Automobile Trade Journal, 1917,
    June **6.00**
Barnum & Bailey, 1956 . . . . **10.00**
Collier, October 24, 1936, Maxfield
    Parrish illustrated **25.00**
Cosmopolitan, 1893, Nov. . . **30.00**
Cosmopolitan, 1939, March, E
    Hemingway article **27.00**
Esquire, 1942, July, Varga illus-
    trated **10.00**
Fur, Fish and Game; 1947, Septem-
    ber **3.00**
Godey's Ladies Magazine, 1867,
    June **12.00**
Harper's Weekly, 1887, February
    12 . . . . **12.50**

Screenland, Lana Turner on cover, February 1952, $8.00.

Harper's Weekly, 1887, March 19,
    EX **8.50**
Harper's Weekly, 1905, June 10,
    Japan's Victory **9.50**
International Socialist Review,
    1911, August, Eugene V Debs,
    EX **45.00**
Jet, 1963, May, Would Negro Stars
    Join Freedom Fight **5.00**
Jet, 1963, November **5.00**
Ladies' Home Journal, 1890, De-
    cember **8.00**
Ladies' Home Journal, 1927, Rose
    O'Neill cover **10.00**
Laff, 1942, May **8.00**
Liberty, 1939, January **16.00**
Life, 1963, DNA molecule cover
    story, NM **8.00**
Life, 1968, April, Martin Luther
    King on cover **22.00**
Life, 1969, September, Coretta Scott
    King on cover **20.00**
Life, 1971, July 23, Clint Eastwood
    on cover **4.00**
Life, 1972, December 8, Diana Ross
    on cover **4.00**
Life, 1972, January 28, John Wayne
    on cover **4.00**

Life, 1972, July 28, Norman Mailer on cover 2.00
Life, 1972, March 3, Mao-Nixon on cover 3.00
Look, 1938, August 30, Duke of Windsor on cover 5.00
McCall's, 1929, Zane Grey novel, NM 5.00
Newsweek, 1955, October 3, World Series cover 8.00
Photohistory, 1937, War in Spain, NM 5.00
Playboy, 1976, November, Jimmy Carter interview 35.00
Ramparts, 1970, January ...8.00
Saturday Evening Post, 1939, October 15.00
Saturday Evening Post, 1942, May, William Faulkner story. 25.00
Saturday Evening Post, 1943, Dec, J Frank Dobie story ...12.00
Saturday Evening Post, 1944, February 25.00
Saturday Evening Post, 1944, March 15.00
Saturday Evening Post, 1946, April 6 ....25.00

Saturday Evening Post, 1957, November 19.00
Saturday Evening Post, 1960, April, Ray Bradbury story ...18.00
Saturday Evening Post, 1978, February 10.00
Screen Guide, 1941, September, Carole Landis on cover .17.00
Texas Monthly, 1977, April ..5.00
Thrill, 1942, January 8.00
Time, 1969, March 3 ....4.00
Town & Country, 1909, January, EX 5.00
TV Guide, 1960, May 7, Elvis Presley on cover 10.00
TV Guide, 1963, July 27, Muppets on cover 4.00
Weird Tales, 1932, August .70.00
Woman's Home Companion, 1904, EX 5.00
Workbasket, 1957, April 2.00
Workbasket, 1960, Nov 2.00
Yank, 1945, Eisenhower on cover, NM 5.00

Majolica

The type of majolica earthenware most often encountered was made during the 1880s, reaching the height of its popularity in the Victorian period. It was made abroad and in this country as well. It is usually vividly colored, and nature themes are the most common decorative devices. Animal and bird handles and finials and dimensional figures in high relief were used extensively.

Ash tray, snake charmer with snake on Persian rug 80.00
Bowl, centerpiece; flowered garland with wicker decor, Wedgwood, large 550.00
Bowl, Morning Glories, napkin form, 5½" 75.00
Bread tray, Twin Shells on Wave, 14" 225.00

Saturday Evening Post, Lyendecker cover, December 28, 1929, $20.00.

Pitcher, wild roses, 8", $150.00.

Butter pat, Shell & Seaweed, unmarked Etruscan, EX .. **65.00**

Chamber pot, Avalon, large. **230.00**

Cheese keeper, cherub with large crane, 12½" **300.00**

Cuspidor, Bamboo, 8" **230.00**

Figurine, cupid carrying shell, Minton, 8" **600.00**

Fruit dish, Shell & Seaweed, Etruscan **150.00**

Humidor, Arab **85.00**

Humidor, Black boy **150.00**

Oyster plate, 6 sunflowers, 10" diameter **175.00**

Pitcher, Basketweave & Bamboo Flower, 7½" **95.00**

Pitcher, Dogwood, pink on cream, 7¾" **100.00**

Pitcher, flowers, berries & leaves, English, 6¼" **70.00**

Pitcher, palm leaves on barrel shape, 6" **70.00**

Pitcher, trout figural, 12" . **150.00**

Pitcher, Water Lily, 6" ... **130.00**

Planter, Floral & Fern, unmarked, 7" **195.00**

Plate, Bird & Cherry Trees, unmarked, 8" **60.00**

Plate, Fern & Floral, 8" **80.00**

Plate, oyster; turquoise shells, Minton, 10" **225.00**

Plate, Shell & Seaweed, Wedgwood, 9" **150.00**

Plate, Water Lily, green, Minton, 9" **125.00**

Plate, Wheat & Flowers, with bows, 8" **70.00**

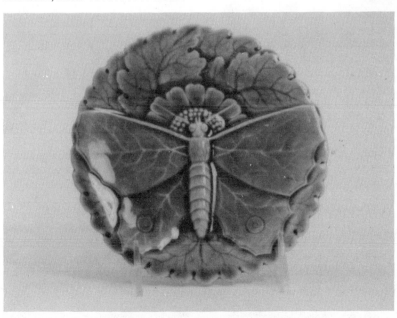

Plate, moth, marked Schultz, 6½", $45.00.

Platter, Blackberry, light blue & tan, 14" 135.00
Platter, ferns & leaves, open handles, 12" 130.00
Platter, shells on turquoise wicker, Wedgwood, 23" 450.00
Sauce dish, Lily of the Valley, Germany 30.00
Spoon holder, Fan, 5" 90.00
Sugar bowl, Cauliflower ..175.00
Sugar bowl, Leaf & Bow, 4" 90.00
Teapot, Bamboo, Griffin-Smith-Hill, 6" 175.00
Teapot, Cauliflower 175.00
Tile, multicolor floral, 6x6" .40.00
Tray, bread; Give Us This Day, 12x11" 200.00
Vase, bird on branch, 7" ..175.00
Waste bowl, Blackberry ...85.00

Toby pitcher, 6", $200.00.

Marbles

Because there are so many varieties of marbles that interest today's collectors, we suggest you study a book on that specific subject such as the one by Edward Grist, published by Collector Books. The larger marbles (1½" to 2¼") are the most expensive, especially the Lutz type with gold flaking, the Onionskins, Micas, and some of the rare Sulfides (clear glass marbles with figures inside). Condition is extremely important. Naturally, chips occured; and, though some may be ground down and polished, the values of badly-chipped and repolished marbles are low.

Agate, 1¾" 50.00
Banded Opaque Swirl, ¾" ..60.00
Banded Transparent Swirl, ¾" 5.00
Bennington, brown & blue mottle, 1¾" 10.00
China, decorated, 1¾" 300.00
Clambroth, blue/white, ¾".. .75.00
Clear Swirl, Lutz-type, clear with gold & white swirls, ¾" .65.00
Comic Strip, Betty Boop ...55.00
Comic Strip, Orphan Annie. 40.00
Coreless Swirl, ¾" 15.00
Cork Screw, machine-made .1.00
End of Day, pontil, ¾" 60.00
Indian Swirl, ¾" 75.00
Indian Swirl, 1¾" 300.00
Latticino Core Swirl, ¾" ...10.00
Lobed Core Swirl, ¾" 25.00
Mica, blue, ¾" 20.00
Mica, cobalt, ½" 30.00
Mica, gold, ¾" 35.00
Onionskin, with mica, ¾" ..65.00
Onionskin, with mica, 1¾". 350.00
Onionskin, yellow & red, 1¾" 250.00
Onionskin Lutz, with gold flakes, ¾" 125.00
Onionskin Lutz, 1¼" 300.00
Opaque Swirl, ¾" 35.00
Peppermint Onion, ⅞" 35.00
Peppermint Swirl, red, white, & blue opaque, ¾" 75.00
Peppermint Swirl, with mica flakes, ¾" 100.00

Ribbon Core Transparent Swirl, ¾", $25.00; 1¾", $150.00.

Ribbon Core, Lutz-type, clear on transparent colors, 1¾" **500.00**
Solid Core Swirl, ¾" **15.00**
Solid Opaque, pink, ¾" **20.00**
Steelie, ½" **15.00**
Steelie, ¾" **20.00**
Sulfide, baboon, 1⅜", VG .. **165.00**
Sulfide, baby in a basket, 2" **300.00**
Sulfide, bird, 2", EX **150.00**
Sulfide, child in dress, 2" . **275.00**
Sulfide, dog begging, 1¼" .. **75.00**
Sulfide, dog with bushy tail, 1⅝" **125.00**
Sulfide, dove on post, 1⅛" . **275.00**
Sulfide, eagle, 1⅝" **185.00**
Sulfide, lion, light purple glass, 1⅝" **275.00**
Sulfide, number 7, 1¼" ... **250.00**
Sulfide, pair of doves in blue glass, 1¼" **700.00**
Sulfide, pig, 1¼" **60.00**
Sulfide, pony, 1¼" **95.00**
Sulfide, rooster, 1¾" **155.00**

Match Holders

Because early matches were eas-
ily combustible, they were stored in match holders, usually wall-hanging or table-top models. Though the safety match was invented in 1855, the habit was firmly entrenched, and match holders remained popular well into the 20th century.

Acorns & oak leaves, brass, wall mount, 5½x6½" **85.00**
Boot, amber glass, striker .. **36.00**
Bucket, blue opalescent, cut pattern, tab handles, 3" ... **45.00**
Cowboy boot, copper, 4" **17.50**
Devil, cast iron figural, EX . **65.00**
Double, lady in knickers on unicycle, silverplate, 8" .. **145.00**
Girl at garden gate, lithograph on tin, wall mount **10.00**
Hanging game bag with horn, painted cast iron, Patent dated, 8" **35.00**
Hat, green paint on tin, black trim, 2⅜" **50.00**
Indian head, silver, 2½" **50.00**
Lacy scrolls & fleur-de-lis, cast iron, Patent dated 1870, wall mount **65.00**
Maltese Cross, tin, double, wall mount **20.00**

Man holding barrel, bisque, Germany **45.00**
Parrots, parian **45.00**
Shoe, Quimper **45.00**
Smoking pipe, milk glass, 4".**12.00**
Venus & cupid, cast iron, wall mount, V&M, 1915 . . . .**95.00**

Lady's boots, cast metal, 4", $28.00.

Match Safes

Before cigarette lighters were invented, matches were carried in pocket-size match safes, as simple or elaborate as the owner's financial status and flair for fashion dictated.

Arm & Hammer, advertising gutta percha, oval **40.00**
Book, brass figural **35.00**
Dog, relief on chrome **44.00**
Gutta percha, plain, 1⅝x3" .**20.00**
Kidney shape, sterling **35.00**
Man riding horse, relief on silverplate **85.00**
Men gambling & drinking at a table, sterling, 1¾x2¼" **100.00**
Milk pail, brass figural . . .**185.00**
Pig, brass figural **110.00**
Spaniel, relief on chrome, celluloid trim **50.00**
Violin, brass figural **75.00**
Walnut, brass figural **200.00**

Sterling, embossed Nouveau figures, $75.00.

McCoy

A popular collectible with flea market goers, McCoy pottery has been made in Roseville, Ohio, since 1910. They are most famous for their extensive line of figural cookie jars, more than two hundred in all. They also made amusing figural planters, etc., as well as dinnerware, and vases and pots for the florist trade. Though some pieces are unmarked, most bear one of several McCoy trademarks.

Bank, Woodsey Owl **25.00**
Bookends, lilies **30.00**
Coffee mug, El Rancho Bar-B-Que line **12.00**
Cookie jar, Animal Crackers.**30.00**
Cookie jar, Apple on Basketweave bottom **30.00**
Cookie jar, Bananas **45.00**

Cookie jar, Barnum's Animals, circus wagon **85.00**
Cookie jar, Bobby Baker . . . **25.00**
Cookie jar, Caboose **60.00**
Cookie jar, Circus Horse . . . **95.00**
Cookie jar, Clown Bust **25.00**
Cookie jar, Clown in Barrel **45.00**
Cookie jar, Coffee Grinder . **20.00**
Cookie jar, Coffee Mug **20.00**
Cookie jar, Cookie Cabin . . . **45.00**
Cookie jar, Cookstove **20.00**
Cookie jar, Corn **75.00**
Cookie jar, Dalmations in Rocking Chair **125.00**
Cookie jar, Elephant **65.00**
Cookie jar, Friendship **65.00**
Cookie jar, Frontier Family . **40.00**
Cookie jar, Grandfather Clock, marked USA **45.00**
Cookie jar, Hen on Nest . . . **55.00**
Cookie jar, Hillbilly Bear . **250.00**
Cookie jar, Kitten on Basketweave bottom **45.00**
Cookie jar, Kittens on Ball of Yarn, 1955 . . . . **55.00**
Cookie jar, Liberty Bell **30.00**
Cookie jar, Lollipop **35.00**

Cookie jar, Mammy with Cauliflower **250.00**
Cookie jar, Oaken Bucket . . **20.00**
Cookie jar, Pears on Basketweave bottom **30.00**
Cookie jar, Pineapple **35.00**
Cookie jar, Potbelly Stove, black matt **20.00**
Cookie jar, Quaker Oats . . **125.00**
Cookie jar, Sad Clown **35.00**
Cookie jar, Snoopy on Doghouse, 1970 . . . . **85.00**
Cookie jar, Old Strawberry, 1955-1957 . . . . **25.00**
Cookie jar, Tepee **110.00**
Cookie jar, Tulip on Flowerpot, tulip finial **35.00**
Cookie jar, Upside Down Bear, panda **18.00**
Cookie jar, Windmill **55.00**
Cookie jar, Wishing Well . . . **25.00**
Cookie jar, Woodsy Owl **75.00**
Creamer, Grecian **9.00**
Decanter, Apollo Len **40.00**
Ice tub, El Rancho Bar-B-Que line, 1960 . . . . **25.00**
Planter, alligator **12.00**

Cookie jars: Raggedy Ann, $35.00; Colonial Fireplace, $50.00.

Planter, bird dog **10.00**
Planter, pear **10.00**
Planter, Robin Hood **15.00**
Planter, spinning wheel ...**12.00**
Spoon rest, butterfly **30.00**
Tea set, Pine Cone, 3-piece .**40.00**
Vase, double tulips **14.00**
Wall pocket, grapes **15.00**
Wall pocket, umbrella **15.00**

Salt and pepper shakers, $12.00.

Medical Collectibles

What used to be of interest to those in the medical profession only is today regarded as a significant part of the early American way of life and as such is being collected by many. Especially fascinating are the 'quack' devices that used violet ray and electricity to 'cure' a variety of aches and pains.

Bleeder, bone handle with 3 blades, NM **95.00**
Bottle, WT & Co, square base with stopper, 11" **10.00**
Broadside, WW Gavitt's Medical Co 1880, 15x5½" **12.50**
Cork press, ornate cast iron lever type, bench mount **60.00**
First Aid cabinet, Johnson's Industrial, tin, 11x16x6½" ...**40.00**
First Aid kit, Johnson & Johnson, tin, with contents, 7½" ..**8.00**
Herb cutter, roller knife style, 20" long **40.00**
Medicine case, Lee's Family Tourist, with contents **30.00**
Mortar & pestle, turned wood, early, 9x6" **45.00**
Ointment jar, blue with gold trim, #1122, 10½" **45.00**
Pamphlet, Circular #2 War Department Surgeon General's Office, 1869 ....**12.00**
Pill machine, brass & wood, handle, unmarked, 15x13x6" ..**95.00**
Pill machine, Whitehall Tatum Co 196, 12x7½" **110.00**
Prescription boxed scale, Torsion Balance Co, 1891 .....**45.00**
Quassia cup, wood, used in pharmacy for fever cure **35.00**

Extracting forceps, fancy handles, F. Arnold, 1850s, $50.00.

Suppository mold, 3-part, brass, makes 12, VG **25.00**
Test tube holder, brass, 8" .. **5.00**
Tin, Dr Hobson's Eczema Ointment, 2½" diameter **6.00**

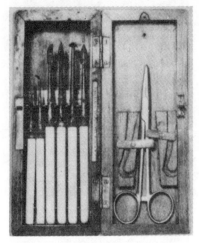

Dental scaling kit, ivory-handled instruments, J. Williken, London, ca 1840, $250.00.

Metlox

Since the 1940s, the Metlox company of California has been producing dinnerware lines, cookie jars, and decorative items which today have become popular collectibles.

Antique Grape, creamer & sugar bowl, with lid **12.50**
Antique Grape, plate, 10½" .. **6.00**
California Ivy, creamer & sugar bowl, with lid **18.00**
California Ivy, cup & saucer . **7.50**
California Ivy, plate, 6" **3.50**
California Provincial, bowl, divided vegetable **30.00**
California Provincial, bread tray, oblong **35.00**
California Provincial, gravy boat **25.00**
Cookie jar, lamb's head **24.00**

Cookie jar, Raggedy Andy .. **35.00**
Cookie jar, Topsy **50.00**
Homestead Provincial, candlestick, pair **25.00**
Homestead Provincial, match holder, wall hanging ... **25.00**
Homestead Provincial, mug . **12.00**
Homestead Provincial, platter, oval, 13½" **17.50**
Poppy Trail, carafe, orange, wood handle **12.00**
Poppy Trail, tumbler, juice; 3-ring design **9.00**
Red Rooster Provincial, ash tray, 8" **10.00**
Red Rooster Provincial, egg cup, footed **15.00**
Red Rooster Provincial, plate, salad; 7" **5.00**
Sculptured Grape, creamer & sugar bowl, with lid **17.50**
Sculptured Grape, soup, flat soup bowl, 8" **7.00**

Cookie jars, Bear, $32.00; Squirrel on stump, $28.00.

Milk Glass

Milk glass has been used since the 1700s to make tableware, lamps, and novelty items such as covered figural dishes and decorative wall plaques. Early examples were made with cryolite and ring with a clear bell tone when tapped.

Bottle, duck, Atterbury ... **250.00**
Bottle, Statue of Liberty, 10" **60.00**

Covered dish, Uncle Sam on Battleship, $80.00.

Bowl, Tree of Life, crimped, 4x8"
diameter **55.00**
Butter dish, Blackberry **65.00**
Butter dish, Roman Cross . . **45.00**
Cake plate, hand-painted floral
design **20.00**
Cake stand, hand stem, footed, At-
terbury **70.00**
Celery vase, Sawtooth, 9¾". . **30.00**
Compote, Jenny Lind, 7½" . **55.00**
Creamer, Grape & Cherry, blue,
with lid **30.00**
Creamer, owl, 3⅝" **35.00**
Egg cup, Bird in Cattails . . . **15.00**
Fruit jar, owl, screw-on cap, Atter-
bury **110.00**
Goblet, Blackberry **35.00**
Lamp, Goddess of Liberty . **100.00**
Mug, birds, square handle . **14.00**
Novelty, baby's shoe **15.00**
Plate, Columbus **35.00**
Plate, Cupid & Psyche **38.00**
Plate, Easter rabbit **30.00**
Plate, Fan & Circle, 10½" . . **28.00**
Plate, Indian, lacy edge, 7" . **20.00**
Plate, Mother Goose, 6¼" . . **70.00**
Plate, Scroll, McKee **40.00**
Plate, Woof-Woof **50.00**

Plate, 3 Bears, 7¼" **38.00**
Platter, Retriever, dog after bird,
13¼" **95.00**
Salt cellar, divided basket shape,
master **25.00**
Sauce dish, Blackberry, 4" . . **8.00**
Shaker, grapes relief, 4-sided, origi-
nal top with celluloid . . **22.00**
Shaving mug, florals **10.00**
Tray, Diamond Grille **40.00**
Tumbler, Apple Blossom . . . **37.50**

Molds

The two most popular types of
molds with collectors are chocolate
molds and ice cream molds. Chocolate molds are quite detailed and
are usually made of tin or copper.
While some are flat backed, others
make three-dimensional shapes.
Baskets, Santas, rabbits, and those
with holiday themes are abundant.
Ice cream molds are usually made
of pewter and come in a wide variety
of shapes and styles.

Acorn, small **35.00**

Basket, tapered, 4½x8" **45.00**
Birds, group of 3 with plumes, medium **55.00**
Boy in tux & top hat, 2-part mold, 7½" **50.00**
Chick, hatching, small **70.00**
Easter bunny, standing, 7½x4½x 1¾" **40.00**
Egg, embossed rabbit decoration, medium **45.00**
Eggs, embossed decoration, set of 3, large **25.00**
Fish, hinged, 4½" **20.00**
Heart, 3-part, 8½x9" **40.00**
Heart & flower, sheet style, Fabriek, 21½x9½" **125.00**
Lamb, standing, medium .. **50.00**
Monkey, medium **60.00**
Peafowl, 11x10" **125.00**
Rabbit, dressed, medium ... **45.00**
Rabbit, E-8351, 3½x6½" ... **50.00**
Rabbit, with basket on back, tin, 2-part, 17" **115.00**
Santa, 2-piece, MIG, 10" .. **225.00**
Tin, melon, 2-piece **20.00**
Walnut, 3¼x2½" **48.00**

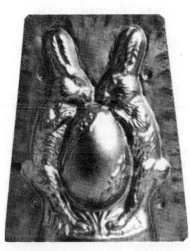

Two-piece rabbit molds, unmarked, 9", $70.00.

Food

Cast iron, pig **85.00**

Copper, eagle relief, oval, heavy, 9½x7¼" **150.00**
Copper, simple sunburst, individual, with cover **14.00**
Copper, swirled, 4" **60.00**
Copper & tin, lion, 6½" ... **120.00**
Copper & tin, rose, 7" **90.00**
Copper & tin, turtle, 10½" . **165.00**
Copper & tin, 3 fruits, oval fluted skirt **125.00**
Tin, fish, curved, 12½" **60.00**
Tin, fish, oval, 9" long **55.00**
Tin, hen on nest, 7x7" **85.00**
Tin, melon, 2-piece **20.00**
Tin, plum pudding, oval, 2-piece, large **30.00**
Tin, teddy bear, 5" **85.00**
Wood, rooster, deeply carved pine, 8½" square **240.00**

Ice Cream

Ace of Spades, #444 .... **30.00**
Alligator, S-394 .... **50.00**
Aster, #236 .... **32.00**
Banana, #157 .... **30.00**
Basketball, E-1150 ...... **25.00**
Beehive, K-251 .... **48.00**
Bride, E-1148 .... **42.00**
Calla lily, E-357 .... **28.00**
Cannon, S-273 .... **45.00**
Chicken, E-625 .... **58.00**
Christmas bell, #404 ...... **65.00**
Daisy, #363 .... **35.00**
Eagle trophy, with shield & cannons, K-517 .... **65.00**
Fish, 5¾" **55.00**
Groom in high hat, E-1149 . **60.00**
Hyacinth, E-356 .... **30.00**
Lemon, pewter **20.00**
Mandolin, S-547 .... **50.00**
Melon, #307 .... **30.00**
Orange, E-307 .... **32.00**
Pear, pewter **20.00**
Pumpkin, E-309 .... **28.00**
Rabbit, crouching, E-658 ... **45.00**
Rooster, 11½" **400.00**
Santa, pewter, 4¼" **55.00**

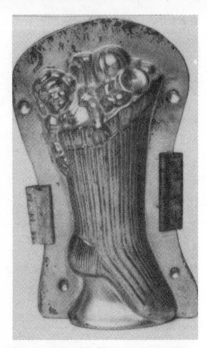

Ice cream mold, Christmas stocking, 2-piece, #59+4271, marked Larrosh Schw. Gmund., rare, 8", $125.00.

Tangerine, pewter 20.00
Turkey, #429 ....30.00
Washington bust, E-1084 ..52.00

Mortens Studios

Animal models sold by Mortens Studios of Arizona during the 1940s are some of today's most interesting collectibles, especially among animal lovers. Hundreds of breeds of dogs, cats, and horses were produced from a plaster-type composition material constructed over a wire framework. They range in size from 2" up to about 7" and most are marked.

Beagle, tan, ivory, & black, standing, 6" 65.00
Black panther on rocks, Dura-Stone, early 58.00

Cocker and Terrier, 3", $30.00 each.

Boxer, brown, 2½x4" 35.00
Dachshund, black male, standing, 9" 44.00
Dalmation, ivory & black, standing, 5½x7½" 75.00
French Poodle, 5" 45.00
German Shepherd, tan & charcoal, recumbent, 7x4", NM ..65.00
Irish Setter, rust, standing, 6x7", M 70.00
Pomeranian, tan, standing, 2".30.00
Sealyham Terrier, standing, 4x5¾", EX 65.00
Springer Spaniel, ivory & black, 5x 5½", M 65.00

Movie Memorabilia

Anything connected with the silver screen and movie stars in general is collected by movie buffs today. Posters, lobby cards, movie magazines, promotional photos, souvenir booklets, and stills are their treasures. Especially valuable are items from the twenties and thirties that have to do with such popular stars as Jean Harlow, Bella Lugosi, Carol Lumbard, and Gary Cooper. Elvis Presley and Marilyn Monroe have devoted fans who often limit their collections to them exclusively.

Advertising blotter, Philadelphia Story, 1941 ....7.00
Book, Hunchback of Notre Dame, 1925 Movie Edition ...25.00

Book, King Kong, 1932 Movie Edition **25.00**
Lobby card, Coggan's Bluff, Clint Eastwood, 1968 .... **2.00**
Lobby card, Cool Hand Luke, Paul Newman, 1967 .... **5.00**
Lobby card, Little Rascals in Fishy Tales, 1951, 11x14" ... **12.50**
Lobby card, The Ghost & Mrs Muir, Rex Harrison & Gene Tierney, NM **24.00**
Magazine, Carnival, Jayne Mansfield, March 1956 ..... **13.00**
Magazine, Modern Screen, Jean Harlow, August 1935 .. **15.00**
Magazine, Modern Screen, Myrna Loy, September 1939 .. **15.00**
Magazine, Modern Screen, Ricky Nelson, November 1958 .**8.00**
Magazine, Modern Screen, Robert Taylor, January 1937 .. **15.00**
Magazine, Movie Mirror, Ginger Rogers, Sept. 1937 .... **20.00**
Magazine, Movie Story, Esther Williams, July 1946 ... **10.00**
Magazine, Photoplay, Doris Day, September 1960 .... **5.00**

Limited edition print, Roy Rogers, autographed, artist proof, 30x24", $60.00.

Magazine, Screen Life, Ann Sheridan, April 1940 .... **10.00**
Magazine, Silver Screen, Susan Haywood, Sept 1944 .... **8.00**
Photoplay book, Susannah of the Mounties **10.00**
Photoplay book, Wizard of Oz, original version **35.00**
Poster, Fun in Acapulco, Elvis Presley, 1963 .... **30.00**
Poster, Public Enemy, James Cagney **35.00**
Poster, Summer Stock, Judy Garland & Grace Kelly, 1950, 14x36" **55.00**
Poster, The Westerner, Gary Cooper **36.00**
Pressbook, Apple Dumpling Gang, 1979 .... **3.50**
Pressbook, City Lights, Charlie Chaplin, 1931, 16-pg. .. **35.00**
Pressbook, Dr No, Sean Connery & Ursula Andress, 1963 .. **42.00**
Pressbook, Gaslight, Ingrid Bergman, 1944, 64 -pg, 11½ x16" **59.00**

Poster, Singing in the Rain, 40x27", $50.00.

Pressbook, Revenge of the Pink
Panther, 1978 ....**6.50**
Program, Gone With the Wind, 1940,
20-pg **29.00**
Program, The Birth of a Nation, ca
1916 ....**25.00**
Program, Woodstock, 1970 .**25.00**
Studio teaching packet, Black Cal-
dron, 1985, 16-pg **30.00**
Title card, Suddenly Last Summer,
Elizabeth Taylor, 1960 .**28.00**
Window card, Revenge of the Crea-
ture, John Agar, 1955, 14x22",
NM **27.00**
Window card, The Incredible
Shrinking Man, 1957, 14x22",
NM **46.00**

Music Boxes

Early music boxes were made in
models that play either a disk or a
cylinder. Some were housed in ornate inlaid cases, sometimes with
extra features such as bells or mechanical birds. The largest manufacturers of music boxes were Regina, Polyphon, and Symphonion;
these are treasured by today's collectors. Condition is always an
important factor; well-restored
examples bring the best prices.

Ariston, 13" cardboard disk, EX
original condition **200.00**
Bremond Mandolin, octagonal case,
13" 8-tune cylinder .**1,600.00**
Criterion, 12" disk, cherry case, EX
original condition ..**1,350.00**
Helvetia, 12", VG **1,000.00**
Komet, 20¾" disk **3,750.00**
Langdorf et Fils, lever wind, 6" cylinder, 12x6x5" **650.00**
Nickelodeon, Nat'l, 8-roll changer,
with 150 rolls **2,650.00**
Olympia, #5-B, mahogany table
model, 15½" disk, coin-op, EX
original condition ..**1,100.00**

**Polyphon, walnut with inlaid lid,
double comb with twelve bells,
restored, 12x25", $4,700.00.**

Polyphon, upright, 19⅝" disk, EX
original condition ..**4,600.00**
Polyphon, walnut case, 15½" single
comb **1,800.00**
Regina, #22, oak, single comb, 8½"
disk, 10 disks, 12" **685.00**
Regina, #33, elaborate oak case,
changer, 27" **1,100.00**
Regina, #36, flat oak changer, 15½",
EX condition **9,000.00**
Regina, #40, mahogany case, console, double comb ...**6,000.00**
Regina, #60, 12" disk, EX original
condition **1,500.00**
Regina, mahogany case, single
comb, 5¢ coin-op table top, EX
original condition ..**3,500.00**
Regina, oak case, double comb,
15½" disk, 10 disks .**2,400.00**
Regina Hexaphone, #102, EX original condition **3,950.00**
Stella, oak console, 17¼" disk, with
27 disks **7,000.00**
Swiss, gold plated, original tune
card, 8-tune, restored .**600.00**
Symphonion, #106, carved case,
17⅝" disk, restored .**8,000.00**

Napkin Rings

Figural silverplated napkin rings were popular in the late 1880s, and today's collectors enjoy finding hundreds of different designs. Among the companies best known for their manufacture are Meriden, Wm. Rogers, Reed and Barton, and Pairpoint (who made some of the finest). Kate Greenaway figurals, those with Kewpies or Brownies, and styles with wheels that turn are especially treasured.

Baby crawling, supports ring on back **150.00**
Bear on stool, paws rest on ring, scalloped base, Middletown #68 .... **195.00**
Beaver sits on leaves & branches, Toronto **60.00**
Bird, fledgling atop nest, mouth open for feeding **65.00**
Bird on ring held by ornate footed base, Meriden #187 ... **95.00**
Boy in work clothes rolls ring, Meriden #161 .... **175.00**
Boy removes sock aside ring, Derby #341 .... **250.00**
Boy with cookie, dog begging, Meriden **185.00**

Greenaway girl, #32, 2¾", $195.00.

Branches form chair, ring rests on seat **125.00**
Brownie climbing up side of ring **145.00**
Bud vase with spout on ring, round base, Reed & Barton #1337 .... **150.00**
Bulldog, glass eyes **145.00**
Butterfly on leaf, Tufts **78.00**
Cat pushing ring with his paws, no base **75.00**
Cat with arched back atop ring, dog on circle base aside, Rogers #262 .... **195.00**
Cherub, cockatoo, & urn with flowers, Middletown #109 . **165.00**
Cherub atop ring guides butterfly on flower, Simpson-Hall-Miller #201 .... **275.00**
Cherub on top of ring holds rein on robin **200.00**
Cherub wears cap, sits against ring, Pairpoint #52 ...... **125.00**
Chick on end of wishbone, Rococo base, ring elevated **65.00**
Chicken pulls ring on wheels, scarce **215.00**
Child with shovel holds upright pole with ring atop, Redfield & Rice **155.00**
Cow by ring, with tipped-over pail, flower-covered base, Meriden #268 .... **195.00**
Cow stands by jagged-edge ring, Wilcox #01538 ...... **225.00**
Crocodile carries ring on back, Meriden #0202 ...... **125.00**
Doe on circular base with ring aside, Toronto #1106 ...... **195.00**
Dog chases bird up ring, oval base, Reed & Barton #1110 . **100.00**
Dog pulls sled with greyhound design embossed on sides, Meriden **150.00**
Dog with bushy tail, forepaws on latticed ring, square & footed base **125.00**
Fireman's helmet at side of ring, Pairpoint #81 .... **100.00**

Monkey musician, 2", $195.00.

Fox pulling cart, wheels turn around 250.00
Frog perched on leaf base, ring behind 75.00
Frogs lean against ring, lily-leaf base, Meridan 250.00
Girl wearing bonnet holds ring, octagonal base, Simpson-Hall-Miller 150.00
Girl with gun on shoulder stands on square base 375.00
Grapes, leaf hangs on side of ring, raised round base 70.00
Greek man carries ring barrel, tiered base, Tufts #1517 ....200.00
Greenaway boy with bat & ball 235.00
Greenaway girl with bonnet & hood sits by ring, Derby ...195.00
Horse pulls ring on movable wheels, Meriden 280.00
Horseshoe on ring, with horse's head & Good Luck embossed. 85.00
Lady stands behind ring, 6 leaves on footed base, Tufts .200.00
Lion, lies on rectangular base, ring on back, no mark 150.00
Lion stands at side of ring with shields, circular base .125.00
Monkey in man's clothes, Tufts 295.00
Monkey plays violin, stands by large repousse ring 235.00
Owl sits on scroll-footed square base, ring on back 195.00
Parrot on wheels, Simpson-Hall-Miller 175.00

Pear with branch & leaves by ring, leaf forms base 80.00
Poodle on haunches shares base with floral ring, Tufts 140.00
Rabbit sits under log tree, ring atop, Reed & Barton #1520 .200.00
Rooster crows from atop shovel that holds ring, Meriden ..120.00
Spanish comb on ring 70.00
Sphinx with ring on back, Meriden #165 ....150.00
Sunflower base, octagonal, Meriden #37 ....65.00
Tennis racquet & ball by ring, Pairpoint 95.00
Vulture perched on leafy branch, Toronto 95.00
Water lily pad holds ring, Meriden #166 ....65.00
2 dolphins support ring between tails 95.00
2 large rabbits on square base, aquatic decoration on ring 375.00
2 Oriental fans embossed with flowers & hummingbirds form ring 95.00

Napkin Rings, Catalin

For a less formal setting, Catalin napkin rings add a cheerful bit of color to the table. Often found in delightful animal shapes and comic chartacter forms, these whimsical accessories are gaining in popularity. Red and orange rings are most often in demand, with blue a close second. Dark green, ivory, salmon pink, light green, yellow, and mottled butterscotch can also be found. Buyers beware! Many of these are being reproduced and sold for the "old" prices.

Angelfish 25.00
Chicken or bird 15.00
Cottontail rabbit 20.00

Donald Duck	**55.00**
Duck	**20.00**
Elephant #1	**23.00**
Elephant #2	**20.00**
Goldfish	**20.00**
Mickey Mouse	**55.00**
New York World's Fair, trylon & perisphere	**45.00**
Penguin	**40.00**
Popeye	**85.00**
Rabbit	**18.00**
Rocking horse	**40.00**
Schnauzer dog	**20.00**
Scotty dog	**18.00**

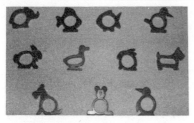

Catalin napkin rings, see listings for specific values.

Nazi Collectibles

An area of militaria attracting a growing following today, Nazi collectibles are comprised of anything related to the Nazi rise and German participation in World War II. There are many facets to this field; among the items hunted most enthusiastically are daggers, medals, badges, patches, uniforms, and toys with a Nazi German theme.

Ammo pouch, K-98, dated 1942, pair **14.00**
Arm band, Custom Official . **24.00**
Badge, Infantry Assault, bronze metal **28.00**
Badge, Luftwaffe Flak, silver metal finish **70.00**
Badge, Luftwaffe Glider . . **116.00**
Badge, Luftwaffe Paratrooper, Assmann hallmark **125.00**

**Battle badge, Krim, 1941-1942, 2½",
$65.00.**

Badge, RAD Health Service Specialty **13.00**
Badge, Tank Assault, silver metal finish **34.00**
Bayonet frog, K-98, 1943 . . . **20.00**
Brooch, WWII **26.00**
Buckle, Army EM, 1943 . . . **16.00**
Buckle, Police EM **20.00**
Buckle, RLB, 1st Pattern . . **27.00**
Canteen & cup, Luftwaffe . . **32.00**
Cap, Hitler Youth Overseas. **26.00**
Cap, visor; Artillery EM . . **120.00**
Cap, visor; Reichwehr for parade uniform **35.00**
Dagger, Luftwaffe, 1st Model, no sheath **175.00**
Field flashlight, dated 1944. **22.00**
Field pack, small assault, tan canvas, D-ring type **14.00**
Flag, Swastika, double-sided, 17x14" **26.00**
Gas mask, civilian, resembles woman's purse **24.00**
Gloves, motorcycle; gray leather & cloth, dated 1942 ..... **38.00**
Hat, Luftwaffe Pilot, peaked crown, NM **150.00**
Helmet, Luftschutz, gladiator type with chinstrap **45.00**

Helmet, Luftwaffe Jet Pilot 350.00
Medal, Iron Cross, 2nd Class 27.00
Medal, Olympic Games Commemorative, with ribbon 55.00
Medal, Russian Front, Winter Campaign, with ribbon. 20.00
Newspaper, Volksdeutches Abendblatt, Brunn, October 16, 1939, NM 20.00
Pennant, Swastika, double-sided, 5x9" 24.00
Plaque, Hilter, metal profile on wood, signed, 4½" 58.00
Plate, for helmet, NSKK ... 18.00
Post card, Duhr Fuhrer & Wein, dated 1938 .... 12.50
Post card, U-boat, full-color photo, French text, 4x6" 12.00
Print, Battleship Bismark, artist signed, 18x24" 52.00
Shoulder straps, marked SS. 30.00
Shoulderboards, Waffen SS Panzer EM 40.00
Songbook, 1936 Olympics, 48 pages, NM 40.00
Sword, Army Officer, Roon Pattern, no scabbard 165.00

Sword, Police, with scabbard, EX 185.00
Wings, Pilot, WWII Croation 26.00

New Martinsville

Operating in New Martinsville, West Virginia, from 1901 until 1944 when it was purchased by the Viking Company, this company produced not only dinnerware lines but beautiful glass animal models, all of which are highly collectible.

Moondrops in amber: cocktail shaker, $20.00; handled shot tumbler, $8.00.

Bookend, nautilus shell 85.00
Bookends, elephant, pair ... 60.00
Bookends, sailing ship, pair. 80.00
Box, Martha Washington, pink satin, with lid 95.00
Cake plate, Prelude, pedestal foot (or standard) 45.00
Candlestick, figure of a seal, small 40.00
Candlestick, swan form, forest green, pair 25.00
Champagne, Prelude 12.00

Plaque, DDAC (German Auto Club), $60.00.

Cocktail, Carlton **12.50**
Cocktail, Prelude **12.00**
Cruet, Janice, light blue ... **65.00**
Cup, Prelude **10.00**
Figurine, fish, teal, tall **22.00**
Figurine, horse, head up ... **95.00**
Figurine, squirrel, no base . **50.00**
Finger lamp, Nosegay, applied
   handle **40.00**
Goblet, Carlton **12.50**
Old Fashioned, Prelude **16.00**
Pitcher, water, Radiance, amber,
   10" **120.00**
Vase, Dove, crystal **60.00**
Vase, Radiance, ruby, 10" .. **55.00**

Niloak

Produced in Arkansas by Charles
Dean Hyten from the early 1900s
until the mid-1940s, Niloak (the
backward spelling of kaolin, a type
of clay) takes many forms — figural
planters, vases in both matt and
glossy glazes, and novelty items of
many types. The company's most
famous product and their most collectible is their swirl or Mission
Ware line. Clay in colors of brown,
blue, cream, red, and buff are swirled
within the mold, the finished product left unglazed on the outside to
preserve the natural hues. Small
vases are common; large pieces or
unusual shapes and those with
exceptional coloration are the most
valuable.

Ash tray, Mission Ware, 5" . **45.00**
Bowl, red, with label, 1¾x3" . **9.50**
Canoe, rose, 10¾" long **28.00**
Elephant standing on circus tub,
   yellow, 5½" **27.50**
Jar, Mission Ware, with pierced lid,
   4" **175.00**
Mug, pink gloss, 3½" **8.00**
Pitcher, lemonade; MissionWare,
   8" **165.00**

**Planter, donkey and clown, 6½",
$30.00.**

Pitcher, yellow, art mark, 3". **12.00**
Planter, camel, 3" **22.00**
Planter, elephant, white ... **18.00**
Planter, frog sitting on a lily pad,
   blue **37.00**
Planter, parrot, orange on white
   matt **10.00**
Planter, swan, rose gloss,
   7" **16.00**
Planter, wishing well, burgundy
   matt **10.00**
Vase, bud; Mission Ware, 6". **35.00**
Vase, Mission Ware, hourglass form,
   6½" **55.00**
Vase, Mission Ware, 7¾" ... **85.00**
Vase, with handles, burgundy matt,
   7" **16.00**

Nippon

In compliance with American im-
portation regulations, from 1891 to
1921 Japanese manufacturers
marked their wares 'Nippon,' mean-
ing Japan, to indicate country of
origin. The term is today used to
refer to the highly decorated porcelain vases, bowls, chocolate pots,
etc., that bare this term within their
trademark. Many variations were
used. In the following listings marks
are indicated by numbers: #1, China
E-OH; #2, M in wreath; #3, Rising
Sun; and #4, Maple Leaf.

Jar, floral reserve, 7½", $175.00.

Basket, violets, gold trim & handle, 6½" **90.00**

Butter dish, pink & green flowers, gold trim, green mark . .**55.00**

Candlestick, leaves & beads in relief, gold bands, 7" **75.00**

Cheese & cracker, colored florals & gold on white, marked . .**15.00**

Chocolate pot, gold tracery & beading, blue mark #4 . . . .**225.00**

Cup, landscape, 3-handle, marked, small **27.50**

Egg warmer, 6-egg, brown, green, & white, mark #3 . . . . . .**185.00**

Ferner, multicolor flowers on light green, gold trim, 8½" . .**175.00**

Ferner, squirrel in tree reserve, mark #2, 5¾" **200.00**

Humidor, canister form, Wedgwood type, mark #2, 6½" . . .**800.00**

Humidor, hexagonal, Indian in canoe, 5½x6½" **300.00**

Jar, scent; roses, 6" **30.00**

Mustard with tray, roses on cream, elaborate gold trim, mark #4 . . . .**42.50**

Plaque, blown-out buffalo, mark #2, 10½" **900.00**

Plaque, watermelon & fruit, artist signed, mark #2, 12" . .**275.00**

Plaque, 3 blown-out horses, mark #2, 10½" **1,100.00**

Plate, blown-out child's face, 6¾" **75.00**

Plate, pink roses on tan, gold border, blue mark #4, 9" .**110.00**

Plate, scene of lake, boat, & woods, brown rim, 7¾" **30.00**

Plate, white with heavy gold & enamel beading, 8¾" . .**18.00**

Relish dish, oval, Wedgwood type, mark #2, 7½" **175.00**

Salt & pepper shakers, green with gold trim, pair **25.00**

Salt cellar, roses, heavy gold, master **15.00**

Stein, 6 blown-out dogs, green mark #2 . . . .**850.00**

Syrup with underplate, floral on yellow border, mark #4 **50.00**

Tankard, red roses on cobalt with gold trim, marked, 13".**275.00**

Tea strainer, flowers, green .**40.00**

Vase, crysanthemum relief with basketweave, 9" **300.00**

Vase, lily of the valley, green with gold handles, 6¾" **125.00**

Vase, orchids on white, blue mark #4, 10½" **300.00**

Mug, playing cards, 5", $250.00.

198

Vase, scene with sailing ships,
Imperial mark, 9½" ..**235.00**
Vase, Wedgwood type, urn shape,
green mark #2, 7½" ..**425.00**

Noritake

Since the early 1900s the Noritake China Company has been producing fine dinnerware, occasional pieces, and figural items decorated by hand in delicate florals, scenics, and wildlife studies. One of their most popular dinnerware lines, Azalea, is listed in the category by that name.

Ash tray, blown-out horse heads,
4½" diameter **200.00**
Ash tray, Indian chief, folded rim,
green wreath mark ...**170.00**
Ash tray, lady, skirt forms bowl,
wreath mark, 5¼" **245.00**
Bowl, vegetable; Wild Ivy, Cook & Serve, with lid **18.00**
Bread tray, modeled as ear of corn,
7x12" **50.00**
Cake plate, Tree in Meadow, pierced handles **35.00**

Moriage basket vase, 5¼" tall, $375.00.

Bonbon, White and Gold line, 6", $15.00.

Cheese dish, sampan scene, with slanted lid, tree crest mark,
6¼" long **80.00**
Cigarette holder, bell shape, bird finial, wreath mark ..**125.00**
Creamer and sugar bowl, Tree in Meadow **30.00**
Cup & saucer, Bahama **20.00**
Humidor, blown-out bulldog smoking pipe **495.00**
Humidor, Tree in Meadow. **295.00**
Inkwell, clown figural, red M in wreath mark, 4" **245.00**
Mug, river scene, earth tones, green, wreath mark, 3¼" **65.00**
Night light, lady figural, orange lustre dress, M in wreath mark,
10" **800.00**
Plaque, man on camel, cobalt with gold rim, 8½" **150.00**
Plaque, stream, trees, & mountains,
10" **100.00**
Platter, Wild Ivy **20.00**
Salt cellar, butterfly figural. **28.00**
Sugar bowl, Nana Rose #98218, with lid **20.00**
Sugar shaker, girl figural .**150.00**
Tea set, Pagoda & Willow, 15-piece **110.00**
Vase, blown-out squirrel on branch, wreath mark, 5¼" **180.00**
Vase, deco lady on red lustre, red M in wreath mark, 8½" ..**135.00**

Wall pocket, applied bird at top, bird & flowers, 8¼" . . . **120.00**
Wall pocket, applied butterfly & bee, red wreath mark, 8¼" . . **80.00**
Wall pocket, birds, cream with gold trim **45.00**
Wall pocket, butterflies on orange lustre, red M in wreath mark, 9" **85.00**
Wall pocket, poppies, red M in wreath mark **35.00**
Wall pocket, sailing ship scene, Art Deco, red mark **55.00**

Wall pocket, nest with babies and mother bird, 5x8", $195.00.

Nutcrackers

Of most interest to collectors are nutcrackers marked with patent information or those made in the form of an animal or bird. Many manufacturers chose the squirrel as a model for their nutcrackers; dogs were also popular. Cast iron examples are most often encountered; but brass, steel, even wood was also used.

Alligator, brass, marked China, 8½" **35.00**
Alligator, cast iron, original paint, 1890s, 13" **85.00**
Cherub, brass, old, EX **75.00**
Crocodile, brass, 8" **27.50**
Dog, cast iron, scalloped footed base, tail handle **55.00**
Dragon, brass **48.00**

Dog, nickel-plated cast iron, Made in England, Pat'd 1863, 9" long, $55.00.

Elephant, cast iron with red paint, twine tail, 9¾" **100.00**
Jester's head, brass **75.00**
Monkey's head, brass **35.00**
Parrot, brass **25.00**
Pliers type, cast iron with wooden handle **12.00**
Ram, glass eyes, carved wood, 8½" **65.00**
Squirrel, cast iron, 1913 . . . **25.00**
Twist & screw type, nickel-plated cast iron, 5" **12.00**

Occupied Japan

Items with the 'Occupied Japan' mark were made during the period from the end of World War II until April, 1952. Porcelains, novelties, paper items, lamps, silverplate, lacquer ware, and dolls are some of the types of exported goods that may bear this stamp. Because the Japanese were naturally resentful of the occupation, it is felt that only a small percentage of their wares were thus marked. Although you may find identical items marked simply 'Japan,' only those with the 'Occupied Japan' stamp are being collected.

Ash tray, dog hydrant, No Parking, 2x2¼" **5.00**
Ash tray, wash line **7.50**
Atomizer, pink glass, embossed MIOJ mark **22.50**

Bank, bisque elephant, 2x3". **30.00**
Bookends, pagodas in relief, heavy metal, 5¾", pair **30.00**
Bookends, penguin, bisque, 4", pair **35.00**
Bowl, octagonal, pansy on blue, marked G in wreath, 7". **15.00**
Bracelet, pearls, with label .**20.00**
Cigarette lighter, camera shape, lightweight metal **35.00**
Cigarette lighter, gun, 2" ..**17.50**
Cookie jar, cottage, marked Maruhon Ware, 8x6¼" **75.00**
Cow creamer, 8" **35.00**
Cup & saucer, child's; tomato, red & green **5.00**
Cup & saucer, demitasse; dragon on blue **20.00**
Dinner set, china, service for 6, with serving pieces **250.00**
Doll, china baby, 3" **17.50**
Figurine, ballerina with net dress, 4½" **25.00**
Figurine, Black fiddler, 5" ..**32.50**
Figurine, Black serenading couple, 4½" **17.50**
Figurine, cat, 2" **7.50**

Figurine, Chinese couple, common base, 5¼" **22.50**
Figurine, couple waiting for rain, 5½" **25.00**
Figurine, Dutch girl with milk can, 6" **22.50**
Figurine, Eskimo, 3" **15.00**
Figurine, frog, 4½" **15.00**
Figurine, girl on fence, 4" ..**10.00**
Figurine, guitar player, 4½".**15.00**
Figurine, Monkeys, Speak no evil...Hear no evil, each .**7.50**
Figurine, Oriental coolie, 4".**15.00**
Figurine, Oriental dancers, 8⅛", pair **65.00**
Figurine, Oriental lady with flowers, 5½" **20.00**
Figurine, puppies in wicker basket, 2½" **12.50**
Figurine, seated couple, marked Paulux, 5½", pair **90.00**
Jewel box, metal, deer on top, with lid **15.00**
Mug, cannibal handle, 4¼" .**35.00**
Nativity set, 7-piece, 2½" ...**40.00**
Planter, birds on floral branch, 3½x4½" **15.00**
Planter, dog with shoe, 2" ...**7.50**
Planter, Donald Duck, 3" ..**15.00**
Planter, Mexican guitar player, 4¼" **15.00**
Plaque, colonial couple, bisque, marked Paulux, 6½x6" .**45.00**
Plaque, Dutch boy, chalkware, marked Yomake **22.50**
Plate, painted rose, lattice edge, Rossetti, Chicago USA .**25.00**
Powder box, blue oval with applied rose on top, bisque, 3½". **10.00**
Rosary beads, metal cross, stamped MIOJ, 30" **35.00**
Salt & pepper shakers, deer, pair **15.00**
Salt & pepper shakers, pigs in sty, pair **22.50**
Salt & pepper shakers, Scottish couple, pair **17.50**
Shelf sitter, cowboy couple, 3½" & 3¾", pair **30.00**

Mug, outdoor scene with man, 5½", $12.50.

Oriental couple, large, $50.00.

Shelf sitter, man with mandolin,
4" **15.00**
Stein, man with inscription, 'Bei
trunk un scherz,' 7⅛" . . **22.50**
Teapot, cobalt on ivory, bee final,
4½" **35.00**
Toby, scarf lady, 2½" **17.50**
Wall plaque, cup & saucer, floral on
white with gold, 3¼" **7.50**

Old McDonald's Farm

Made by the Regal China Co.,
items from this line of novelty ware
designed with characters and animals from Old McDonald's farm can
often be found at flea markets and
dinnerware shows.

**Salt and pepper shakers, figural
heads, $22.00.**

Butter dish, cow's head **35.00**
Canister, large **95.00**
Canister, medium **85.00**
Canister, spice; small **35.00**
Creamer, rooster **35.00**
Grease jar, pig figural **65.00**
Pitcher, cow's head, tankard form,
milk size **200.00**
Shakers, churn shape, pair . **18.00**
Shakers, feed sacks with sheep's
head, pair **35.00**
Shakers, figural heads, pair. **22.00**
Sugar bowl **35.00**
Teapot, duck's head **135.00**

Old Sleepy Eye

Both the Sleepy Eye Milling
Company and the Minnesota town
where it was located took their name
from the Sioux Indian Chief who
was born there in 1789, Old Sleepy
Eye. In the early 1900s, the milling
company contracted with the Weir
Pottery Co. to make four pieces of
blue and gray stoneware — a salt
bowl, butter crock, vase, and stein
— each decorated with the likeness
of the old chief. One of these pieces
was given as a premium inside each
barrel of their flour. Weir was one of
six companies that in 1906 merged
to form the Western Stoneware
Company. There the line was produced in blue and white, and several more items were added. These
early pieces, along with advertising
items such as pillow tops, post cards,
match holders, signs, labels, etc.,
are today highly collectible.

Calendar, 1904 . . . . **350.00**
Cookbook, loaf of bread . . . **250.00**
Fan, ca 1900 . . . . **175.00**
Flour sack, paper **100.00**
Label, egg crate **25.00**
Letter opener, bronze **850.00**
Match holder, white **850.00**
Milk carton **18.00**
Mirror, advertising, 1935 . . **35.00**

Mug, blue & white, 4¼" ... **175.00**
Pitcher, #1 .... **150.00**
Pitcher, #2 .... **185.00**
Pitcher, #3 .... **250.00**
Pitcher, #4 .... **275.00**
Pitcher, #5 .... **300.00**
Pitcher, gold & brown, 1981, club
    issue **125.00**
Post card **90.00**
Salt crock, Flemish **350.00**
Stein, cobalt **750.00**
Stein, Flemish **475.00**
Teaspoon, Indian-head handle, sil-
    ver-plated **100.00**
Thimble **2.00**
Vase, blue & white **425.00**

Pillow top, audience with President Monroe, $600.00.

Opalescent Glass

Pattern-molded tableware and novelty items made from glassware with a fiery opalescence became popular around the turn of the century. It was made in many patterns by several well-known companies.

Alaska, banana boat, blue . **250.00**
Alaska, bowl, 8 scallops, clear, 7¾"
    diameter **50.00**
Alaska, butter dish, vaseline, with
    cover **250.00**
Alaska, celery tray, blue .. **135.00**

Alaska, cruet, blue **265.00**
Alaska, pitcher, water; vaseline,
    9" **375.00**
Arabian Nights, tumbler, water,
    cranberry **85.00**
Argonaut Shell, butter dish, blue,
    with cover **275.00**
Argonaut Shell, spooner,
    blue **150.00**
Beaded Cable, rose bowl,
    blue **150.00**
Beatty Rib, creamer, individual;
    clear **20.00**
Beatty Swirl, butter dish, blue, with
    cover **150.00**
Block & Flower Band, bowl, trian-
    gular, clear, 5½" **20.00**
Bubble Lattice, pitcher, water; blue,
    9" **135.00**
Buttons & Braids, pitcher, water;
    blue **135.00**
Cabbage Leaf, vase, 3-footed, green,
    6" **47.00**
Chrysanthemum Base Swirl,
    spooner, blue **75.00**
Circled Scroll, compote, open,
    green **125.00**
Circled Scroll, table set, green, 4-
    piece **475.00**
Coin Spot, pitcher, water; blue,
    9" **120.00**
Coral, bowl, vaseline **55.00**
Daisy & Fern, pitcher, water; blue,
    9" **165.00**

Bowl, Pearl Flowers, green, 4¾", $60.00.

203

Pitcher, Spanish Lace, blue, $250.00.

Diamond Spearhead, butter dish, vaseline **195.00**

Dolly Madison, butter dish, blue, with cover **290.00**

Dolly Madison, spooner, green **45.00**

Double Greek Key, celery vase, blue **115.00**

Drapery, pitcher, blue, 9" . **135.00**

Everglades, berry set, vaseline, rare, 7-piece **285.00**

Fish-in-the-Sea, vase, blue . **45.00**

Flora, celery, blue **110.00**

Fluted Scroll, bowl, triangular, footed, blue **24.00**

Gonterman Swirl, sugar bowl, blue **160.00**

Good Luck, bowl, ruffled rim, aqua **70.00**

Greek Key & Scales, bowl, ruffled, blue **35.00**

Honeycomb & Clover, bowl, blue, large **30.00**

Idyll, tumbler, blue **85.00**

Intaglio, compote, jelly; open, vaseline **39.00**

Iris with Meander, sugar bowl, blue, with cover **150.00**

Iris with Meander, tumbler, vaseline **55.00**

Jackson, pitcher, water; vaseline, 9" **185.00**

Jewelled Heart, pitcher, water; clear, 9" **95.00**

Many Loops, bowl, scalloped, blue, 8¾" **25.00**

Ocean Shell, bowl, footed, blue **45.00**

Poinsettia, pitcher, water; blue, tankard form **225.00**

Regal, celery vase, blue **90.00**

S-Repeat, bowl, master berry; green, large **55.00**

Scroll with Acanthus, pitcher, water; vaseline **350.00**

Seaweed, sugar bowl cover only, blue **16.00**

Sunburst on Shield, tumbler, water, blue **100.00**

Swirl, rose bowl, clear **36.50**

Water Lily & Cattails, creamer, blue **45.00**

Wild Bouquet, berry set, clear, 6-piece **145.00**

Windows, pitcher, blue ... **200.00**

Novelty wall pocket, light blue, 7", $175.00.

Paper Dolls

Though the history paper dolls can be traced even farther back, by the late 1700s they were being mass produced. A century later, paper dolls were being used as an advertising medium by retail companies wishing to promote sales. The type most often encountered are in book form — the dolls on the cardboard covers, their wardrobe on the inside pages, published since the 1920s. Those representing famous people or characters are popular; condition is very important. Those in original, uncut folders are most valuable.

American Family, Grinnell Lithographic Co Inc, #C1002, 1940 . . . . **25.00**

Ann & Joe, MA Donohue & Company, #80C **20.00**

Ava Gardener, uncut **35.00**

Baby Dress-Up Kit, Colorforms, #176, 1964 . . . . **6.00**

Baby Jane, Gertrude Breed, 1927 . . . . **17.50**

Baby Merry, Merry Manufacturing Company, #4350, 1964 . . **8.00**

Beautiful Dolls for Children to Dress, Platt & Peck, . . . **30.00**

Betty, Complete Wardrobe & Trunk, Ritt-Miller Company, 1932 . . . . **25.00**

Betty & Dick Tour the USA, Standard Toykraft, #D100, 1940 . . . . **17.50**

Betty Marie, Londy Card Corporation, #5F, 1932 . . . . **5.00**

Bible Children Paper Dolls, Standard Publishing Company, #2590 . . . . **5.00**

Bible Land Children, Near East Foundation, 1934 . . . . . . **8.00**

Bible Think & Do, CR Gibson Company, #4936 . . . . **3.00**

Big Sister, Londy Card Corporation, #5J, 1932 . . . . **5.00**

Billy Boy, The Stecher Lithographic Company, #7029 . . . . . . **35.00**

Blondie, The DeJournette Mfg Company, #R-30 . . . . **6.00**

Bob & Nan, MA Donohue & Company, #80A **20.00**

Bobby, Doll to Dress, MS Publishing Company, #900 . . . . **20.00**

Bobbsey Twins, Samuel Lowe Co., ca 1950, $10.00.

Brenda Lee, Merry Manufacturing Company, #4360, 1964 . **12.00**

Brownies From Bingo-Land, Albert Whitman & Company, 1922 .... **30.00**

Children of God's World, Standard Publishing Co, #2591 ... **5.00**

Circus Day, Stephens Publishing Company, #135, 1946 ... **6.00**

Circus Twins, National Paper Box Company Inc, #N12-29 .. **5.00**

Cleopatra, Blaise Publishing Company, #1000, 1963 ..... **15.00**

Crepe Paper Doll Outfit, Dennison Manufacturing, #36 ... **30.00**

Daisy Dolly, Goldsmith Publishing Company, #516, 1922 .. **17.00**

Dancing Priscilla, Gertrude Breed, 1927 .... **17.50**

Dearie Dolls, Charles E Graham & Company, #0212 ...... **15.00**

Debbie, Avalon Industries Inc, #701-2 .... **4.00**

Debutante, Jan, C&M Publishing Company **5.00**

Design-A-Doll Joan, Dennison Mfg #11, 1950 .... **8.00**

Dolls of all Nations, New York Book Company, 1911 ...... **20.00**

Dolls to Make & Dress, George Sully & Company, #51, 1919 . **40.00**

Dolly's Kut-Out Klothes, American Toy Works, #3081 ..... **10.00**

Dotty & Danny on Parade, Burton Playthings, Inc, #875, 1935 .... **22.50**

Fashion Art Dolls, Art Award Company, #6000 .... **4.00**

Fluffy Ruffles, J Ottmann Lithograph Company, 1907 . **60.00**

Forget-Me-Not Paper Dolls, Charles Thompson COmpany, 1912 .... **30.00**

Friendship Paper Dolls, Friendship Press **25.00**

Fun Farm Frolics, International Paper Goods, #60, 1932. **35.00**

Glenn, Janex Corporation, #2002, 1971 .... **5.00**

Grandmother's Dolls, Frann Paper Dolls, 1955 .... **18.00**

Hansel & Gretel, The DeJournette Mfg Company, #1440 .. **18.00**

Hello, I'm Adeline, Animated Book Company, 1944 .... **18.00**

Ivy, Janex Corp, #2001, 1971. **5.00**

Judy, Magic Wand Corporation, #104 .... **6.00**

June Bride, Stephens Publishing Company, #136, 1946 ... **7.00**

Lacey Daisy, Kits, Incorporated, #1050, 1949 .... **7.00**

New Puss in Boots Paper Doll, E.H. Horsman, $75.00.

Sister Ruth, 1915, Kaufmann & Strauss, $40.00.

Let's Play Eskimo, Rand McNally & Company, #211, 1937 . . **15.00**

Life-Like Doll Set, Simplex Toys, #100 . . . . **15.00**

Li'l Miss Designer Kit, Suntex Corporation, 1953 . . . . **7.00**

Li'l Pearl, Grinnell Lithographic Co, Inc, #C1001, 1940 . . . . . 25.00

Linda the Ballerina, Avalon Industries Inc, #801-1, 1969 . . **4.00**

Little Betty Gad-About, American Colortype Co, #622 . . . . . **8.00**

Little Polly Dress-Up, American Colortype Company, #629 . . . . **25.00**

Little Red Riding Hood, The DeJournette Mfg Company, #901 . . . . **10.00**

Little Sister, The Dandyline Company, 1918 . . . . **18.00**

Look Who I Am, Hart Publishing Company, 1952 . . . . . . **10.00**

Lullaby Twins, National Paper Box Company Inc, #N10-29 . . **5.00**

Magic Mary, Milton Bradley Company, #4132, 1946 . . . . . **10.00**

Magic Mary Jane, Milton Bradley Company, #4010-3, 1950. **7.00**

Magnetic Missy, Smethport Specialty Company, #53 . . . . **5.00**

Magnetic Troll, Smethport Specialty Company, #116, 1965 . . . **5.00**

Mardi Gras, Einson Freeman Company, Inc, #432, 1935 . . **35.00**

Margie, Avalon Industries Inc, #811 . . . . **18.00**

Marquerite Clark, Percy Reeves, 1920 . . . . **45.00**

Mark Antony, Blaise Publishing Company, #1001, 1963 . **15.00**

Martha Ann, Winthrop-Atkins Co Inc, #6310 . . . . **10.00**

Miss America, Reuben H Lilja & Company, Inc, #900, 1941 . . . . **25.00**

Mother Daughter Dolls, The DeJournette Mfg Co, #60. **6.00**

Mother Goose Village, Harter Publishing Company, #H-164, 1935 . . . . **12.00**

Movieland, Reuben H Lilja & Company, Inc, #906, 1947 . . **12.00**

Mr & Mrs Hawaii, Schattel's, 1955 . . . . **10.00**

My Own Dolls To Color & Dress, Treasure Books, 1952 . . . **7.00**

Nancy & Jane, Howell, Soskin Publishers, Inc. 1945 . . **15.00**

New Puss in Boots Paper Doll, EH Horsman Company **75.00**

Nurse & Twins, Grinnell Lithographic Co, Inc, #C1003, 1940 . . . . **25.00**

Nursery Rhymes, Childrens Press, Inc, #R1000, 1950 . . . . . . **3.50**

Pam & Jeff, Transogram Toy Company, #4102, 1963 . . . . . **10.00**

Paper Doll Outfit, American Toy Works, #102 . . . . **20.00**

Patsy, Children's Press, Inc, #3002, 1946 . . . . **15.00**

Patty's Party, Stephens Publishing Company, #175 . . . . **6.00**

Penny & Her Dolly, DeJournette Mfg Co, #90 . . . . **6.00**

Playtime Pals, Current Inc, #5607, 1982 . . . . **4.00**

Primrose Paper Dolls, Charles Thompson Co, 1912 . . . **30.00**

Progressive Sewing Set, Progressive Toy Corporation, #502, 1941 . . . . **15.00**

Rag Doll Sue, Harter Publishing Company, #H-100, 1931. **30.00**

Sally Dimple, Burton Playthings, Inc, #975, 1935 ...... **22.50**

School Days, National Syndicate Displays, #77-1, 1943 .. **10.00**

Sister Ruth, Kaufmann & Strauss Company, #11, 1915 ... **40.00**

Snow White, J Pressman Toy Corporation, #1214 ...... **15.00**

Stitch & Sew, J Pressman Toy Corporation, #1205 .... **6.00**

Suzie Sweet, Samuel Gabriel Sons, #D94 .... **10.00**

Sweet Sue, Magic Wand Corporation, #108 .... **5.00**

Teddy Bear & His Friends, Platt & Munk Company, Inc, #190 .... **40.00**

Teena the Teenager, Avalon Industries Inc, #701-2 ...... **4.00**

The Bride Doll, Frann Paper Dolls, 1955 .... **18.00**

The Dolly Twins, The DeJournette Mfg, #500 .... **10.00**

The Make-It Book, Rand McNally & Co, #RM 103, 1928 ..... **3.00**

The Old Fashioned Doll, Colorforms, #525, 1970 .... **3.00**

The Three Bears Home, Mcloughlin Brothers, #517, 1933 .. **25.00**

The Wardrobe Book, The World Publishing Company, #R-501, 1952 .... **17.00**

Tina the Talking Paper Doll, Colorforms, #5550 .... **10.00**

Tiny Dolls, Charles E Graham & Company, #0214 ...... **15.00**

Triple-Joy-Book, Pinkham Press, 1927 .... **25.00**

Wendy Walks, Merry Manufacturing Company, #6504, 1965 .... **10.00**

Wendy's Wardrobe, Jak Pak, #301 .... **2.00**

When I Grow Up, Current Inc, #3216, 1980 .... **5.00**

Winky Winnie, Jaymar Specialty Co, #994 .... **12.00**

Pattern Glass

As early as 1820 glassware was

Glitter Dolls, Playtime House, $12.00.

being pressed into patterned molds to produce tablewares and accessories. The process was perfected, and by the latter part of the century, dozens of glass houses were making hundreds of patterns. This type of glassware retained its popularity until about 1915. Two types of glass were used: flint, the early type made with lead to produce a good clear color and resonance; and non-flint, the later type containing soda lime. Generally, flint glass is the more expensive.

Actress, compote, with lid, frosted
   dome, 6¼x9½" **145.00**
Alabama, celery vase **30.00**
Alabama, relish dish **15.00**
Alligator Scales, goblet,
   flint **28.50**
Almond Thumbprint, creamer, non-
   flint **37.50**
Amazon, creamer, mini **28.00**
Amazon, tumbler, etched .. **26.00**
American Beauty, tumbler, green,
   gold trim **23.00**
Anthemion, pitcher, 8¼" ... **35.00**
Apollo, sauce dish, with matching
   stand **12.00**
Apollo, sugar bowl, etched, with
   lid **40.00**
Aquarium, pitcher, water;
   green **290.00**
Arched Grape, goblet **25.00**
Argus, egg cup, handled ... **70.00**
Argus, sauce dish, flint, 4¼" . **9.00**
Arrowsheaf, pitcher, water . **42.00**
Art, cake stand, 7¾" **52.00**
Art, pitcher, milk; ruby
   stain **97.50**
Ashburton, claret, flint **55.00**
Ashburton, compote, open, low stan-
   dard, 7½" **64.00**
Ashburton, mug, 7" **120.00**
Ashland, plate, 6" **10.00**
Atlas, creamer, flat base ... **17.00**
Atlas, salt cellar, individual . **10.00**

Atlas, tumbler, water **30.00**
Austrian, bowl, 8" **47.50**
Austrian, wine, vaseline .. **125.00**
Ball & Swirl, creamer **23.00**
Baltimore Pear, celery vase. **35.00**
Baltimore Pear, sugar bowl, with
   lid **50.00**
Banded Portland, vase, 9" .. **40.00**
Bar & Diamond, compote, fluted,
   low stem, 8⅜" **15.00**
Bar & Diamond, jug, original stop-
   per, 10" **37.00**
Barberry, bowl, oval **18.00**
Barberry, bread plate **23.00**
Barberry, goblet **30.00**
Barley, celery vase **37.50**
Barred Forget-Me-Not, cake
   plate **20.00**
Barred Forget-Me-Not, celery vase,
   footed, handled **34.00**
Barrel Honeycomb, champagne,
   flint **25.00**
Basket Weave, goblet **23.50**
Basket Weave, plate, round handles,
   8¾" **12.50**
Beaded Band, goblet **25.00**
Beaded Grape, creamer,
   green **38.00**

Beaded Grape Medallion, spoon holder, $30.00.

Beaded Grape Medallion, castor jar,
   mustard **17.00**
Beaded Grape Medallion, sugar
   bowl, with lid **45.00**
Beaded Tulip, goblet **42.50**

Beaded Tulip, wine **28.00**
Beehive, goblet **60.00**
Bellflower, bowl, flat, flint,
7½" **95.00**
Bellflower, compote, low, flint,
7" **58.50**
Bellflower, honey dish, flint. **12.50**
Bellflower, wine, flint **75.00**
Bethlehem Star, sugar bowl. **30.00**
Bevelled Diamond & Star, bowl, flat,
7" **12.50**
Bevelled Diamond & Star, cheese
dish **40.00**
Bigler, goblet, flint **30.00**
Bigler, tumbler **57.00**

Birch Leaf, compote, $50.00.

Birch Leaf, egg cup, milk
glass **18.00**
Bird & Harp, mug, 3⅛" **20.00**
Bird & Strawberry, bowl, oval,
footed, 9¼" **32.00**
Bird & Strawberry, sauce dish,
footed, 4" **17.50**
Birds at Fountain, goblet .. **50.00**
Blackberry, butter dish with lid,
milk glass **30.00**
Blaze, bottle, oil; original stopper,
6" **40.00**
Blaze, champagne, flint **65.00**
Bleeding Heart, egg cup ... **40.00**
Bleeding Heart, bowl, oval, 6x9¼"
long **39.50**
Bleeding Heart, goblet **35.00**

Block & Fan, bowl, footed, collared,
8" **20.00**
Block & Fan, bowl, 4½x6¾" . **20.00**
Block with Thumbprint, goblet,
footed **18.00**
Bow Tie, bowl, shallow **15.00**
Bow Tie, cake stand, 9" **47.00**
Bradford Grape, goblet, flint. **50.00**
Brazen Shield, goblet **30.00**
Brittanic, castor bottle **27.00**
Broken Column, creamer .. **28.00**
Broken Column, cruet, original
stoper **55.00**
Bryce, plate, 8¼" **18.00**
Bryce, spooner **20.00**
Buckle, goblet **22.50**
Buckle, sugar bowl, with lid,
flint **57.00**

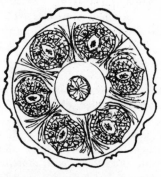

**Buckle with Star, sauce dish,
$30.00.**

Buckle with Star, wine **26.50**
Budded Ivy, goblet **32.50**
Bull's Eye, wine, flint **55.00**
Bull's Eye with Diamond Points,
sauce dish, flat, 4¼" **8.00**
Button Arches, punch cups; ruby
stained **17.50**
Button Arches, spooner **25.00**
Button Arches, tumbler, water; ruby
stained **32.50**
Button Arches, wine, footed, clam-
broth **27.00**
Button Band, creamer & sugar bowl,
open **30.00**
Cabbage Rose, compote, with lid,
7" **58.00**

Cabbage Rose, tumbler **45.00**
Cable, butter dish **125.00**
Cable, plate, 6" **85.00**
Cane, waste bowl, amber .. **30.00**
Cape Cod, goblet **40.00**
Cardinal Bird, creamer **20.00**
Cardinal Bird, sugar bowl, with
    lid **47.00**
Carlonia, pitcher, milk **37.50**
Cathedral, bowl, relish; fish shape,
    ruby stained **56.00**
Cathedral, wine **30.00**
Chain, butter dish **14.00**
Chain & Shield, creamer ... **16.00**
Champion, pitcher, water .. **52.00**
Chandelier, creamer **40.00**
Cherry & Cable, creamer .. **25.00**
Cherry & Cable, pitcher, wa-
    ter **62.00**
Classic, creamer **100.00**
Classic, goblet **196.00**
Colonial, champagne, flint . **45.00**
Colorado, bowl, footed, green,
    7½" **29.50**
Colorado, butter dish, with lid,
    blue **225.00**
Colorado, toothpick holder . **30.00**
Columbian Coin, spooner . **400.00**
Cord Drapery, bowl, oval, 8¼"
    long **25.00**
Cord Drapery, butter dish, footed,
    with flange **60.00**
Cottage, champagne **50.00**
Cottage, creamer **20.00**
Croesus, cruet, green **175.00**
Croesus, sugar bowl, with lid, purple
    with gilt trim **200.00**
Crossed Block, goblet **18.00**
Crystal Wedding, banana
    stand **75.00**
Crystal Wedding, spooner .. **70.00**
Crystal Wedding, sugar bowl, with
    lid, ruby stained **65.00**
Cube with Fan, goblet **15.00**
Cupid & Venus, butter dish. **42.50**
Cupid & Venus, mug **20.00**
Curled Leaf, celery, clear with gold
    trim **30.00**
Currant, cake stand, 10½" . **80.00**

Currant, creamer **60.00**
Currier & Ives, goblet **22.50**
Currier & Ives, tray, wine; balky
    mule, 9½" **68.00**
Cut Log, bowl, relish **13.00**
Cut Log, celery vase **34.50**
Dahlia, cake plate **22.00**
Dahlia, tray, bread; oval,
    handled **40.00**
Daisy & Button, bottle, scent; origi-
    nal stopper **22.50**
Daisy & Button, cake basket, yel-
    low, 7x5½" **126.00**
Daisy & Button, plate, salad; am-
    ber, 7" **15.00**
Dakota, butter dish, etched . **55.00**
Dakota, compote, with lid, etched,
    6" **68.00**
Dakota, sugar bowl, with lid,
    etched **57.50**
Deer & Dog, goblet **65.00**
Delaware, banana boat, rose with
    gilt trim, 5½" **45.00**
Delaware, finger bowl, clear with
    gold trim **22.00**
Delaware, punch cup, green with
    gold trim **22.50**
Dew & Raindrop, cordial ... **15.00**

Diamond Point, spill holder, $60.00.

211

Diagonal Band with Fan, champagne **30.00**
Diamond Cut with Leaf, wine, footed **25.00**
Diamond Point, salt cellar, master; flint **30.00**
Diamond Point, sugar bowl, with lid **66.00**
Diamond Prisms, goblet ... **65.00**
Diamond Quilted, bowl, flat, amber, 7" **17.50**
Diamond Thumbprint, butter dish, flint, 4½" **150.00**
Divided Heart, egg cup, etched top, flint **55.00**
Dot & Dash, sugar bowl ... **40.00**
Dotted Loop, pitcher, water . **18.00**
Drapery, egg cup **20.00**
Drapery, sugar bowl, lid ... **30.00**
Egg in Sand, goblet **30.00**
Egg in Sand, tray, swan & flowers in base, 7¾x5" **30.00**

Egyptian (Parthenon), bowl, footed 8", $30.00.

Egyptian, compote, with lid, 8" diameter **195.00**
Eight-O-Eight, plate, 8¼" .. **20.00**
Eight-O-Eight, wine **20.00**
Essex, water set, 7-piece .. **145.00**
Etched Band, wine **12.50**
Eugenie, champagne, flint . **78.00**
Eugenie, goblet **35.00**
Eureka, goblet, flint **30.00**
Eureka, salt cellar, master . **25.00**

Eyewinker, butter dish **70.00**
Eyewinker, cake stand **55.00**
Eyewinker, plate, square, 8". **20.00**
Fan with Diamond, butter dish, with lid **38.00**
Fancy Loop, bottle, water .. **65.00**

Feather (Fine Cut and Feather; Indiana Swirl; Swirl; Doric; Feather Swirl; Prince's Feather), syrup, $55.00.

Feather, bowl with lid, footed, 4⅞" **17.00**
Feather, celery vase **32.50**
Feather cruet, original stopper **85.00**
Feather Duster, tumbler, water; green **12.00**
Feeding Swan, tumbler, water; etched **20.00**
Fern Garland, wine **12.00**
Fine Cut, waste bowl, yellow. **33.00**
Fine Cut & Panel, sauce dish, footed, yellow **15.00**
Fine Rib, decanter, bar lip, quart **95.00**
Fishscale, bowl, square, 9" . **20.00**
Fishscale, cake stand **30.00**
Fishscale, pitcher, milk **26.00**
Flamingo Habitat, compote, open, 8x7¼" **17.50**

212

Flat Diamond, spooner **27.00**
Flattened Sawtooth, spill ..**35.00**
Fleur-de-Lis & Drape, celery vase, flat, 10¼x4½" **17.50**
Fleur-de-Lis & Drape, tray, relish; green, 8x5¼" **17.00**
Florida, plate, 7½" **15.00**
Florida, spooner **18.00**
Flower & Pleat, sugar shaker, original lid **65.00**
Flower Pot, creamer **30.00**
Flower Pot, sauce dish, low foot, 3¾" **10.00**
Flying Stork, goblet **56.00**
Four Petal, sugar bowl, pagoda, dome top, with lid, flint. **52.00**
Frosted Circle, creamer & sugar bowl, with lid **70.00**
Frosted Circle, tumbler **25.00**
Frosted Eagle, sugar bowl .**250.00**
Frosted Roman Key, sugar bowl, with lid **97.50**
Fuchsia, goblet, stippled ...**36.00**

Galloway (Virginia; Mirror), cruet, $30.00.

Galloway, butter dish, with lid **60.00**
Galloway, sauce dish **12.00**
Garden Fruits, creamer, applied handle **24.00**
Garden Fruits, sugar bowl, with lid, applied handles **30.00**

Garden of Eden, sauce dish, footed, 4⅛" **8.00**
Garfield Drape, pitcher, water **60.00**
Giant Sawtooth, goblet, flint **95.00**
Gooseberry, tumbler **25.00**
Gothic, wine **137.00**
Grand, bread plate **22.00**
Grand, celery vase, footed ..**25.00**
Grape & Festoon, egg cup, stippled leaf **30.00**
Grape Band, creamer, applied handle, non-flint **35.00**
Grape Band, salt cellar, master; non-flint **25.00**
Grasshopper with Insect, celery tray, oblong **35.00**
Hairpin, celery vase **40.00**
Hamilton, goblet **45.00**
Hamilton, sauce dish, flat, flint, 4" **10.00**
Hand, cordial **86.00**
Hand, syrup **30.00**
Hanover, plate, 10" **18.00**
Hartley, sauce dish, low foot, blue **15.00**
Hawaiian Lei, compote, jelly; open **12.50**
Hawaiian Lei, wine **23.00**
Heart with Thumbprint, tumbler, water **22.00**
Heart with Thumbprint, wine **55.00**
Heavy Gothic, goblet, ruby stained **55.00**
Hercules Pillar, egg cup, cobalt blue **30.00**
Hexagon Block, tumbler ...**33.00**
Hexagon Block, tumbler, water; amber stained, etched .**35.00**
Hexagonal Bull's Eye, wine. **40.00**
Hickman, compote, open ...**20.00**
Hickman, goblet, gilt trim .**35.00**
Hidalgo, celery vase, flat base, amber stained **33.00**
Hidalgo, pitcher, water **50.00**
Hinoto, tumbler, whiskey; handled, rare **46.00**

Holly, bowl, flat, small **45.00**
Holly, creamer **110.00**
Honeycomb, goblet, footed, etched, flint **22.50**
Horn of Plenty, compote, 8" **50.00**
Horseshoe, compote, with lid, 8x 9" **75.00**
Horseshoe, creamer, hotel type, 6½" **97.00**
Horseshoe, relish bowl, oblong, 9x 5" **12.50**
Huber, champagne, flint ...**25.00**
Huber, egg cup, 10-panel ..**20.00**
Hummingbird, tumbler, bar; amber **47.00**
Hummingbird, water set, amber, 7-piece **365.00**
Illinois, basket, 11½x7" ...**100.00**
Illinois, toothpick holder ...**20.00**
Interlocked Hearts, goblet .**33.00**
Inverted Fern, champagne, flint **150.00**
Inverted Fern, goblet **40.00**
Inverted Thumbprint & Star, goblet, blue **30.00**
Iowa, sauce dish, 4½" **7.00**
Ivy, butter dish, flint **95.00**
Ivy in Snow, creamer **25.00**
Ivy in Snow, syrup **70.00**
Jacob's Ladder, butter dish .**45.00**
Jacob's Ladder, pitcher, water; bulbous **165.00**
Jacob's Ladder, spooner ...**30.00**
Jersey Swirl, compote, with lid, flint, 11¾" **75.00**
Jewel with Dewdrop, compote, open **35.00**
Jewelled Moon & Star, cruet **20.00**
Jumbo, butter dish, oblong, no handle **465.00**
Kentucky, plate, square, 7" .**17.50**
Kentucky, punch cup, green. **15.00**
Kentucky, toothpick holder .**27.00**
King's Crown, castor set, ruby stained **25.00**
King's Crown, tumbler, water; etched **40.00**
Klondike, butter dish **270.00**

Lacy Daisy, creamer, $20.00.

Lacy Daisy, butter dish **33.00**
Lacy Daisy, creamer & sugar bowl, with lid **40.00**
Ladder with Diamonds, tumbler, ruby stained with gilt ..**25.00**
Lady Hamilton, plate, 6" ...**18.00**
Late Block, butter dish, ruby stained **60.00**
Late Block, decanter, original stopper **175.00**
Late Panelled Grape, goblet. **19.00**
Leaf & Dart, egg cup **20.00**
Leaf & Dart, spooner **25.00**
Leaf & Dart, wine **28.00**
Lee, goblet, flint **165.00**
Liberty Bell, goblet, footed, with knob stem **35.00**
Liberty Bell, relish dish, shell handles, 7x11¼" **67.50**
Liberty Bell, tray, relish; states motif **36.00**
Lily of the Valley, creamer, footed **75.00**
Lily of the Valley, cruet ...**110.00**
Lion, bowl, relish; lion handles **40.00**
Lion, celery vase, frosted ...**95.00**
Log & Star, goblet **20.00**
Log Cabin, sugar bowl **300.00**
Loop, salt cellar, master; flint, NM **22.50**
Loop & Block, creamer **45.00**
Loop & Block, goblet **47.00**
Loop & Dart, sauce dish, 4" ..**7.00**
Loop & Moose Eye, egg cup, flint, rare **30.00**
Maine, butter dish **23.00**

Manhattan, sauce dish, pink with gilt, set of 6 . . . . **60.00**
Manting, goblet, flint **37.50**
Manting, tumbler, bar; flint. **47.00**
Maple Leaf, plate, blue, 10½" **45.00**
Maple Leaf, platter, yellow, 13x 9" **36.00**
Marquisette, goblet **25.00**
Maryland, goblet **28.00**
Maryland, pitcher, milk; 7" . **27.00**
Maryland, sauce dish, flat . . . **7.50**
Mascotte, basket, with handles, 9½" **30.00**
Mascotte, compote, 5x7" . . . **30.00**
Mascotte, sauce dish, low foot, 4" **9.00**
Massachusetts, cruet **40.00**
Massachusetts, olive dish, 3½x 5" **9.00**
Massachusetts, plate, 8" . . . **25.00**
Medallion, bread plate, openwork rim **25.00**
Medallion, goblet **25.00**
Melrose, plate, 8" **9.50**
Melrose, sugar bowl **32.50**
Melrose, wine, etched **22.00**
Memphis, pitcher, water . . . **78.00**
Michigan, celery vase, pink blush **85.00**
Michigan, sauce dish, flat, 5". **6.00**

Mirror Star (Old Glory), pitcher, $45.00.

Millard, spooner, ruby stain. **40.00**
Minerva, goblet **85.00**
Minnesota, cruet **33.00**
Mioton, sugar bowl, open . . **20.00**
Mirror, wine, flint **40.00**
Missouri, mug, green **40.00**
Missouri, plate, 9½" **15.00**
Mitered Diamond, wine, footed, amber **33.00**
Monkey, bowl, scalloped, 4½x 8" **400.00**
Monkey, pitcher, water . . . **425.00**

Moon and Star, (Star and Punty; Bulls-Eye and Star; Palace), pitcher, $65.00.

Moon & Star, goblet **38.00**
Morning Glory, wine, rare **175.00**
Nail, bowl, shallow, 6" **17.00**
Nail, cake stand **25.00**
Nailhead, compote, with lid, 6¼x 6¼" **40.00**
Nailhead, sugar bowl, open . **13.00**
New England Pineapple, egg cup, flint **40.00**
New England Pineapple, wine **137.00**
New Hampshire, creamer & sugar bowl, breakfast size . . . **25.00**
New Jersey, pitcher, water . **75.00**
New Jersey, plate, 8" **12.50**
Oak Leaf Band, mug **40.00**
O'Hara Diamond, plate, green, 10" **17.00**
One Hundred & One, goblet. **25.00**
One Hundred & One, plate, luncheon, 7" **12.50**

Open Rose, goblet, $30.00.

Open Rose, compote, 8x4" . . **33.00**
Open Rose, egg cup **18.00**
Opposing Pyramids, spooner, green
　with gold trim **65.00**
Oregon, butter dish **60.00**
Oriental, butter dish **35.00**
Oval Mitre, goblet, flint **36.00**
Paddlewheel, cruet **22.50**
Palmette, butter dish **60.00**
Palmette, pitcher, water . . **125.00**
Panelled Acorn Band, creamer,
　applied handle **40.00**
Panelled Daisy, plate, 9" . . . **17.50**
Panelled Grape Band, creamer,
　applied handle **40.00**
Panelled Oval, egg cup **35.00**
Pathfinder, tumbler, water . **10.00**
Pathfinder, wine **10.00**
Pavonia, butter dish **60.00**
Pavonia, pitcher, water; etched,
　9½" . . . . :**85.00**
Peerless, platter, clear & frosted,
　13x9" **30.00**
Pennsylvania, punch cup . . . **9.00**
Pennsylvania, sauce dish . . . **8.00**
Pentagon, wine **17.50**
Pillar, goblet, flint **40.00**
Pillar, tumbler, ale; flint . . . **43.00**
Pineapple & Fan, tray, celery; ob-
　long **25.00**
Pineapple & Fan, wine **20.00**
Pittsburgh Daisy, cake stand, footed,
　8½" **20.00**
Pittsburgh Fan, goblet **15.00**

Pleat & Panel, goblet **28.00**
Pleat & Panel, sugar bowl . . **25.00**
Plume, cake stand, 8¼" **50.00**
Pogo Stick, plate, 7" **9.00**
Pointed Jewel, goblet **150.00**
Polar Bear, goblet **150.00**
Popcorn, pitcher, water; with ears
　of corn **18.00**
Powder & Shot, egg cup . . . **46.00**
Powder & Shot, salt cellar, master;
　flint **40.00**
Powder & Shot, spooner . . . **33.00**
Pressed Diamond, creamer, canary
　yellow **20.00**
Pressed Leaf, goblet **17.50**
Primrose, relish dish, 8x5" . **12.50**
Primrose, tray, blue, 10" . . . **30.00**
Princess Feather, plate, 6" . **37.50**
Princess Feather, spooner . . **24.00**
Psyche & Cupid, goblet **52.50**
Punty & Diamond Point, biscuit
　jar **75.00**

**Queen (Sunk; Pointed Panel; Pan-
elled Daisy and Button), pitcher,
$65.00.**

Queen, compote, with lid,
　12" **46.00**
Queen, goblet, blue **40.00**
Queen, wine **23.00**
Rainbow, wine **12.50**
Raindrop, creamer, blue . . . **30.00**
Ramsay Grape, pitcher, water;
　amber **48.00**
Reverse Torpedo, bowl, berry;
　ruffled top, 10¾" **65.00**

Reverse Torpedo, compote, open, 6½x7¾" 57.50

Ribbed Ivy, sauce dish, 4" ..12.50

Ribbed Palm, creamer 145.00

Ribbon, spooner 22.00

Ribbon Candy, cake stand ..35.00

Ripple, creamer 40.00

Roman Key, champagne, frosted 78.00

Roman Key, goblet, flint ...30.00

Rope Bands, goblet 28.00

Rose in Snow, butter dish ..40.00

Rose in Snow, mug, Remembrance, yellow, 3¼" 47.50

Rose Leaves, goblet 21.00

Rose Sprig, boat, relish 20.00

Rosepoint Band, goblet 30.00

Rosette, bowl, flat, 7⅜" 11.50

Roman Rosette, creamer, $50.00.

Rosette & Palms, spooner ..25.00

Rosette & Palms, sugar bowl, with lid 45.00

Sandwich Star, bottle, bar; flint, quart 58.00

Sandwich Star, spill, clear .35.00

Sawtooth, creamer, flint ...85.00

Sawtooth, sauce dish, flat, canary, 4" 25.00

Scalloped Tape, wine 12.00

Scroll, egg cup 18.00

Sequoia, tray, 12x7½" 20.00

Serrated Prism-Banded, wine, footed 8.00

Shell & Tassel, tray, ice cream 47.50

Sheraton, bread plate, blue, 10½x 8" 25.00

Sheraton, goblet, blue 45.00

Shimmering Star, tumbler .18.00

Shoshone, butter dish, amber stained 48.00

Shrine, salt shaker 22.00

Shrine, tumbler, pattern under base, 4⅞" 40.00

Skilton, bowl, flat, 7¾x2½" .14.00

Skilton, compote, ruby flashed 55.00

Skilton, tumbler, water; ruby stained 28.00

Snail, bowl, flat, 2¾x9" 35.00

Snail, butter dish 76.00

Snail, syrup 80.00

Spearpoint Band, bowl, flat, flint, 7" 70.00

Spirea Band, goblet 28.00

Spirea Band, sauce dish, flat, blue, 4" 12.50

Sprig, wine, 3⅝" 32.00

Squirrel, sauce dish, 4¼" ...18.00

Star Band, creamer 16.00

Star Rosetted, sugar bowl, with lid 40.00

Stedman, sauce dish, flat, flint, 4" 15.00

Stippled Band, goblet, flint .22.50

Stippled Chain, sauce dish, flat, 4½" 5.00

Stippled Cherry, bowl, shallow, 2½x8¼" 16.00

Stippled Cherry, bowl, 8" ..22.00

Stippled Grape & Festoon, sugar bowl, open 28.00

Stippled Medallion, goblet .30.00

Strawberry, goblet 40.00

Strawberry, pitcher, water; bulbous 110.00

Strawberry, sauce dish, flat, milk glass, 4" 12.50

Strigil, wine, gold trim 15.00

Sunburst, plate, 8" 12.00

Sunburst, sauce dish, 5", with handle 7.50

Sunk Daisy, carafe **40.00**
Sunk Prism, cake stand ... **22.00**
Swan, creamer **40.00**
Swirled Column, butter dish,
    green **45.00**
Tackle Block, goblet, flint .. **33.00**
Tarantum's Atlanta, cruet . **20.00**
Teardrop, goblet, etched ... **22.00**
Teardrop, tumbler, etched . **22.50**
Teardrop & Tassel, creamer. **38.50**
Texas, creamer **10.00**
Texas, pitcher, water **175.00**
The Prize, tumbler, water .. **19.00**

Thousand Eye (Daisy), pitcher, $40.00.

Thousand Eye, cruet, am-
    ber **175.00**
Thousand Eye, toothpick holder,
    amber **35.00**
Thousand Eye, tumbler, water; light
    amber **25.00**
Three Face, creamer **125.00**
Three Face, saucer, cham-
    pagne **150.00**
Tidy, pitcher, water; bul-
    bous **50.00**
Torpedo, bowl, flat, 8½x2¾" . **16.00**
Torpedo, compote, jelly **28.00**
Torpedo, creamer **40.00**
Tree of Life, compote, with lid, 6x
    8" **67.50**

Tree of Life, cruet, original stopper,
    milk glass **30.00**
Tree of Life, tumbler **30.00**
Triangular Prism, spooner,
    flint **30.00**
Triangular Prism, wine **16.00**
Triple Triangle, butter dish, ruby
    stained **75.00**
Truncated Cube, salt cellar . **12.50**
Tulip, celery vase **40.00**
Tulip with Sawtooth, salt cellar,
    master **30.00**
Tulip with Sawtooth, wine . **30.00**
Two Panel, goblet, amber .. **35.00**
Two Panel, goblet, footed, apple
    green **35.00**
US Coin, bowl, berry; large. **375.00**
US Coin, sauce dish, flat,
    frosted **120.00**
Valencia Waffle, tray, amber,
    13¼x9½" **47.50**
Valencia, goblet, footed, apple
    green **40.00**

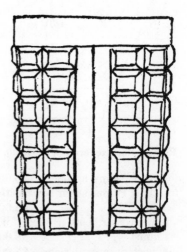

Waffle, tumbler, $40.00.

Virginia, cake stand, 8½" .. **70.00**
Waffle, decanter **85.00**
Waffle, salt cellar, master;
    flint **60.00**
Washboard, butter dish, with
    lid **50.00**

Washington, decanter, original stopper, flint, quart 200.00
Washington, Early; egg cup, flint 80.00
Washington Centennial, compote, open 40.00
Waterlily & Cattails, tray, water 18.00
Wedding Ring, goblet 35.00
Wedding Ring, sauce dish, flint, 4" 9.00
Westmoreland, cruet, original stopper 23.00
Westward Ho, creamer, dog handle 135.00
Westward Ho, sauce dish ..30.00
Wheat & Barley, salt shaker, blue 40.00
Wild Rose with Bowknot, tumbler, frosted 20.00
Wildflower, butter dish 60.00
Wildflower, tumbler, water; amber or yellow 30.00
Willow Oak, compote, 6½" ..18.00
Willow Oak, compote, with lid, 6¼x10½" 47.50
Willow Oak, pitcher, milk ..32.00
Windflower, sugar bowl, with lid 50.00
Wisconsin, celery vase 38.00
Wisconsin, pitcher, water ..60.00
Wisconsin, plate 15.00
Wooden Pail, match holder, amber, handled 20.00
Wooden Pail, tumbler, bar; amethyst 36.00
X-Logs, goblet 20.00
Yoked Loop, goblet, footed, green, flint 18.00
Yoked Loop, tumbler, whiskey; handled, flint 25.00
Zig Zag, goblet 20.00
Zig Zag, salt cellar 8.50
Zig Zag, wine 15.00
Zipper Slash, wine 20.00
Zippered Block, salt shaker, ruby stained 36.00
Zippered Block, tumbler, water; ruby stained 40.00

Pennsbury

From the 1950s through the 1970s, dinnerware and novelty wares produced by the Pennsbury company were sold through tourist gift shops along the Pennsylvania turnpike. Much of their ware is decorated in an Amish theme. Barber shop singers were also popular, and a line of bird figures was made, very similar to Stangl's.

Tea tile, 4½", $20.00; Mug, 4½", $22.50.

Ash tray, Constitution, oval, medium size 30.00
Bowl, Amish, 9" 35.00
Bowl, cereal; rooster motif, red, 5½" 14.00
Cake stand, Harvest, 4½x12" diameter 39.00
Cruet, Amish couple, figural-head stoppers, pair 125.00
Mug, Here's Looking at You .20.00
Pitcher, tulip, 3-quart 65.00
Plaque, Sweet Adeline, 5" ..30.00
Plate, rooster, 10" 30.00
Platter, black rooster motif, oval, 13½x11" 38.00
Sugar bowl, rooster motif, with cover 25.00
Tray, relish, Laurel Ridge, oblong, 9½" 30.00
Wall pocket, blue flowers with green border 35.00

Peters and Reed

Peters and Reed founded a pottery in Zanesville, Ohio, around the turn of the century. By 1922, the firm became known as Zane Pottery. Several lines of artware were produced which are today attracting the interest of pottery collectors: High Glaze Brown Ware, decorated with in-mold relief; Moss Aztec, relief designs molded from red clay with a green-washed exterior; Chromal, with realistic or suggested scenics done in soft matt colors; Landsun; Shadow Ware; and Wilse Blue.

Vase, Moss Aztec, 10", $45.00.

Bowl, dragonfly relief, shallow, 6" **25.00**
Bowl, Moss Aztec, pine cones, signed Ferrell, 3x6¼" **35.00**
Flower frog, Pereco, turtle figural, light green **45.00**
Hanging basket, Moss Aztec, roses relief, with chains **35.00**
Jardiniere, Moss Aztec, grape border, signed Ferrell, 8" ..**50.00**
Jug, Brown Ware, grapes & leaves, bulbous, 6¼" **65.00**
Loving cup, Brown Ware, lion's head & florals, 3-handle **85.00**
Pitcher, Brown Ware, man with banjo, 4" **55.00**
Tankard, Brown Ware, grapes & leaves, 17" **170.00**
Vase, Brown Ware, floral, 3-footed, squat, 5" **50.00**
Vase, bud; Sheenware, Zaneware, 10" **30.00**
Vase, Chromal, large trees in foreground, bulbous, 6¾" .**195.00**
Vase, Chromal, scenic, stylized, pastel matt, 7" **165.00**
Vase, dark green with light green drip, 4¾" **35.00**
Vase, Landsun, 5" **45.00**
Vase, Moss Aztec, 12" **65.00**
Vase, Shadow Ware, brown-blue drip over tan, 8¾" **75.00**
Wall pocket, Moss Aztec, signed Ferrell, 7½" **45.00**

Pewter

A metal alloy combining tin, lead, copper or brass, pewter was molded or spun to form utensils, tableware, lamps, inkwells, and miscellaneous items of every sort. Artisans in England marked their wares with touchmarks, signs or initials used to identify themselves or their companies, and until the Revolution provided America with nearly all of the pewter on the market. With the end of the war and the abolition of the English law restricting the import of raw materials needed for its production, the Colonists themselves began to make pewter on a much larger scale. This practice continued until the Civil War.

Basin, marked JC Konn 1801, 2¼x8⅞" **65.00**
Bowl, Flagg & Homan, footed, 5⅝x9½" **25.00**
Candlesticks, removable bobeche, brass trim, 10¾", pair .**100.00**

Chamberstick, scalloped & beaded
edge, 5¼" diameter **95.00**
Chamberstick, whale oil burner,
2⅛" **175.00**
Charger, eagle touchmark, Thomas
Badger, Boston, 12¼" . .**95.00**
Charger, thistle & shell touchmarks,
English, 14½" **50.00**
Coffee urn, Reed & Barton, brass
spigot, 16½" **150.00**
Dish, with hinged lid, marked AG,
1¾x4⅜" diameter **220.00**
Flagon, angel touchmark, Continental, 9¾" **65.00**
Flagon, crowned rose mark, footed,
English, 10" **175.00**
Flagon, fleur-de-lis touchmark,
French, 10⅛" **87.50**
Hand lamp, ear handle, American,
3¼" **95.00**
Inkwell, with hinged lid, English,
insert missing, 2½x4" . .**55.00**
Measure, set of 6; English, 1⅝" to
3¾" **195.00**
Pan, 2 loop handles, English, ca
1800, 11" diameter **20.00**
Plate, Ashbil Griswold, American,
7⅞" **150.00**
Plate, Blakslee Barns, American,
7⅞" **230.00**

**Lighthouse coffeepot, Rufus
Dunham, Maine, 1837-1861, 11", EX,
$350.00.**

**Fluid lamp, attributed to Capen &
Molineux, New York and
Massachusetts, 1856-1850, 7½",
$325.00; Pigeon-breasted teapot,
Isaac C. Lewis, Connecticut, 1834-
1852, 9", $400.00.**

Plate, crowned rose touchmark with
IS, 8" **125.00**
Plate, Edward Danforth, American,
7⅞" **210.00**
Plate, Josiah Danforth, American,
8" **200.00**
Plate, rose touchmark with London, English, 8" **25.00**
Plate, Thomas Badger, American,
7⅞" **65.00**
Salt box, hanging, applied cast head
crest, French, 7¼" **45.00**
Tall pot, eagle touchmark, Connecticut, 11" **150.00**
Tall pot, R Dunham, American,
hinged lid, 11¾" **300.00**
Tall pot, Reed & Barton, wood
handle & finial, 13½" .**150.00**
Teapot, individual; pear shaped,
wood handle, 6¼" **150.00**
Teapot, James Dixon & Sons, wood
handle & final, English, 10¾",
EX **85.00**
Teapot, marked John Phillips & Co,
Glasgow; footed, 8¼" .**150.00**
Teapot, touchmark McQuilkin,
7½" **250.00**
Teapot, unmarked, pear shape,
6⅜" **200.00**
Teaspoon, marked Charles Parker
& Co, 5⅞" **55.00**
Tumbler, touchmark of Ashbil
Griswold, 3" **25.00**

Phoenix Bird China

Since early in the 1900s, Japanese potteries have been producing a line of blue and white china decorated with the Japanese bird of paradise and vines of Chinese grass. The design will vary slightly, and newer ware is whiter than the old, with a more vivid blue.

Bowl, berry; 1¼x4¾" 8.00
Bowl, sauce; oval, 1½x8½" . .28.00
Bowl, serving; scalloped, 9" .40.00
Casserole, oval, Japan, with cover,
   2½x6¼x4½" 50.00
Chocolate pot, crown border, scalloped base, 9" 85.00
Creamer, long spout, 2¾" . .15.00
Cup & saucer 12.00
Egg cup, double, 3⅛" 18.00
Egg cup, single, 2¼" 15.00
Ginger jar, 5" 15.00
Gravy boat, with separate 9" underplate 48.00
Ladle, 6¼" 22.00
Mustard, with cover 40.00
Plate, dinner; 9¾" 40.00
Platter, oval, 15" 75.00
Teapot, 8" 85.00
Tray, relish; handled, 10" . .30.00
Tureen, oval, 2-handle, with cover,
   4⅞x12" 68.00

Phoenix Glass

Sculptured artware vases made during the 1930s and 1940s by the Phoenix Glass Company of Monaca, Pennsylvania, are very similar to a line made by the Consolidated Company of nearby Corapolis. It is very difficult to distinguish between the two. Though there are exceptions, as a general rule Phoenix added color to the background, while Consolidated left the background plain and added color to the raised design.

Bachelor Button, vase, dark blue on crystal, 6" 60.00
Box, covered 3-part, floral, green on crystal, 8" 60.00
Dancing Girl, vase, mother-of-pearl nudes on red, 11½" . . .250.00
Dancing Girl, vase, slate blue on white, 12" 265.00
Dancing Nymph, plate, white on crystal, 8" 32.00
Fern, lamp, slate blue with mother-of-pearl fronds 85.00
Jewel, vase, mother-of-pearl floral on light blue, 5" 45.00
Lace Dew Drop, bowl, milk glass, with lid, 8½" 30.00
Lace Dew Drop, compote, blue on milk glass, with lid, 12". 45.00

Creamer and sugar bowl, $42.00.

Light shade, Flame, crystal satin, #5069, 8" long, 3" fitter . **35.00**

Madonna, vase, white sculptured form on blue, 10¼" . . . **125.00**

Pine Cone, vase, (no cones), brown on white, 6½" **75.00**

Reuben, vase, goldfish on dark blue, pillow form, 9" **150.00**

Tiger Lily, bowl, red over milk glass, 11½" **100.00**

Wild Geese, vase, mother-of-pearl over milk glass, marked PG Co, 1976 . . . . **50.00**

Wild Geese, vase, pink on green background, ovoid, 9" . **135.00**

Wild Rose, vase, mother-of-pearl floral on light green, sticker, 10" **85.00**

Zodiac, vase, red on white, mother-of-pearl figures on red over milk glass, 10" **450.00**

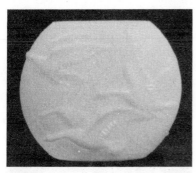

Vase, Wild Geese, white with opalescence, 9½", $120.00.

Photographica

Early cameras and the images they produced are today becoming popular collectors' items. The earliest type of image was the daguerrotype, made with the use of a copper plate and silver salts; ambrotypes followed, produced by the wet-plate process on glass negatives. Tintypes were from the same era as the ambrotype but were developed on

japanned iron and were much more durable. Size, subject matter, esthetics, and condition help determine value. Stereo cards, viewing devices, albums, photographs, and advertising memorabilia featuring camera equipment are included in this area of collecting.

Album, velvet covered, elaborately faced front **110.00**

Album, velvet covered, portrait pages, 10x8", VG **25.00**

Albumen print, home of Thomas Alva Edison at Menlo Park, 22x18" **675.00**

Albumen print, Rain Sculpture at Salt Creek Canon, Utah; 1872 . . . . **450.00**

Albumen print, Sugar Loaf Mountain, on card, 6x9" **90.00**

Albumen print, 4 Union Army staff officers, ca 1862, 7x9" . **275.00**

Ambrotype, full plate, Niagara Falls & sightseers **375.00**

Ambrotype, 4th plate, curly-haired girl in gingham dress . . **55.00**

Cabinet photo, Alica Placide, Wild West star, J. Wood photo, $250.00.

Bank, cast iron, box Brownie form, 1940s, 4x5x2¾" **350.00**

Camera, #3-A Autographic Folding Kodak, leather case . . . **15.00**

Camera, Ansco Buster Brown, folding, 1910-1920 . . . . **10.00**

Camera, Brownie #1, adjustable view finder, with box . **100.00**

Camera, Brownie Model A, ca 1909, 8½" long **22.00**

Camera, Cirofles TLR, 120 film, 1950s **40.00**

Camera, Colly, miniature . . . **3.50**

Camera, Duca, 35mm, mini-movie camera type, 1950s **85.00**

Camera, Folding Scout 3-A Seneca Camera Co, in case **30.00**

Camera, Hawk-Eye Special #2, tooled leather sides **45.00**

Camera, Jem Jr, box type, with Jem Flash unit, late 1940s . **55.00**

Camera, Kodak #2, 1890s . **325.00**

Camera, Kodak Bullet **7.50**

Camera, Kodak Girl Scout #620, no case **25.00**

Camera, Kodak Junior 6-20, folding, original box & manual, 1920s **25.00**

Camera, Kodak Model B-4, ca 1902, no case **40.00**

Camera, Minolta 16, miniature type, no case **22.50**

Camera, Petie, marked Kunick & Frandfurt, 1958 . . . . . **550.00**

Camera, Polaroid 95 . . . . . . **14.50**

Camera, Powell, used for stereo views, 1850s, G **750.00**

Camera, Super Rocoh-Flea, in leather case **35.00**

Camera, Whittaker 16MM Micro 16, in case, 2x1x3" **15.00**

Camera, Whittelsey Detective, no case **750.00**

Camera, Zeiss Icon Contessa, 35mm, folding, 1950s **200.00**

Carte de visite, Gen George Custer, seated, uniformed **150.00**

Carte de visite, Gen Sheridan, facing front, half-length . . **40.00**

Catalog, Photo Tools & Accessories for Amateurs, '03, 3x6" . **12.00**

Daguerreotype, 6th plate, Massachusetts soldier **150.00**

Daguerreotype, 6th plate, Zouave soldier **550.00**

Foto Reel, metal, with 26 views on reel **35.00**

Locket, portrait daguerreotype, gold filled, 1¼x1¾" **85.00**

Platinum print, Gen Ulysses S Grant, 1880s, oval, 7¼". **70.00**

Sign, Kodak, light-up, red & black on yellow, 3½x10x3½" . . **12.00**

Silver print, Jean Harlow, signed, in MGM envelope **125.00**

Slide projector, Executive 500, in original case & instructions, 8" **12.00**

Slide projector, tin & cast metal, 1899, Enterprise **50.00**

Stanhope, Niagara Falls souvenir, soapstone, 6", $90.00.

Stanhope, alabaster barrel, Niagara Falls scene **28.50**

Stanhope, cross, bone, WWI soldiers in trenches, bone **55.00**

Stereo view, Civil War soldier shaved by Black man . . **65.00**

Stereo view, Steamer Martha's Vineyard, ochre mount . **18.00**
Tintype, cooper with his tools, 2¼x3½" **40.00**
Tintype, 9th plate, Maine Civil War soldier wearing kepi . . . **35.00**
Viewer, Cosmorama, table model drawer base, 1850s . **1,650.00**

Pickard

When first founded in Chicago in 1897, the Pickard China Company was merely a decorating studio. Because they imported blanks from European firms such as T&V Limoges, Noritake, and Haviland, you may find the manufacturer's backstamp alongside Pickard's. Much of their ware was decorated with hand-painted fruits, florals, and scenics, often signed by the artist. By the late 1930s, Pickard had developed their own formula for a fine china body, and began producing their own blanks.

Ash tray, allover gold etched floral, 5" **25.00**
Bottle, scent; forget-me-nots, gold stopper, 1912 . . . . . . **175.00**

Bowl, filbert nuts in shallow shell form **98.00**
Bowl, fruit, much gold, signed Gasper, with cover, 9" **300.00**
Bowl, red Nouveau poppies on gold, 10" **160.00**
Candle holder, allover gold etched floral, 2½", pair **25.00**
Coffeepot, allover gold etched floral, 8" **85.00**
Creamer & sugar, cherries & leaves, signed **110.00**
Creamer & sugar, flowers, signed Challinor **65.00**
Cup & saucer, large red poppies, signed **105.00**
Marmalade jar, blackberries, artist signed, 7" **78.00**
Marmalade jar, strawberries, signed Yeschek **135.00**
Plate, cake; roses, artist signed, handles **95.00**
Plate, floral, artist signed, Haviland, 8" **65.00**
Plate, multicolor floral, signed James, 8½" **75.00**
Plate, outdoor scene on matt, signed, 8¾" **170.00**
Plate, green shamrocks, 10" . **90.00**
Tea set, stylized design, artist signed on handle, 3-piece **300.00**

Breakfast set, Aura Argenta Linear, 5 pieces, pot: 7", $550.00.

Vase, multicolor floral, heavy gold,
early, 8¾" **150.00**
Vase, scenic, matt finish, artist
signed, 7¼" **235.00**

Pickle Castors

Popular table accessories during
the Victorian era, pickle castors
consist of a fancy silverplated frame
with a glass insert, either pressed
pattern glass or art glass, and tongs
or a pickle fork.

Beaded Dart, citron, Webster frame
with embossed base & ornate
fretwork **195.00**
Beaded Drape, lime green frost,
silverplated holder . . . **325.00**
Block, elaborate silverplated holder,
marked, with tongs . . **110.00**
Broken Column, ruby stain, footed
silverplate holder **395.00**
Cane, amber, exotic birds & fountain on silverplated holder, with
tongs **185.00**
Cane, amber, silverplated holder,
with tongs, signed Web-
ster **165.00**
Cobalt with etched decor, ornate
footed holder **225.00**
Cone, pink cased, silverplated
holder, with tongs **255.00**
Daisy & Button, blue/clear, marked
silverplated holder . . . **145.00**
Diamond Point, vaseline, silverplated Homan holder . **160.00**
Pigeon blood, original Forbes holder
with braid handle **295.00**
Quilted pink satin, bird atop, Wilcox
holder **550.00**
Swirl, cranberry with florals,
silverplated Benedict hol-
der **195.00**
Swirl Rib, clear & frosted, marked
Rogers tree-bark holder, with
tongs **150.00**
Vaseline opal, ornate footed holder,
attributed to Webb . . . **450.00**

Daisy and Button, sapphire, Tufts,
11", $225.00.

Pin Back Buttons

Most of the advertising buttons
prior to the 1920s were made of
celluloid and so are called 'cellos.'
Many were issued in sets on related
topics. Some buttons had paper
inserts on the back that identified
the company or the product they
were advertising. After the 1920s,
lithographed metal buttons were
produced; these are referred to as
'lithos.' Political buttons are listed
in the section called Campaign
Collectibles.

Andy Gump **25.00**
Beatles **6.00**
Breyer's Ice Cream **16.00**
Chew Bull Dog, multicolor bulldog,
early 1900 . . . . **8.00**
Colt Firearms Factory Guard, Tif-
fany NY, 1900 . . . . **45.00**
De Laval Cream Separators, multi-
color, 1900 . . . . **45.00**

Dick Tracy **15.00**
Dodson-Braun Pickles **15.00**
Ford, 1937 . . . . **15.00**
Heinz Pickles, 1930s **10.00**
I Say Butternut, child with loaf of
   bread, red & white, 1930. **8.00**
I'm Looking for a Thrill, dated 1940,
   with ribbon, 1¼" **5.00**
Imperial Plow **28.00**
Iver Johnson Cycles **25.00**
JI Case Eagle **15.00**
Muggs McGinnis **15.00**
Omaha Lightning Rods, Victorian
   house **20.00**
Oshkosh Trucks **20.00**
Phantom's Club Member, multicolor
   phantom, 1940s **65.00**
Philip Morris **18.00**
Pogo, I Go Pogo **15.00**
Popeye, Paramount, 1955 . . **35.00**
Remember Pearl Harbor, patriotic
   with flag, 1940s **12.00**
Sharples Cream Separators. **15.00**
Shmoo, figure on green background,
   1940s **20.00**
South Bend Watch Co **20.00**
Sterling Bicycles **20.00**
Vote for Buster Brown, '20s . **12.00**
Warren Harding **6.00**
Workers' Alliance, 1939 . . . . . **7.50**
Yellow Kid #5 . . . . **25.00**

Pink Pigs

Made in Germany, these amusing pigs and piglets are portrayed driving a roadster, sitting in a suitcase, bowling, beside the feeding trough, or typing on a typewriter. While some figurines are easy to find, others are scarce and may bring prices in excess of $100.00.

Climbing out of an oval bucket, little
   pig at window **85.00**
Climbing out of cup **65.00**
Holding frypan, & wearing chef's
   costume, with basket . . **80.00**

Bank, pig inside satchel, 3½", $75.00.

Laying in bathtub **90.00**
Mother bathes baby in tub...**115.00**
Reclining on an ash tray . . . **70.00**
Riding on a train, 4½" **125.00**
Sitting behind a 3" trough . . **55.00**
Sitting on a log **65.00**
Two in a purse **75.00**
Two on top of pouch bank, on a
   seesaw **75.00**

Planters Peanuts

Since 1916, Mr. Peanut has represented the Planters Peanuts Company. Today he has his own fan club of collectors who specialize in this area of advertising memorabilia. More than fifteen styles of the glass display jars were made; the earliest was issued in 1926 and is referred to as the 'pennant' jar. The rarest of them all is the 'football' jar from the early '30s. Premiums such as glass and metal paperweights, pens, and pencils were distributed in the late 1930s; after the war, plastic items were offered.

Plastic Mr. Peanut salt and pepper shakers, 3½", $12.50.

Alarm clock, Mr Peanut ...**55.00**
Ash tray, glass **10.00**
Blotter **18.00**
Champagne glass, green plastic, footed **10.00**
Charm bracelet, celluloid ..**34.00**
Coloring book, 1950 ....**8.00**
Comic book, 1956 ....**9.50**
Cutter, metal with razor blade insert **5.00**
Jar, Barrel, running Mr Peanut, paper label **225.00**
Jar, Fish Bowl, rectangular label, ca 1930 ....**100.00**
Jar, Football, peanut finial.**275.00**
Jar, Leap Year, original lid .**50.00**
Jar, octagon, embossed Pennant 5¢ on 8 sides **175.00**
Jar, peanut butter, early Mr Peanut on tin lid, scarce ...**25.00**
Jar, Pennant 5¢, 6-sided, paper label, ca 1926 ......**175.00**
Jar, Streamline, tin lid **50.00**
Jar, 6-sided, yellow printed label, later issue **60.00**
Mr Peanuts cloth doll, 21" .**18.00**
Nut chopper **15.00**
Nut scoop, tin, 1½-ounce ...**65.00**
Paint book, 1926, EX **20.00**
Peanut butter grinder **30.00**
Pencil, mechanical; Mr Peanut, clip marked Planters, 5½" ..**28.00**

Salt & pepper, plastic, Mr Peanut, 4" pair **12.50**
Spoon, Mr Peanut figural handle, gold finish **22.00**
Tin, key-open top, copyright 1838, A Handy Coaster on top .**8.00**
Tin, pennant on front, 10-pound, 10x8½" **150.00**
Tin, with nut chopper in lid, blue, yellow & white, 1938 ..**50.00**
Whistle, 3½" **10.00**
Wristwatch **50.00**

Jar, large blown-out peanuts on 4 corners, peanut finial, 14", $300.00.

Post Cards

The first post cards were printed in Austria in 1869, but it was the Columbian Exposition in 1893 that started the post card craze that swept the country for years to come. Today's collectors tend to specialize in cards of a particular theme or by a favorite illustrator. Among the famous artists whose work you may find are Rose O'Neill, Philip Bouileau, Alphonse Mucha, and John Winsch.

Attwell, Mabel Lucie; I'll Learn 'Em to Learn Me Music, girl .8.00

Aviation, Whitley Bomber, #4850, Bannister 8.00

Bears, The Roosevelt Bears at the Theatre, on stage 20.00

Brundage, The Snow Maiden, girl pulling sled 23.00

Canadian, SS Halifax, Halifax, NS; scene in life preserver .16.00

Clapsaddle, Birthday Blessings & Cradle Roll poem 20.00

Clapsaddle, Christmas, Santa listening to girl's prayer ...7.50

Clapsaddle, Easter, girl in red dress & hat holds egg 10.00

Clapsaddle, New Year, boy in red coat & top hat in snow .10.00

Clapsaddle, Valentine's Day, boy offering ring to girl 12.00

Coin, 10 coins of Hungary, publisher Walter Erhard, M 15.00

Epp, Nature Series, The Frog, shows 9 growth stages, M 15.00

Fisher, Harrison; Luxury, woman reading in bed 14.00

French verse, dressed lady frog sits on washtub, unused ...15.00

Gassaway, Katherine; 3 Years, girl with spade in garden ..12.00

Gibson, American Picturesque, lady seated on beach, unused 12.00

Kewpies sit on mailbox with note, Gartner & Bender 7.00

King, Hamilton; Ocean Grove Girl, unused 9.00

Langsdorf, Christmas, red-robed Santa empties toy bag for children 15.00

Monkey in tree, with real wire spring forming tail 7.50

Patriotic, Remember Pearl Harbor, linen, 1943 ....9.00

Photo, train wreck, Haverhill, NH, March 1908 ....9.00

Real hair, lady with feather in hair, unused 15.00

Russell, Charles; Boss of the Herd, cowboy on horse 22.00

State capitol, Pennsylvania, #43, NM 8.00

Bernald's Overall Boy Series, Me and Jack, $5.00; Advertising, Girl of the Pingree Shoe, $8.00.

All Joy to You This Eastertide, $5.50; Happy Eastertide, $5.50.

Train on Trestle at Canyon Diablo, AZ **4.00**

Tuck, Call of Flag, #8862 . . **15.00**

Tuck, Donaldini, Steeplechasing Series, Going to Post . . **10.00**

Tuck, Educational Series, Zebra, #401 .... **12.00**

Tuck, Kept In at School, 2 bears on schoolroom bench **12.00**

Wain, Louis; The Twins Mascot, pair of cats **20.00**

Watermelons, The Darkie's Delight, 6 women eat in field **7.50**

WWI, After the German Retreat, allies view destruction . . **6.50**

Yellow Kid, calendar for Oct 1911, fishing scene **15.00**

Posters

The most collectible posters are those from the early days of the circus, war posters or those with a patriotic theme, early advertising posters, or those illustrated by noted artists such as Parrish, Fisher, Flagg, and Christy. Condition is important, also consider subject matter. Foxing and fading colors, as with any print, detract from their value.

Advertising, Ault & Wiborg Company, 1897 .... **65.00**

Advertising, Bull Durham Tobacco, bull atop Earth **50.00**

Advertising, Grand Cherry-Brandy Cointreau, 48½x37" . . **100.00**

Advertising, Gold Dust Twins, A Word to the Wife **28.00**

Advertising, Green River Whiskey, 1935, 23x17" **300.00**

Advertising, Gulfpride Oil, ca 1940, 40x30" **22.00**

Advertising, Le Thermogene, ca 1930, 40x30" **85.00**

Advertising, Moxie, man on white horse in open car, 1916 . **35.00**

Advertising, O'Baby Chocolate Dairy Drink, 22x14" ... **80.00**

Advertising, Peerless Hair Dressing, ca 1935, 20x15" . . **100.00**

Advertising, Raissac & Cie Revell, ca 1905, 47x32" **75.00**

Advertising, Regency Wine & Liquor, 37x27" **225.00**

Advertising, Saturday Evening Post, 1935 ....**50.00**

Advertising, Shaker's Imperial Rose Balm, 15x17½" **110.00**

Advertising, Shell Tractor Oils, 29x40" **55.00**

Advertising, White Slave by Bartley Campbell, '11, 27x38" .**300.00**

Art exhibition, Midnight Sun, Mark Chagall, 1977, 30x20" .**43.00**

Alligator border, Horseless Carriage, 2 Black women in cart **27.00**

Circus, Kelly & Miller Brothers, 28x42" **25.00**

Clapsaddle, Halloween, mechanical, girl in white robe **25.00**

Clapsaddle, To My Valentine, kaleidoscope, unsigned ...**28.00**

Fantasy, Edouard VII, skull made of nudes, unused **35.00**

Fisher, Harrison; A Midsummer Reverie, woman in swimsuit **20.00**

Hold-to-light, St Louis World's Fair, 1904 ....**28.00**

Pectoral de Anacahuita, patent medicine advertising, Lanman Kemp Litho, 1909, 29x14", $110.00.

Kirchner, Rosabla, lady in red swim suit on diving board ...**45.00**

Magazine, Bachelor of Arts, May 1898, 18x13" **25.00**

Magic, Kar-Mi, Magician of India, ca 1914, 28x40" **85.00**

Mucha, Alphonse; Four Ages of Man, set, unused ....**.800.00**

Philips, Coles; Home Ties, woman on white wicker stool ..**25.00**

Philips, Coles; Such Stuff as Dreams Are Made Of **28.00**

Political, Roosevelt with children, by Christy, 17x26", EX .**27.00**

Political, State of Israel, 1949, 11x 9" **20.00**

Printer's proof, Cabinet Export Beer, Bastian Bros, 19x25" .**250.00**

Printer's proof, Keiffer Brothers Shoes, 25x19" **325.00**

Religious, Judaica, 15x20" .**15.00**

Remington, A Fight for the Water Hole, cowboys with rifles **30.00**

Russell, Charles; Kill, Indian on horseback attacks buffalo **24.00**

Sports, Champion Boxing, ca 1945, 22x28" **25.00**

Theatrical, Cramer Baletten, 39x 27" **60.00**

Theatrical, Gayety Girls of 1930, 28x20" **45.00**

Theatrical, Simone Frevalles, 1923 67x32" **175.00**

Theatrical, To Die at Dawn, 78x 43" **150.00**

Travel, Bern, Switzerland, 40x 30" **40.00**

Travel, La Province de Quebec, 40x30" **20.00**

Travel, Monte Carlo Beach, ca 1925, 32x47" **100.00**

Travel, Norway, 40x30" **35.00**

Travel, Porto Ramos, Pinto, 15x 25" **35.00**

Travel, Taussat-Les Dimanches D'Ete a La Mer, ca 1930, 31x 45" **60.00**

Tuck, Flags & Ships of Different Nations, set of 6 . . . . . **100.00**
War, Flag Raising at Iwo Jima, 1945, 36x26" **40.00**
War, Have You a Red Cross Flag, 1918, 30x21½" **70.00**
War, Keep Him Free, Buy War Savings Stamps, 20x30", NM **35.00**
War, Order Coal Now, ca 1914, 30x20" **300.00**
War, Sure We'll Finish the Job, 1918, linen backed, 26x38" . . **60.00**
War, They Give Their lives, WWI, colorful **10.00**
War, Till We Meet Again, soldier waves from ship, 1942 . **66.00**
War, Use It Up, Wear It Out, Make It Do!, 22x28" **20.00**
War, V, blue & white on red, WWI, linen backed, 19x30" . . **10.00**

If You Want To Fight, Howard Chandler Christy, $210.00.

Primitives

From the early days of our country until the industrial revolution of the latter 1800s, tools, utensils, furniture, and even toys were made almost entirely by hand from read-ily available materials. Even factory-made items were finished by carvers, smithies, and other artisans who augmented the basic work of the machine with their handiwork. Primitives are evaluated by age, condition, workmanship, uniqueness of form, and desire to own.

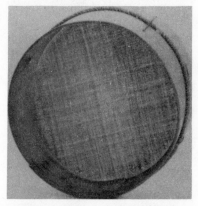

Cheese drainer, horsehair sieve, attributed to the Shakers, 10" diameter, $50.00.

Bed warmer, brass, engraved lid, wood handle, 46" long . **175.00**
Bed wrench, wood, 13½" . . . **65.00**
Candle box, sliding lid, old green painted pine, 12" **95.00**
Candle stand, wood, adjustable ratchet, 27½" **155.00**
Cheese drainer, hard wood, 9x29" diameter **90.00**
Cheese ladder, chestnut, mortised & pinned, 9x17" **52.00**
Cobbler's bench, leather seat, some repair, 16x25x37½" . . . **270.00**
Dipper, deep bowl, hook handle, 9" long **35.00**
Dough box, pine, old red paint, with lid, 16x28¾" **100.00**
Dough scraper, wrought iron, shaped blade, 3¼" wide. **35.00**
Drying rack, pine, worn red paint, 3 bars, 34x37" **85.00**
Flax break, wood, 58" long . **75.00**

Foot warmer, tinware, 8½" wide, $120.00.

Foot warmer, punched tin in wooden
    frame, 8½" long **125.00**
Niddy-noddy, 17¾" **85.00**
Sugar bucket, wood staved, worn
    blue paint on lid, 10" . . **90.00**
Toaster, wrought iron, 2-section
    rack, wooden handle . . . **65.00**
Wash board, glazed pottery in wood
    frame, Bennington . . . **165.00**

Prints

Prints, as with any article of collectible ephemera, are susceptible
to certain types of damage. Staining
and foxing (brown spots caused by
microscopic mold) are usually present to some extent and should be
weighed against the desirability of
the print. Margin tears may be
acceptable if the print is a rare one,
but avoid tears that affect the image itself. If margins have been
trimmed to less than ¾", the value is
considerably lowered.

Currier & Ives

Alice, small folio **60.00**
American Homestead, Autumn,
    small folio **400.00**
Apples & Plums, small . . . **125.00**
Battle of Bull Run, small . **170.00**
Battle of Fair Oaks, large . **725.00**

Currier & Ives, Hudson River — Crow Nest, small folio, $225.00.

Battle of Pea Ridge, small .**150.00**
Battle of Williamsburg, large folio,
    NM **725.00**
Bear Hunting, small folio .**400.00**
Betrothed, small folio **50.00**
Bower of Roses, large folio. **175.00**
Bully Team, small folio . . .**295.00**
Burial of the Bird, small . . .**75.00**
Byron & Marianna, small . .**50.00**
Charley Is My Darling, small folio,
    NM **55.00**
City of Chicago, large . . .**2,000.00**
Cooling Stream, medium .**350.00**
Cornwallis Is Taken, small folio,
    NM **600.00**
Darktown Hook & Ladder Corps,
    small folio **225.00**
Darktown Wedding-The Send Off,
    small folio **250.00**
Dead Game, small folio . . .**170.00**
Express Train, small . . .**1,500.00**
First Under the Wire, small folio,
    NM **300.00**
Garfield Family, small folio . **60.00**
George Washington, small. **150.00**
Good Times on the Old Plantation,
    small folio **450.00**
Grandpa's Cane, medium .**125.00**
Grant & His Generals, medium fo-
    lio **150.00**
In Full Bloom, small folio . .**50.00**
Ivy Bridge, small folio **125.00**
John Adams, small folio . .**150.00**
Landing of Pilgrims at Plymouth,
    small folio **195.00**
Little Manly, small folio . . .**55.00**
Magic Lake, medium folio .**125.00**
Maj Gen Phillip H Sheridan, small
    folio **125.00**
Midnight Race on the Mississippi,
    small folio **450.00**
Moonlight in the Tropics, small fo-
    lio **125.00**
Moosehead Lake, small . . .**250.00**
Nettie, small folio **60.00**
Playful Family, small folio .**75.00**
Puppies with a Bowl of Milk, yard
    long **165.00**
Queen of Beauty, small folio . **50.00**

Queen of the Turf Lady Thorn, small
    folio **350.00**
Quit Your Fighting & Lets All Be
    Friends, ca. 1915, 7½x
    19½" **47.50**
Robert Burns & His Highland Mary,
    small folio **60.00**
Royal Mail Steam Ship Arabia,
    23¼x30" **325.00**
Scenery of the Upper Missis-
    sippi, an Indian Village; 13x
    16" **200.00**
Sinking of the Steamship Ville Du
    Havre, small folio **225.00**
Stanch Pointer, small folio. **250.00**
Summer Evening, small . .**225.00**
Summer Morning, medium.**250.00**
West Point, 19x25" **75.00**
Wild Duck Shooting, small. **425.00**
Woodcock, 11x14" **150.00**
Yankee Doodle on his Muscle, small
    folio **225.00**
Yo-Semite Falls, small . . .**275.00**
Young Cavalier, small folio .**50.00**

Louis Icart

After the Raid, signed, blindstamp,
    framed **1,795.00**
Bathing Beauties **1,950.00**
Conchita, signed, blindstamp,
    framed **1,495.00**
Don Juan, signed, blindstamp,
    framed **1,250.00**

**Icart, Thais, 1927, 21x16", NM,
$3,000.00.**

Girl in Crinoline, signed, blind-
stamp, framed **1,500.00**
In the Nest, framed **950.00**
Laughing, signed, blindstamp,
framed **1,050.00**
Peacocks, signed, blindstamp,
framed **1,350.00**
Untitled, seated lady with cat,
signed **675.00**
Wisteria **2,200.00**

Nutting, Wallace

All Smiles, lady at mirror, interior,
7x9" frame **110.00**
Cold Day, lady sits beside hearth,
framed, 14" **115.00**
Hesitancy, man in red jacket, rare
subject **400.00**
Litchfield Minister **75.00**
Maple Sugar Cupboard, original
frame, 12x15" **125.00**
Mending the Quilt, 4x6", in 12½"
frame **110.00**
Pergola, panoramic Italian scene,
11" frame **110.00**
Pilgrim's Daughter **85.00**
Swimming Pool, pond, reflections,
foliage, 17" frame **65.00**
Under Old Apple Trees, weather-
beaten house, exterior .**85.00**
Where Grandma Was Wed .**65.00**

Maxfield Parrish

Advertising, Ferry Seeds, 1919,
NM **45.00**
Advertising, Swifts Premium Ham,
1920s, 14x11" **125.00**
Afterglow, 7x9" **55.00**
Air Castles, in frame, 1904, 15½x
11½" **135.00**
Atlas, original frame, 1908, 11x13",
NM **90.00**
Book, Arabian Knights, '41 .**95.00**
Book, Poems of Childhood, original
issue **95.00**

Maxfield Parrish, Wild Geese,
13x16", $185.00.

Bookplate, Golden Age & Dream
Days, 7¾x6" **15.00**
Bookplate, Jester, Knave of Hearts,
1925, 12½x10½" **70.00**
Calendar, Evening, Brown & Bige-
low, 1947, 10x8", EX ...**95.00**
Calendar, Venetian lamplighter,
Edison-Mazda, 1924, 18x9",
complete **150.00**
Calendar, Village Brook, Brown &
Bigelow, 1941, complete, 17x
12¾" **125.00**
Dinkey Bird, nude on swing, 1905,
12½x17½" **130.00**
Dreaming, ca 1960, framed, 14¾x9",
NM **115.00**
Label, crane & mountains, Crane's
chocolate, 1915, 5½x8" .**85.00**
Land of Make Believe, original
frame, 11x8½" **75.00**
Lute Players, ca 1924, in frame,
30x18" **400.00**
Poster, Idiot, Municipal Arts Dept,
ca 1967, 21½x13" **55.00**
Prince, House of Arts, ca 1925, in
frame, 12x10" **115.00**
Puzzle, Queen's Page, 1925, com-
plete in original box ...**85.00**
Reveries, ca 1926, in frame, 16x
14" **120.00**

Reveries, large **350.00**
Romance, knave & maiden on bal-
   cony, 1925, 23½x14" . . **450.00**
Rubaiyat, 1917, in frame . . **230.00**
Sea Nymphs, '08, 16½x12" **100.00**
Twilight, framed, 18x12" . . **125.00**
Twilight, 8x10½" **50.00**
Wild Geese, 13x16" **185.00**

Purinton

Popular among collectors due to its 'country' look, Purinton Pottery's dinnerware and kitchen items are easy to learn to recognize due to their bold yet simple fruit and flower motifs created with basic hand-applied colors on a creamy gloss.

Canister, Apple, small **15.00**
Coffeepot, Apple, 8-cup **20.00**
Cookie jar, Apple, oval **25.00**
Cookie jar, Pear, wood lid . . **30.00**
Creamer, Apple & Pear **5.00**
Cup & saucer, Apple **7.00**
Grease jar, Apple & Pear . . **20.00**
Honey jug, red flowers **8.00**
Jug, Apple, Dutch, 2-pint . . **12.50**
Jug, Apple, 5-pint **20.00**
Mug, beer; Intaglio, brown . **30.00**
Plate, Apple, 11½" **12.00**
Plate, snack; Apple **5.00**
Saucer, Intaglio, brown **2.50**
Shakers, Apple, 4", pair **6.00**
Shakers, Normandy Plaid, jug type,
   pair **8.50**

Cookie jar, Apple and Pear, $25.00.

Sugar bowl, Apple, open **5.00**
Teapot, Apple, 2-cup **12.00**
Teapot, Apple & Pear, 2-cup. **12.00**
Tumbler, Apple, 12-oz **12.00**

Purses

From the late 1800s until well into the 1930s, beaded and metal mesh purses were popular fashion accessories. Flat envelope styles were favored in the twenties, and bags featuring tassels or fringe were in vogue. Enameled mesh bags were popular in the late twenties and into the thirties, decorated in Art Deco designs with stripes, birds, or flowers. Whiting and Davis and the Mandalian Manufacturing Company were two of the most important manufacturers.

Lucite, green with mica, 6", $24.00.

Alligator, ca 1940 . . . . **34.00**
Beaded, black & white diamonds on
   1 side, fringe **30.00**
Beaded, black clutch style, ca 1920,
   small **25.00**
Beaded, black velvet with silver
   closure **35.00**

Silver-colored lead mesh, 5x3½", $30.00; Gold-colored mesh, 5", $35.00.

Beaded, floral, 8" **28.00**
Beaded, floral with butterfly, multi-
    color, 9" **48.00**
Beaded, geometric & floral on jew-
    eled frame with chain, 11x
    7" **125.00**
Beaded, silver, with gold fringe,
    drawstring **40.00**
Cord, black pouch, ca 1940 .**10.00**
Crochet, clasp top with chain handle,
    waistband hook **35.00**
Leather, hand-tooled clutch style,
    1915 ....**25.00**
Mesh, elaborate design, ca 1890, by
    Gorham **75.00**
Mesh, floral design, chain on metal
    frame, Whiting & Davis.**60.00**
Mesh, gold, Art Deco style, Whiting
    & Davis **40.00**
Mesh, gold with rhinestone closure,
    Whiting & Davis **38.00**
Petit point, embroidered multicolor
    floral on black silk, Whiting &
    Davis **50.00**
Rattlesnake skin **25.00**
Rhinestones, satin lined, chain
    handle **60.00**

Satin, black with compact top, ca
    1920 ....**25.00**
Tapestry, embossed figures on gold
    frame, round **45.00**
Velvet, round metal top with mirror
    in lid **25.00**

Puzzles

Of most interest to collectors of
vintage puzzles are those made of
wood or plywood, especially the early
hand-cut examples or those that
are character related or have a
special interest theme.

Automobile, McLoughlin, 1903,
    25x18" **250.00**
Beehive, wood, 14-piece **8.00**
Country Scenes, McLoughlin, 4x
    4½x4" **45.00**
Indian Chief, wood, ca 1930. **30.00**
Locomotive, ca 1900, in box. **65.00**
Map of the US, Milton Bradley, in
    box **20.00**
Norman Rockwell, 1931 ...**15.00**

Peg Solitaire, 1940, 6x6" ...**12.00**
Popeye, 1932, set of 4, in original
box **65.00**
Puzzle Parties Game, Gilbert, 1920,
in box **22.00**
Roy Rogers, with Trigger & Bullet,
Whitman, ca 1950 .....**18.00**
White Sewing Machines & Bicycles,
in box **125.00**
Winter Moonlight, wood, 150-piece,
in original box **15.00**

Quilts

The appreciation of quilting as an art form and the popularity of 'country' antiques have caused an increase in the sale of quilts; and prices, especially on the finer examples, have risen dramatically. There are several basic types of quilts: (1) appliqued — having the decorative devices applied onto a solid top fabric; (2) pieced — having smaller pieces that have been cut out in a specific pattern, then stitched together to form the quilt top; (3) crazy quilts — made by stitching pieces of various sizes and shapes together following no orderly design; (4) trapunto — devised by stitching the outline of the design through two layers of fabric, one very loosely woven, and inserting padding into the design through openings made by separating the loose fibers of the underneath fabric.

Condition of a quilt is important; intricacy of pattern, good color composition, and craftsmanship contribute to its value. These factors are of prime concern whether evaluating vintage quilts or those by contemporary artists.

Amish

Black with light blue sateen, doll
size, 20x25" **300.00**

Double Peony, tan diamonds on
white, 1900, 160x80" .**300.00**
Nine Patch, grayish-brown with
maroon & gray print, 70x80",
EX **270.00**
Ocean Wave, shades of blue & white,
machine-stitched binding,
66x72" **325.00**
Pinwheel, quilted vine & bird border, 86x86" **600.00**
Star medallions, solid border, Pennsylvania, 80x94" **450.00**
Sunshine & Shadow, shades of blue,
feather quilted border, unused,
80x81" **1,150.00**
Triangle block pattern, green border, ca 1945, 80x100" .**425.00**

Appliqued — red and green tea roses, brier stitch design, blue binding, EX, $275.00.

Appliqued

Carolina Lily, sawtooth border,
feather wreath quilting, 83x86",
NM **750.00**
Chimney Sweep, alternating polka
dot & calico squares, 136x160",
NM **250.00**
Compass star center in red grid,
stars & buds surround, 77x94",
NM **150.00**
Floral, green & red calico, puffed
buds borders, 90x96" .**360.00**

Appliqued — florals in red and green calico on homespun, stitched flowers and foliage in white squares, EX, $500.00.

Floral Basket, red, yellow-green, & yellow, EX quilting, 86x108", NM **200.00**

Geometric, red, goldenrod & deep teal blue, 82x82", EX . **600.00**

Hearts, flowers, & foliage, red & green on white, unused, ca 1920, 83x84" **500.00**

Log Cabin, color prints & solids, light wear, 76x78" ... **125.00**

Medallion, stylized, red, gold, & blue on white, 82x82" **600.00**

Medallions, red calico, red & green vine border, 82x89" .. **200.00**

Pine Tree, calico flowers & wreaths on solids, 78x90" **175.00**

Pinwheel, red, blue, & yellow on white, 160x144" **190.00**

Pinwheel, red, green, & yellow on ivory, 1963, 84x84" ... **175.00**

Poinsettias, red, green, & yellow on white, 1940, 72x88" .. **325.00**

President's Wreath with Acorns, flower & vine border, 88x72", NM **750.00**

Star, sawtooth border, goldenrod, blue, & salmon, ca 1920, 76x79", EX **1,000.00**

Sun medallions, gold & red, design quilted hearts & wreaths, 87x88" **350.00**

Pieced

Arrow Point, prints & solids, white background, ca 1950 .. **175.00**

Basket, blue & gold on white background, 82x82" **450.00**

Baskets, red on white background, 44x102" **200.00**

Chintz, floral border, trapunto feather inner border, center has chintz applique with trapunto wreath, signed Ellen Mary, Made by her affectionate Mother, 1846, EX, $3,000.00; Appliqued — floral, meandering feather-stitched border, NM, $950.00.

Birds, flying, colorful prints on white, 78x78" **285.00**
Bow Tie, colorful prints, mostly blue & brown, 74x78" **135.00**
Bow Tie, maroon & white on navy, 64x73" **325.00**
Chevron design, red calico on white, cut-out corners, for poster bed, 76x83" **250.00**
Crazy, silk, satin & velvet, embroidery & paint design, 72x72", NM **65.00**
Double Wedding Ring, yellow & lavender solids & prints, 1940, 82x82" **225.00**
Flower Garden, multicolored flowers, green border, ca 1940, 70x80" **250.00**
Honeycomb patches, colorful prints, red border, 59x72" ...**135.00**
Irish Chain, sawtooth edge, dark colors on gold, 80x80" .**225.00**
Log Cabin, colorful prints & solids, 76x78" **125.00**
Nine Patch, colorful prints on blue polka dots, 78x80" ...**155.00**
Star, simple allover design, gold on blue, 74x80" **225.00**
Star, white, blue & maroon calico, 80x80" **225.00**
Triple Irish chain, blue, green, & red on calico, 64x80" ...**85.00**

Radios

Collectors of vintage radios are especially interested in those made from the twenties through the fifties by companies such as RCA, Atwater Kent, Philco, and Crosley, though those produced by the smaller manufacturers are collectible as well. Cathedral and breadboard styles are popular, so are Art Deco styles and those with a unique type of speaker, power source, or cabinet.

Arborphone, #27 ....**65.00**

Atwater Kent, #12, breadboard, 6-tube, EX **825.00**
Atwater Kent, #37 ....**40.00**
Crosley, red Bakelite **45.00**
Fada, Bullet, amber Bakelite, Deco styling **440.00**
Freed-Eisemann NR-5, '22 .**60.00**
Freshman Masterpiece, EX .**65.00**
General Electric, Ice Box, tube type, EX **75.00**
Hallicrafters World Wide, portable, AC-DC **75.00**
Kennedy, XV, EX **160.00**
Majestic, #130, VG **45.00**
Philco, #511, metal case with tubes, EX **35.00**
Philco, #87, EX **185.00**
Philco A, clock type **165.00**
Radiodyne, #WC-11, EX ...**55.00**
Radiola, #33, EX **55.00**
RCA #4T, cathedral, EX ..**100.00**
Revere, #300, camera-case type, EX **45.00**
Scott Imperial All Wave, 1936, rare, VG **400.00**
Sentinel, white plastic, '30s. **75.00**
Spartan, #5218, NM **85.00**
Steinite, #410, EX **165.00**
True Tone, plastic, 1930s ..**35.00**
Westinghouse, brown Bakelite, miniature floor-standing model, 9x5" **35.00**
Westinghouse, Grandfather clock radio **325.00**
Zenith, #160, EX **185.00**
Zenith, table, wood cabinet, battery operated **20.00**
Zenith White, Bakelite **22.00**

Sparton #558, in peach mirror glass, $2,400.00; in blue mirror glass, $1,800.00.

Railroadiana

Memorabilia relating to the more than 175 different railway companies that once transversed this great country of ours represents one of the largest and most popular areas of collecting today. Because the field is so varied, many collectors prefer to specialize. Lanterns, badges, advertising, dinnerware, silver, timetables, locks, and tools are only a sampling of the many types of relics they treasure. Some enjoy toy trains, prints showing old locomotives — in short, virtually anything that in any way represents the rapidly disappearing railway system is of value.

Calendar, Chicago Rock Island & Pacific, 1888, unused, 22x14", $100.00.

Dinnerware

Ash tray, pink & yellow flowers, GN, back stamped, 3½" diameter **45.00**

Bowl, baked apple; Mimbreno, ATSF, back stamp **75.00**
Bowl, berry; California Poppy, ATSF, Syracuse, 6¼" ..**30.00**
Bowl, cereal; Peacock, CMStP&P, 6" **22.50**
Bowl, cereal; Streamliner, UP **16.00**
Bowl, cereal; Traveler, CMStP&P, 6" **12.50**
Butter pat, Atlantic Coast Line 1952 Carolina **30.00**
Butter pat, Historical, UP ..**87.50**
Butter pat, Indian Tree, Pullman, top mark **60.00**
Butter pat, Winged Streamliner, Santa Fe **15.00**
Celery dish, Flora of the South, ACL, back stamp, 9½" **185.00**
Cup, bouillon; National, Amtrak **6.00**
Cup & saucer, demitasse; Centenary, B&O, bottom mark. **45.00**
Cup & saucer, Desert Flower, UP, back stamp **65.00**
Cup & saucer, tea; Cavalier, N&W **35.00**
Ice cream shell, DeWitt Clinton, NYC, back stamp **42.50**
Ice cream shell, Streamliner, UP **28.00**
Mug, California Poppy, ATSF, Syracuse **20.00**
Plate, Cavalier, N&W, 6½" .**32.50**
Plate, Challenger, UP, 6" ..**18.00**
Plate, Eagle, MP, back stamp, bread & buter, 6½" **32.00**
Plate, Flora of the South, ACL, back stamp, 7¾" **75.00**
Plate, George Washington, C&O, back stamp, 6½" **35.00**
Plate, Mountains & Flowers, GN, back stamp, 7" **30.00**
Plate, Platinum Blue, NYNH&H, back stamp, 7" **35.00**
Plate, Purple Laurel, PRR, back stamp, 10" **55.00**
Plate, Winged Streamliner, UP, 10½" **45.00**

Flares, Baltimore & Ohio, 10", $20.00; no mark, 9", $14.00.

Platter, California Poppy, bottom stamp, ATSF, 11" **60.00**

Platter, Feather River, WP, 7½" long **48.50**

Platter, Glory of the West, GN, back stamped, 10½x7½" **60.00**

Platter, Mountains & Flowers, GN, oval, 9x7½" **55.00**

Teapot, gold logo on blue, BC&Q, Hall **95.00**

Teapot, Winged Streamliner, UP, with lid **75.00**

Silverplated Flatware

Fork, Albany, bottom stamp, Santa Fe **12.00**

Fork, Cromwell, bottom stamp, Santa Fe **12.00**

Fork, dinner; Hutton, top mark, INT'L **12.00**

Fork, dinner; Sierra, bottom mark, R&B **16.00**

Fork, oyster; Cromwell, top mark, INT'L **18.00**

Knife, Belmont, top mark, D& RGW **4.00**

Knife, Broadway, top mark, PRR, 9½" **10.00**

Knife, butter; Albany, hollow handle, INT'L **15.00**

Knife, butter; Silhouette, bottom mark, NPR **25.00**

Knife, Cromwell, bottom stamp, Santa Fe **12.00**

Knife, dinner; Embassy, bottom mark, R&B **16.00**

Spoon, soup; Broadway, top mark, PRR **10.00**

Tablespoon, Embassy, top mark logo, bottom mark NPR. **18.00**

Silverplated Holloware

Bowl, CM&StP border design, bottom mark, marked Reed & Barton, 5" **65.00**

Bread tray, top mark, marked Gorham, 6" **125.00**

Change tray, bottom stamp, Alaska Railroad **45.00**

Change tray, top center mark logo, MP, ca 1955 ....**65.00**
Coaster, bottom stamp, BR .**12.00**
Coffeepot, bottom mark, GN, 14-ounce **75.00**
Coffeepot, bottom stamp, UP, 1-pint, individual **50.00**
Coffeepot, Challenger finial, SK, ca 1946, 10-ounce **55.00**
Crumber, Albany, bottom stamp, Santa Fe **55.00**
Finger bowl, bottom stamp, RI **45.00**
Gravy boat, bottom stamp, C&NW, 6-ounce **35.00**
Ice cream shell, tab handle, bottom stamp, UPRR, ca 1950 .**35.00**
Pitcher, water; hinged lid, bottom mark, INT'L, 4-pint ..**120.00**
Sherbert, pedestal base, bottom stamp, UP **20.00**
Spoon, ice tea; Silhouette, top mark, GNR **25.00**
Spoon, ice tea; top mark Monad logo, bottom mark NPR **20.00**
Spoon, ice tea; Winthrop, top mark, GN **25.00**

Spoon, serving; Aristocrat, top mark, Burlington Route.**15.00**
Spoon, serving; Silhouette, bottom mark, NPR **22.00**
Sugar bowl, with lid, bottom stamp, GN, issued 1929 .....**250.00**
Sugar bowl, with lid, bottom stamp, UP, 8-ounce **55.00**
Sugar bowl, 2 handles, bottom stamp, NP, ca 1930 ....**42.50**
Sugar tongs, Reed & Leaf, top mark, UP **65.00**
Syrup pitcher, with attached tray, bottom stamp, UP **45.00**
Tip tray, bottom stamp, Lackawanna, 1947 ....**70.00**
Toothpick holder, footed, back mark, Reed & Barton, 3¼" ...**75.00**
Tray, top mark, Santa Fe in script, oval 12x9" **95.00**

Miscellaneous

Air hammer, N&W **16.50**
Almanac, Milwaukee, 1941 ..**5.00**
Annual pass, Iowa Central Railway Co, 1900 ....**12.00**
Ash tray, brass, hinged cover has cigarette rests, mounts to seat **25.00**
Ash tray, china, ca 1940, Chinchfield Railroad **32.50**
Ash tray, enamel over brass, mounts to wall, Pullman Company **37.50**
Ash tray, Silhouette, side mark, 7 x3¼" **65.00**
Axe, Plumb Mfg Co, N&W. **15.00**
Baggage check, brass, Illinois Central Railroad System ..**37.50**
Baggage tag, PRR, 4¾x2½" ..**7.00**
Baggage tag, Ship It by Railway Express, 1942, 5x3" **1.00**
Book, First 5 Years of Railroad in Colorado, '48, 214 pages .**5.00**
Book, Railroad Red Book, January 1923, 370 pages **50.00**
Book, UP Railroad Indoor Sports & Games, 1899 ....**15.00**

Poster, Lake Shore & Michigan Southern Ry., advertising fast mail, 1875, 30x22", $1,300.00.

Switch lock, N&W Ry cast on entire back side, heart shape, no maker's mark, 1952, $40.00.

Booklet, Color Light Signals Aspects, 1976, 6x8" **4.00**
Booklet, 1955 C&NW System Timetable **10.00**
Button, C&O for Progress, yellow & black, 1½" **10.00**
Button, flat silver uniform type, CStPM&O **3.00**
Button, gold domed, conductor's, large **2.50**
Button, Junior Railroader, from SR, 1½" **5.00**
Button, Southern Railway, logo & train, 2½" **1.25**
Caboose backup whistle, brass, patent 1910, Sherburne Mfg Co **40.00**
Calendar, Chessie, 1947, 15x 24" **70.00**
Candle holder, brass, bracket wall mount, no chimney, 8" .**35.00**
Cap badge, gold, conductor's, Boston & Maine **32.50**
Deodorizer jug, stoneware, corn cob stopper, marked Pullman Co **44.00**
Doorknob, coach, ornate, cast brass, L&NRR **31.50**
Flashlite, black hard rubber, UP, 7" **15.00**
Hammer, caboose; marked, N& W **12.50**

Hard hat, safety, with logo of SR on front **16.50**
Hat, B& O Trainman, with silver finish metal badge, ca 1910 .... **70.00**
Hat, chef; paper, NWP **5.00**
Hat badge, enamel letters on gold, Conrail **22.50**
Inspection certificate, Cripple Creek-CO Springs Railway, 1915 .... **2.00**
Insulator, white porcelain, embossed CPR on top, 3¾" .**5.00**
Lantern, Adlake Adams, beehive, drop fount, 1889, NYN H&H **130.00**
Lantern, Adlake Kero, clear globe etched ACL, ca 1933 ...**65.00**
Lantern, Adlake Kero, clear short globe, 1947, N&W **35.00**
Lantern, Adlake Model #250, clear globe, Wabash **50.00**
Lantern, Adlake Reliable, clear etched 5⅜" globe, C& NW **70.00**
Lantern, Armspear, bell bottom, clear marked globe, PRR **100.00**
Lantern, Dietz #39, clear globe, N&W **50.00**
Lantern, Dietz Vesta, clear unmarked globe, 1937, P& LE **60.00**

Centennial medallion, $85.00.

Switch stand lamps, $125.00.

Lantern, Dressel Arlington, red fresnel globe, Reading . **48.00**

Lantern, Handlan, red etched 3½" globe, B&ORR **50.00**

Lantern, Keystone Casey, wire-ring base, red marked globe, HV, EX **180.00**

Lantern, Rayo Pony #15, brass **125.00**

Lantern, Vesta, clear unmarked globe, B&M **35.00**

Letter opener, nickel, white handle, SCL **3.00**

Magazine, Railroad, March, 1949, NM **2.25**

Mail bag, RI, Mail Dept printed on canvas, 36" **25.00**

Medal, veteran; N&W, with ribbon, oval 2¼" **28.00**

Medallion, WWI Service, Pennsylvania RR **37.50**

Menu, double-fold dinner; 1963, Burlington Rte **10.00**

Menu, single-card luncheon, 1962, NP **15.00**

Napkin, dinner; Santa Fe in blue thread, 16" square **7.50**

Oiler, original paint, Eagle, 24" spout **27.50**

Paperweight, Empire State Express, NYC&HR **47.50**

Paperweight, glass, MP ... **22.50**

Paperweight, photo of Chicago's Union Station under glass, ca 1918 .... **20.00**

Pass, Gavelston, Houston, & Henderson, 1879 .... **18.00**

Pass card, employee's, ATSF, 1869, NM **8.00**

Pin, gold circle, for 16 years of service, SR **17.50**

Pin, gold with blue stone, for 40 years of service, Seaboard System **22.50**

Playing cards, bicentennial, SCL, in box **5.00**

Playing cards, Frisco **17.50**

Playing cards, SP **12.00**

Playing cards, WP&YR, 1900, original box **62.00**

Post card, NP **5.00**

Post card, Tennessee Southern, ca 1918 .... **2.00**

Poster, Lackawanna, ca 1915, 11x21" **95.00**

Rule book, May 1, '09, L&N. **20.00**

Signal lock, Yale, brass, heart shape, no railroad mark, EX .. **10.00**

Signal lock, Yale, ornate cast monogram, BR&P, EX **40.00**

Spittoon, nickel over brass, PPC Co. **75.00**

Stationary, RI, logo on envelopes & paper **12.00**
Stereoview card, Keystone, patent 1898 . . . .**15.00**
Switch key, Adlake, with chain, marked 3-62 . . . .**17.50**
Switch key, brass, stamped CPR on 1 side, 2" long **16.00**
Switch key, brass, unmarked. **5.50**
Switch lamp, Adlake, round glass lenses, snow hoods, B-R.**97.50**
Switch lamp, WRRS Type 1880, cast hinged top **67.50**
Switch lock, brass, heart shape, B&O **38.00**
Switch lock, steel, L&N **16.50**
Switch lock, Yale, nickel plated, no railroad mark, EX **18.00**
Syrup pitcher, NYC, tin . . .**18.00**
Ticket punch, nickel **5.25**
Timetable, dated April 1, 1954, Clinchfield **6.50**
Timetable, dated December 1943, NYC **6.50**
Token, Oklahoma Railway, marked Good for One City Fare .**2.50**
Token, Portsmouth, Virginia, marked "One Fare" on both sides **2.00**
Token, Southern Coach Lines, "Good for One Fare" **1.50**
Torch, copper, water can shape, 6" **50.00**
Towel, white, stamped Burlington Rte, 18x14" **5.00**
Towel rack, brass, 33½" long **65.00**
Wall map, 1960, N&WRY . . .**7.50**

Razors

Straight razors are prized for their beautifully decorated blades and handles, often portraying nudes, animals, scenes, or slogans popular at the time of their manufacture. Values are determined by assessing the blade style, pattern of the handle, and manufacturer's mark.

Corn razors, used to remove corns from the feet, are also collectible. An approximate date of manufacture may be arrived at thorough study of various types of blades. Those made before the 19th century were crude wedge-shaped affairs that evolved through many improvements in shape as well as material to the fully hollow-ground blades of the 1880s.

A Arnold, etched Arnold's Surgical-The Lancet on blade . . .**20.00**
A Witte, NY, etched Empire State on blade, ivory tang . . .**20.00**
Blue Steel Special, faux black stag handle, hollow ground blade, EX **18.00**
CA Tabet & Co, nude standing on man's back on handle . .**55.00**
Celebrated Hollow Ground, deer in relief on faux ivory handle **21.00**
Challenge, fancy faux ivory handle, ivory tang **25.00**
Corn razor, JA Henckels Twin Works, Germany, original box **46.00**
Corn razor, rounded bone handle & spacer, wedge blade, in box **36.00**
Corn razor, unmarked, faux ivory handle **27.00**
Dime Safety Razor, New York, patented 1907, 3½", in box..**75.00**
Ern, embossed floral faux ivory handle **37.00**
Ern, faux ivory handle, EX .**30.00**
Frederick Reynolds, embossed Old English Razor on horn handle, EX **20.00**
Frederick Reynolds, mottled horn handle, wedge blade, Sheffield, EX **18.00**
G Savage Double X Razor, wedge blade with thumb grip .**10.00**
G Wostenholm, mottled horn handle, wedge blade . . .**15.00**

F. Fenney, beautifully etched blade, ca 1850, $25.00.

G Wostenholm & Sons, floral relief faux ivory handle, EX . . **15.00**

Gem Minute Man Safety Razor, original box, M **16.00**

Genco, nude on lily pad in relief on handle **35.00**

Geneva Cutlery Co, eagle & Improved Eagle Razor etched on blade **16.00**

H Hobson Warranted, crude bone handle, wedge blade . . . **10.00**

Henry Martin I, faux ivory handle, hollow ground blade, Germany **26.00**

Herman Improved Razor, metal-trimmed green celluloid handle, EX **15.00**

Hibbard, Spencer, Bartlett & Co, tree trunk, pine cones on handle **21.00**

Hibbard, Spencer & Bartlett Hindoo, embossed pink handle, NM **21.00**

J Allen & Sons, mottled green horn handle, wedge blade . . . **20.00**

Jackson Fremont, checkered faux ivory handle **21.00**

Johan Engstrom Eskilstuna, frameback, etched JE 1874 on blade **20.00**

Joseph Elliot's Fine India Steel, black horn handle, ca

1835 . . . . **35.00**

Joseph Rogers & Sons, embossed mottled horn handle, marked Sheffield **10.00**

JR Torrey Co, wrapped rope design on faux ivory handle, etched blade **15.00**

Kampee Bros, New York EX. **12.00**

Laurel Ladies' Boudoir Safety Razor, original box **15.00**

Manhattan Cutlery, embossed black horn handle, Old English Razor **25.00**

Oxford, nude picking grapes in relief on handle, Germany **50.00**

Parex Safety Corn Knife, gutta percha handle, marked Made in USA **25.00**

Penn Safety set, original box, M **34.00**

Pocket safety set, 2-part handle, Made in Austria, in box. **15.00**

Refined Steel, straight mottled horn handle, etched blade . . . **17.00**

Robeson Shuredge, fishscale handle, yellow celluloid tang . . . **37.00**

Schermack, roundhead, faux pearl handle, with booklet & blades **30.00**

Shake Sharp Razor, black celluloid handle, in box **24.00**

Shapleigh Hardware Co, floral metal inlay on faux ivory handle **42.00**

Silver Steel Warranted, round mottled horn handle, wedge blade **10.00**

Simplified Shick Automatic Magazine Razor, gold plated, NM in box **20.00**

Star Safety Corn Knife, gutta percha handle, EX **20.00**

Thomas Mfg Co, swirl handle, etched scene with lion on blade **35.00**

Tonsorial Gem, faux ivory handle, hollow ground blade, Germany **30.00**

Torrey Razor Co, Worcester, Mass, faux ivory handle, small. **36.00**

Universal, frameback, faux ivory handle, engraved blade. **22.00**

Von Cleff Corn Razor, bone handle, in original box, EX **35.00**

W Greaves & Sons, black horn handle with flat scales, ca 1825, NM **10.00**

W Greaves & Sons, straight black horn handle, wedge blade **26.00**

Wade & Butcher, etched blade, You Lather Well, I'll Shave Well, NM **15.00**

Wade & Butcher, etched eagle & American Eagle on blade **30.00**

Warner Hudnut Reelshave Safety Razor, red celluloid handle **22.00**

Weck Safety Corn Razor, faux ivory handle, pat 1909, in box.**35.00**

Reamers

Though made for the simple task of extracting citrus juices, reamers may be found in fanciful figurals as well as the simple utilitarian styles. You may find even wood or metal examples, but the most popular with collectors are those made of glass and ceramics. Fry, Hazel Atlas, Hocking, Jeanette, and McKee are among the largest producers of the glass reamer, some of which (depending on color and rarity) may bring prices well into the hundreds of dollars.

Clown figural, Japan, $42.00.

Cambridge, crystal **10.00**

Clown, ceramic, 7½" **45.00**

Duck, ceramic, baby's **32.50**

Easley's, chisel cone, clear .**50.00**

Federal, amber, paneled, with loop handle **15.00**

Federal, green, with seed dam & tab handle **8.00**

Federal, pink, ribbed, with seed dam & tab handle **85.00**

Fenton, white with rabbit decals, 2-piece **80.00**

Fleur, custard, unembossed **125.00**

Fry, opal, with fluted sides .**35.00**

Fry, pink, ruffled top **125.00**

Germany, ceramic with floral decoration, 2-piece **55.00**

Germany, monkey, ceramic **55.00**

Goebel, orange, ceramic, yellow top, #L-33 .... **35.00**

Hazel Atlas, Crisscross, cobalt, orange reamer **170.00**

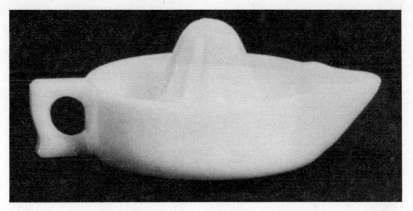

Sunkist, milk glass, block letters, $45.00.

Hazel Atlas, pitcher & reamer, pink, 2-cup **125.00**

Hocking, green, 2-quart, fruit juice reamer **20.00**

Hocking, green clambroth, with tab handle **75.00**

Indiana, pink **85.00**

Japan, beige with floral design, 2-piece **40.00**

Japan, frog, ceramic, gray, #F-66 .... **25.00**

Jeannette, crystal, with loop handle **8.00**

Jeannette, green, with loop handle, large **15.00**

Jeannette, green, with tab handle, 5⅛" **18.00**

Jeannette, Jennyware, dark jadite with small loop handle . **25.00**

Jeannette, Jennyware, Delphite, small loop handle **50.00**

Jeannette, pink, with tab handle, 5⅛" **28.00**

McKee, Chalaine blue, grapefruit reamer **250.00**

McKee, custard, pointed cone, unembossed, small **25.00**

McKee, custard, unembossed, large **35.00**

McKee, Seville yellow, grapefruit reamer **180.00**

Radnt, crystal **70.00**

Silver & Co, NY, Little Handy Lemon Squeezer, 6½" . . **85.00**

Sunkist, black with embossed Sunkist **500.00**

Sunkist, Seville yellow, ... **40.00**

Sunkist, white, embossed Thatcher Mfg Co **13.00**

US Glass, amber, with stick handle **300.00**

Valencia, green, embossed Valencia **125.00**

Westmoreland, frosted crystal, baby's 2-piece **50.00**

Records

Records that made it to the 'Top Ten' in their day are not the records that are prized by today's collectors, though they treasure those few which best represent specific types of music: jazz, rhythm and blues, country and western, rock and roll, etc. Instead they search for those cut very early in the career of artists who later became super stars, records cut on rare or interesting labels, or those aimed at ethnic groups.

Alabama Jug Band, Crazy Blues, Decca, #7042 .... **10.00**

Alfred Lewis, Friday Moan Blues, Vocalion, #1498 .... **30.00**

All Star Band, The Blues, Victor, #26144 .... **2.50**

Anonymous, Battleship Kate, Grey Gull, #1701 . . . . **8.00**

Arcadian Serenaders, Carry It On Down, Okeh, #40538 . . **17.00**

Arkansas Trio, Boll Weevil Blues, Edison, #51373 . . . . **7.00**

Atlanta Merrymakers, Sweet Little Sis, Madison, #50024 . . . **8.00**

Bailey's Dixie Dudes, I'm Satisfied, Gennett, #5577 . . . . **7.00**

Barbecue Pete, Avenue Strut, Champion, #15904 . . . . **42.00**

Ben's Bad Boys, Wang Wang Blues, Victor, #21971 . . . . **10.00**

Bert Johnson, Nasty But Nice, Brunswick, #7136 . . . . . **40.00**

Bertha Henderson, Six Thirty Blues, Paramount, #12511 . . . **37.00**

Bertha Idaho, Move It On Out..., Columbia, #14437-D . . . **17.00**

Bill Hawley, Delores, Victor, #21383 . . . . **8.00**

Bing Crosby, At Your Command, Brunswick, #6140 . . . . . . **8.00**

Blue Jay Boys, My Baby, Decca, #7240 . . . . **12.00**

Blythe's Blue Boys, Tell Me, Cutie, Champion, #40115 . . . . **15.00**

Bob Call, Thirty-One Blues, Brunswick, #7137 . . . . **62.00**

Bob Fuller, I Ain't Got Nobody, Brunswick, #7006 . . . . . **12.00**

Bobby's Revelers, Mojo Blues, Silvertone, #3552 . . . . **43.00**

Boots & His Buddies, Ain't Misbehavin', Bluebird, #7241 . **8.00**

Broadway Rastus, Rock My Soul, Paramount, #12764 . . . **45.00**

Buck & Bubbles, Rhythm for Sale, Columbia, #2873-D **12.00**

California Poppies, What a Wonderful Time, Sunset, #506-507 . . . . **100.00**

California Vagabonds, Waitin' for Katy, Gennett, #6426 . . **12.00**

Candy & Coco, China Boy, Vocalion, #2849 . . . . **18.00**

Cannon's Jug Stompers, Wolf River Blues, Victor, #23272 . . **82.00**

Carolina Collegians, Before the Rain, #6319 . . . . **7.00**

Carolina Dandies, Come ... Go Easy Love, Victor, #22776 . . . . **8.00**

Caroline Johnson, Georgia Grind, Perfect, #103 . . . . **18.00**

Charles W Hamp, Sweetheart's Holiday, Okeh, #41308 . . **7.00**

Choo Choo Jazzers, Snuggle Up a Bit, Ajex, #17038 . . . . . **10.00**

Chubby Checker, Cubby's Folk Album, ca 1963, Parkway Records **10.00**

Connie's Inn Orchestra, Milenberg Joys, Crown, #3212 . . . **20.00**

Cookie's Gingersnaps, Love Found You for Me, Okeh, #40675 . . . . **40.00**

Deppe's Serenaders, Falling, Gennett, #20012 . . . . **17.00**

Dick Porter & His Orchestra, Poor Robinson Crusoe, #3478. **10.00**

Dixie Four, Five O'Clock Stomp, Paramount, #12674 . . . **62.00**

Dixieland Thumpers, Oriental Man, Paramount, #12595 . . **140.00**

Dixon & Channey, Sweet Patunia, Paramount, #12471 . . . **62.00**

Dubin's Dandies, In My Wedding Gown, Banner, #6507 . . . **7.00**

Edith Evans, My Kinda Love, Brunswick, #4291 . . . . **8.00**

Edmonia Henderson, Jelly Roll Blues, Paramount, #12239 . . . . **45.00**

Elzadie Robinson, Driving Me South, Paramount, #12900 . . . . **50.00**

Ermine Calloway, Do Something, Edison, #14024 . . . . **12.00**

Ethel Finnie, Hula Blues, Ajax, #17027 . . . . **17.00**

Fats Domino, When I'm Walking, 1969, Columbia **12.50**

Five Hot Chocolates, Memphis Stomp, VanDyke, #71786 . . . . **20.00**

Frances King, She's Got It, Okeh, #40854 . . . . **8.00**

Frank Mater, Let's Do It, Harmony, #808-H 8.00

Fred Astaire, A Foggy Day, Brunswick, #7982 .... 7.00

Frisco Syncopators, Sweet Harry, Puritan, #11271 .... 9.00

Georgia Strutters, It's...Here for You, Harmony, #468-H.. 20.00

Gulf Coast Trio, Grand Opera Blues, Buddy, #8041 .... 20.00

Guy Lumpkin, Decatur Street Rag, QRS, #7078 .... 62.00

Harry's Happy Four, Western Melody, Okeh, #8266 ..... 17.00

Henry Brown, Blues Stomp, Paramount, #12934 .... 62.00

Herwin Hot Shots, Salty Dog, Herwin, #93015 .... 87.00

Horsey's Hot Five, Weeping Blues, Gennett, #6722 .... 42.00

Jewell Nelson, Beating Me Blues, Columbia, #14390-D ... 14.00

Joe's Hot Babies, Beans & Greens, Paramount, #12783 ... 40.00

Judy Garland, Sleep, My Baby, Sleep, Decca, #1796 .... 7.00

Katherine Handy, Loveless Love, Paramount, #12011 ... 17.00

Kentucky Hott Hoppers, Red Head Blues, Perfect, #15022 .. 9.00

KYXZ Novelty Band, Bugle Call Rag, Bluebird, #5852 ... 8.00

Laura Bryant, Dentist Chair Blues, QRS, #7055 .... 62.00

Lill's Hot Shots, Drop That Sack, Vocalion, #1037 .... 87.00

Lillian Goodner, Chicago Blues, Ajax, #17020 .... 12.00

Louisiana Stompers, Hop Off, Paramount, #12550 .... 42.00

Major & His Orchestra, Blue Evening Blues, Hollywood, #1028 .... 62.00

Memphis Jug Band, Jazzbo Stomp, Okeh, #8955 .... 50.00

Miami Lucky Seven, Slippery Elm, Gennett, #3174 .... 10.00

Mississippi Trio, Doin' That Thing, Supertone, #9528 ..... 50.00

Mount City Blue Blowers, High Society, Champion, #40103 .... 10.00

Nap Hayes, Somethin Doin', Okeh, #45231 .... 18.00

New Orleans Five, Memphis Blues, Oriole, #371 .... 8.00

Nobby Neale & Al Lyons, Go to It, Paramount, #12775 ... 17.00

North-West Melody Boys, Rain, Champion, #15365 .... 17.00

Okeh Melody Stars, Look Out, Mr Jazz, Okeh, #8282 .... 17.00

Original Indiana Five, Indiana Shuffle, Banner, #1931 .8.00

Original Tampa Five, Heebie Jeebies, Dandy, #5248 .... 16.00

Paramount Pickers, Salty Dog, Paramount, #12779 ... 85.00

Porter Grainger, In Harlem's Araby, Ajax, #17039 ..... 25.00

Ray Charles, Genius Hits the Road, 1964, ABC Paramount .15.00

Raymond Barrow, Walking Blues, Paramount, #12803 ... 50.00

Red Hot Syncopators, Jackass Blues, Bell, #445 ...... 18.00

Red Russell's Rhythm, Mood Indigo, Superior, #2719 ..... 18.00

The Ambassadors, Military Mike, Vocalion, #15156 .... 7.00

The Andrews Sisters, Just a Simple Melody, Decca, #1496 ... 7.00

The Big Aces, Cherry, Okeh, #41136 .... 15.00

The Blues Chasers, Sweet Georgia Brown, Perfect, #14428 .7.00

The Chicago Footwarmers, Oriental Man, Okeh, #8548 .. 50.00

The Harlem Footwarmers, Jungle Jamboree, Okeh, #8720. 30.00

The High Steppers, Please, Crown, #3394 .... 8.00

The Home Towners, Let's Get Together, Cameo, #9130 ... 7.00

The Hot Dogs, Steady Roll, Silvertone, #3574 .... 90.00

The Jim-Dandies, Shake That Thing, Harmony, #55-H .7.00

The Lumberjacks, Black Beauty,
Cameo, #8352 . . . . **7.00**
The Mariners, Happy Feet, Okeh,
#41433 . . . . **8.00**
The Mills Brothers, Diga Diga Doo,
Brunswick, #6519 . . . . . **12.00**
The Night Owls, Pump Tillie, Sil-
vertone, #3549 . . . . **40.00**
The Rhythm Kings, You Rascal, You,
Victor, #2379 . . . . **25.00**
The Rounders, Lovable & Sweet,
Domino, #4386 . . . . **7.00**

Red Wing

Taking their name from the location in Minnesota where they located in the late 1870s, the Red
Wing Company produced a variety
of wares, all of which are today
considered noteworthy by pottery
and dinnerware collectors. Their
early stoneware lines, Cherry Band,
and Sponge Band (Gray Line), are
especially valuable and often fetch
prices of several hundred dollars on
today's market. Production of dinnerware began in the thirties and
continued until the pottery closed
in 1967. Some of their more popular
lines — all of which were hand
painted — were Bob White, Lexington, Tampico, Normandie, Capistrano, and Random Harvest. Commercial artware was also produced.
Perhaps the ware most easily associated with Red Wing is their Brush-
ware line, unique in its appearance
and decoration. Cattails, rushes,
florals, and similar nature subjects
are 'carved' in relief on a stoneware
type body with a matt green wash
its only finish.

Dinnerware

Blossom Time, cup & saucer . **8.00**
Blossom Time, fruit bowl, 5" . **5.00**

Pitcher, deer and pine trees, made
for Hamm's Brewery, $25.00.

Blossom Time, plate, 6½" . . . **3.00**
Bob White, cookie jar **50.00**
Bob White, cup & saucer . . . **16.00**
Bob White, divided vegetable bowl,
large **25.00**
Bob White, pie plate **10.00**
Bob White, pitcher, 12" **25.00**
Bob White, plate, 10½" **7.50**
Bob White, relish dish **35.00**
Bob White, sugar bowl **25.00**
Bob White, teapot **40.00**
Capistrano, divided vegetable bowl,
large **10.00**
Capistrano, platter, 13" **12.00**
Driftwood, cereal bowl, 6½" . . **7.00**
Driftwood, cup & saucer **8.00**
Driftwood, platter, 13" **15.00**
Hearthside, salt & pepper shakers,
tall, pair **6.00**
Iris, creamer **5.00**
Iris, French casserole **30.00**
Iris, plate, 10x10" **10.00**
Lexington Rose, chop plate . **10.00**
Lexington Rose, teapot **35.00**
Lexington Rose, vegetable bowl,
deep **10.00**
Lotus, plate, 10½" **5.00**
Lute Song, cup & saucer **6.50**

Magnolia, chop plate, 13x11". **6.00**
Morning Glory, dinner plate. **6.50**
Orleans, platter **10.00**
Orleans, salt & pepper shakers,
pair **5.00**
Pepe, plate, 7½" **3.50**
Picardy, cup & saucer **7.50**
Plum Blossom, platter **9.00**
Provincial Oomph, pitcher, with
lid **20.00**
Random Harvest, cake plate. **20.00**
Smart Set, divided vegetable bowl,
large **10.00**
Tampico, casserole **18.00**
Tampico, gravy boat **12.50**
Tampico, plate, 10½" **8.50**
Tampico, platter, 15" **16.00**

Stoneware

Beater jar, plain **25.00**
Beater jar, with advertising. **85.00**
Bowl, Gray Line, 10" **75.00**
Bowl, Greek Key, 6" **45.00**
Butter jar, brown, marked Minne-
sota, 2-pound **40.00**
Butter jar, marked North Star, ½-
pint **150.00**
Casserole, Saffron, with cover,
small **100.00**
Chamber pot, blue bands on white
background **65.00**
Cookie jar, Gray Line **350.00**
Crock, leaf design on salt glaze, with
lid, 3-gallon **65.00**
Cuspidor, brown & white, marked
Minnesota, large **265.00**
Custard cup, Spongeband .. **85.00**
Jug, common, marked Minnesota,
1-gallon **65.00**
Jug, white, with bail, marked Red
Wing, 1895, 1-gallon .. **125.00**
Milk pan, brown, marked North
Star, large **75.00**
Mug, Transportation, blue & white,
relief design **65.00**
Pitcher, Cherry Band, 8" .. **145.00**
Pitcher, Cherry Band, with adver-
tising, 9" **165.00**

Pitcher, Western Cattail, bulbous,
7" **100.00**
Reamer, Gray Line **375.00**
Salt crock, hanging; Gray Line, with
lid **500.00**
Spittoon, dark brown, marked
Minnesota on bottom . **325.00**
Spittoon, salt glaze **250.00**
Water cooler, with stenciled wing,
5-gallon **225.00**

Miscellaneous

Butter dish, chicken shape . **32.00**
Cookie jar, Katrina **45.00**
Cookie jar, Monk, Thou Shalt Not
Steal, yellow & brown . **50.00**
Lye dispenser, McCormick Deering,
2-gallon **175.00**
Mug, Hamm's Beer **25.00**
Vase, Egyptian, 15½" **48.00**
Vase, green with white interior,
8" **10.00**
Vase, light green, 12" **13.50**
Wall pocket, shell, light blue with
pink interior **15.00**

**Vase, profile of man, stylized deer,
8", $45.00.**

Wall pocket, violin **25.00**

Redware

Simple utilitarian ware made from easily accessible deposits of red clay was a staple of the early American settlers. Though available throughout the country, it was utilized to its fullest extent in Pennsylvania, Ohio, and southern Appalachia. Occasionally yellow slip was used to add decorations of straight or wavy lines or simple outlines of birds or tulips. Value is determined by size and form, age, decoration, and condition.

Bank, apple shape, worn red & green paint, 2½" **105.00**
Bank, rooster shape, stylized, initialed, 3", VG **40.00**
Bowl, brown sponging, 4¾x11¾", NM **60.00**
Bowl, milk; green slip with brown sponging, 3¼x11⅝" **85.00**
Bowl, yellow slip decorated, 3¾x 12¼" **165.00**
Charger, yellow slip pinwheel decoration, 12¼" **75.00**
Colander, rim handles, 3 applied feet, 7x9¾" **300.00**
Cup, brown spots on deep red, strap handle, 4½" **55.00**
Dish, yellow slip decoration, 2x 10½" diameter **160.00**
Dog, seated, free-standing front legs, red-brown glaze, 9" ...**100.00**
Flask, brown glaze, 7" **115.00**
Flowerpot, black glaze, attached saucer, 4⅜" **25.00**
Flowerpot, brown glaze, ovoid shape, attached saucer, 6½" ..**25.00**
Flowerpot, brown spots on amber glaze, no saucer, 4½" ..**85.00**
Jar, brownish-red glaze, applied rope twisted handles, 6½" **200.00**

Plate, yellow slip wavy lines on clear glaze (orange-brown ground), rim chips, 10", $400.00.

Jar, preserving; brown spots on amber glaze, 8½" **275.00**
Jug, brown glaze, strap handle, incised 18 on bottom, 8½" **165.00**
Jug, dark brown glaze, ovoid form with strap handle, 7¼".**185.00**
Jug, dark brown glaze, wide strap handle, ovoid, 11¾" **95.00**
Jug, green glaze, strap handle, incised lines, 5¼" **155.00**
Jug, greenish-amber glaze, strap handle, 4⅛" **75.00**
Jug, puzzle; white slip decoration, initialed WW, 6⅞" **100.00**
Mold, food; turk's head, brown spotches in glaze, 7⅞" ..**55.00**
Mold, food; turk's head; clear glaze, scalloped sides, 7" **105.00**
Pie plate, crimped edge, pumpkin glaze, 8¼" **30.00**
Pie plate, yellow line slip decor, 10¼" **175.00**
Pie plate, 3 wavy lines in yellow slip, 7½", NM. **265.00**
Pie plate, 3 wavy lines on yellow slip, coggled edge, 11¾", EX **175.00**
Pie plate, 4 wavy lines on yellow slip, 11", EX **195.00**
Pitcher, black spots on clear glaze, strap handle, 7¼" **195.00**

Vase, sgraffito design, fan shape,
7¼" **100.00**

Riviera

Made by the Homer Laughlin
China Company, Riviera was a line
of colored dinnerware that was sold
through Murphy's dime stores from
1938 until sometime in the late
1940s. A sister line to Fiesta, Riviera was lighter in weight, unmarked,
and inexpensive.

Handled tumbler, $40.00.

Bowl, fruit; 5½" **6.00**
Butter dish, ½-pound **50.00**
Casserole, with cover **48.00**
Creamer, regular **6.00**
Cup & saucer **9.00**
Jug, with cover **55.00**
Nappy, 9¼" **13.00**
Plate, deep, 8" **11.00**
Plate, 7" **6.50**
Platter, 11" **9.00**
Sauce boat **11.00**
Sugar bowl, with cover **11.00**
Teapot **50.00**
Tumbler, juice size **35.00**
Tumbler, with handle **40.00**

Rockingham

A type of utilitarian ware favored
in America from the early 1800s
until after the 1920s, Rockingham
is easily identified by its mottled
brown sponged-on glaze. While some
items are simple and unadorned,
many are molded with high relief
designs of animals, vines, leaves,
cherubs, and human forms. Figural
hound handles are often found on
pitchers. Some of the finest examples
of Rockingham were made at the
Vermont potteries of Norton and
Fenton, and you may find ill-in-
formed dealers and collectors that
mistakenly refer to this ware as
'Bennington.' However, hundreds of
potteries produced goods of a very
similar appearance; and proper
identification of the manufacturer
is often difficult, if not impossible.

Bottle, shoe with embossed laces,
figural, 6¼" **65.00**
Bottle, man wearing turban, figu-
ral, 5" **95.00**
Bowl, embossed, 3x5¼" **75.00**
Bowl, mixing; 4¼x10½" . . .**145.00**
Bowl, oval, 2x7¼x10" **150.00**
Bowl, oval, 5¾" **70.00**
Bowl, oval, 8" **125.00**
Compote, solid brown, footed, 3x
5¼" **200.00**
Cuspidor, shells in relief . .**135.00**
Dish, embossed hearts around bot-
tom edge, 6⅞" **55.00**
Dish, washtub shape with open
handles, 3½" diameter .**85.00**
Dog, seated, free-standing front legs,
11" **250.00**
Foot warmer, cylinder shape, 14"
long **100.00**
Goblet, 4½" **275.00**
Jar, embossed designs, handles,
7½", VG **115.00**
Jar, with lid, 2⅞" **85.00**
Mug, oversize, 5½" **150.00**
Mug, 2¾" **100.00**
Pitcher, embossed peacock on front,
8" **145.00**

Mixing bowl, 13", $170.00; Food mold, 10", $135.00.

Pitcher, embossed vintage scene with cherubs, 7" **125.00**

Plate, 8½" **120.00**

Platter, 13½" **275.00**

Soap dish, embossed design of leaves, 6" **110.00**

Teapot, Rebecca at the Well, with lid, 7¼" **125.00**

Window stop, lion's head figural, 5", NM **175.00**

Rockwell, Norman

His first *Saturday Evening Post* cover was published in 1916; launching him on a lifetime career. He became famous for his ability to portray through his illustrations keen insight and understanding of the American way of life. In addition to his magazine covers, he illustrated advertisements and sheet music. All are highly collectible. Modern applications of his original art — collector plates, figurines, Christmas ornaments, etc. — are also valued.

Ad, Elgin Watch Co, ca 1920 .**6.00**

Blotter, Fisk Tires, 1924 ...**25.00**

Book, Adventures of Tom Sawyer, 1936, EX **75.00**

Calendar, Boy Scouts of America Special Bicentennial ...**10.00**

Calendar, Looking Out to Sea, 11x13½" **14.00**

Display card, Pepsi Santa Claus, 24" **55.00**

Figurine, Bedtime, Rockwell Museum **42.50**

Figurine, Carolers, Dave Grossman Co **35.00**

Figurine, Celebration, Rockwell Museum **127.50**

Figurine, Discovery, Dave Grossman **100.00**

Figurine, Jolly Coachman, Gorham **60.00**

Figurine, Lovers, Dave Grossman **60.00**

Figurine, Missed, Gorham .**85.00**

Figurine, No Swimming, Gorham Co **45.00**

Figurine, Bride & Groom, Rockwell Museum, Music Hall ..**55.00**

Figurine, Sweet Sixteen, Rockwell Museum **58.50**

Figurine, The Toss, Dave Grossman **125.00**

Figurine, Tiny Tim, Gorham Company **60.00**

Letter signed, to magazine editor, 1965, EX **85.00**

Magazine, American Boy, April, 1920 ....**22.50**

Magazine, Literary Digest, November 17, 1923, EX **20.00**

Magazine, Look, July 14, 1964, EX **18.00**

Magazine, McCalls, December, 1964, EX **20.00**

Magazine, Saturday Evening Post, June 6, 1959 ....**8.00**

Sterling silver Christmas card, 1972, $25.00.

Magazine, Saturday Evening Post, November 3, 1945 . . . . . **15.00**

Magazine, Woman's Day, June, 1965, Sketchbook of Dog Portraits **4.00**

Plate, Teenagers Together, Sweethearts edition **65.00**

Poster, A Good Sign All Over the World, 1967, 17x22" . . . **15.00**

Print, Audubon Paints the Passenger Pigeon, signed . . . **275.00**

Print, Brooks Robinson, Rawlings, signed, 24x30" **350.00**

Print, GI Homecoming, unframed, 20x24" **25.00**

Print, Portrait of JFK, 1 of limited signed edition of 223. **1500.00**

Print, Scuffleton Barber Shop, signed, 20x24" **250.00**

Print, You Got To Be Kidden, 18x 24" **475.00**

Sheet music, Little French Mother, Good-bye **28.00**

Sheet music, Over Yonder Where the Lilies Grow **25.00**

Tray, tin, Who's Having More Fun?, kids eating corn **35.00**

Rookwood

Fine art pottery was produced by the Rookwood Pottery Company, established in Cincinnati, Ohio, in 1879 by Maria Longworth Nichols Storer. Though it is not at all impossible to find examples of the early art lines at flea markets, the type most often encountered is their mass-production vases, bookends, paperweights, etc., made after the turn of the century, machine molded and relying upon in-mold details for their decorations. The company was faithful in marking their wares — the most familiar mark is the reverse R and P device with the flame points above it. First used in 1886, each flame represents the succeeding years up to 1900. Roman numerals were used in addition to the flames from that time on. Early artware lines are judged and evaluated by scarcity of line and finesse of the artwork involved.

Basket, Standard, signed Van Briggle, 1887, 16" long, $375.00.

Ash tray, Standard, 1901, cigarette & leaves, 1¼x4¾" **70.00**
Ash tray, 1943, owl, cream gloss, 4" **85.00**
Bookends, 1922, Oriental girls, seated, turquoise, 9" . . **325.00**
Bookends, 1951, panther, green gloss **170.00**
Bowl, Jewel Porcelain, 1920, blue cobalt, with mustard interior **70.00**
Bowl, Limoges, butterflies & swirls, gold rim, M Rettig . . . **400.00**
Bowl, Wax Mat, 1927, multicolor floral, S Coyne, 5x7" . . . **70.00**
Creamer, Standard, 1903, leaves & berries, S Coyne, 3" . . **245.00**
Ewer, Standard, 1889, wild roses, Anna Valentien, 9" . . . **220.00**
Flower frog, 1927, frog figural, medium green **70.00**
Inkwell, Mat, 1906, lily pad shape, green, 7½" long **110.00**
Jug, Limoges, 1884, outdoor scene, 4½" **175.00**
Lamp, Porcelain, ca 1940, red floral on white & gray, 10" . . **100.00**
Match holder, Mat, shields with lions, signed ST, 5" **60.00**
Mug, Mat, 1905, Arts & Crafts incising, C Duell, 5" **70.00**
Mug, Standard, 1890, blossoms on orange-brown, 4½x5" . **165.00**

Mug, 1887, commemorative of Washington DC, 5" . . . **150.00**
Paperweight, 1935, Potter at the Wheel, green mat **65.00**
Paperweight, 1947, yellow bird figural, 3⅞" **55.00**
Pitcher, Iris, 1901, florals, Sara Sax, 5" **420.00**
Pitcher, Standard, 1882, poppies, Sally Toohey, 7" **500.00**
Plaque, Vellum, 1922, On the River, ET Hurley, 9x7" **900.00**
Platter, blue sailing pirate ships, oval, 13" **60.00**
Potpourri, Vellum, 1922, floral with berries, L Asbury, 4" . **275.00**
Teapot, Porcelain, 1915, blue gloss, large **110.00**
Vase, Bisque, 1887, roses, sage clay, Valentien, 8", EX **200.00**
Vase, Iris, 1901, 2 handles, floral, Sara Sax, 4" **260.00**
Vase, Jewel Porcelain, 1931, floral, Jens Jenson, 7½" **600.00**
Vase, Mat, 1923, leaves, mold #1903, 5¼" **95.00**
Vase, Porcelain, 1930, geometric design, Sara Sax, 5½" . **175.00**
Vase, Sea Green, 1901, daffodils, S Coyne, 7" **800.00**
Vase, Standard, 1900, tulips, C Schmidt, 5½" **395.00**

Paperweight, galleon on waves, ochre-yellow, $125.00.

Vase, Wax Matt, signed Wilhelmine Rehm, 6", $400.00.

Vase, Standard, 1901, magnolias, Leona Van Briggle, 7". **175.00**

Vase, Vellum, 1905, primroses, F Rothenbusch, 6" **225.00**

Vase, Vellum, 1911, trees, Katherine Van Horn, 8" **440.00**

Vase, Vellum, 1914, snow scene at bottom, S Coyne, 7" . . **175.00**

Vase, Vellum, 1920, floral, Elizabeth McDonald, 15" . . **600.00**

Vase, Wax Mat, 1922, bluebells, Vera Tischler, 9" **550.00**

Vase, Wax Mat, 1931, stylized floral, E Lincoln, 7x5" . . . **180.00**

Vase, 1925, floral design at neck, #2811, 4¼" **45.00**

Vase, 1941, birds in relief, light pink, 5" **40.00**

Vase, 1944, gray with green drip gloss, 7¼" **250.00**

Vase, 1945, floral in relief, light turquoise, 9½" **60.00**

Vase, 1948, butterflies in relief, green gloss, 4½" **25.00**

Vase, 1952, leaves in relief, dark green, 3½" **20.00**

Wall sconce candle holder, Mat, 1922, large stylized rose in relief **100.00**

Rose Medallion

A lovely pattern of dinnerware first exported from China in the early 1800s, Rose Medallion is decorated in a rose palette with figures, butterflies, and florals within paneled reserves. It sold well into the 20th century and is evaluated by age, condition, form, and color. Early examples were sometimes decorated with gold or heavily reticulated. Such items bring premium prices.

Bowl, ca 1920, marked Made in China, 6¼" **52.00**

Bowl, rice; with trivet base, ca 1900, 2½x4½" **30.00**

Box, 3¼" diameter **95.00**

Butter pat, early **35.00**

Candlestick, no mark, 6" . . **200.00**

Charger, 13¾" **180.00**

Creamer, Made in China, 4". **42.00**

Cup & saucer, demitasse; no mark, ca 1850 . . . . **60.00**

Cup & saucer, scalloped rim, no mark, early **45.00**

Flowerpot, square with undertray, with gold trim, Canton, 5x 3⅜" **300.00**

Ginger jar, 12" **175.00**

Mug, ca 1830 . . . . **400.00**

Plate, late, 8½" **35.00**

Plate, Made in China, 7" . . . **30.00**

Platter, ca 1800, 13" **450.00**

Punch bowl, ca 1850, 6¾x15½" diameter **800.00**

Teapot, with gold trim, Canton, ca 1850, 5½" **400.00**

Vase, with gold trim, Canton, ca 1850, 14" **500.00**

Punch bowl, ca 1950s, 15 ¾", $800.00.

Rosemeade

Novelty items made by the Whapeton Pottery Company of North Dakota from 1941 to 1960 are finding an interested following among collectors of American pottery. Though smaller items (salt and pepper shakers, figurines, trays, etc.) are readily found, the larger examples represent a challenge to collectors who prize them highly. The name of the novelty ware, 'Rosemeade,' is indicated on the paper labels (many of which are still intact) or by the ink stamp.

Ash tray, Indian head **40.00**
Basket, powder blue, 2" . . . **18.00**
Bowl, with figural deer flower-
    holder **30.00**
Figurine, elephant, seated, gray,
    miniature **15.00**
Figurine, male pheasant, 12"
    long **150.00**
Flower frog, frog shape **18.00**
Pie bird, peacock, blue & green,
    paper label, 4½" **45.00**
Planter, swan, powder blue . **20.00**
Salt & pepper, pheasants, paper
    label, pair **12.50**
Salt & pepper, prairie dogs, paper
    label, pair **18.00**

**Donkey figure, rust glaze, 4½",
$25.00.**

Salt & pepper, rabbits, running,
    gray, pair **25.00**

Roseville

Founded by George Young in 1892, the Roseville Pottery Company produced hand-decorated artware, utility ware, and commercial artware of the finest quality until they closed in the 1950s. Of the major American potteries, Roseville's production pieces are among the finest, and it is a rare flea market that will not yield several excellent examples from the 'middle period.' Some of the early artware lines require perseverance to acquire, while others such as their standard brown-glazed 'Rozane' is easy to locate. During the twenties and thirties they produced several lines of children's serving dishes decorated with Santa Claus, chicks, rabbits in jackets, Sunbonnet Babies, and various other characters, which are today treasured by their own band of devotees. While many pieces of Roseville are marked with some form of the company name, others that originally had paper labels are otherwise unmarked. Careful study of Roseville lines may result in your finding one of the few bargains left at the flea markets today.

Apple Blossom, tea set, #371, 3-
    piece **145.00**
Artwood, vase, #2053, 8" . . **15.00**
Autumn, jar with lid, 10" . **270.00**
Autumn, jardiniere, 9½" . . **400.00**
Aztec, lamp, 11" **275.00**
Aztec, pitcher, 5½" **250.00**
Azurean, mug, floral **450.00**
Baneda, vase, 6" **55.00**
Bank, buffalo, 3x6" **150.00**
Bank, dog's head, 4" **150.00**

Bittersweet vase, 10", $60.00.

Bittersweet, basket, with handle, #810, 10" **75.00**

Bittersweet, bud vase, slim form, #873, 6" **40.00**

Blackberry, candlestick, #1086, 5", pair **195.00**

Blackberry, jardiniere & pedestal, 10" **1,300.00**

Blackberry, vase, with handles, 10" **290.00**

Bleeding Heart, basket, with handle, #361, 12" **150.00**

Bleeding Heart, ewer, blue, #972, 10" **95.00**

Burmese, bookends, white figural, pair **125.00**

Burmese, candle holders/bookends, #70B, black, pair **150.00**

Bushberry, basket, #370, 8". **65.00**

Bushberry, ewer, #1, 6" **45.00**

Capri, basket, tan, 10" **60.00**

Carnelian I, console bowl, 14" diameter **35.00**

Carnelian II, bowl, handles, 3x9" diameter **30.00**

Cherry Blossom, candle holder, 4", pair **185.00**

Cherry Blossom, vase, low foot, 8" **100.00**

Chloron, candle sconce, warrior, 17" **400.00**

Clematis, cookie jar **125.00**

Colonial, pitcher, 11" **285.00**

Columbine, vase, #13, 6" ... **30.00**

Corinthian, candlestick, 8" .**50.00**

Cosmos, console bowl, 12" .. **45.00**

Creamware, chocolate pot, with cherry decal, 10" **225.00**

Creamware, mug, Quaker people, 5" **175.00**

Cremo, vase, 7" **500.00**

Crocus, vase, 7" **350.00**

Dahlrose, triple bud vase, 6".**50.00**

Dahlrose, vase, square, 6" ..**55.00**

Dawn, vase, 8" **52.00**

Dogwood I, vase, 6" **55.00**

Dogwood I, wall pocket, 9 .**110.00**

Donatello, bowl, 2¾" **22.00**

Donatello, candlestick, 8" .. **65.00**

Dutch, humidor, & lid, 5" .**150.00**

Dutch, tankard & 6 mugs .**495.00**

Early Pitchers, Cow, 7½" ..**145.00**

Early Pitchers, Mill, 8" ... **175.00**

Early Pitchers, Poppy, 9" .**100.00**

Early Pitchers, Tulip, 7½" ..**50.00**

Egypto, lamp base, elephants & riders, 10" **400.00**

Rosecraft Panel, vase with nude, 6½", $180.00.

261

Pine Cone candle holders, 4", $80.00 for the pair.

Elsie the Cow, plate, 7½" . . **110.00**
Ferella, bowl, red, 12" **175.00**
Florentine, basket, with handle,
    #332, 8½" **125.00**
Forget-Me-Not, dresser set, cream-
    ware with floral **300.00**
Foxglove, bud vase, 4½" **30.00**
Freesia, basket, #390, 7" . . . **50.00**
Freesia, flowerpot, #670, 5" . **40.00**
Fuchsia, bowl, handles, 5" . . **52.00**
Fuchsia, vase, #896, 8" **65.00**
Futura, candle holder, 4" . . **95.00**
Gardenia, basket, 8" **75.00**
Holland, mug, 4" **45.00**
Holland, shaving mug **75.00**
Imperial II, vase, bulbous, rings at
    shoulder, blue, 8" **100.00**
Iris, basket, #354, 8" **85.00**
Iris, bookends, pair **95.00**
Ivory II, vase, 10" **50.00**
Ixia, basket, #346, 10" **65.00**
Jonquil, basket, 9" **150.00**
Jonquil, vase, footed, 4" **35.00**
Juvenile, mug, chick, 3½" . . **50.00**
La Rose, bowl, 6" **45.00**
Laurel, vase, blue/green, 7" . **50.00**
Luffa, vase, 6" **50.00**
Magnolia, ewer, #13, 6" **40.00**

Magnolia, tea set, 3-piece . **125.00**
Mayfair, planter, #1113, 8" . **30.00**
Ming Tree, conch shell **46.00**
Monticello, basket, with handle,
    blue, 6½" **150.00**
Moss, console bowl, 13" **55.00**
Moss, wall pocket, 10" **150.00**
Novelty Steins, each **175.00**
Olympic, pitcher, Ulysses at the
    Table of Circle, 7" . . **2,250.00**
Panel, pillow vase, 6" **50.00**
Panel, vase, 9" **75.00**
Peony, vase, #70, 18" **165.00**
Persian, bowl, 3x7" **75.00**
Pine Cone, triple candle holder,
    #1106, 5½" **85.00**
Pine Cone, wall plate, blue. **200.00**
Raymor, relish tray **25.00**
Rosecraft, vase, 8" **50.00**
Rosecraft Black, vase, handles,
    10" **125.00**
Royal Capri, planter, 7" . . **100.00**
Rozane Light, tankard, grapes, C
    Mitchell, 11" **450.00**
Rozane Royal, candlestick, floral, J
    Imlay, 9" **175.00**
Rozane Royal, letter holder, floral,
    G Neff, 3½" **200.00**

Rozane Royal, vase, floral, pillow form, V Adams, 8½" . . **175.00**
Russco, cornucopia, 8⅜" . . . **26.00**
Russco, vase, rust, 14½" . . . **95.00**
Savona, vase, 12½" **225.00**
Silhouette, basket, #708, 6" **35.00**
Smoker Sets, ash tray, 2" . . **50.00**
Sunflower, vase, 6" **80.00**
Teasel, vase, 15" **150.00**
Thornapple, basket, with handle, #342, 10" **90.00**
Thornapple, planter, 5" . . . **45.00**
Topeo, vase, blue, 9" **100.00**
Tuscany, bowl, 10" **40.00**
Tuscany, vase, handles, 8" . **40.00**
Vista, basket, 12" **135.00**
Volpato, vase, 6" **85.00**
Water Lily, vase, #81, 10" . . **70.00**
White Rose, vase, #146, 6" . **50.00**
Windsor, candlestick, handles, 4½", pair **175.00**
Wisteria, vase, 7" **125.00**
Wisteria, wall pocket, 8" . . **250.00**
Zephyr Lily, vase, #138, 10". **55.00**
Zephyr Lily, vase, 12" **60.00**

Rowland and Marcellus

Souvenir and commemorative plates marked Rowland and Marcellus or with an R & M within a diamond were manufactured by various Staffordshire potteries for these American importers who added their own backstamp to the blue-printed wares that were popular in gift shops from the 1890s until 1920. Plates are encountered most often, though cups and saucers, pitchers, etc, were also made.

Plate, Charles Dickens, rolled rim, 10" **45.00**
Plate, Historical Philadelphia, rolled rim, 10" **60.00**
Plate, Miles Standish Monument, rolled rim **45.00**

Plate, Niagara Falls, rolled rim, 10½" **36.00**
Plate, Old Albany Fort, Frederick, rolled rim **50.00**
Plate, Robert Burns **48.00**
Plate, San Francisco, 10" . . **45.00**
Plate, Thomas Jefferson, Florida souvenir, rolled rim, 10½" **60.00**

Plate, Landing at Hendricks, Hudson, 10", $50.00.

Royal Copley

Produced by the Spaulding China Company of Sebring, Ohio, Royal Copley is a line of novelty planters, vases, ash trays, and wall pockets modeled after appealing puppy dogs, lovely birds, innocent-eyed children, etc. The decoration is airbrushed and underglazed; the line is of good quality and is well-received by today's pottery collectors.

Ash tray, leaf form, pink with yellow flower, 5" **5.00**
Creamer, duck, pink hat & blue wings, 4½" **10.00**
Figurine, dove, 5" **10.00**
Figurine, spaniel, brown, 6". **15.00**
Figurine, wren, 6¼" **20.00**
Pitcher, daffodil, 8" **20.00**
Planter, black cat & tub . . . **14.00**

Parrot, 8", $24.00.

Planter, Dutch girl with bucket, maroon & blue **7.00**
Planter, hummingbird on flower, 5¼" **10.00**
Planter, mallard duck & tree stump, 8" **15.00**
Planter, Oriental girl leaning on vase, red & green 6" **9.00**
Planter, teddy bear, 6½" ...**16.00**
Planter, water lily, green, 6" .**7.50**
Planter, woodpecker, 6½" ...**7.00**
Vase, dragon, gray & pink, footed, 5½" **10.00**
Wall pocket, bamboo **12.00**
Wall pocket, lady's bonnet with flowers **35.00**

Roycroft

Elbert Hubbard, whose name is familiarly associated with the Arts and Crafts movement, established a community called Roycroft in New York at the turn of the century. There, in addition to the original print shop, furniture, metal items, leather goods, and a variety of other items were made, bearing the 'R-in-circle' mark of the Roycrofters.

Billfold, hand-tooled leather, 2½x 3¾" **82.50**

Inkwell, glass insert, 4", $75.00.

Book, Last Ride, Robert Browning, 1900, vellum cover ...**450.00**
Book, Little Journeys, Memorial Edition, 1928, set of 14 .**90.00**
Book, Philosophy, 1930 ....**25.00**
Bookends, copper, with 3 feet, 3x7", pair **95.00**
Bowl, acid-etched copper, 4½x12¼" diameter **60.00**
Box, flower relief on lid, rectangular, with logo, 7" wide ..**65.00**
Catalog, leather items, photos & prices, 1909, 48 pages .**39.00**
Cigarette package holder, lacquered finish, ring handles ...**45.00**
Crumb set, hammered copper, 2-piece **75.00**
Desk set, copper, 6-piece ..**250.00**
Frame, brass finish, 5x3" ..**55.00**
Humidor, hammered copper, shape #635, 4x5" **290.00**
Jug, pottery, brown, 5½" ...**25.00**

Inkwell, glass insert, 4", $75.00.

Letter opener **35.00**
Pen tray, copper, 4½x12" ...**45.00**
Scrapbook, 1921 .... **25.00**
Vase, bud; American Beauty, brass wash, some copper left exposed, 7" **200.00**
Vase, copper, flared, 5" **95.00**
Vase, hammered copper, 7" **150.00**

Royal Haeger, Haeger

Manufactured in Dundee, Illinois, Haeger pottery has recently become the focus of much collector interest, especially the artware line and animal figures designed by Royal Hickman. These were produced from 1938 through the 1950s and are recognized by their strong lines and distinctive glazes.

Bookends, lily, R-47, pair ..**18.00**
Bowl, console; grape clusters, pedestal foot, 14" long **25.00**
Bowl, green swirl, with flower frog, marked **18.00**

Candle holders, stalks with grapes, R-473, 10", pair **15.00**
Centerpiece, mermaid, pink & white, 13½x20½" **65.00**
Figurine, matador with cape, red or black, #6343, 11¼" **20.00**
Figurine, panther, black & colors, R-733, 13" long **15.00**
Figurine, tall pony, brown & green, R-234, 13" **16.00**
Flower frog, double angelfish, any color, R-360, 11½" **22.00**
Lamp, table; figurine, with finial, complete **50.00**
Lamp base, buffalo, lavender & blue, label, 15" long **55.00**
Planter, girl with basket leans over pool, 10x12½x6½" **35.00**
Vase, basket, floral border, any color, R-386, 12" long **18.00**
Vase, cock, fighting, oxblood agate, R-790, 11½" **25.00**
Vase, deer, cream, 7" **15.00**
Vase, gladiola; peacock, any color, 15½" **45.00**
Vase, Pegasus, blue, 12" ...**22.00**
Vase, pouter pigeon, any color, R-108, 7½" **25.00**

Bookends, lily, R-47, $22.00 for the pair.

Vase, swan, head down, any color,
R-36, 16" **35.00**
Vase, swan, head down, wings out,
R-414, 12" long **25.00**
Vase, swan, lavender, 8¾" . .**15.00**

Leopard, 11", $40.00.

Rugs, Hooked

Today recognized and admired as folk art, vintage hooked rugs as well as contemporary examples are prized for their primitive appeal, workmanship, and originality of design.

Acorns & oak leaves, brown, green,
&black on olive, 25x63". **65.00**
Cat with 3 kittens & ball of yarn,
24x35½" **725.00**
Floral, multicolor on black, oval,
24x35½" **65.00**
Flower basket on gray, Welcome,
22x44" **95.00**
Folk design with tulips, multicolor,
23x39" **65.00**
Geometric, dark colors with red &
green floral, 22x32" . .**125.00**
Horse, wide border, 40x46".**275.00**
Owl on branch, Welcome, semi-
circle, 24x34" **185.00**
Pair of stags, stylized mountain
landscape, 20x53" **120.00**
Polo player, black, green, brown, &
red, 19x37" **175.00**
Rooster & hen in barnyard, 22½x
36¾" **300.00**
Vining floral, blue with yellow &
green leaves, 27½x44" .**85.00**

Russel Wright Dinnerware

Dinnerware designed by one of America's top industrial engineers is today attracting the interest of many. Some of his more popular

Dog, bird, and tree, American, 1892, 27x53", VG, $275.00.

lines are American Modern, manufactured by the Steubenville Pottery Company (1939-'59), and Iroquois, introduced in 1944.

American Modern, bowl, vegetable; #318, open **15.00**
American Modern, carafe, #311, with stopper, rare **95.00**
American Modern, coffeepot, #322, with lid **65.00**
American Modern, creamer . **8.00**
American Modern, pitcher, water; #320 .... **40.00**
American Modern, plate, dinner; #302 .... **20.00**
American Modern, plate, salad; #301, 8¼" **8.00**
American Modern, relish, #309, divided **45.00**
American Modern, salt & pepper, #323, pair **10.00**
American Modern, saucer ...**3.00**
American Modern, stacking server **80.00**
American Modern, teapot, #316, 6x10" **45.00**
Highlight, creamer **15.00**
Highlight, cup **15.00**
Highlight, plate, dinner **15.00**
Highlight, platter, round ...**25.00**
Iroquois, bowl, cereal; 5" **6.00**

Iroquois, bowl, fruit; 9½-ounce, 5½" **5.00**
Iroquois, bowl, soup; 5¼" **8.00**
Iroquois, casserole, 2-quart .**20.00**
Iroquois, coffeepot **65.00**
Iroquois, cup & saucer, tea; 7-ounce **10.00**
Iroquois, mug, restyled, tall, 9-ounce **35.00**
Iroquois, plate, dinner; 10" ..**6.00**
Iroquois, salt & pepper, stacking, pair **12.00**
Sterling, bouillon, 7-ounce ..**8.00**
Sterling, cup & saucer **12.00**
Sterling, pitcher, cream **12.00**
Sterling, plate, service; 12". **15.00**
Sterling, platter, oval, 10½". **15.00**

Salesman's Samples

Commonplace during the late 1800s and early 20th century, salesman's samples were small-scale copies of a particular product, often exact working models that enabled the salesman to demonstrate his wares to potential customers.

Anvil **30.00**
Carrying case, 3-section, leather handle, 22x10x7" **32.00**

American Modern, coffeepot, $65.00; teapot, $45.00.

Lounge chair, folding, 14" long, $250.00.

Eyeglass Case & Testing Outfit, complete, 12x9" case . . **100.00**

Grinder, cast iron **45.00**

Ice cream freezer, Shepard's Lightning, with wood tub . . . **60.00**

Jacob's Custom Built Shirts, fabric samples, ca 1915 . . . . . . **15.00**

Milk cooler, Copeland, complete, 4 milk cans, 6x8x13" . . . **220.00**

Paint color cards, National Lead Co, Dutch Boy on original case, NM **10.00**

Stove, Kelsey Warm Air Generator, 8" **125.00**

Swing, 2-seat in frame, red & green paint, 23" **85.00**

Table, unfinished wood, in original box **28.00**

Trivet, brass, solid metal under 3 sides, openwork top . . . **24.00**

Waffle iron, Wagner, 1910 . **85.00**

Salt Shakers

Though salt has always been a valuable commodity, shakers as we know them today were not used until 1863 when a patent was issued for a mechanism capable of breaking up the lumps of salt in a bottle. In 1901 a method was developed that rendered the salt less apt to absorb moisture, and salt shakers began to be produced literally by the thousands in any available material — art glass, ceramics, wood, silver, brass, pot metal, and plastic.

Acorn, pink to white, Hobbs, ca 1890, pair **70.00**

Argus Swirl, cranberry . . . **150.00**

Atterbury Twin, milk glass, combination shaker, 1873 . . . **85.00**

Basket, milk glass, hand-painted decoration **25.00**

Beaded Dahlia, green opaque, original tops, pair **32.50**

Bevelled Diamond & Star . . **25.00**

Bow Tie, Thompson Glass Co, ca 1889 . . . . **35.00**

Bull's Eye & Daisy Variant, green eyes **24.00**

Christmas, amber, barrel shape, Sandwich, pair **175.00**

Clover Leaf, blue opaque, original tops, pair **50.00**

Corn Barrel, opaque white & custard **55.00**

Cosmos, short, condiment set, 4-piece **195.00**

Cotton Bale, green opaque . **30.00**

Currier & Ives, blue **55.00**

Diamond with Peg, custard, original tops, pair **85.00**

Eureka, ruby stain, pair . . . **48.00**

Fine Cut, yellow, pair **50.00**

Fluted Scrolls, blue opal with decoration, pair **85.00**

Heart, milk glass, pair **90.00**

Jewel & Flower, blue opalescent with gold **75.00**

Leaf & Spear, hand-painted opalware, Wave Crest, pair **165.00**

Scroll, pink, 3½", $30.00; Quilted Phlox, green, $30.00.

Novelty, deep-sea diver attached to base, fish are shakers, $15.00.

Many Petals (Periwinkle), New Martinsville **35.00**

Nail, red flashed, etched, original top **40.00**

Novelty, Blk head with watermelon, ceramic, pair **27.50**

Novelty, bride & groom, Occupied Japan, pair **18.00**

Novelty, cactus, ceramic, gr with yel stripes, pair **6.50**

Novelty, cat, lustreware, pair. **7.50**

Novelty, corn, ceramic, yel with green shucks, '40s, pair . **7.50**

Novelty, fox, ceramic, realistic, Relco, Japan, pair **12.00**

Novelty, gingham dog & calico cat, ceramic, pr **9.00**

Novelty, horse & jockey, ceramic, pair **9.00**

Novelty, Jack & Jill, ceramic, bright colors, pair **9.00**

Novelty, kissing couples on benches, ceramic, pair **12.50**

Novelty, owls in doctor's clothing, ceramic, pair **10.00**

Novelty, pilgrim boy & girl, ceramic, pair **7.50**

Novelty, Popeye & Olive Oyl, ceramic, 1950s, pair **25.00**

Novelty, rooster & hen, ceramic, bright colors, pair **7.50**

Novelty, sailboats in a wave, ceramic, pair **7.50**

Novelty, Vess soda, green glass, red top, pair **10.00**

Novelty, windmill, ceramic, black, yellow & red, pair **7.50**

Panelled Scroll, green **20.00**

Pineapple & Fan, pair **30.00**

Reverse Swirl, clear with opalescent motif **48.00**

Sequoia, blue, in stand, pair. **85.00**

Sunset, milk glass **15.00**

Swag with Brackets, amethyst with gold, pair **80.00**

Tarentum's Victoria, custard, ca 1900, pair **110.00**

Woven Neck, kitten in grass decoration, Wave Crest **55.00**

Samplers

Samplers were designed and embroidered by very young ladies from colonial times until the late 1800s. Many signed their efforts with their names, their ages, and the date the sampler was completed. Through the application of various stitches, the less-complicated examples display the alphabet, numbers, or a simple verse; but, depending upon the skill and dedication of the seamstress, others depict buildings of brick, American eagles, all sorts of animals and other birds, and complete family registers.

Signed, dated as finished in 1814, EX color, 12x13", $650.00.

Adam & Eve, flowering trees, subjects from nature, signed, 1851, 19x19¾" **225.00**

Alphabets, animals, flowers, signed, dated 1836, 21½x22½". **450.00**

Alphabets, birds, flowers, house, signed, 8⅝x18⅝" **305.00**

Alphabets, birds, flowers, trees, dated 1831, 18½x23" .**175.00**

Alphabets, border stripes, wool needlepoint, dated 1876, 15x17", EX **160.00**

Alphabets, figure with staff & bird, 1786, 12x13" **400.00**

Alphabets, flowers, signed, 1809, unframed, 19½x22" ..**325.00**

Alphabets, geometrics, signed, 1773, 13¼x15" **625.00**

Alphabets, geometrics, signed, 1887, 12½x13" **225.00**

Alphabets, linen, signed, dated 1863, 9x11½" **75.00**

Alphabets, moralistic verse, signed, dated 1846, 21½x21" .**400.00**

Alphabets, poem, homespun, signed, dated 1827, 19x20½" .**200.00**

Alphabets, strawberries, signed, dated 1826, 13¾x19" .**275.00**

Alphabets, stylized designs, initialed, 1831, 18x23" ..**175.00**

Alphabets, stylized flowers, signed, 1820, 11½x13" **230.00**

Alphabets, verse, homespun, signed, dated 1815, 14x17¾" .**225.00**

Alphanumerics, animals, flowers, dated 1817, 22x22¾" .**375.00**

Alphanumerics, homespun, signed, dated 1835, 13¾x14" .**250.00**

Alphanumerics, signed, 1851, 10¼" square **235.00**

Family record, vining border, signed, ca 1840, 14½x19" **275.00**

Family record, vining floral border, signed, 1815, 19x19" ..**475.00**

Floral designs & border, signed, 1838, 20¼x20½" **425.00**

Flowers, trees, birds, homespun, signed, 1839, 13x16" ..**600.00**

Geometric, stylized flowers, animals, & birds, 23x33" .**195.00**

Mourning, vining strawberries, needlepoint, dated 1842, 21x23", EX **150.00**

Verse, strawberry border, homespun, signed, 1834, 13¼x13¼", EX **425.00**

Signed, dated 1815, 22x15", $750.00.

Schoop, Hedi

From the 1940s through the '50s, Hedi Schoop managed a small operation in North Hollywood, California, where she produced novelty wares such as figurines, lamps, and other decorative items.

Lady with fan and basket, 13", $35.00.

Bowl, formed by lady's skirt, #418, 13" diameter **65.00**
Figurine, debutante, 12½" .. **35.00**
Figurine, Dutch boy, 11½" .. **35.00**
Figurine, girl standing, with vase in arm, 9" **20.00**
Figurine, lady with basket leads large poodle, 10" **25.00**
Figurine, Oriental man in black & white jacket, tall **35.00**
Flower holder, peasant woman figural, 12" **35.00**
Lamp, TV; Comedy & Tragedy, rare, large **150.00**
Planter, geisha with umbrella, blue, #223 .... **24.00**

Scouting Collectibles

Founded in England in 1907 by Major General Lord Baden-Powell, scouting remains an important institution in the life of young boys and girls everywhere. Recently scouting-related memorabilia has attracted a following, and values of many items have escalated dramatically in the last few years. Early first edition handbooks often bring prices of $100.00 and more; vintage uniforms are scarce and highly valued; and one of the rarer medals, the Life Saving Honor Medal, is worth several hundred dollars to collectors.

Booklet, Annual Report of the Scout Executive, 1938 .... **5.00**
Boy Scout Official Firemaking Equipment, orig box ... **30.00**
Calendar, shows scouts with emblem, 1953, 23x11" **14.00**
Catalog, 1946 Girl Scout **8.00**
Compass, black Bakelite with clear plastic center, 2" **10.00**

World Jamboree jacket patches, R1: 1975, $10.00; 1971, $12.00. R2: 1967, $14.00; 1979, $30.00. R3: 1979, $15.00; 1967, $12.00.

Neckerchiefs: BSA Issue Eagle Scout, $10.00; National Eagle Scout Association, $5.00.

Compass/sundial, Sunwatch, brass, original box, 3x2" **20.00**

Diary, dated 1950, unused ..**5.00**

First Aid Kit, tin, ca 1930 ..**22.00**

Game, Game of Boy Scouts .**30.00**

Handbook, Boy Scout of America, 1962, EX **7.00**

Medal, God & Country; red, white, & blue on blue ribbon ..**10.00**

Medal, War Service 1945 Gen Eisenhower Waste Paper Campaign **27.00**

Merit badge sash, with 10 patches, circa 1960 ....**10.00**

Neckerchief slide, brass, reads Onward for God & Country, 1950 ....**10.00**

Patch, pocket; 1977 Boy Scout National Jamboree **5.00**

Poster, recruiting; Loyalty Like Thrift ...., ...**10.00**

Ring, sterling silver, insignia on top, early **8.00**

Shirt, with insignia, green cotton, ca 1955 ....**12.00**

Statue, cast metal Boy Scout, signed K Tait McKenzie, 15½" .**26.00**

Statue, cast metal Boy Scout on black celluloid base, 7" .**16.00**

T-Shirt, Boy Scout National Jamboree 1953 ....**6.00**

Thermometer, Cub Scout, tin, with mercury tube **45.00**

Watch, Official Girl Scout, original box, ca 1930 ....**55.00**

Sebastians

Sold primarily in gift stores in the New England states since the 1930s, Sebastian miniatures were designed by Prescott W. Baston who withdrew the line from production in 1976. At that time, one hundred of the more than four hundred original models were selected to continue in production by the Lance Corporation. The discontinued figures have become highly collectible.

Becky Thatcher, green label. **35.00**

Benjamin & Debora Franklin, Marblehead label, pair.**175.00**

Bringing Home the Tree ...**20.00**
Chestnut Hill Mall, Marblehead
    era, no label **225.00**
Christmas Morning **45.00**
Concord Minuteman, Marblehead
    label **100.00**
Dutchman's Pipe **125.00**
Family Picnic **50.00**
Grandma at the Cookstove, green
    label **35.00**
Huckleberry Finn, Marblehead
    label **60.00**
In the Candy Store (Necco). **180.00**
Jello-O Moose **300.00**
John Hancock, pewter **40.00**
Madonna, chair, green label. **40.00**
Olivea **90.00**
Outboard Fishers, bl label .**40.00**
Pilgrims, Marblehead label .**65.00**
Priscilla Alden, Marblehead
    label **90.00**
Sam Houston, blue label ...**40.00**
St Theresa **125.00**
Victorian Couple, Marblehead la-
    bel **55.00**
Watchman, green label **35.00**
Weighing the Baby, Marblehead era,
    no label **200.00**

Dame and Rip Van Winkle, 3", $30.00 each.

Sewing Items

Sewing notions from the 1800s
and early 20th century, such as
whimsical figural tape measures,
beaded satin pincushions, blown
glass darning eggs, and silver and
gold thimbles are pleasant reminders of a bygone era — ladies' sewing
circles, quilting bees, and beautifully hand-stitched finery.

Book, Sewing Book for Children's
    and Girls' Clothes, 1900.**10.00**
Box, heart shape, 1 drawer, with
    pincushion, 12" long ..**100.00**
Box, pine, imitiation burl, gold sten-
    cil, tray, 11½" long **35.00**
Button, embossed Cupid, gold
    dipped, signed **5.00**
Catalog, Home Needlework, 1916,
    EX **8.00**
Crochet ball holder, woven sweet
    grass **30.00**
Darning egg, wood with fancy ster-
    ling handle **45.00**
Glove darner, wood, fancy sterling
    handle, ca 1865, 4½" ...**42.00**
Knitting sheath, hand-carved
    wood **70.00**
Lace bobbin, wood with heading, ca
    1870 ....**8.00**
Needle case, brass, ca
    1790 ....**170.00**
Needle case, umbrella, ivory &
    black celluloid **75.00**
Needle case, with stanhope, carved
    bone **75.00**
Needle sharpener, book shape, Fairy
    Tales, ca 1850 ....**35.00**
Needle sharpener, strawberry
    shape, ca 1870 ......**25.00**
Pincushion, duck, gun metal,
    1½" **75.00**
Pincushion, fainting couch, brass,
    2½" **65.00**
Pincushion, lady's slipper, with red
    velvet, spelter **22.00**
Pincushion, painted floral & Friend-
    ship on ivory, ca 1840 ..**40.00**
Pincushion, souvenir, transfer on
    china, shield shaped ...**22.50**
Sewing bird, brass, elabor-
    ate **245.00**
Sewing bird, brass & iron, 2
    cushions with red velvet,
    4½" **200.00**

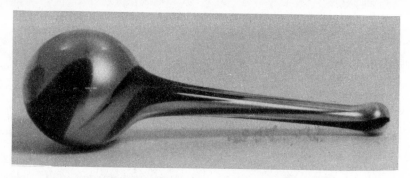

Darner, gold and red swirled glass, 9½", $185.00.

Spool caddy, wood, 3-tiered, pincushion at top, 6" **25.00**
Tape measure, chicken, celluloid
figural **65.00**
Tape measure, clock figural, pull
tape & hands move, 1x1¼"
square **55.00**
Tape measure, clown figural, Germany, 2" **38.00**
Tape measure, drum, painted brass,
2" **140.00**
Tape measure, egg with rooster
atop **95.00**
Tape measure, elephant, cloth with
glass eyes, 2½" **38.00**
Tape measure, fish, celluloid, Ja-
pan, 4½" **40.00**
Tape measure, helmet, white deco-
rated black plastic, 1½". **85.00**
Tape measure, house with 2 wheels,
brass, 2" **125.00**
Tape measure, pig, celluloid, Ger-
many **65.00**
Tape measure, turtle, brass,
2" **120.00**
Tatting shuttle, advertising, Lydia
Pinkham **35.00**
Thimble, blue enameling over
silver **48.00**
Thimble, child's; brass **10.00**
Thimble, engraved Only a Thimble
Full, sterling, 2" **38.00**
Thimble, sterling, embossed flower
border, dated 1926 ....**85.00**
Thimble, tailor's; sterling ..**45.00**
Thimble, sterling, with 14K gold
wash, marked France ..**75.00**

Thimble, 14K, beading with engraved band **80.00**
Thimble, 14K, engraved scene with
house, marked **175.00**
Thimble holder, blue glass slipper
with steel thimble, 2" ..**95.00**
Thimble holder, brass house
with glass roof that opens,
2½" **95.00**
Thimble holder, brass slipper with
felt pad & steel thimble,
2" **85.00**
Thimble holder, embossed brass
bucket with chain, 1" ..**48.00**

**Tape measure, monkey figural,
marked Germany, $40.00.**

274

Thread holder, marked Wilcox, silverplate **45.00**

Shaker Items

Made by an all-but-vanished religious sect that was founded in America in 1776, Shaker items are exquisitely simple and are prized for their flawless construction and originality of design. The Shakers established self-contained communities, each of which produced all the necessities required for day-to-day living. They were weavers, brick makers, printers, farmers, and cabinetmakers. Besides their furniture, which collectors value highly, finger-constructed boxes, finely woven baskets, original handmade clothing, and advertising items relating to the sale of their seeds are the most sought after memorabilia.

Butter scales, all wood, 24" . **65.00**
Carrier, bentwood with handle, copper tacks & rivets, oval, 3" long **275.00**
Chair, apple sorting; low ladderback, turned finials . . **200.00**
Coat hanger, wooden, Mt Lebanon, NY, 46" **90.00**
Coffeepot, tin, 19th-century American, 10" **100.00**

Bowl, for food chopping, old red paint on maple, turned, New Lebanon, NY, $80.00; Food masher, tiger maple, knob end, Pleasant Hill, KY, 13", $180.00; Sugar scoop, maple, Hancock, ca 1940, 10", $250.00.

Dusting brush, worn gray paint, 13¾" **65.00**
Footstool, spint seat, Mt Lebanon, 9¾x11¼x14¼" **135.00**
Footstool, wood, turned legs, original finish, Mt Lebanon, NY **250.00**
Kitchen tool, twisted wire with wood handle, 10½" **50.00**
Lap board, pine, signed, ca 1910, 12¼x24" **75.00**
Maple syrup dipper, tin, Enfield, New Hampshire, 11½" . **25.00**
Measure, bentwood, copper tacks, turned handle, original finish, 7¼" diameter **215.00**
Rocker, with original stenciled label, original finish . . . **600.00**
Sewing box, walnut with square nails, china knob, 6" . . . **85.00**

Sieve, wooden, open-weave splint, old patina, 21" diameter, $150.00.

Shaving Mugs

Often as elegant as the handlebar mustache sported by its owner, the shaving mug was usually made of china or earthenware, well decorated with floral sprays, gold trim, depictions of the owner's trade, or his name. Today, the 'occupationals' are most highly valued, especially those representing an unusual trade or fraternal affiliation.

Oriental man, Bavaria, 4", $110.00.

Advertising, Thomas Hughes Co,
white porcelain **25.00**
Advertising, Use Tonique Delux,
Germany **75.00**
Advertising, Washington Dairy
Lunch, portrait & flags **20.00**
Character, grinning Black man
wearing straw hat, soap ledge
in mouth **170.00**
China, white & green floral, Homer
Laughlin **35.00**
Coat of Arms, RH Caldwell with
shield, France **100.00**
Fraternal, Elk's head over clock face,
gold trim **80.00**
Fraternal, Knights of Pythias, suit
of armor **95.00**
Fraternal, Masonic, blue flowers
highlighted with gold .. **60.00**
Fraternal, Odd Fellows, emblem &
TB Dick on front **45.00**
Occupational, banker, silver nickel
on front, Limoges **65.00**
Occupational, barber, interior work-
ing scene **400.00**
Occupational, boot maker, high-
button boots, France .**200.00**
Occupational, buggy maker, riding
buggy with name **200.00**
Occupational, carpenter, tools of
trade, Austria **200.00**
Occupational, dentist, working on
patient in chair **425.00**
Occupational, farmer, horse-drawn
buggy & dog **175.00**

Occupational, farmer, tied horse
with bow & shamrocks, Aus-
tria **125.00**
Occupational, harness maker, man
at work **225.00**
Occupational, milk man, horse-
drawn milk wagon, Knech Mfg
Co. **275.00**
Occupational, musician, trumpet &
MF Beach **125.00**
Occupational, musician, 5-string
banjo, marked T&V ..**325.00**
Occupational, stone cutter, man
chipping marble slab, marked
Austria **275.00**
Occupational, tinsmith, gold trim
at top rim **155.00**
Occupational, waiter, at work in
resturant, Germany ..**675.00**

**Floral mug and brush in original
box, $85.00.**

Shawnee

The novelty planters, vases,
cookie jars, salt and pepper shakers, and 'Corn' dinnerware made by
the Shawnee Pottery of Ohio are
attractive, fun to collect, and are
still available at reasonable prices.
The company operated from 1937
until 1961 marking their wares with
'Shawnee, U.S.A.' and a number
series, or 'Kenwood.'

Ash tray, squirrel **12.00**
Bank, tumbling bear with paper
label **65.00**

Bookends, geese, pair **25.00**
Candlestick holder, with platinum
   trim, #3026 .... **22.00**
Cookie jar, Clown **75.00**
Cookie jar, Drummer Boy .. **85.00**
Cookie jar, Dutch Girl, with blue
   dress **55.00**
Cookie jar, Elephant, with white
   collar **25.00**
Cookie jar, Puss 'N Boots, green &
   yellow with gold trim .. **50.00**
Cookie jar, Smiley Pig, blue ban-
   dana **60.00**
Corn, bowl, #6 .... **18.00**
Corn, casserole, small **32.00**
Corn, creamer, #70 ...... **12.00**
Corn, cup, #90 .... **22.00**
Corn, mug, #69 .... **25.00**
Corn, plate, #68, 10" **23.00**
Corn, platter, #96 .... **25.00**
Corn, salt & pepper shakers, large,
   pair **15.00**
Corn, salt & pepper shakers, small,
   pair **12.00**
Corn, teapot, 30-ounce **42.00**
Creamer, elephant, gold trim &
   decals **18.00**
Figurine, rabbit **10.00**
Pitcher, Bo Peep, gold trim & de-
   cals, large **90.00**
Pitcher, Smiley, pig, red flower,
   large **45.00**
Planter, boy at stump **12.00**

Planter, Polynesian girl, #896, $16.00.

Planter, chihuahua at doghouse,
   marked USA **15.00**
Planter, coal bucket, USA .. **12.00**
Planter, cornucopia **10.00**
Planter, doe & fawn, #669 .. **14.00**
Planter, house, #J543P **15.00**
Planter, man with push cart. **12.00**
Planter, piano, #528, green . **16.00**
Planter, rabbit with turnip . **16.00**
Planter, shell, #665 .... **7.00**
Planter, water trough **16.00**
Salt & pepper shakers, flowerpot,
   gold trim, pair **20.00**
Salt & pepper shakers, Little Chef,
   gold trim, pair **16.00**
Salt & pepper shakers, milk can,
   pair **6.00**
Salt & pepper shakers, owl, gold
   trim, pair **25.00**
Salt & pepper shakers, Smiley Pig,
   small, pair **5.00**
Salt & pepper shakers, watering
   can, pair **18.00**
Salt & pepper shakers, wheelbar-
   row, pair **12.00**
Sugar bowl, fruit, #81 ..... **20.00**
Teapot, Granny Anne, with green
   apron **50.00**
Teapot, Tom Tom, with white &
   brown base **40.00**
Vase, #890, large **14.00**
Vase, tulip, gold trim **12.00**

Corn line salt and pepper shakers, large, $15.00 for the pair.

Wall pocket, birds at birdhouse,
#830, marked **10.00**
Wall pocket, grandfather clock, gold
trim **22.00**

Sheet Music

The most valuable examples of sheet music are those related to early transportation, ethnic themes, Disney characters, a particularly popular artist or composer, or with a cover illustration done by a well-known artist. Production of sheet music peaked during the 'Tin Pan Alley Days,' from the 1880s until the 1930s. Covers were made as attractive as possible to lure potential buyers, and today's collectors sometimes frame and hang them as they would a print. Flea markets are a good source for sheet music, and prices are usually very reasonable. Most are available for under $5.00. Some of the more valuable examples are listed here.

Ben Hur March, chariot race on
cover **6.50**

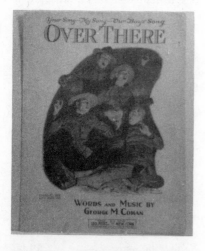

Over There, Rockwell illustration, copyright 1918, $25.00.

Beside You, Bob Hope & Dorothy
Lamour **6.00**
Carry Me Back to Old Virginny,
Blacks relaxing, 1900 . . **10.00**
Comrades, I Am Going Home; 1866,
5 pages **12.50**
Coon's Breach of Promise Cakewalk,
1898 . . . . **18.00**
Cupid's Awakening Waltzes, sleepy
cupid on flowers, 1899 . **75.00**
Curly Top, When I Grow Up, Shirley
Temple **24.00**
Dashing Cavaliers, soldiers on
horseback, 1911 . . . . . . **30.00**
Don't Be a Baby, Baby; Mills Broth-
ers, 1946 . . . . **6.50**
Don't Cry Dolly Grey, publisher
Remmick & Company . **25.00**
Don't Fence Me In, 1944, Cole Por-
ter **4.00**
Down Home Rag, Black children in
cotton balls, 1916 . . . . . **10.00**
Forty Second Street, Shuffle Off to
Buffalo **25.00**
Gal in Calico, picture Dennis Mor-
gan, Janice Paige, 1946 . **5.00**
Hesitation Waltz, ballroom scene,
1914 . . . . **50.00**
Hurricane, men grasping mast of
ship in storm, 1906 . . . . **28.00**
I'm Forever Thinking of You, Rolf
Armstrong illustration . **12.00**
If You Were Only by My Side, cupid
ringing bells, 1898 . . . . **95.00**
It's Magic, from Romance on High
Seas, Doris Day cover . . **10.00**
Leaf by Leaf the Roses Fall, pub-
lished by Lyon & Healy, 1867,
NM **17.50**
Little Buttercup's Song, 1895. **5.00**
Lucky Lindy, 1927 . . . . **20.00**
Masquerade, party scene with bor-
der of party favors, '07 . **30.00**
Mexicali Rose, Bing Crosby shown
on cover **7.00**
Midnight Fire Alarm, horse-drawn
fire engine, 1900 . . . . . . **15.00**
Midnight Flyer, Colorado Express
train, 1903 . . . . **45.00**

Tears Tell, by C.&.F. Wilson, Armstrong illustration, 1919, $15.00.

Moonlight & Shadows, Dorothy Lamour & Ray Milland cover, 1936 ....7.00

My Wild Irish Rose of Killarney, 1907 ....5.00

Race Course, horse race scene, 1910, ET Paull cover 45.00

Richard Carvel Waltzes, photo of Andrew Robson, 1901 ..45.00

Ring Out, Wild Bells; Father Time flying in winter, 1912 ..45.00

Shuffle Off to Buffalo, Ginger Rogers 25.00

Silver Sleigh Bells, horse-drawn sleigh at night, 1906 ...35.00

Snow White, Heigh-Ho, Disney Studio, 1937 ....13.00

That Dixie Rag, Black people dancing jig, ca 1900 ......10.00

The Kissing Bandit, Frank Sinatra on cover 20.00

There's a Star in My Window for You, 1945 ....12.00

Tipperary Guards, soldiers fighting & marching, 1915 .....18.00

Turkey in the Straw, Black man with banjo, 1921 ......10.00

We'll Stand by the Flag, Admiral Dewey, Gen Lee, 1898 .30.00

When My Ship Comes In, copyright 1915 ....8.00

You're the Only Star, from Enoch Light, Gene Autry 15.00

Slot Machines

Now legal in many states, old 'one-arm bandits' are being restored, used for home entertainment, or simply amassed in collections. Especially valuable are those from the turn of the century, rare or unique models, and those with unusually fancy trim.

Aristocrat 25¢ Mechanical Wizard, EX original 700.00

Bailey Hold & Draw, EX original 500.00

Bally 5¢ Draw Bell 575.00

Bally 5¢-25¢ Double Bells, EX original 3,000.00

Buckley Criss Cross, 1947, EX original 1,400.00

Caille Doughboy, 1935 ..1,200.00

Caille Jumbo Success ...1,600.00

Champion, gumball & token machine, 3-reel 550.00

Groetchen Corona Blue Bell, 1950, EX original 600.00

Groetchen Twin Falls, bell console, 1947 ....800.00

Groetchen-Columbia, 1936, EX original 800.00

Jennings 25¢ Standard Chief , EX original 1,250.00

Jennings 5¢ Electovender, EX original 1,950.00

Jennings 5¢ Mints of Quality, side vendor, future pay ..1,600.00

Jennings 5¢ Silver Moon Chief, half-moon on front, 1941 1,600.00

Keeney Pyramid 2,200.00

Mills Baseball 1,500.00

Mills 1¢ QT Bell, red & yellow, restored 1,250.00

Mills 10¢ Black Cherry .1,500.00

Caille 25¢ Victory Bell, 3-reel, cast iron with nudes, 1919, restored, $3,500.00.

Mills 10¢ Hightop **1,200.00**
Mills 25¢ War Eagle, EX. **1,600.00**
Mills 5¢ Black Cherry, 1931, EX
  original **1,500.00**
Mills 5¢ Cherry Front . . **1,500.00**
Mills 5¢ Diamond Front, 1939, M
  restored **1,500.00**
Mills 5¢ Futurity, 1936 . **2,800.00**
Mills 5¢ Horsehead Bonus, M re-
  stored **1,900.00**
Mills 5¢ Poinsettia **1,500.00**
Mills 5¢ Puritan, 1904, countertop
  size **750.00**
Pace 1¢ Bantam, 1928, EX orig-
  inal **1,200.00**
Pace 5¢ Comet **1,300.00**
Pace 5¢ Deluxe Chrome, 1947, EX
  original **1,500.00**
Rockola 5¢ FOK with jackpot, origi-
  nal **1,000.00**
Rockola 5¢ War Eagle, NM orig-
  inal **1,900.00**

Skelly Candy Boy, 1925 . **2,000.00**
Superior Golden Bell, 1934, EX
  original **2,000.00**
Watling 5¢ Brownie **4,500.00**
Watling 5¢ Rol-A-Top, EX orig-
  inal **2,600.00**
Watling 5¢ Twin Jackpot, 3-reel,
  1931 . . . . **1,800.00**

Snuf-A-Rette Ash Trays

Made in the late thirties and early forties for railroads, hotels, world's fairs, various businesses, and for general home use, Snuf-A-Rette ash trays are gaining in popularity largely because of their Deco styling. Available in various shapes and colors, the railroad, world's fair, and advertising trays are most popular and command higher prices.

#25, Stacy China Co **11.00**
#26, Stacy China Co **11.00**
#801, National Porcelain Co. **17.50**
#802, National Porcelain Co. **10.00**
#810, Ekstrand Mfg Co **20.00**
#818, Ekstrand Mfg Co **14.00**
#820, Ekstrand Mfg Co **17.50**
#821, Ekstrand Mfg Co **17.50**
#834, Ekstrand Mfg Co **14.00**
#835, Ekstrand Mfg Co **17.50**
#841, Ekstrand Mfg Co **20.00**
#842, Ekstrand Mfg Co **20.00**
#852, Ekstrand Mfg Co **14.00**
Advertising, all styles, range from
  $30 to **60.00**

See listings for current values.

Railroad, all styles, range from $25
up to **50.00**
World's Fair, all styles, range from
$25 up to **30.00**

Soda Fountain Collectibles

The days of the neighborhood ice
cream parlor are gone; the soda jerk,
the mouth-watering confections he
concocted, the high counter and bar
stools a thing of the past — but
memories live on through the soda
glasses, ice cream scoops, milk shake
machines, and soda fountain signs
that those reluctant to forget treasure today.

Book, Ice Cream, hardcover, illus-
trated, 1928, 407 pages. **30.00**
Carton, Real Velvet Ice Cream, 1941,
1-quart **4.00**
Catalog, Soda Fountain Supplies &
Repair Parts, '39, 6x9" . **22.00**
Dipper, hot fudge; aluminum, Her-
shey's on handle, 8½" .. **15.00**
Dish, banana split; boat shape,
crystal **4.00**
Flavor board, Quality Dairy Ice
Cream, 7 inserts, glass front, ca
1940s **50.00**
Ice cream sandwich mold, alumi-
num, 3x3¾x¾", with 3" long
handle **22.00**
Ice cream scoop, Clipper Fountain
Supply **320.00**
Ice cream scoop, Dover Manufac-
turing, 2-way action .. **125.00**
Ice cream scoop, Gilchrist #31, wood
handle, 10" **32.00**
Ice cream scoop, Gilchrist #33, wood
handle, 10½" **90.00**
Ice cream scoop, Hamilton Beach
Mfg Co. **30.00**
Ice cream scoop, Indestructo #3,
wood handle **45.00**
Ice cream scoop, Indestructo #6,
wood handle **50.00**

Strawholder, tin lid, 12", $135.00.

Ice cream scoop, Kingery, brass with
squeeze handles, 1894. **150.00**
Ice cream spoon, silverplated lily
pattern with twist handle, set
of 8 .... **32.50**
Ice pick, Gilchrist #50, 6-prong, wood
handle, 9" **14.00**
Ice scoop, metal, 2 drainage holes,
7" **4.00**
Ice shredder, Yankee #27, serrated
blade, cast iron, 7¾" ... **27.00**
Magazine, The Liquid Bottler, Feb-
ruary 1914, 7x10" **12.00**
Menu holder, Arctic Ice Cream, blue
& white, weighted base . **8.00**
Post card, picture; Chamberlain Ice
Cream Co, ca 1920, M .. **5.00**
Ruler, Breyer's Ice Cream, wood,
12" **6.00**
Shaker, tinware, marked Double
Malted **8.00**
Soda glass, Nestles in red at top,
syrup line, 6¼" **8.00**
Soda spoon, Su Su Nut Krumbles
Sundae on handle, marked Wm
Rogers, 8" **6.00**

Straw holder, clear, slim cylinder
with flared base **200.00**
Straw holder, clear pattern glass,
Bakelite finial, nickel-plated
base **300.00**
Straw holder, green glass, nickel-
plated base, 1930s . . . **350.00**
Syrup bottle, Cherry Smash 5¢,
metal top, 12" **110.00**
Syrup bottle, Mint, glass label, origi-
nal cap, 11" **60.00**
Tip tray, Telling's Ice Cream, couple
at freezer, 6" diameter . **70.00**
Trade card, White Mountain
Freezer, girl, 3x4" **3.00**
Tray, Justrite Ice Cream, Western
Dairy & Ice Cream Co . **27.00**

Spongeware

Utility earthenware from the last
quarter of the 1800s decorated with
sponged-on colors is popular with
today's collectors, especially those
interested in primitives, country
antiques, and American pottery.
Usually the color was applied at
random, although occasionally
simple patterns were attempted.
Blue on white are the most treasured colors; but red, green, rust,
black, and tan were also used,
sometimes in combination. You may
find some items trimmed with gold.

Bean pot, blue & white, with lid,
M **375.00**
Bowl, batter; yellow over blue, with
bail handle, 7½x4½" . . **120.00**
Bowl, blue & rust on white, blue
banded top, 5" **65.00**
Bowl, blue & white, 3x7" . . **125.00**
Bowl, brown & green on cream,
4½x9½" **35.00**
Bowl, mixing; blue & white, em-
bossed, 6x13" **160.00**
Bowl, yellow & rust, 9½" . . . **65.00**
Casserole, blue & rust on cream,
with lid **80.00**

Pitcher, brown and blue sponging,
3 embossed bands, 9", $70.00.

Creamer, blue & white, 4" . **125.00**
Crock, butter; blue & gray, no lid,
6x9" **185.00**
Cup, blue & white with gold band,
5" diameter **55.00**
Mug, blue & white, 3½" . . . **155.00**
Pitcher, blue & white **120.00**
Pitcher, brown & green on yellow,
fluted sides, 6" **75.00**
Plate, blue & white, scalloped, 10"
diameter **125.00**
Platter, blue & white, 13½"
long **225.00**
Soap dish, blue & white . . **145.00**
Vase, blue & white, 4⅜" . . . **90.00**

Spoons

Since the 1890s, spoons have been
issued as souvenirs, to commemo-
rate an event, in honor of a famous
person, or on the occasion of a holiday. Today's collectors prefer those
with high relief designs on handle
as well as bowl, Indian or other full-
figure handles, enameled or gold-
washed trim, and spoons that are

dated or from a limited edition. While the design is more important than the material, silver is preferred over silverplate.

Angel Moroni handle, Mormon Temple in bowl **65.00**

Apollo XIII, Not a Moon Landing But..., 4½" **6.00**

Atlantic City & scene in bowl, holly & berries on handle ...**40.00**

Belmar NJ embossed in bowl, rose & foliage handle **12.00**

Boston, Edwin Booth in wreath on handle, etched bowl ..**185.00**

Brooklyn/handle, City of Churches in bowl, Gorham **65.00**

Capitol building, cannon shape handle, embossed bowl .**95.00**

Carnegie Institute, Elkhart, Indiana **35.00**

Catalina, sterling **30.00**

Chicago, figural Indian handle, gold-washed bowl **32.50**

Chick hatching from egg embossed in bowl **10.00**

Cincinnati, OH, engraved bowl, state seal handle **15.00**

Cordele, GA, Black boy eating watermelon, Stolen Sweets, 5½" **85.00**

Delaware, OH, Gray Chapel, gold-washed bowl, scrolled handle **35.00**

Dixieville Notch & Gloriette Lake, scene in bowl, 3¾" **15.00**

Denver Mint, Gen. James Denver on handle, sterling, 6", $18.00.

Elk with blue & white enamelled clock handle, plain bowl.**49.00**

Eston, WV, St Paul's Episcopal Church in bowl **35.00**

General Meade handle, view of Devil's Den in bowl **29.00**

General Putnam on handle, plain bowl **18.00**

Idaho state seal handle, St Maries engraved in bowl **15.00**

Indiana, cut-out letters on handle, embossed view in bowl .**18.00**

Jamestown Centennial 1800-1900, embossed scene with log cabin in bowl **35.00**

Liberty, full-figure on handle, embossed scene & quote in bowl **125.00**

Los Angeles, sterling **25.00**

Mexico on handle, Mexico's flag in enamel bowl, Wendell Mfg **95.00**

Mount Hood, figural salmon handle, foreign building embossed in bowl **55.00**

Niagara Falls view embossed in bowl, head on handle ..**38.00**

Niagara Falls view embossed in bowl, scroll handle **15.00**

Order of the Eastern Star, 1903 ....**22.50**

Osceola, NB, sterling **25.00**

Palm Beach, Florida, embossed in bowl, alligator handle ..**38.00**

Petoskey, MI, engraved in bowl, 1902 on back, 4" **15.00**

Philadelphia, Penn Treaty, gold-washed bowl **30.00**

Plattsburg, NY, in bowl, full-figure Indian handle **34.00**

Portland, OR, state seal on handle, scene on bowl back, 4" .**15.00**

Prospector & pick, full-figure handle, plain bowl **55.00**

South Haven, MI, floral handle, dated 1898, 4" **15.00**

Spokane Falls, WA, sterling. **25.00**

St Louis in bowl, horn of plenty, cut-out handle, 4⅛" **18.00**

Statue of Liberty handle, gold-washed bowl, Tiffany . **125.00**
Stork, full-figure handle, engraved birth data in bowl, 5¾" . **18.00**
Summit Pikes Peak engraved in gold-washed bowl **15.00**
Texas Centennial, 1936 . . . . **12.00**
Toreador, full-figure handle, Corrida de Torres in bowl . **95.00**
Trenton, NJ, embossed in bowl, leaves on handle **14.00**
Uncle Tom's Cabin in bowl, sterling, ca 1910, 6" **95.00**
Virginia on handle, Old Capitol Williamsburg in bowl . . **18.00**
Warren, PA, Episcopal church, gold-washed bowl **35.00**
Washington, DC, landmarks on handle, Capital in bowl. **15.00**
Wesleyan University emblem on handle, plain bowl, 4⅜". **12.00**
William Penn, full-figure handle, embossed Independence Hall view **45.00**
William Penn, full-figure handle, gold wash overall, 4⅜" . **35.00**
Zodiac, April & Taurus, Gorham Mfg, 5⅞" **25.00**

Sports Collectibles

Memorabilia related to sports of any kind — hunting, fishing, golfing, baseball, bicycling, etc. — is attracting a following of collectors, many of which specialize in the particular sport that best holds their interests. See also Fishing Collectibles.

Baseball bat, Louisville Slugger Navin Field, Detroit . . . **20.00**
Book, Yogi Berra's Baseball Guidebook, 1966, 80 pages **5.00**
Button, Joe Lewis World's Champion, photo, 1¼" **16.00**
Dodgers Program, 1964 . . . . **12.50**

Bicycle carbide lamp, 1897, original box, $85.00.

Game, Jack Armstrong, Big Ten Football, Wheaties premium, 1936 . . . . **22.00**
Homecoming banner, football player, ca 1935, 35x23". **45.00**
Nodder, Dallas Cowboys, composition body on wood base . **25.00**
Pin, Dizzy Dean Winners, baseball & bat in center, 2" long. **15.00**
Score book, Comiskey Park, 1917, NM **22.00**
Sugar Bowl Program, 1963, 104 pages **17.50**
Token, Mikey Mantle **5.00**
World Series Program, 1974. **15.00**
Yearbook, Pittsburgh Pirates, 1964, M **5.00**

Staffordshire

The Staffordshire district of England is perhaps the best known pottery-producing area in the world. Since the early 1700s, hundreds of potteries have operated there, producing wares as varied as their names. While many examples are extremely rare and expensive, it is still possible to find small but interesting Staffordshire items at nearly any good market. See also Historical Blue Ware.

Bank, eagle figural **225.00**
Bust, clergyman, black marbleized plinth, 8½" **195.00**
Chamber pot, pink & green floral swags on cream, 9" **75.00**

284

Cottage with bird, 1840, 2". **145.00**

Creamer, cow, copper lustre trim, ca 1830, 4¾x6¼" **250.00**

Cup plate, gazebo scene, purple, 3¾" **40.00**

Cup plate, Oriental scene, green, Adams, 4" **40.00**

Cup plate, soldier aims rifle, purple, 4" **45.00**

Figurine, cat on cushion, black & white, 1850, 5½" long . **700.00**

Figurine, cockerel, blue on white, ca 1770, 5½" **385.00**

Figurine, couple seated under arbor, 14½" **100.00**

Figurine, fireman, 9" **135.00**

Figurine, girl riding on back of goat, 12½" **150.00**

Figurine, lion, glass eyes, 14" long, pair **350.00**

Figurine, Prodigals Return, 13½", NM **150.00**

Figurine, Robin Hood group, strong colors **150.00**

Figurine, Uncle Tom & Eva, 1850, 10" **250.00**

Figurine, Widow, Walton, ca 1830, NM **350.00**

Figurine, zebra, opposing pair, 6¼" **150.00**

Flask, fish form, dark brown & salt glaze, 8½" wide **200.00**

Inkwell, dog & pup recumbent on pillow, scroll-leg base, repaired, 4" long **135.00**

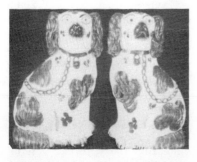

Dogs, copper lustre spots with green highlights, facing pair, 9", $125.00.

Goat on scrolled base, 7x8", $200.00.

Jug, Bacchus mask, florals, monkey handle, 1830, 7½" . **165.00**

Mug, dancing & drinking scenes, hand painted, 3½" **165.00**

Mug, train, brown transfer with red & green enamel, 4" . . . **165.00**

Pastille burner, cottage, applied flowers, ca 1860, 5" . . . **185.00**

Plate, Caledonia, green & black, 7½" **15.00**

Plate, girl feeds chickens, black on white, ca 1840, 5¼" **30.00**

Plate, toddy; temperance meeting black transfer with multicolor, 5", EX **115.00**

Platter, peacock, creamware, feather edge, 1810, 16". **550.00**

Spill vase, Red Riding Hood & wolf, 10" **200.00**

Teapot, with lid, gaudy 4-color swags, 6½" **110.00**

Tureen, hen on nest figural, with lid, ca 1870, 8½" **175.00**

Vase, figural couple with basket between, 8" **75.00**

Wash bowl, Baltimore, marked Meigh, tall **335.00**

Stangl

Originally known as the Fulper Pottery, the Stangl company was founded in 1913 and until its closing in 1972 produced many lines of dinnerware as well as various types of artware. Birds modeled after the prints of Audubon were introduced in the early 1940s. More than one hundred different birds were produced, most of which are marked with 'Stangl' and a four-digit number to identify the species. Though a limited few continue to be produced, since 1976 they have been marked with the date of their production.

Allen Hummingbird, #3634 **45.00**
Bird of Paradise, #3408 .... **80.00**
Blue Jay with leaf, #3716 . **350.00**
Blue-Headed Vireo, #3448 . **40.00**
Bluebird, #3276 .... **65.00**
Cardinal, #3444, matt red .. **90.00**
Cardinal, #3444, pink **65.00**
Carolina Wren, #3590 ..... **65.00**
Cerulean Warbler, #3456 .. **50.00**
Chestnut-Backed Chickadee. **75.00**
Cliff Swallow, #3852 ...... **60.00**
Cock Pheasant, #3492 .... **130.00**
Cockatoo, #3405 .... **45.00**
Duck, #3250B **35.00**
Duck, Flying; #3443 ..... **225.00**
Duck, Quacking; #3250-F .. **35.00**
Evening Grosbeak, #3813 . **100.00**
Golden-Crowned Kinglets, #3853, rare **325.00**

Cardinal, #3444, 7", $90.00.

Kentucky Warbler, #3598 .. **40.00**
Key West Quail Dove **220.00**
Kingfisher, #3406 .... **45.00**
Lovebirds, #3404D **100.00**
Painted Bunting, #3452 .. **100.00**
Parrot, #3449 .... **135.00**
Penguin, #3274, Terra Rose, rare **180.00**
Rooster, #3445, yellow **95.00**
Titmouse, #3592 .... **40.00**
Turkey, #3275 .... **300.00**
Wrens, #3401D **85.00**

Parrot, #3449, 5", $135.00.

Dinnerware

Butter dish, Thistle **20.00**
Casserole, Blueberry, with lid, individual **12.00**
Chop plate, Star Flower, 12½" diameter **20.00**
Coffeepot, Blueberry **15.00**
Cream soup, Magnolia **5.00**
Creamer, Blueberry **9.00**
Creamer, Golden Harvest ... **8.50**
Cup, Country Garden **10.00**
Gravy boat, Thistle, with matching liner **20.00**
Pitcher, Fruit, 1-quart **25.00**
Plat, Thistle, 10" **12.00**
Plate, Blue Daisy, 10" **12.00**
Plate, Magnolia, 6" **4.00**
Shakers, Magnolia, pair ... **10.00**
Sugar bowl, Colonial **8.00**

Sugar bowl, Orchard Song . **10.00**
Teapot, Colonial **24.00**

Stoneware

From about 1840 and throughout the next hundred years, stoneware clay was used to pot utility wares such as jugs, jars, churns, and pitchers. Though a brown Albany slip was applied to some, by far the vast majority was glazed by common salt that was thrown into the kiln and vaporized. Decorations of cobalt were either slip trailed, brushed on, or stenciled; sgraffito (incising) was used on rare occasions. The complexity of the decoration has a great deal of bearing on value, and examples bearing the mark of a short-lived company are often at a premium.

Batter jug, one gallon, F.H. Cowden, Harriburg, Pennsylvania, ca. 1887-1895, $575.00.

Churn, elaborate floral in cobalt on salt glaze, E&LP Norton, 3-gallon **475.00**
Churn, Whites Utica, NY, bands, wavy lines & #3 in cobalt, 15¼", NM **175.00**
Cooler, Cyrus Felton, ear handles & lid, floral in cobalt, 24½" **650.00**
Cooler, foliage & elves with mugs in cobalt, no lid, 12" **250.00**
Cooler, Gast Crofts, blue sponging, black transfer, 16¼" . . **185.00**
Cooler, Whites Utica 5, double-ear handles, bung hole, 8¼" **475.00**
Crock, #3 in cobalt, ovoid . . **65.00**
Crock, butter; with lid, vining floral in cobalt, 8½" **450.00**
Crock, Cowden & Wilcox, tulip in cobalt, ovoid, 7½" **110.00**
Crock, E&LP Norton, floral in cobalt, 2-gallon, EX **275.00**
Crock, FT Wright & Son, long-tailed bird on stump in cobalt, 11" **400.00**

Crock, Fort Edward Stone Ware Co, bird in cobalt, 11¼" . . . **145.00**
Crock, J Fisher, brushed leaf & #3 in cobalt, 10¼" **75.00**
Crock, James Morehead, single flower in cobalt, 7¼" . . **150.00**
Crock, Ottman Bros Co, bird on branch in cobalt, 10⅝". **400.00**
Crock, pecking chicken in cobalt, 9⅜" **350.00**
Crock, quillwork floral & #4 in cobalt, 12" **200.00**
Crock, quillwork sunflower & #6 in cobalt, 14¼" **250.00**
Crock, simple floral on stem in cobalt, 7" **65.00**
Funnel, gray salt glaze, 5" . **40.00**
Jar, #4 with 4 lines underneath in cobalt, 15" **55.00**
Jar, apple butter; cobalt on handle, Albany slip interior, 7" . **65.00**
Jar, Belmont Ave Pottery, bird in cobalt, 2-gallon, 12" . . **200.00**
Jar, Burger & Lang, quillwork tulip & #4 in cobalt **170.00**
Jar, C Crolius, incised design, applied open handles, 12½" **300.00**
Jar, canning; #2 in grayish-blue, 12" **195.00**

Jar, canning; cobalt design on shoulder, incised I, 10" **65.00**
Jar, canning; Hamilton & Jones, Greensboro, PA, 9⅞" ..**100.00**
Jar, canning; Janson Bros Pure French Mustard, 9½" .**105.00**
Jar, canning; McCarthey & Hayless, 8" **200.00**
Jar, canning; stenciled shield & line design in cobalt, 8¼" ..**275.00**
Jar, canning; Uhrig & Stuckhorr, Dealers in Dry Goods, 9¾" **275.00**
Jar, canning; WW Field, ovoid, 9½" **75.00**
Jar, Cowden & Wilcox, Harrisburgh, flower in cobalt, 9" ...**125.00**
Jar, double flower in cobalt, applied handle, 6-gallon **225.00**
Jar, Hamilton & Jones, floral & stripe, 2-gallon **225.00**
Jar, Hamilton & Jones, stenciled & brushed label, 24" **175.00**
Jar, Hamilton & Jones, stenciled label, 2-gallon **150.00**
Jar, Harrington & Burger, floral in cobalt, 2-gallon **170.00**
Jar, IM Mead, cobalt on handles & label, #2, ovoid, 11½" ..**65.00**
Jar, IM Mead, cobalt on handles & label, ovoid, 9¼" **85.00**
Jar, John Burger, Rochester, quillwork flower, 4-gallon .**185.00**
Jar, pig shape, tan glaze, 9¾" long, NM **175.00**
Jar, RT Williams, New Geneva, PA, ovoid, 9⅛" **170.00**
Jar, swags in cobalt, incised line design, handles, 12½" .**200.00**
Jar, TF Reppert, cobalt stenciled & brushed label, handles, 16½" **150.00**
Jar, WH Lehew & Co, leaf design at in cobalt, 11" **85.00**
Jar, white flowers on Albany slip, narrow mouth, 8" ...**100.00**
Jar, Williams & Reppert, blue stencil on gray, handles, 24½" **350.00**

**Jug, large bumblebee on front, 20",
EX, $130.00.**

Jar, WJ & EO Schror, sgraffito birds, dated 1873, 7⅜" **450.00**
Jar, Wm Porter, S Co on bottom, ovoid, 12¾" **70.00**
Jug, B Bosworth, incised label, floral in cobalt, 13½" **160.00**
Jug, Bayless, McCarthey & Co, stenciled label, 11¼" ...**75.00**
Jug, bird on leaf in cobalt, E&LP Norton, 2-gallon, EX .**375.00**
Jug, brownish-tan, 8½" **85.00**
Jug, brushed floral design in cobalt, impressed #2, 14½" ...**150.00**
Jug, Bullard & Scott, floral in cobalt, 18¾" **125.00**
Jug, Burger Bros & Co, NY, flower & #3 in cobalt, 16¾" ..**130.00**
Jug, Chelsea, foliage in cobalt, 2-gallon, 12½" **100.00**
Jug, cobalt quillwork & #3 in cobalt, 14" **85.00**
Jug, Cowdon & Wilcox, floral in cobalt, ovoid, 3-gallon, 15¾" **400.00**
Jug, CW Braun, Buffalo, NY, 11¼", NM **85.00**

Jug, double-ear handles, cork top, ovoid, 5-gallon **175.00**

Jug, E Purdy, brushed cobalt design, ovoid, 2-gallon . . . **80.00**

Jug, floral design & #3 in cobalt, 15", EX **90.00**

Jug, FT Wright & Son, brushed leaf in cobalt, 11" **125.00**

Jug, H & G Nash, Utica, brushed flower in cobalt, 15" . . **175.00**

Jug, Hartford, ovoid, 10⅞" **155.00**

Jug, harvest; FH Cowden, ear handles & spout, tin lid, 9½", NM **150.00**

Jug, harvest; K Soper, sgraffito design, Albany slip, 8¾" **390.00**

Jug, J Norton & Co, bird on branch in cobalt, 14" **300.00**

Jug, John Berger, Rochester, feather plumes in cobalt, 2-gallon **115.00**

Jug, New York Stoneware Co, flower in cobalt, 11½" **130.00**

Jug, Nicholas Baldes, bird on branch in cobalt, 13⅝" **270.00**

Jug, S Hart, Fulton, pair of dotted birds in cobalt, ovoid, 12" **600.00**

Jug, splashes of cobalt, marked #4, ovoid, 16¾" **110.00**

Jug, WD Graves, Westmoreland, 2 hearts & #2, 14¼" **175.00**

Jug, WH Farror & Co, NY, flower & #2 in cobalt, 13¾" **185.00**

Jug, Whites, Utica, floral in deep cobalt, 13¾" **275.00**

Jug, Whites Utica, long-tailed bird on perch in cobalt, 12". **275.00**

Jug, Whites Binghamton, flower in cobalt, 11¼" **265.00**

Jug, Williams & Reppert, stenciled label, 2-gallon **150.00**

Pitcher, cobalt bands, Albany slip interior, 8½" **150.00**

Pitcher, Cowden & Wilcox, flower in cobalt, 9" **750.00**

Pitcher, incised design filled with cobalt, pewter lid, 13" . . **95.00**

Pitcher, Mrs. Schoene, blue sponging & black transfer on white **500.00**

Pitcher, Pat Sexton, flower & bird in cobalt on buff, 8¾" . **105.00**

Pitcher, cobalt daubs, 12⅜". **180.00**

Punch bowl, embossed foliage & Bardwell's Root Beer, 9¾x 19" **295.00**

Store Collectibles

Items that once were part of the country store scene are being collected and enjoyed by many, especially those whose interest's focus on primitives or advertising memorabilia. Today small glass and oak showcases often display collections of miniatures, or they may be used as coffee tables, filled with green plants and a few special pieces of glass or pottery.

Broom holder, wall mount, cast iron, EX **12.00**

Cash register, National, #313, EX original **595.00**

Counter case, ribbon; oak with dividers & glass lid **67.00**

Counter jar, Barsam Bros, embossed glass, octagonal, 10" . . . **55.00**

Counter jar, W & S Cough Drops, embossed glass, on pedestal base **35.00**

Boye Hooks, wooden case, 9x8", $35.00.

Fly chaser, cast iron frame with netted paddles, 29" **95.00**
Pickle barrel, wood with original mustard-colored paint. **150.00**
Scales, candy; National Specialties, 2-pound, 1910 . . . . . . **225.00**
Scoop, pickle; glass **15.00**
Shoe display, Hamilton Brown Shoe Co **45.00**
Shoe display, Peters Shoes & Diamond Brave, tin **65.00**
Shoe horn, Shinola **35.00**
Shoe horn, White House Shoes, advertising **35.00**
Showcase, glass framed with oak, oak shelves, 72" long . **125.00**
Sign, Butter & Egg, blue & yellow painted tin, 9x13" **15.00**
Spool cabinet, Belding's Silk, oak, 3-drawer, with brass hardware, EX **260.00**

String Holders

Until the middle of this century, spools of string contained in devices designed for that purpose were a common sight in country stores as well as many other businesses. Early examples of cast iron or wire and

Baby face, chalkware, $20.00.

those with advertising are the most desirable and valuable, but later chalkware or ceramic figurals are also quite collectible.

Apple, chalkware **22.00**
Beehive, cast iron, original paint, NM **35.00**
Bird in birdhouse, ceramic . **30.00**
Chef, ceramic **35.00**
Court jester, plaster **40.00**
Kitten with ball, chalkware. **25.00**
Lovebirds **18.00**
Mammy, full-figure, Japan . **65.00**
Pumpkin with winking eyes, ceramic, Japan **35.00**

Sugar Shakers

Once a commonplace table accessory, the sugar shaker was used to sprinkle cinnamon and sugar onto toast or muffins.

Acorn, opaque pink to white, original lid **150.00**
Baby Thumbprint, amberina, original lid **200.00**
Beatty Rib, blue opalescent . **90.00**
Bulging Loops, blue cased . **195.00**
Coin Spot, blue opalescent, 9-panel, original lid **110.00**
Cone, glossy pink cased **90.00**
Cone, pink satin **100.00**
Daisy & Fern, blue **80.00**
Egg shape, pansies on peach to white, Mt WA **195.00**
Frosted Circle **35.00**
Jumbo & Barnum **145.00**
Leaf Mold, yellow satin . . . **175.00**
Leaf Umbrella, spatter, Northwood, original lid **165.00**
Melligo, blue opaque **80.00**
Panelled Sprig, milk glass with green decoration **50.00**
Reverse Swirl, canary opalescent, original lid **135.00**
Ribbed Pillar, satin spatter **115.00**

Royal Oak, clear & frosted **100.00**
Sawtooth Band, US Glass . . **45.00**
Windows, blue opalescent . **150.00**

China ware, 6", $55.00 each.

Syrups

Syrup dispensers have been made in all types of art glass, china, stoneware, and in many patterns. Together they make a lovely collection.

Apple Blossom, Northwood. **175.00**
Argus Swirl, peachbloom . **265.00**
Banded Portland **75.00**
Bulging Loops, pink satin . **250.00**
Bull's Eye, scalloped, pewter lid, large **50.00**
Chrysanthemum Leaf, chocolate slag **750.00**
Columbia Coin, frosted . . . **225.00**
Cone, pink satin, squatty . **150.00**
Cone, yellow, dated 1882 . . **135.00**
Cord & Tassel **125.00**
Eyewinker **120.00**
Feather, green **345.00**
Feeding Swan, applied handle, etched **78.00**
Frosted Stork **85.00**
Grape & Leaf, blue opaque . **75.00**
Grape & Leaf, green opaque, pewter lid **200.00**
King's 500, clear & frosted . **85.00**

Late Block, ruby stained, Duncan, original lid **195.00**
Lincoln Drape, flint, eagle embossed on tin lid **195.00**
Maine, green **210.00**
Medallion Sprig, green to clear, original lid **265.00**
Moon & Star **125.00**
Pansy, milk glass **65.00**
Royal Oak, clear rubena . . **375.00**
States **65.00**
Utah, tin lid **75.00**
Valencia Waffle, amber . . . **100.00**
Wild Iris **70.00**
Wildflower, clear **90.00**
Zipper Border, ruby stained, fern etching **195.00**

Milk glass with hand-painted floral, pewter top, $65.00.

Target Balls

Blown glass target balls were commonly used from the 1840s until the early 1900s at shotgun competitions. Common examples are often unmarked. The following listings are for items in mint condition.

Black Pitch, CTB Co. 250.00
Borgardus' Glass Ball Pat'd April
10, 1877, amber 250.00
Embossed ribs, amber 150.00
English, shooter embossed in 2
round panels, clear . . . 300.00
English, shooter embossed in 2
round panels, green . . 300.00
English shooter embossed in 2 round
panels, purple 300.00
For Hockey's Patent Trap,
green 500.00
Great Western Gun Works,
amber 600.00
Gurd & Son, London, Ontario,
amber 400.00
Ira Paine's Filled Ball Pat Oct 23
1877, amber 250.00
Ira Paine's Filled Ball Pat
Oct 23, 1877, other than am-
ber 500.00
NB Glass Works Perth, pale green,
almost clear 200.00
Plain, amber 65.00
Plain, clear, mold marks. 1,000.00
Plain, cobalt 100.00
Plain, purple 100.00
WW Greener St Mary's Works
Birm/ 68 Haymarket
London 250.00

Tea Leaf Ironstone

Ironstone decorated with a copper lustre design of bands and leaves
became popular in the 1880s. It was
produced by potters in both England and America until the early
1900s.

Bacon rasher, rectangular, Meakin,
5⅝x3⅞" 30.00
Bone dish, scalloped, Meakin,
6½x3¼" 65.00
Bowl, vegetable; Fish Hook, with
cover, Meakin 125.00
Butter dish, Bamboo, insert & cover,
Meakin 125.00

Butter dish, Mellor-Taylor. 145.00
Chamber pot, ribbed, Mellor-Tay-
lor, no cover 125.00
Creamer, beaded handle, rectangu-
lar, East End Co., 4¼" . 75.00
Creamer, bulbous, marked
Wedgwood 95.00
Cup & saucer, Cable, Shaw . 80.00
Cup & saucer, farmer's; marked
Meakin 65.00
Cup & saucer, handleless; Pepper
Leaf Variant 75.00
Gravy boat, Fish Hook, marked
Meakin 45.00
Pitcher, Alcock, 8⅜" 125.00
Pitcher, milk; Fish Hook, Meakin,
7" 165.00
Plate, Pepper leaf, Elsmore & For-
ster, 7½" 14.00
Plate, Wedgwood, 7¾" . . . 15.00
Platter, rectangular, Wilkinson,
13x9" 45.00
Relish dish, Bamboo, handle,
Meakin 35.00
Shaving mug, Grape, 12-sided,
Shaw, 3¼" 145.00
Sugar bowl, Pepper Leaf, Elsmore
& Forster, 7" 100.00
Sugar bowl, with lid Wilkinson,
6½x6½" 85.00
Teapot, Chinese shape, marked
Shaw, 9½" 195.00
Toothbrush holder, Bamboo,
Meakin, 5x2⅜" 145.00
Tray, bread; open handles, marked
Shaw 75.00
Tureen, soup; Davenport . 300.00

**Compote, marked Royal Patent
Ironstone, 5x9", $395.00.**

Wash bowl & pitcher, marked Burgess **350.00**
Waste bowl, Meakin **55.00**

Teapots

Since the discovery of tea in China, special serving pieces have been made to serve this wonderful drink. Some teapots are known for their great beauty and style; others may be whimsical and quite novel, while some are purely functional. All seem to be popular with collectors.

Austria Victoria Carlsbad, fine china with florals **30.00**
Dragon, Japanese coralene, marked DM, 6-cup **20.00**
Monterey, made in California, pink spatter, large **20.00**
Old English Sampler, marked, H&K England, 6-cup, EX **45.00**
Sadler, pink oval with small flowers, marked, 6-cup **35.00**
Sutherland, England, silver lustre, marked, 6-cup **60.00**
SYP, 'Simple Yet Perfect,' brown earthenware, ca 1905 .. **95.00**
Wedgwood, Jasperware, blue & white, ca 1784, 2-cup . **210.00**
WS George, yellow with gold, round, marked, 6-cup, EX **18.00**

Teddy Bears

Only teddies made before the 1940s can be considered bona fide antiques, though character bears from more recent years are also quite collectible. The 'classic' bear is one made of mohair, straw stuffed, fully jointed, with long curving arms tapering at the paw and extending to the knees. He has very long skinny feet, felt pads on all paws, embroidered claws, a triangular, proportionately small head, a long pointed snout, embroidered nose and mouth, and a hump on the back torso at the neck. But above all, he is adorable, endearing, cuddly, and he loves you.

Bear, gold haircloth, glass eyes, jointed body, 22" **110.00**
Bear, gold haircloth, leather paw pads, jointed, worn, 15 . **95.00**
Bear, gold velvet haircloth, marked Great Britain, 18" **90.00**
Bear, handmade, wool, 14" . **20.00**
Bear, Miss Amy, gold mohair, straw stuffed, Made in England, ca 1934, 33" **275.00**
Bear, mohair, straw stuffed, glass eyes, standing, Made in Germany, 15" **180.00**
Bear, Panda, rayon plush, straw stuffed, made in Japan, ca 1950, 9" **35.00**
Bear, pink haircloth, jointed head & forearms, sitting, 8¼" .. **45.00**
Bear, polar; white mohair, felt pads, plastic eyes, 1960, 5" .. **90.00**

Curly mohair, glass eyes, straw stuffed, replaced paw pad, wear, 39", $300.00.

Teddy Bear school room, $325.00.

Bear, white & black cotton plush, Germany, ca 1948, 13" . **75.00**
Bear, Winnie the Pooh, Disney, Japan, ca 1965, 10" **65.00**
Bear, wire jointed, early, 3" . **20.00**
Book, Aunt Louisa's Big Picture ..., hand sewn, ca 1885 . . . **75.00**
Book, The Story of the Three Bears, ca 1934, 10 pages **10.00**
Cup & saucer, bears writing on fence **45.00**
Feeding dish, ceramic, I go here says the fork, 1930, 7¼". **25.00**
Hand puppet, Chad Valley Bear, black ears, embroidered nose, 10" **55.00**
Hand puppet, dark brown mohair gold muzzle, Steiff . . . **110.00**
Marionette, tan dralon & cotton fur, Steiff, ca 1979 . . . . **75.00**
Mug, silverplated, footed . . . **45.00**
Night light & bank, full figure, celluloid, 7" **35.00**
Nursing bottle, glass, embossed on side **65.00**
Perfume bottle, gold mohair over metal form, jointed, 5". **250.00**
Pin, figural, painted bisque, jointed, 1½" **70.00**
Pin, figural, pearl tummy & rhinestone eyes, 1950, 1½" . . **22.00**

Pull toy, bear, wood, on red wheels, Steiff, ca 1965 . . . . **65.00**
Sand pail, tin, Chein **35.00**
Toothbrush holder, ceramic Germany **45.00**

Telephones

Early phones are quite different in appearance than those we have become accustomed to, and the various stages of advancement over the years since the telephone was invented have resulted in hundreds of modifications. Oak wall phones, simple or with ornate carvings, are only one type that is highly sought. Collectors also seek related memorabilia such as Bell Company paperweights, public telephone signs, and advertising ephemera.

American Electric, wall, oak case, 20x7½x12" **250.00**
American Telephone & Telegraph, candlestick, 1913, 12". **100.00**
Automatic Electric, #40 . . . . **45.00**
Bell, series 304, black plastic body, circa 1940 . . . . **20.00**

Candlestick, black, dial ...**78.00**
Candlestick, with Hush-A-Phone
attachment **200.00**
Danish, French horn, 1913 .**55.00**
Leich Electric, wall, oak case, ca
1920s **180.00**
Railroad dispatcher, candlestick
type **75.00**
Western Electric, candlestick, brass
& black metal, 1904 ..**135.00**
Western Electric, candlestick, nickel
plated & black, ca 1904 .**70.00**
Western Electric, wall, oak, model
1894 ....**250.00**

Tinware

From 1800 until the early 20th
century, American tinsmiths imported sheets of tin plate from Europe from which they hand fashioned kitchenware items, foot warm-
ers, lamps, etc. Some pieces, such as
lamps and lanterns, were sometimes
decorated with simple pierced designs. Often they were painted, either freehand or stenciled; this type
of decoration is referred to as tole.
Cookie cutters, very popular with
today's collectors, were made in
every shape imaginable. The very
early, more unusual detailed forms
sometimes sell for well in excess of
$100.00. See also Toleware.

Apple corer, wood knob **18.50**
Bank, can shape, embossed floral &
heart design, ...**40.00**
Bath tub, with seat, arched wide
rim, old paint **160.00**
Boiler, with lid, tin washed, copper
bottom, 15x11x22" **45.00**
Cake box, painted oak-like grain, ca
1890 ....**35.00**
Candle mold, 4-tube, hung by
leather strap **48.00**
Candle snuffer, scissors style, dark
patina **35.00**

**Candle holder with saucer and
snuffer, 4x8½", $135.00.**

Chamber stick, with push-up, 3¾",
pair **90.00**
Chandelier, 4 arms, punched & cut-
out leaves, paint, 21" .**625.00**
Cheese drainer, with sieve, 18" di-
ameter **35.00**
Cheese mold, punched, 2 handles, 3
loop feet, 6x6" **55.00**
Cookie cutter, Christmas tree, ca
1910, 7x3½" **26.00**
Cookie cutter, hollow ball, cuts 6
different animals **110.00**
Cookie cutter, deer, 4½" ...**55.00**
Cup, child's; From Papa, silver on
black japanning **45.00**
Food carrier, 4 units stack, handle
at top, dated 1884 .....**85.00**
Grater, flat, with open handle,
7x11" **30.00**
Hot plate, punched-out compass star
design, 6¾" diameter .**160.00**
Lamp, skater's, 6¾" **23.00**
Lamp filler, hinged lid, angled pour-
ing spout **75.00**
Lantern, Paul Revere style, punched
work, 16" **115.00**
Lard pail, with lid, copper band at
top & bottom **25.00**
Lunch pail, oval cup on top, wire
bail , marked Brethern .**30.00**
Milk can, with lid, side strap,
marked Kreamer, quart. **22.50**
Ornament, 9-point dimensional
star, 6" **175.00**
Pastry board, hangs on wall. **75.00**
Picture frame, decorated front,
stand at back, 2¾x2⅛" .**30.00**
Pie lifter, punched work blade, wood
handle, 12½" **70.00**

Rolling pin, with wooden handles, dark patina **90.00**

Sugar shaker, strap handle **20.00**

Tinder box, hinged, with damper & striker **325.00**

Toddy warmer, dark tin ..**145.00**

Torch lamp, horizontal cylinder font, curved reflector, 12" ..**125.00**

Tobacciana

Now gone the way of the barber shop and the ice cream parlor, the cigar store with its carved wooden Indian at the door and the aroma of fine tobacco in the air is no more. But the clever figural cigar cutters, the hand-carved Meerschaum pipes, the cigar molds, and humidors are still enjoyed as reminders of our country's younger days and for the workmanship of long-ago craftsmen.

Cigar cutter, Peter Schuyler Cigars, 7½", $150.00.

Cigar box, Lucke's Telescopes, interior & exterior labels ..**25.00**

Cigar cutter, Bergner & Engel Brewing Co, mechanical **50.00**

Cigar cutter, embossed sterling, marked Germany, 6" ..**53.00**

Cigar cutter, Handmade Export 5¢ Cigar, cast iron, 8" **50.00**

Cigar cutter, knight's helmet, miniature **70.00**

Cigar cutter, lady's slipper, nickel plated **30.00**

Cigar cutter, Smoketts 5¢ Cigars, EX **65.00**

Cigar cutter, sterling silver, fob type **30.00**

Cigar holder, Meerschaum, branch shape, amber tip, 4" ...**15.00**

Cigar holder, Meerschaum, bull on stem, amber tip, 4" **40.00**

Cigar press, marked Wearever, wood, small **65.00**

Cigar press box, with 10 trays, 8x6x18" **30.00**

Cigarette case, celluloid base, metal lid, dolphin handle **20.00**

Cigarette holder, claw, carved from ivory **35.00**

Cigarette lighter, airplane, stainless steel, 6" **45.00**

Cigarette lighter, golf bag shape, 5", NM **40.00**

Cigarette lighter, Manning-Bowman, electric, 1911 ....**65.00**

Cigarette roller, Brown & Williamson, red metal, ca 1930 .**25.00**

Cigarette silk, Sunbonnet Baby, Zira **35.00**

Humidor, sailor's head with pipe, china, 5¼" **75.00**

Humidor, skull, cream-glazed porcelain **55.00**

Pin-back button, Hassan Cigarettes, ca 1910 ....**9.00**

Pipe, American Colonist's, pottery, ca 17th century **15.00**

Pipe, briar, carved Uncle Sam's face, 6" **30.00**

Pipe, burl, brass fittings & cap, twig stem, marked Ross **40.00**

Pipe, clay, lady's head with large hat, 5" **15.00**

Pipe, clay, ca 1700, 7½" **25.00**

Pipe, Meerschaum, horse, in original case, small **50.00**

Pipe, Italian briar, monkey head, $35.00.

Pipe, Meerschaum, Swiss peasant, low relief, 12" **17.50**
Pipe, painted china, brass fittings, Bavarian twig stem ...**45.00**
Pipe tamp, ball & chain, brass, 2¾" **15.00**
Pipe tamp, ivory handle, 3" .**30.00**
Pipe tamp, Robin Hood, brass, marked England, 2¼" ..**30.00**
Pipe tamp, wood boot, 1½" .**30.00**
Plug cutter, Standard **35.00**
Plug cutter, Triumph.......**45.00**
Tin, Pedro Cut Plug Smoking Tobacco, red & black on yellow, 8" NM **45.00**
Tobacco card, New's Boy, ca 1890, NM **5.00**
Tobacco card, Player's Cigarettes, miniature, 25 in set **8.50**
Tobacco card, Sub Rosa Cigarettes, ca 1890 ....**25.00**

Toleware

Hand-painted or stencil-decorated tinware is refered to as 'tole.' The most valuable was made by the Pennsylvania Dutch in the 17th century. Color, design, age, and condition are the most important worth-accessing factors.

Beaker, dark japanning with yellow & red, 3¾" **105.00**
Box, florals & shells, 3-color on black, oval, 5" **225.00**

Canister, Bartlett & Sons, Bristol, gold trim on green, 17" .**85.00**
Coffeepot, floral, 3-color on dark brown, worn, 11" **575.00**
Creamer, brushstrokes, red, yellow, green, brown, 4", VG ..**90.00**
Cribbage board, with brass ball feet, 2⅜x10⅛" **105.00**
Deed box, dome top, original japanning with stencil **195.00**
Deed box, embossed lid, japanning & cherries, 9½" **100.00**
Deed box, floral, 2-color on black, dome lid, 11", EX **250.00**
Deed box, floral, 3-color on brown, dome top, 9", EX **350.00**
Mug, japanning with red & yellow floral design, 4¼" **275.00**
Mug, green with yellow, red, dark green decoration, 2" ..**185.00**

Pitcher, green and ivory with multicolor florals, late, 12", VG, $135.00.

Spice box, 6 interior canisters, 3-color, 9½" **65.00**
Sugar bowl, brushstrokes, 4-color, with lid, 4", EX **500.00**
Teapot with lid, floral, red & green on brown, oval, straight spout, 5½" **185.00**
Tray, floral with red & green wedges, ca 1850, 26" diameter .**75.00**

Tea caddies, mounted as lamps, Oriental figures on red ground, 1825, 17", $900.00 for the pair.

Tray, multicolor exotic birds & florals, scalloped, 1850s, 14" diameter **350.00**

Tools

Considering the construction of early tools, one must admire the hand-shaped wood, the smithy-wrought iron, and the hand-tooled leather. Even factory-made tools from the late 1800s required a good deal of hand finishing. Most desirable to tool collectors are those with the touch mark of the craftsman or early examples marked by the manufacturer. Value is determined by scarcity, condition, usefullness, and workmanship.

Axe, broad; 10¾" **25.00**
Axe, felling; wrought iron, 5" blade **8.00**
Clapboard guage, 3x7" **40.00**
Cloth tape, surveyor's, in leather case, 50 feet **10.00**
Cotton comb, 11x4½" wood base with metal bristles **15.00**
Crank brace, with gears, marked Millers Falls #182 ..... **32.00**
Draw knife, Keen Kutter, 8". **25.00**

Draw knife, unmarked, 16" wide **8.00**
Float, cabinetmaker's, W Drummond & Sons, 14" **65.00**
Froe, splitting; 10" blade ... **20.00**
Hammer, sawyer's, 5½" head **50.00**
Hand router, Stanley #71 .. **85.00**
Hay hook, wrought, oak handle **400.00**
Hoof rest, farrier's, 19" **33.00**
Ice hook, 72" **10.00**
Jointer, metal, Stanley #7, Pat 1910 .... **50.00**
Kit, wood-carver's, 7 tools fit in handle, 1883 .... **30.00**
Level, with brass end plates, marked Pat 12-20-04, 26" **12.00**
Level, wood, brass trim Davis & Cook, NY, 26" **45.00**
Mitre jack, mahongany, 30". **58.00**
Plane, block; Sargent #5206. **30.00**
Plane, bullnose; Stanley, cast iron body, 1x4" **18.00**
Plane, bullnose; steel, 1¼x 4¾" **55.00**
Plane, hand beader, Stanley Universal, 1-blade **35.00**
Plane, plow; Stanley #45 ... **85.00**
Plane, rabbit; Stanley, 8" long, 1½" wide **28.00**
Plane, spill; dark beech, 9¾". **40.00**
Plane, spoke; Stanley, cast iron, 10" **22.00**
Punch, leather; cast iron, Patent October 9, 1900 .... **15.00**
Push drill, Johnson & Tainters, Boston, 1869 .... **35.00**
Ring dog, logger's, wrought iron, 10" **16.00**
Rule, 2-fold, steel, Chesterman, Sheffield, England, 24" **14.00**
Saw, piercing; jeweler's, beech handle, 12" **40.00**
Saw, salt; zinc blade, marked W Marples & Sons, 20" ... **60.00**
Saw, stair; 15" **36.00**
Scorp, wrought iron, open, 16" **60.00**

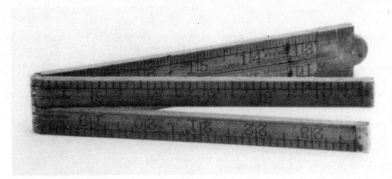

Ruler, boxwood with brass mountings, Stanley, $35.00.

Screw box, cherry, marked MM Rice, 2¾x8" **35.00**

Screwdriver, brass ferrule, Winchester **23.00**

Shears, cast iron, 14" **12.00**

Square, steel, Eagle, 24" . . . **12.00**

T-Square, mahogany with brass, adjustable, 37" **28.00**

Tape measure, Stanley, in early leather case **15.00**

Tooth router, beech, 5" **40.00**

Vise, jeweler's **85.00**

Whetstone, in wood case, 7" . **7.50**

Wrench, Model T Ford; marked, 5" long **5.00**

Toothpick Holders

Toothpick holders have been made in hundreds of designs, in art glass, pattern glass, opalescent, and translucent glass of many colors, in novelty designs and figural forms. Today they are all popular collectibles, relatively easy to find and usually affordable.

Argonaut Shell, custard . . **275.00**

Bead & Scroll, ruby stain . . **35.00**

Beatty Honeycomb, blue opalescent, 2½" **45.00**

Bees on Basket, black **60.00**

Bull's Eye & Fan, clear, with gold trim **40.00**

Champion, green **45.00**

Corset, amber **75.00**

Daisy & Button, amber **30.00**

Daisy & Button, amberina. **185.00**

Delaware, green with gold . **40.00**

Francesware Swirl, frosted, amber trim **75.00**

Gaelic, clear with gold **22.00**

Hobnail, vaseline opal **55.00**

Iris with Meander, blue opalescent, 2¼" **75.00**

Lacy Medallion, green with gold decoration **27.50**

Iris with Meander, sapphire blue with gold trim, $55.00; Forget-Me-Not, peachblow, $50.00.

Paddle Wheel **22.00**

Paddle Wheel & Star **35.00**

Pineapple, pink satin **75.00**

Prize, ruby stain **115.00**

Reverse Swirl, vaseline satin opalescent **95.00**

Sawtoothed Honeycomb . . **30.00**

Shoshone, clear with gold . . **25.00**

Swirl & Panel **18.00**

Twist, blue opalescent **60.00**
Washington **30.00**
Zippered Swirl & Diamond .**25.00**

Toys

Toy collecting is a very popular hobby; and, if purchases are wisely made, there is good potential for investment. Toys from the 1800s are rarely if ever found in mint condition but should at least be working and have all their original parts. Toys manufactured in the 20th century are evaluated more critically. Compared to one in excellent condition, original box intact, even a slightly damaged toy may be worth only about half price. Character-related toys, space toys, toy soldiers, and toy trains are among the more desirable.

Guns

American, cast iron, Kilgore, 1940, 9⅝" **45.00**
Boss, cast iron, Kenton, 1925, 6¼", NM **19.00**
Daisy Defender BB gun, #140, NM **60.00**
Dandy, cast iron, Hubley, 1935, 5¾" **18.00**
Federal, cast iron, Kilgore, 1920, 5½" **18.00**
Mascot, cast iron, automatic, Kilgore, 1936, 4" **18.00**
Star, cast iron, Stevens, 1910, 6¼" **30.00**

Penny Toys

Black man in cart drives ostrich, Lehmann **285.00**
Delivery wagon, with sacks, boxes, & driver, 3¼", EX **125.00**
Goose, hand-painted tin, German, 4" **100.00**

Penny toy, mule cart, tin litho, Germany, 6" long, $110.00.

Ocean liner, lithographed tin, 4½", EX **250.00**
Pistol, Ives, UM3 ....**45.00**
Pool player, lithographed tin, 4", VG **125.00**
Sedan, lithographed tin, German, NM **125.00**
Sulky, 3¼" **130.00**
Woman pushes baby carriage, lithographed tin, 3" ..**275.00**
Zeppelin, Los Angeles, lithographed tin, German, 3⅞", EX .**500.00**

Toy Soldiers

Barclay, advancing, rifle is level, #21, NM **22.00**
Barclay, bugler, #709 .....**18.00**
Barclay, cowboy with pistol, #96, NM **10.00**
Barclay, digging, cast helmet, #781, NM **25.00**
Barclay, flagbearer, tin helmet, #701, NM **12.00**
Barclay, officer, with sword, #708, NM **15.00**
Barclay, soldier hitting with rifle, tin helmet, #766 ......**15.00**
Barclay, soldier sitting, with rifle, tin helmet **15.00**
Barclay, typist, with typewriter & wooden table, #961 ....**15.00**
Britains, Egyptian Lancers, #115, 1950 ....**100.00**

Britains, Japanese Infantry, charging, #134 . . . . .180.00
Britains, Royal Navy Bluejackets, #78, 1930 . . . . .125.00
Britains, Turkish Cavalry, #71, in box 215.00
Grey Iron, Boy Scout saluting, #72, early, EX 12.50
Grey Iron, man, #1, EX 5.00
Grey Iron, officer, US Cavalry, #8MA 20.00
Grey Iron, pirate, with hook, #16/4, NM 15.00
Grey Iron, US Infantry officer, #12, early, EX 12.00
Manoil, bicycle dispatch rider, #79, NM 18.00
Manoil, farmer with scythe, #136, NM 20.00
Manoil, soldier, grenade thrower, #56, EX 18.00
Manoil, nurse, #36, NM 10.00
Manoil, parachute jumper, #88, EX 17.00
Manoil, soldier with gun, charging, #37 . . . . .20.00
Manoil, young girl, to sit on bench, #130, NM 8.00

Toy soldiers by Manoil, VG/EX, $8.00 each.

Miscellaneous

AC Gilbert, Big Boy tool chest, #6, NM 15.00
AC Gilbert, Erector Set #4, 1919, with box 35.00

AC Gilbert, Helicopter Set #10181, NM 40.00
AC Gilbert, Rocket Launcher, #10053 . . . . .65.00
Amico, Moon Scout, battery-operated, with box 40.00
Arcade, airplane, cast iron, 6" long, NM 85.00
Arcade, airport limousine, rubber, 8" 10.00
Arcade, Roper range, worn green & white paint, 6" 35.00
Arcade, truck, open bed, red painted cast iron, 2½x6" 75.00
Arcade, windmill, cast iron, 15¼", NM 150.00
Ashai Cadillac, battery-operated, 3 actions, 1949 . . . . .50.00
Chein, Musical Church, tin, circa 1937 . . . . .45.00
Fisher-Price, #16 duck cart .65.00
Fisher-Price, #305 walking duck cart 30.00
Fisher-Price, #407 chick . . .75.00
Fisher-Price, #476 Mickey Drummer 75.00
Fisher-Price, #605 Donald Duck cart, NM 50.00
Fisher-Price, Bucky Burro, pull toy, NM 60.00
Fisher-Price, Cackling Hen, white, pull toy 30.00
Fisher-Price, Happy Hippo .25.00
Fisher-Price, Leo the Drummer, pull toy 60.00
Fisher-Price, Looky Fire Truck, pull toy 20.00
Fisher-Price, Snoopy Sniffer.50.00
Fisher-Price, Timmy Turtle .40.00
German, cat, fur, glass eyes, pull-string squeaker, 6" . . .275.00
German, harmonica, Jolly Jack, 4" long 20.00
German, horse & carriage, tin litho windup, early, 10" . . .190.00
German, man at forge, tin, steam driven, 7" 300.00
GMC, Greyhound Scenicruiser Bus, 1957, 6" 6.00

Hibbard Playmate wagon, wood, 31" long, $125.00.

Hartland, Cochise, #816, EX . **7.50**

Hartland, horse, Appaloosa family mare, 7", EX **10.00**

Hartland, horse, for Chief Thunderbird, black pinto Chubby, VG **4.00**

Hartland, horse, for General Lee, creamy white, EX **7.50**

Hartland, horse, for Matt Dillon, black molded bridle, EX . **4.00**

Hartland, horse, for remuda, white, EX **6.00**

Hartland, horse, rearing, for Roy Rogers, with reins, VG . **10.00**

Hartland, Roy Rogers on Trigger, #806, NM **24.00**

Hubley, car, 4-door, worn paint, nickel-plated trim, 6" . . **75.00**

Hubley, motorcycle, policeman rider, cast iron, rubber tires, VG **225.00**

Hubley, race car, die-cast, black rubber tires, 3", EX . . . **50.00**

Hubley, sleigh, horse drawn, cast iron with EX paint, 1921, 15½" **550.00**

Hubley, stake truck, cast iron, 1930s, 3½", M **55.00**

International, K11 Oil Tanker, 1946, 6" **10.00**

Ives, cannon, cast iron, with brass barrel **20.00**

Ives, mechanical bear, patented 1872 . . . . **700.00**

Japan, Jupiter Jyro 24, battery-operated, with box **30.00**

Japan, Moon Globe Orbiter, tin litho, battery-operated **150.00**

Japan, Solar-X #7 Space Rocket, battery-operated, tin . **160.00**

Japan, Space Copter, tin litho, friction, with box **35.00**

Japan, TPS Robot, plastic, windup, 3¾" **25.00**

Linemar, Calypso Joe, battery-operated, 1950s **125.00**

Marx, Ambulance, with siren, tin windup **125.00**

Marx, fireman on ladder, tin windup, 24" **175.00**

Marx, Home Town Movie Theatre, tin litho , '30s **35.00**

Marx, Jolly Joe Jeep, tin litho windup, 6", EX **75.00**

Marx, Looping Plane, #182, tin windup **35.00**

Marx, Subway Express, tin windup, 1950s **55.00**

Marx, Turn Over Tank, #3, tin windup **20.00**

Marx army tank, tin litho windup, 10", $50.00.

Noah's Ark, removable roof, 7 windows, door, 38" **350.00**
Schoenhut, catalog, 1903 . **115.00**
Schoenhut, doll cottage, 14½x11", EX **200.00**
Schoenhut, donkey, painted eyes, reduced, EX **55.00**
Schoenhut, elephant, painted eyes, reduced, EX **55.00**
Schoenhut, lion tamer, regular, EX **185.00**
Schoenhut, painted eyes, regular, EX **550.00**
Schoenhut, piano, 10x10x8", EX **85.00**
Schoenhut, piano, 6x6x5" .. **60.00**
Schoenhut, ringmaster, regular, replaced clothes, VG .. **120.00**
Structo, dump truck, tin litho, 18", EX **75.00**
Structo, steam shovel, 21" . **175.00**
Structo, tank, #48, 11" **225.00**
Structo, telephone, black metal case, wood receiver, 10" **15.00**
Structo, Toyland Garage Truck, tin windup **55.00**
TN Co, Bulldozer, battery-operated, 5 actions, 1950s **45.00**
TN Co, Charlie Weaver, battery-operated, 1962, 12" **30.00**
Tonka, Volkswagon **30.00**
Tootsie Toy, Chevrolet, coupe, #6201, 1926 .... **30.00**
Tootsie Toy, fire engine, #4652, with hook & ladder, M **75.00**
Tootsie Toy, Lincoln wrecker, #6016, 1936 .... **145.00**

Tootsie toy, racer with driver, #23, VG **50.00**
Traveleer, Land Coach Traveler, Trailer Co LA, 1927 .. **100.00**
Turner, dump truck, friction, 15½" long **130.00**
Tykie Toy, Baby Bunny, Catalin, #100, M paint on face .. **75.00**
Tykie Toy, Baby Cannibal (Black boy), Catalin, #200, M paint on face **100.00**
Tykie Toy, Bobby Bear, Catalin, #202, M, paint on face. . **75.00**
Tykie Toy, Eddie Egg, Catalin, #204, M paint on face **90.00**
Tykie Toy, Katie Kitten, Catalin, #203, M paint on face .. **75.00**
Tykie Toy, Peepo the Clown, Catalin, #70, M paint **75.00**
Tykie Toy, Settie Lou, Catalin, #90, M paint on face **75.00**
Tykie Toy, Sweater Boy, Catalin, #85-S, M paint on face . **75.00**
Wilkins, roadster, with driver, tin windup, 9" long **200.00**
Williams, steamroller, 1930s, 5½", EX **50.00**
Wolverine, Diving Submarine, 13" long **50.00**
Wyandotte, dump truck, 1930s, 12½" long **25.00**
Wyandotte, Red Ranger Ride 'Em Cowboy, tin windup, ... **75.00**
Wyandotte, sedan, ca 1940, 6" long, NM **15.00**
Wyandotte, Stake Truck, battery-operated lights, 10" ... **30.00**

Tramp Art

Tramp art is a type of folk art attributed to the 'tramps' and 'hobos' from the era around the turn of the century. Made from whatever materials were at hand, it is not uncommon to find original cigar box labels still intact inside the drawers or walls of jewelry or sewing boxes.

These boxes and picture frames are the most commonly-found examples, but occasionally even tables or other items of furniture are reported.

Box, cigar; on pedestal with stepped base **70.00**
Box, 2 drawers, hinged lid, 13" long, ca 1890's **100.00**
Cross, with stanhope in brass center, dated 1879, 1¼" ... **65.00**
Dresser, mirror & china knobs, 2 drawers, 2 doors, 30" .. **65.00**
Frame, crisscross work at corners, gold trim, 18½" square .**90.00**
Frame, 12x15" **35.00**

Picture frame, gilt trim, 18", $90.00.

Traps

Recently attracting the interest of collectors, old traps are evaluated primarily by their condition. Traps listed here are in fine condition, that is with the trademark legible in its entirety, with strong lettering.

Allsteel #3, double long spring, EX trademark **35.00**
Austin Humane Killer #1 .. **20.00**
Automatic Trap Co, steel rattrap, trademark legible **12.00**
Bigalow, 6" **8.00**

Bridell, 7-hole pan **18.00**
Champion #1½, single long spring, fine stamping **18.00**
Cinch Mole Trap **15.00**
Crescent #3, double long spring, strong lettering **110.00**
Cyclone, metal mousetrap .. **20.00**
Dahlgreen Shur Pelt, 7" Killer, legible trademark **15.00**
Diamond #1 Jump **10.00**
Easy Set Triumph #3, double coil spring **12.00**
Elgin, steel rattrap **15.00**
Gomber Beaten Path, metal rattrap **30.00**
Goshen, fish & game trap . **200.00**
IT Mouse Choker, metal ... **20.00**
Katch Kwik Mouse, mousetrap with wood snap **8.00**
Little Sampson, iron rattrap.**75.00**
Lucife, wood snap mousetrap, France **6.00**
Nebraska, trail trap **265.00**
Newhouse #0, single long spring, EX stamping **35.00**
Phillips, gopher trap **30.00**
Sargent #24, with teeth, double long spring **250.00**
Snappy Mouse Trap, Harvard, IL, clear markings **10.00**
Taylor Special #1, single long spring, good trademark **5.00**
Webley #1½, disheye spring .**6.00**
Wyoming Trap #XX, with teeth **35.00**
Zip, metal snap mousetrap .**15.00**

Van Briggle

Van Briggle pottery has been made in Colorado Springs since 1901. Fine art pottery was made until about 1920 when commercial wares and novelties became more profitable products. The early artware was usually marked with the date of production and a number indicating the shape. After 1920 'Colorado Springs' in script letters was used; after 1922 'U.S.A.' was added. Van Briggle is most famous for his Art Nouveau styling and flat matt glazes.

Ash tray, Indian girl with corn, turquoise, 6" **75.00**
Bookends, squirrels, pair ..**85.00**
Candlestick, turquoise, 3" ..**20.00**
Conch shell, maroon, 9" **35.00**
Creamer & sugar bowl, turquoise, individual **30.00**
Cup, demitasse; turquoise ..**20.00**
Figurine, bull, sitting **45.00**
Figurine, spirited horse, Persian Rose **50.00**
Pitcher, Persian Rose, 3½" .**40.00**
Planter, with frog, Persian Rose, scalloped, 6" **40.00**
Plaque, Big Buffalo, maroon.**75.00**
Salt & pepper shakers, barrel shape, white, pair **9.50**
Tile, stylized floral, gray, green, yellow on red clay, 5½" .**65.00**
Vase, bird of paradise, white, Colorado Springs, 8¾" **18.00**
Vase, brown, marked Colorado Springs #645, 4¼" **32.00**
Vase, floral, blue, dated 1920, 4" **65.00**
Vase, floral, green on brown, with handles, 3½" **45.00**
Vase, floral, rose & blue, 8" .**75.00**
Vase, leaves, maroon, 3½x4".**45.00**
Vase, moths, brown & green, 1918, 7" **105.00**
Vase, Persian Rose, 1905, 5".**95.00**
Vase, yucca leaves, dark blue & maroon, #774 ....**140.00**
Wall pocket, parrot, AA CS .**65.00**

Vernon Kilns

From 1931 until 1958, Vernon Kilns produced hundreds of lines of fine dinnerware, which today's collectors enjoy reassembling. They also made novelty items designed by famous artists such as Rockwell Kent and Walt Disney, examples of which are at a premium.

Ash tray, Chicago Fair, red .**25.00**
Brown-Eyed Susan, gravy ..**15.00**
Calico, spoon rest **20.00**
Chinz, chop plate, 14" **18.00**

Fleur-de-lis charger, 14", $65.00.

Early California, cup & saucer **9.00**
Early California, pitcher, tankard shape, 3-pint **25.00**
Fantasia, dinner plate, ...**40.00**
Fantasia, figurine, #14 Unicorn, sitting **175.00**
Fantasia, figurine, #25, Elephant, 1940 ....**100.00**
Fantasia, salt & peppers, Mushroom, 1941, pair **100.00**
Fantasia, sugar bowl with lid, individual **25.00**
Gingham, butter dish **18.00**
Gingham, chop plate, 12" ..**15.00**
Hawaiian Coral, divided vegetable bowl, 10" **8.00**
Hawaiian Flowers, cup **14.00**
Hawaiian Flowers, tumbler, 13-ounce **20.00**
Homespun, butter pat **6.00**
Homespun, carafe **18.00**
Lei Lani, cup Ultra shape ..**20.00**
Linda, creamer **10.00**
Modern California, muffin tray with lid **40.00**

Modern California, sauce . . **10.00**
Monterey, bowl, 5½" **3.00**
Monterey, platter, 12" **12.00**
Organdie, plate, 6½" **2.00**
Organdie, tumbler **10.00**
Plate, Abraham Lincoln Memorial,
   8½" **18.00**
Plate, Alaska Husky, miniature,
   4½" **15.00**
Plate, Colorado **10.00**
Plate, Maine, blue **10.00**
Plate, New Mexico, red, 10½". **8.00**
Plate, Remember Pearl Harbor, On
   to Victory, unmarked . . **22.00**
Plate, Will Rogers **12.00**
Salamina, cup **20.00**
Salamina, plate, 8½" **75.00**
Salamina, plate, 10½" **95.00**
Salamina, plaque, 14" . . . **235.00**
Tam-O'-Shanter, water pitcher, 2-
   quart **25.00**
Tam-O'-Shanter, platter, oval,
   12½" **9.00**
Vernon Rose, platter, 16" . . **18.00**
Yosemite, demitasse cup . . . **12.00**

Watch Fobs

Watch fobs were popular during
the last quarter of the 19th century
and remained in vogue well into the
20th. Retail companies issued advertising fobs, and these are especially popular with collectors. Political, commemorative, and souvenir fobs may also be found. They
were made from brass, cast iron,
bronze, copper or celluloid.

Acme, lyre in wreath on triangular
   point shape **60.00**
Allis Chalmers, earth mover tractor
   shape & relief **20.00**
Alpha Portland Cement . . . **15.00**
American Accident Insurance
   Company, NE **50.00**
Arrowhead shape, with inserted
   compass **45.00**

Big Brute **35.00**
BPOE Greenfield, MA, 1923. **40.00**
Bronco buster on horse, no adver-
   tisement **30.00**
Buick, blue enameled letters on
   porcelain over metal . . . **45.00**
DeLaval Cream Separator . **80.00**
Drydene Motor Oil **50.00**
Elastica Standard Varnish . **75.00**
Elks, shield shaped **35.00**
Euclid Earth Moving Equipment,
   silver **13.00**
First National Bank, PA, embossed
   building **45.00**
GM Diesel Power **25.00**
Great Western **14.00**
Green River Whiskey, man with
   horse **25.00**
Gun in holster, sterling **42.00**
Heinz Pure Food Products, '57' in
   center **28.00**
Hyatt Bearings, Chicago . . . **90.00**
Independent Telephone Co candle-
   stick phone relief **90.00**
International Stock Exposition,
   Chicago 1920, silver . . . **25.00**
Jaeger Products, relief cement-
   mixing truck **35.00**
John Deere Plows, deer & plow,
   brass **90.00**

**Top: Holt Mfg. Co. Combines,
$200.00; Left: Dead Shot Powder,
$185.00; Right: LeTourneau
Certified Operator, worn, $90.00.**

Johnson Tractor Company . **40.00**
Keen Kutter **55.00**
Kellogs, Toasted Corn Flakes, brass,
   enameled **50.00**

Knights of Pythias 30.00
Long Beach, CA 4.00
Lookout Mountain 35.00
Lorain Shovels, Draglines, & Cranes 20.00
Malleable Steel Range 30.00
Michigan Shovels & Cranes .32.00
Mohawk Trail, Indian in headress on arrowhead shape ...22.00
Mountain States Ice Manufacturers' Association 50.00
National Cash Register Co. 125.00
National Sportsman, buck deer in relief on medallion 30.00
New York State Seal, on medallion shape 19.00
Niagara Falls 20.00
Pacific Coast Steamship Company, celluloid, 2" diameter ..20.00
Pershing, 1918 ....20.00
Police, FOP; 5-point star, brass 15.00
Porter Hay Carrier 45.00
Portraiture bust of a lady, set in circle, no advertising ..40.00
Rainbow Packing, colorful enamel on porcelain 45.00
Red Man Cider 60.00
Rumely Oil, with world, EX .65.00
Souvenir of Texas, brass circle, 1914 ....21.00
Starrett Tools 20.00
Studebaker, colorful enamel on porcelain 95.00
To War, silver metal shaped like Roman helmet 5.00
Town Talk Flour, fleur-de-lis in center 60.00
Tractor tire, plain 60.00
Travelers Protection Association, Portland, ca 1920 .....35.00
Union Tool 40.00
Woodman of the World 35.00
WOW (Wobblies of the World), raised WOW on square .40.00
YMCA Pontiac Michigan Boy's Conference 15.00
Yukon Pacific Exposition, Seattle, 1909, silver 15.00

Watt

Since making an appearance a few years ago in a leading magazine on country decorating, Watt Pottery has become highly collectible. Easily recognized by it's primary red and green brush-stroke patterns on glossy buff-colored backgrounds, these items often carry a stenciled advertising message in addition to designs of apples, tulips, starflowers, and roosters. It was made in Crooksville, Ohio, from about 1935 until the plant was destroyed by fire in 1965.

Bean pot, Apple, #76 ......65.00
Bean pot, Bleeding Heart ..40.00
Bean pot, Flower Bud, #76 .55.00
Bowl, Apple, #55, large 45.00
Bowl, Apple, #65 ....48.00
Bowl, Flower Bud, #6, 4½" .30.00
Bowl, Pennsylvania Dutch, mixing, #65 ....50.00

Pitcher, Apple, with advertising, 6", $40.00.

Bowl, Rooster, #73, with advertising 38.00
Bowl, Starflower, #67 .....20.00
Bowl, Tulip, mixing, #65 ...50.00
Casserole, Apple, #601, with cover, 9½" 55.00
Casserole, French; Rooster .65.00
Cookie jar, Apple 95.00

Ice bucket, Apple, ...**75.00**
Mug, Starflower, #501 .....**55.00**
Pie plate, Apple **85.00**
Pitcher, Leaves, #16 ......**40.00**
Shakers, Rooster, with advertising,
   pair **100.00**
Sugar bowl, Rooster, #98, with cover
   & advertising **75.00**

Weil Ware

The figurines, wallpockets, and other decorative novelties made from the 1940s through the mid-1950s by Max Weil are among the several similar types of California-made pottery that has today become the focus of much collector attention.

Bowl, dogwood, white on gray, oval,
   10" **6.00**
Casserole, floral on green, square,
   with cover **25.00**
Cigarette box, Bamboo, blue &
   white, with cover **22.50**
Compote, floral, footed **14.00**
Figurine, girl with lifted chin, sgraf-
   fito floral on skirt, tall .**30.00**
Planter, boy, 11" **20.00**
Planter, bust of lady, hand-painted
   fan in hand, 8" **25.00**
Plate, Bamboo, dinner size ..**5.00**
Plate, Rose, square, 10" **4.50**
Tidbit tray, Bamboo, 2-tier .**10.00**

**Oriental girls with fan vases, 10",
$25.00 each.**

Vase, bonsai pines, 6½x4½" .**25.00**
Vase, bud; Ming Tree, with coralene,
   #946, 6" **18.00**
Vase, Ming Tree, with coralene trim,
   8½" **35.00**
Wall pocket, Oriental girl ..**22.50**

Weller

Sam Weller's company made pottery in the Zanesville, Ohio, area from before the turn of the century until 1948. They made lovely hand-decorated artware, commercial lines, garden pottery, dinnerware, and kitchenware. Most examples are marked with the company name, either in block letters or script.

Ansonia, batter jug, 14½" .**100.00**
Arcadia, bud vase, 7½" **20.00**
Arcadia, fan vase, 15x8" ...**35.00**
Ardsley, candle holders, 3",
   pair **40.00**
Atlas, dish, with cover, #C-2, mark
   Weller, 3½" **80.00**
Aurelian, mug, berries, artist
   signed, 6" **110.00**
Barcelona, oil jar, no mark,
   25½" **850.00**
Barcelona, vase, 7" **55.00**
Blossom, cornucopia, floral on blue,
   8½" **35.00**
Blue Drapery, planter, 4" ..**30.00**
Bouquet, bowl, #B-8, 4" **30.00**
Brighton, chicks, 5" **110.00**
Brighton, hanging parrot, spread
   wings, 15" **600.00**
Burntwood, vase, footed,
   6½" **125.00**
Cactus, monkey, 4" **60.00**
Cactus, snail, 3½" **60.00**
Candis, ewer, mark, 11" ...**45.00**
Chengtu, vase, 9" **60.00**
Classic, wall pocket, 7½" ...**30.00**
Claywood, mug, no mark, 5".**50.00**
Cloudburst, wall pocket, no mark,
   5½" **35.00**

Coppertone, pitcher, fish handle, 7½" 250.00
Coppertone, vase, frogs on base, 12" 165.00
Cornish, bowl, 4" 35.00
Cornish, jardiniere, 7" 55.00
Darsie, vase, 7½" ...'......35.00
Decorated Creamware, jardiniere, floral, 8" 200.00
Delsa, basket, 7" 35.00
Dickens I, mug, Admiral portrait, 5" 800.00
Dickens II, mug, cavalier portrait, 5" 200.00
Dickens II, mug, grape cluster, marked, 5" 125.00
Dickens II, vase, stag & trees, twisted form, 11" 300.00
Dickens III, ewer, Squeers, signed LM, 12½" 600.00
Elberta, cornucopia, 8" 45.00
Eocean, flask vase, dog, artist signed, 7½" 1,000.00
Eocean, vase, floral, artist signed, 13½" 400.00

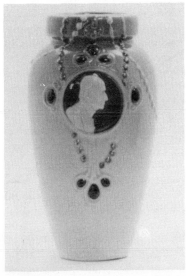

Etna/Jewel, vase with profile medallion of pope, 10½", $150.00.

Etched Matt, vase, boats & 6 fishermen, artist signed, 14". 600.00

Etna, pitcher, floral, 6½" ..100.00
Etna, vase, snake entwined with frog, 6½" 200.00
Evergreen, candle holder, triple, 7½" 65.00
Fairfield, bowl, 4½" 50.00
Flemish, jardiniere, 8" 100.00
Flemish, tub, handles, 4½" .55.00
Fleron, vase, flared rim, 9" .30.00
Florenzo, pillow vase, 4" ...30.00
Floretta, ewer, grapes, 11". 135.00
Forest, tub planter, 6" 65.00
Fruitone, wall pocket, 5½" ..80.00
Garden ornament, gnomes on toadstool, 17" 1,100.00
Glendale, wall bud vase, double, 7" 135.00
Greenbriar, vase, 8" 70.00
Hobart, bowl, 3x9½" 30.00
Hudson, floral signed Pillsbury, 6" 230.00
Hudson, snow scene, signed Pillsbury, 9½" 1,300.00
Hunter, mug, flying ducks, incised fish, fish handle, 5" ...200.00
Ivoris, vase, 7" 35.00
Ivory, wall pocket, ram's head, 10½" 225.00
Ivory, planter, 15½x6" 60.00
Jap Birdimal, inkwell, trees, windmill, & house, 2x4" ...145.00
Juneau, bud vase, 6" 40.00
Klyro, fan vase, 6" 45.00
L'Art Nouveau, vase, lady standing holds flower, 17½" ...300.00
Lido, basket, 8½" 45.00
Loru, vase, 8" 50.00
Louella, bowl, 3" 20.00
Louwelsa, pitcher, floral, artist signed, 5" 150.00
Lustre, bud vase, 6" 25.00
Lustre, candlestick, 9" 15.00
Malvern, pillow vase, 8½" .45.00
Mammy, cookie jar, 11" ...250.00
Marvo, bud vase, 9" 30.00
Melrose, basket, 10" 180.00
Mirror Black, jar 65.00
Muskota, girl with doll, 8" 135.00
Noval, comport, 9½" 120.00

Novelty Line, monkey on peanut,
8x5" **45.00**
Orris, wall pocket **35.00**
Parian, vase, 13" **100.00**
Patra, basket, 5½" **75.00**
Patricia, swan planter, 3½" .**40.00**
Pearl, wall vase, 7" **85.00**
Pumila, bowl, 4" **35.00**
Roma, bowl, handles, 3" . . .**35.00**
Sabrinian, bud vase, 7" **35.00**
Senic, vase, #S-16, 12½" . . .**85.00**
Sicard, mug, 3½" **600.00**
Silvertone, vase, 9" **125.00**
Softone, planter, blue, 8x4" .**35.00**
Souevo, tobacco jar, 6" **200.00**
Sydonia, candle holder, double, with
bud vase, 11½" **90.00**
Trellis, wall shelf, 10½" **55.00**
Turada, umbrella stand . .**750.00**
Tutone, basket, 7½" **85.00**
Voile, fan vase, 8" **75.00**
Wild Rose, candle holder, triple,
6" **50.00**
Wild Rose, vase, floral, handles,
8" **20.00**
Woodcraft, bowl, squirrel on branch,
3½" **75.00**
Woodcraft, fan vase, 8" **30.00**
Xenia, vase, leaves, 9½" .**195.00**
Zona, pitcher, floral, 7½" .**135.00**

Western Collectibles

Items such as chaps, spurs,
saddles, and lariats represent possibly the most colorful genre in the
history of our country, and collectors, especially from the western
states, find them fascinating.The
romance of the Old West lives on
through relics related to those bygone days of cowboys, Wild West
shows, frontier sheriffs, and boom-
town saloons.

Booklet, Origin of Grand Canyon,
1916, 30 pages **15.00**
Bridle, military, with eagle ro-
settes **35.00**

Broadside, Wild West Show with
MT Frank, 24½x32" . . .**25.00**
Bull whip, leather with turned wood
handle, 108", EX **65.00**
Cabinet photo, shows group of
armed Texans, ca 1890 .**35.00**
Cabinet photo, young cowboy, by
George Bigelow **50.00**
Map, Indian Reservations in USA,
1898, 22x33" **25.00**
Map, Kansas, Nebraska, & Colo-
rado, 1864 . . . .**55.00**
Pick, iron mining, 15" **12.00**
Pistol holster & belt, stamped Pat-
ent May 6, 1885, Read & Sons,
EX **120.00**
Playing cards, The Great South-
west, Indians & horses .**20.00**
Print, The Wilds Huntsman, litho-
graph, 1861, 5x9" **13.00**
Roping stirrups, pair **10.00**
Spittoon, copper with wide lip,
complete **30.00**

Westmoreland

Originally an Ohio company,
Westmoreland relocated in
Grapesville, Pennsylvania, where
by the 1920s they had became known
as one of the country's largest
manufacturers of carnival glass.
They are best known today for the
high-quality milk glass which ac-
counted for 90% of their production.

Argonaut Shell, candy dish, ruby,
dolphin handles **45.00**
Ashburton, goblet, green, original
label **8.00**
Beaded Grape, ash tray, milk glass,
roses & bows motif, 4" .**18.00**
Beaded Grape, bowl, milk glass,
square, with cover, 7" . .**32.00**
Beaded Grape, nappy, milk glass,
bell shape, 8" **18.00**
Box, blue opaque, hand-painted
decoration, egg form . . .**22.00**

Covered dish, camel atop, milk glass 100.00

Covered dish, cat, lacy base, milk glass 95.00

Covered dish, dog, milk glass, Westmoreland 65.00

Covered dish, dog, wide-ribbed base, amber 45.00

Covered dish, eagle with young, beaded base, milk glass .85.00

Covered dish, fox, beaded base, blue opaque, large 85.00

Covered dish, fox, lacy base, milk glass, large 125.00

Covered dish, hen on basket base, blue opaque 65.00

Covered dish, hen on basket base, milk glass 35.00

Covered dish, hen on nest, lattice edge, milk glass 75.00

Covered dish, hen on sleigh, milk glass, 5½" 65.00

Covered dish, lamb, blue opaque, Westmoreland 46.00

Covered dish, lion, lacy base, aqua ice, glass eyes, large ... 70.00

Covered dish, rabbit, hand-painted eggs, milk glass, large . 100.00

Covered dish, rooster, lacy base, milk glass, large 75.00

Covered dish, swan, humpback, milk glass 60.00

Covered dish, swan, lacy base, aqua ice, large 100.00

Covered dish, swan, wings up, blue opaque 125.00

Della Robbia, compote, painted decoration 32.00

Della Robbia, goblet, 6" ... 12.00

Della Robbia, salt & pepper shakers, pair 35.00

Della Robbia, sherbet, 4¾" .. 8.00

Dolphin, candlestick, milk glass, 9" (being reproduced) 35.00

English Hobnail, ash tray, milk glass, hat form 10.00

English Hobnail, cruet, milk glass, 4" 17.50

English Hobnail, ivy ball, milk glass, 5½" 18.00

English Hobnail, mustard, milk glass, with lid & ladle .24.00

Oak Leaf, creamer & sugar bowl, milk glass 28.00

Old Quilt, ash tray, milk glass, 4" 20.00

Old Quilt, banana bowl, milk glass, rare 60.00

Old Quilt, bowl, milk glass, flared, 13" 95.00

Old Quilt, butter dish, milk glass, ¼-pound 30.00

Old Quilt, cheese dish with lid, milk glass 55.00

Old Quilt, creamer & sugar bowl, milk glass, with cover .. 50.00

Old Quilt, cruet, milk glass .35.00

Old Quilt, cup, milk glass .. 20.00

Old Quilt, jardiniere, milk glass, cupped, 6½" 40.00

Old Quilt, juice tumbler, milk glass, 3" 15.00

Old Quilt, relish tray, milk glass, 9" 22.00

Old Quilt, salt & pepper shakers, milk glass, pair 25.00

Old Quilt, sandwich plate, milk glass, 8½" 32.00

Old Quilt, syrup pitcher with lid, milk glass 22.00

Old Quilt, vase, aqua ice carnival, ruffled top, footed, 7" .. 35.00

Panelled Grape, bonbon, milk glass, ruffled, footed 22.50

Panelled Grape, bowl, milk glass, footed, with cover, 9" .. 50.00

Panelled Grape, cake plate, milk glass, skirted 60.00

Panelled Grape, candle holder, milk glass, octagonal, 4", ... 10.00

Panelled Grape, candy dish, milk glass, 3-footed, with lid . 32.00

Panelled Grape, creamer, milk glass, 5" 15.00

Panelled Grape, goblet, milk glass, 5¾" 20.00

Panelled Grape, mayonnaise, milk glass, footed 20.00

Panelled Grape, pitcher, milk glass, 1-pint 35.00

Panelled Grape, platter, milk glass, 14" 75.00

Panelled Grape, rose bowl, milk glass, footed, 4" 15.00

Panelled Grape, soap dish, milk glass 45.00

Panelled Grape, sugar & creamer with lid, milk glass 30.00

Panelled Grape, tumbler, milk glass, 4¾" 15.00

Panelled Grape, vase, milk glass, bell shape, 9" 28.00

Panelled Grape, vase, milk glass, 6" 20.00

Panelled Grape, wine, footed, milk glass 15.00

Plate, chicks, milk glass ...34.00

Plate, Indian in headdress, milk glass 42.50

Plate, Zodiac signs, white on blue mist, 5½" 20.00

Ring & Petal, cake plate, milk glass 45.00

Ring & Petal, candlestick, milk glass, pair 30.00

Roses & Bows, card receiver, hand form, hand-painted 28.00

Roses & Trellis, basket with handle, flared, large 45.00

Slipper, blue mist, hand-painted decoration 18.00

Spiral, candlestick, purple slag, 6½" 40.00

Wakefield, cordial, crystal ...8.00

Wildflower & Lace, banana bowl, blue 17.00

Wicker

Wicker became a popular medium for furniture construction as early as the mid-1800s. Early styles were closely woven and very ornate; frames were of heavy wood. By the turn of the century the weaving was looser and styles were simple. Today's collectors prefer tables with wicker tops as opposed to wooden tops, matching ensembles, and

pieces that have not been painted.

Armchair, Gustav Stickley, #60, willow, ca 1907, 39" ..400.00

Armchair, Nouveau styling, Heywood Brothers, Wakefield, 1920s 450.00

Baby basket, 38x11x18" ..125.00

Baby buggy, Victorian, elaborate, NM 600.00

Basket, wall; rattan, 8x8½" .45.00

Breakfast tray, cup holder & paper rack on side 110.00

Bird cage, ca 1890-1910, 17", $350.00.

Chair, breakfast; heavy, dated 1917, set of 4, restored 700.00

Doll carriage 135.00

Doll stroller, Victorian, original paint & upholstery ...495.00

Footstool, square base, upholstered round top, 9½x12" 100.00

Highchair, Victorian, woven braid trim, simple design ...150.00

Loveseat, rocker, 1890s ...300.00

Rocker, loose weave, square back with high arm rest ...240.00

Rug beater 30.00

Silverware caddy 35.00

Table, tight weave, round, with 2 shelves 180.00

Table lamp, with shade, 24". **75.00**
Vanity bench, white paint .**350.00**
Vase, 9½" **18.00**

Willow Ware

Inspired by the lovely blue and white Chinese exports, the Willow pattern has been made by many English, American, and Japanese firms from 1750 until the present. Many variations of the pattern have been noted; mauve, black, green, and multicolor Willow ware can be found in limited amounts. The design has been applied to tinware, linens, glassware, and paper goods, all of which are treasured by today's collectors.

Baking dish, with lid, Hall .**40.00**
Biscuit jar, bail handle **80.00**
Bowl, Allerton's, 10x7¼" ...**45.00**
Bowl, Buffalo, 5" **10.00**
Butter pat, Allerton **18.00**
Butter pat, marked Made in Japan, 3" **13.00**

Butter dish, covered, English, 8"x3½", $140.00.

Canister, Japan, with cover, set of 4 ....**195.00**
Carafe & warmer, marked Japan, 12" **175.00**
Cheese board, tiles in pecan wood server, 1950s, 8x12" ...**45.00**
Coffeepot, Shenango, high loop handle, 7" **75.00**

Creamer, Allerton **40.00**
Cup, demitasse; Japan, 2½" diameter **17.50**
Cup, Homer Laughlin **7.50**
Cup, mush; Buffalo, 1911 ..**50.00**
Cup & saucer, Johnson Bros .**9.50**
Decanter, modern, 8" **25.00**
Egg cup, Buffalo, dark blue .**30.00**
Food warmer, Booth's, 8¼". .**95.00**
Gravy boat, Buffalo, 1911 ..**50.00**
Gravy boat, Wedgwood **35.00**
Hatpin holder, England, ...**20.00**
Infant feeder, England, unmarked, 4" **125.00**
Ladle, soup; Japan **110.00**
Pie bird, no mark **7.50**
Pitcher, with ice lip, 10" ...**55.00**
Plate, Globe Pottery, 9" **7.50**
Plate, grill; Japan **127.50**
Platter, Buffalo, 1911, 16" ..**60.00**
Salt box, Japan, 5x5" **60.00**
Saucer, Buffalo **7.50**
Shaker, sugar; Moriyama ..**32.00**
Spoon rest, Japan **20.00**
Sugar bowl, Occupied Japan, child's size **10.00**
Tea caddy, Rington **175.00**
Tea set, Made in Japan, 1930s, 3-piece **85.00**
Trivet, Japan, square **25.00**
Tureen, Minton, 5½" **65.00**
Vase, Japan, unmarked, 5" .**45.00**
Wall pocket, marked Japan, samovar shape **65.00**
Wash set, Wedgwood, 1880s, 5x16" bowl with pitcher **700.00**
Waste bowl, English, 3x6" ..**40.00**
Waste bowl, marked Maastricht, footed **15.00**

Winchester

Originally manufacturing only guns and ammunition, after 1920 the Winchester Company produced a vast array (over 7,500 items) of sporting goods and hardware items which they marked 'Winchester

Trademark, USA.' The name of the firm changed in 1931, and the use of the trademark was discontinued. Examples with this mark have become collectors' items.

Ash tray, red letters on black glass, club style **5.00**
Battery, radio; ca 1950 .....**6.00**
Brace, heavy duty, with 14" sweep, EX **60.00**
Brace, with standard 8" sweep, EX **50.00**
Bullet mold, 32-165 caliber .**48.00**
Calendar, Llewelyn champion Mars Guy, 1932 ....**400.00**
Carving set, stag handles, silver ferrule, 2-piece, original box, EX **45.00**
Catalog, 1962 ....**20.00**
Catalog #80, 1916, 50th Anniversary copy **65.00**
Comic book, 1950 ....**28.00**
Flashlight, 3-cell, nickel bottom, octagonal top, black ...**18.00**
Golf club, #4 iron, EX **55.00**
Grain scale, bushel measure; brass, EX **200.00**
Hammer, riveting **60.00**
Ice pick #9502, ...**26.00**
Ice skates, pair **25.00**
Knife, butcher, stainless steel, marked, 11½" **45.00**
Oil can, red & yellow **12.50**
Paperweight, 1910 ....**35.00**
Pencil box **75.00**
Pliers, marked, 8" **25.00**
Pocket knife, marble arms, stag handle, 8", VG **175.00**
Post card, 1916 ....**15.00**
Poster, running deer 30x36".**24.00**
Poster, depicts game, 1923, in frame **186.00**
Poster, Winchester the Perfect Shell, 10x18" **80.00**
Razor, straight; #8527 .....**42.00**
Reel #2349, bait casting ...**85.00**
Roller skates, dated 1925 ..**14.00**
Scissors, #9041 ....**25.00**

Sharpening stone **40.00**
Stickpin, Blue Rival **46.00**
Trade stamp, man in red sweater shooting skeet **15.00**
Yardstick, EX **100.00**

Woodenware

Most of the primitive hand-crafted wooden bowls and utensils on today's market can be attributed to a period from late in the 1700s until about 1870. They were designed on a strictly utilitarian basis, and only rarely was any attempt made toward decoration. The most desirable are those items made from burl wood — the knuckle or knot of the tree having a grain that appears mottled when it is carved — or utensils with an effigy-head handle. Very old examples are light in weight due to the deterioration of the wood; expect age cracks that develop as the wood dries.

Apple butter stirrer, cut-out heart in blade, 36¼" long ...**105.00**
Apple peeler, with table clamp, 9½" long **65.00**
Baker's peel, 56½" **105.00**
Bowl, burl, 2⅞x3⅞" **95.00**
Bowl, burl, 3¾x6½" **300.00**
Box, apple; cherry, dovetailed, cut-out handles in sides ..**100.00**
Box, apple; poplar, octagonal, 8½" wide **85.00**
Box, candle; pine, wall mount, red paint, 12½" **85.00**
Box, candle; poplar, dovetailed, sliding lid, 16½" long **65.00**
Box, knife; poplar, 2-piece, cut-out handle in divider, 8x12".**45.00**
Box, pine, dovetailed, wrought iron handles, 19x19x20" ..**205.00**
Box, pine, vinegar graining, brown on yellow , 11" **85.00**
Box, poplar, worn yellow paint, 3⅜", EX **50.00**

Box, salt; poplar, hinged lid, scalloped crest, 10" **110.00**
Box, walnut, dovetailed construction, 10½" long **50.00**
Box, writing; poplar, dovetailed construction wrought iron lock & hasp **325.00**
Butter paddle, curly maple .**75.00**
Butter paddle, curved hook handle, 8¾" long **60.00**
Butter paddle, maple **60.00**
Butter scoop, maple, shaped bowl, 9½" long **35.00**
Cookie board, carved, man on horseback & lion, 12½x14¾" .**55.00**
Cookie board, 1-piece, incised pig & cow, 6x19" **250.00**
Cranberry scoop, fish tail handle, 16¾" long **120.00**
Dipper, hand carved, 6½" ..**80.00**
Knife, hearts, trees, & birds carved in relief, 17¾" **35.00**
Mortar & pestle, burl & poplar, 6½" **195.00**
Mortar & pestle, poplar, 7" .**75.00**
Niddy-noddy, 18" long **40.00**
Paddle, with burl bowl, 9" ..**55.00**
Spice cabinet, hanging; 9 drawers with ivory pulls **240.00**

Maple porringer, one-piece, scrubbed surface, New England, 1700s, rare, 7 " diameter, with 3½" handle, $400.00.

World's Fairs and Expositions

Souvenir items have been distributed from every fair and exposition since the mid-1850s. Examples from before the turn of the century are challenging to collect, but those made as late as for the 1939 New York and San Francisco fairs are also desirable.

1876 Centennial, Philadelphia

Booklet, Centennial Diary 1876, 22 pages, 3x6", VG **25.00**
Handkerchief, 23x28" **75.00**
Plaque, pressed wood, Agricultural Hall, 4x2¾" **45.00**
Stud, metal, embossed building & letters, 1" diameter **27.50**
Ticket, admission, Philadelphia Bank Note Co, EX **15.00**

1893 Columbian, Chicago

Book, History of the World's Fair, 610 pages **38.00**
Coin, Columbian Half Dollar, silver color, 1¼" **15.00**
Medal, Columbus Bust, Father-Savior-Defender **16.00**
Medal, Democratic Presidential Nominees, 1892, embossed aluminum **35.00**
Medal, Ferris Wheel, has 5 fair scenes **24.00**
Medal, Santa Maria, bust of Columbus, copper **15.00**
Opener, watch; Keystone Case, pocket watch form **15.00**
Penny, 1893 Indian Head; rolled out, Columbian Expo ..**12.00**
Playing cards, color drawings of Expo building **30.00**
Spoon, demitasse; Indian handle, building in bowl, 4" **32.50**
Token, Manufacturers & Liberal Arts ....,....**12.00**

1898 Omaha

Album, folds out **20.00**
Knife, made of large nail ...**20.00**
Pin-back button, Pennsylvania Day, Oct 5 1898, celluloid ...**40.00**

Poster, Milwaukee Litho Co, panoramic view, EX **175.00**
Silk, Electric Tower, 10", M. **35.00**
Spoon, US Gov't Building in bowl, angel on handle, 4¼" . . **25.00**

1901 Pan American

Knife, made of large nail . . . **20.00**
Pipe, corn cob bowl, marked Pan-Am Expo, 5½" **15.00**
Program, closing day **15.00**
Silk, Electric Tower, 10" . . . **35.00**
Spoon, Expo buildings in bowl, scene on handle, 4½" **15.00**

1904 St. Louis

Booklet, Important Information for Visitors, contains map . . **8.00**
Change tray, embosed floral, boy & girl in center, 5x3" **27.00**
Stickpin, pendant hanging from spread-winged eagle . . . **10.00**
Token, harvesting machines, brass, 1¼" **20.00**

1915 Panama Pacific

Fan, Shidzouka Teas **25.00**
Pin-back button, Indian on horse, dated Dec 4, 1915 . . . . . **35.00**
Post card album, set of 10 multicolor cards **15.00**
Souvenir View Book, official, 40 pages, 9½x12½" **22.50**
Spoon, sterling, dated **25.00**
Tray, metal, pictures Expo buildings, round, 5" **15.00**

1933 Chicago

Album, A Century of Progress, contains 11 scenes **33.00**
Ash tray, Century of Progress, fair scenes at rim, 4½" **15.00**
Bank, American Can Co, lithograph on tin **23.00**

Booklet, 100 Years of Progress in Modern Railroading . . . **12.00**
Guide Book, official, illustrated, 194 pages **8.00**
Playing cards, The Century of Progress, original box **18.00**
Salt & pepper, Travel & Carillon Buildings, 3", pair **20.00**
Spoon, Century of Progress, with Indian figural handle . . **14.00**
Tie bar, green enamel on nickel plate, 2½", EX **17.00**
Token, Good Luck, embossed brass, 1¼" **12.00**
Tray, crumb; silverplate . . . **35.00**
Tray, illustration of General Exhibits Group, 4" diameter . **20.00**
Viewer, in original box **15.00**

1939 New York

Chair, folding; cane seat, made by Kan-O-Seat, 36" **45.00**
Coaster, paper, embossed, dated, 5" diameter, set of 6 . . . . . . **7.00**
Commemorative plate, made by Homer Laughlin, 10" . . **50.00**
Diary, Trylon & Perisphere on cover, unused, 6½x9" **15.00**
Guide book, official, first edition, 256 pages **15.00**
Handkerchief, maroon, white, blue, green, & yellow silk . . . **20.00**
Map, By Subway & Automobile, 21½x16½" **5.00**
Medallion, World of Tomorrow, chain, 1½" long **9.00**
Newspaper, Today at the Fair, July 24, 1939, 8 pages **8.00**
Paint book, Bag Full of New York World's Fair Pictures . . **25.00**
Pennant, white letters on orange, 18" long **22.00**
Pin-back button, I Have Seen the Future, blue on white . . **12.00**
Post card, Lower Manhattan Skyline, unused **5.00**
Program, American Jubilee, 24 pages, 8¾x11¾" **10.00**

Program, Hot Mikado, illustrated
cover, 9x12" 20.00
Salt & pepper shaker, on holder,
colored plastic, thermometer on
base 15.00
Spoon, fair name & stars in bowl,
engraved handle, 6" . . . 10.00
Spoon, Georgian Section in Court of
States Buildings, ... 15.00
Spoon, Golden Gate Expo, nude on
handle 20.00
Spoon, Marine Transportation, Wm
Rogers, 6" 12.00
Spoon, theme building in bowl,
marked Plymouth Silverplate
Co 15.00
Token, brass, 1¼" diameter . 12.00

1939 San Francisco

Ice pick, wood handle, 8" . . 25 .00
Spoon, 1939 Golden Gate International Expo, silverplate. 12.00
Token, Golden Gate Bridge & Union Pacific logo on sides . 7.00

Wrought Iron

Before cast iron became commonplace in the mid-1800s, hand-forged
(or wrought) iron was the metal
used most extensively. You can often judge the age of an iron piece by
studying its surface. While rusty
wrought iron appears grainy, cast
iron pits to an orange-peel texture.

Candle holder, sticking tommy,
12" 40.00
Fork, 13¼" long 205.00
Pipe tongs, 12¾" long 500.00
Plant stand, tree shaped with 3
shelves for pots, 47" . . 105.00
Skimmer, brass bowl, 21"
long 85.00

Spatula, 10¾" long 30.00
Trivet, heart with 3 shaped feet,
7¾" long 30.00

Yellow Ware

Utility ware made from buff-burn-
ing clays took on a yellow hue when
covered with a clear glaze, hence
the name 'yellow ware.' It is a type
of 'country' pottery that is becoming quite popular due to today's em-
phasis on the 'country' look in home
decorating. It was made to a large
extent by the Ohio potters, though
some was made in the eastern states
as well. Very seldom do you find a
marked piece. Bowls, pitchers, and
pie plates are common; mugs, rolling pins and lidded jars are more
unusual and demand higher prices
— so do items with in-mold decoration or mocha-like decoration.

Bowl, blue & brown with red spat-
ter, 4¼x8⅜" 45.00
Bowl, embossed foliage & scroll,
green & brown, 8" 45.00
Bowl, mixing; brown sponge, 5¾x
12⅜" 55.00
Bowl, mixing; white stripe, 6½x
13¾" 60.00
Casserole, blue bands, with co-
ver 65.00
Crock, white bands, 9" 85.00
Dish, stacking; brown sponge, with
cover, 8½" diameter . . . 55.00
Ginger jar, with cover 100.00
Jar, canning; John Bell, Way-
nesboro, 7¼" 300.00
Pitcher, brown & green sponge
spatter, 4⅝" 50.00
Rolling pin, 14" 285.00
Tub, raised handles, brown ribbed
bands, 7¼" diameter . . 350.00
Washboard insert, 11x11" . 145.00

Index

Schroeder's Antiques Price Guide

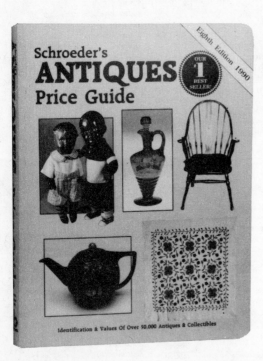

Schroeder's ANTIQUES Price Guide

OUR 1 BEST SELLER!

Eighth Edition 1990

Identification & Values Of Over 50,000 Antiques & Collectibles

Schroeder's Antiques Price Guide has climbed its way to the top in a field already supplied with several well-established publications! The word is out, *Schroeder's Price Guide* is the best buy at any price. Over 500 categories are covered, with more than 50,000 listings. From ABC Plates to Zsolnay, if it merits the interest of today's collector, you'll find it in Schroeder's. Each subject is represented with histories and background information. In addition, hundreds of sharp original photos are used each year to illustrate not only the rare and the unusual, but the everyday "fun-type" collectibles as well. All new copy and all new illustrations make Schroeder's THE price guide on antiques and collectibles. We have not and will not simply change prices in each new edition.

The writing and researching team is backed by a staff of more than seventy of Collector Books' finest authors, as well as a board of advisors made up of well-known antique authorities and the country's top dealers, all specialists in their fields. Prices are gathered over the entire year previous to publication, then each category is thoroughly checked. Only the best of the lot remains for publication. You'll find the new edition of *Schroeder's Antiques Price Guide* the one to buy for factual information and quality.

No dealer, collector or investor can afford not to own this book. It is available from your favorite bookseller or antiques dealer at the low price of $12.95. If you are unable to find this price guide in your area, it's available from Collector Books, P.O. Box 3009, Paducah, KY 42001 at $12.95 plus $2.00 for postage and handling.